DATE DUE			

THE ALTERING EYE

Contemporary International Cinema

ROBERT PHILLIP KOLKER

OXFORD UNIVERSITY PRESS
Oxford New York Toronto Melbourne
1983

Oxford University Press

Oxford London Glasgow
New York Toronto Melbourne Auckland
Delhi Bombay Calcutta Madras Karachi
Kuala Lumpur Singapore Hong Kong Tokyo
Nairobi Dar es Salaam Cape Town
and associate companies in
Beirut Berlin Ibadan Mexico City Nicosia

First published by Oxford University Press, New York, 1983
First issued as an Oxford University Press paperback, 1983

Library of Congress Cataloging in Publication Data
Kolker, Robert Phillip.
The altering eye.
Bibliography: p.
1. Moving-picture plays–History and criticism.
2. Moving-pictures–Philosophy. I. Title.
PN1995.K66 791.43′09′046 81-22488
ISBN 0-19-503126-1 AACR2
ISBN 0-19-503302-7 (pbk.)

Acknowledgment is made to the following
for permission to use copyright material:

The table "Dramatic Theatre–Epic Theatre" from *Brecht on Theatre,* edited and translated by John Willett. Copyright © 1957, 1963, 1964 by Suhrkamp Verlag, Frankfurt am Main. This translation and notes © 1964 by John Willett. Reprinted by permission of Hill and Wang, a division of Farrar, Straus and Giroux, Inc., and Methuen London.

From "To Posterity" in *Selected Poems,* copyright 1947 by Bertolt Brecht and H. R. Hays; copyright 1975 by Stefan S. Brecht and H. R. Hays. Reprinted by permission of Harcourt Brace Jovanovich, Inc., and Ann Elmo Agency, Inc.

Printing (last digit): 9 8 7 6 5 4 3 2
Printed in the United States of America

For

LINDA

and

in Memory of

GLAUBER ROCHA

and

RAINER WERNER FASSBINDER

PREFACE

Narrative film can set out to please its audience, soothe it, meet and reinforce its expectations. Or it can challenge, question and probe, inquire about itself, its audience, and the world that both inhabit and reflect. This is the kind of film that is my subject: film made in a spirit of resistance, rebellion, and refusal; made with desire. These films are made all over the world; they were made in America at one time—in the forties, in the late sixties and early seventies—and I have spoken about them in another book. Here I am concerned with the same periods, but with films made in Europe and Latin America, made in reaction to American cinema, often to America itself, yet dependent upon America, upon the conventions and attitudes of American film and culture, feeding upon them and sometimes spitting them out. These films are part of the modernist movement in twentieth-century art, a movement whose diversity has a common location in the desire to challenge attitudes about the work and place of art, to attack conventions and complacency, to reorder the relationship of the work and the spectator.

The modernist endeavor as a whole does not follow a simple chronological path, but in commercial cinema it concentrates in the movement that started in postwar Italian neo-realism, climaxed in the work of the French New Wave, and extends into the films of the new German cinema. It is various in its manifestations, complex in its forms, and demanding upon its audience. It is, therefore, not very popular. These films run contrary to everything popular cinema has trained us to expect, and present the added difficulty of being spoken in foreign languages, translated with words printed on the screen that distract our attention.

But popularity is a relative thing. In the sixties, when the movement was at its peak, it caused great excitement, much critical and even commercial attention. That attention has now dwindled, as the creative drive of cinema world wide has slackened. Therefore a central function of this book is to attempt both to recapture and re-evaluate that excitement by means of tracing the modernist movement in cinema using the critical apparatus that has been explaining it and that is in fact part of it. (For a key to understanding modernist film is an awareness that the work of imagination is simultaneously a work of criticism and vice versa.) In the course of this study I will examine films of great intellectual and emotional energy, engaged in a struggle to negate traditional cinema while drawing sustenance from that cinema in the process. In fact process itself is my major concern, and while I will look closely at representative works and figures, I will concentrate upon movement and the changing perceptions of the work of cinema.

What follows is a critical progress through progressive film, through a cinema that asks to be taken seriously and assumes that complexity is not a quality that diminishes entertainment. This is a cinema that invites emotional response and intellectual participation, that is committed to history and politics and an examination of culture, that asks for the commitment of its audience; a cinema that offers ways to change, if not the world, at least the way we see it.

Columbia, Md. R.P.K.
June 1982

ACKNOWLEDGMENTS

Although distribution of European and Latin American films in the United States has fallen off in recent years, there are a number of small distributors who still acquire new material, add it to their collection of older films, and help keep the tradition alive. I wish to thank the following distributors who supplied the films that made the writing of this book possible: Cinema Five, Corinth Films, Films Inc.–Audio Brandon, New Line Cinema, New Yorker Films, Unifilm.

The motion picture division of the Library of Congress was, as always, of great help, and the theater division of the American Film Institute gave special assistance.

A number of people assisted me with ideas, research, and technical help, by reading parts of the mansucript, and with good conversation. Thanks especially to Peter Beicken, Maria Coughlin, Douglas Gomery, Danusia Meson, Joe Miller, J. Douglas Ousley, David Parker, Stephen Prince, Adam Reilly, Harvey W. Thompson, Jr., and Katherine S. Woodward, and to many students who worked with me in courses and seminars in contemporary European cinema at the University of Maryland. A Faculty Research Grant from the University of Maryland allowed me a semester off to do the major writing.

ACKNOWLEDGMENTS

Sheldon Meyer and Stephanie Golden at Oxford University Press supplied their support and knowledge in giving this book shape and direction.

While it is an easy matter to thank and acknowledge those whose personal intervention aided my work, it is less easy when it comes to the great number of scholars and critics whose writing has been influential in forming my ideas. The notes to the text indicate some of the debt and the bibliography widens the range of acknowledgement, but can never complete it.

CONTENTS

For the Eye altering alters all.

William Blake,
"The Mental Traveller"

The screen's white eyelid would only need to be able to reflect the light that is its own, and it would blow up the Universe.

Luis Buñuel

We often went to the movies. The screen lit up and we trembled. . . . But more often than not Madeleine and I were disappointed. The pictures were dated, they flickered. And Marilyn Monroe had aged terribly. It made us sad. This wasn't the film we'd dreamed of. This wasn't the total film that each of us had carried within himself . . . the film we wanted to make, or, more secretly, no doubt, that we wanted to live.

Paul, in Jean-Luc Godard's
Masculin-féminin

My father said, "film is the art of seeing." That's why I can't show these films which are mere exploitations of all that can be exploited in human heads and eyes. . . . I won't be forced to show films where people stagger out stunned and rigid with stupidity . . . that kill any joy of life inside them, destroying any feeling for themselves and the world. . . . The way it is now it is better there's no cinema than a cinema the way it is now.

A provincial theater owner in
Wim Wenders's *Kings of the Road*

The Altering Eye

INTRODUCTION

At the beginning of Jean-Luc Godard and Jean-Pierre Gorin's *Tout va bien* (1972), a voice announces: "I want to make a film." Another voice responds: "That costs money." And for many minutes the screen is filled with the image of a checkbook as, one after the other, checks are signed and torn off: makeup, sets, bit players, editing, electricians, sound, the communal apparatus of filmmaking enumerated by cost, deglamorized, and placed in a material context. It is a clear announcement of the state and the problem of contemporary film. Films cost money. And there is a second part to the equation. Films cost money; the people who spend the money want to see it back, with a profit.

The results of this equation are becoming too clear. In cinema world wide those films that do not promise large returns remain unmade or unseen. In the past, particularly in America, the great studio system provided such a large turnover for such a large audience that there was some room for exploration, for the occasional "noncommercial" work. Now every film must stand on its own in the circuit of exchange. It must make money. But European cinema never had quite the kind of studio system that existed in America, which was in fact something unique in history–the mass production of narratives; an assembly line for products of the imagination; art integrated with and often subdued by commerce. America had (and has still) the world for its market, while most European filmmakers have, with rare exceptions, only their own countries. Therefore, the art-commerce tension that existed throughout the history of American movie-making–with commerce now subordinating art–was never as extreme in other countries. The difference must not be exaggerated; there was–and certainly now is–no absolute freedom in filmmaking outside America, just as there neither was nor is absolute tyranny within it. In fact much European filmmaking involves the production of "quota quickies," sex comedies and the like made fast and cheap to satisfy government demand for a certain amount of indigenous product before the more profitable American films can be exhibited. Outside Europe, India and Japan have had entertainment factories almost on the scale of Hollywood.

However, because most countries cannot compete with Hollywood, other opportunities arise for their filmmakers. Instead of trying to compete they have the opportunity to make films quite unlike the standard American product. This opportunity is often supported by the fact that in Europe and elsewhere there is a greater respect for film as an intellectual, imaginative activity, a greater willingness on the part of a producer to allow the filmmaker to work on his or her own, to write, direct, and even edit a film, to release it in the form the filmmaker desires. In recent years, this respect has been demonstrated through state support (particularly through television) for new filmmakers, or for established ones who cannot find commercial distribution. Certainly state support brings with it the problems of state control; but overriding this is the fact that it permits films to get made that otherwise could not. The rebirth of German cinema came about through the patronage of the German government and its television subsidiaries. British cinema is promising to show some signs of life through the support of Regional Arts Councils and the British Film Institute Film Production Board. In past years a variety of films from many countries–the late works of Roberto Rossellini; Bertolucci's *The Spider's Stratagem* (1970); the Taviani brothers' *Padre Padrone* (1977); Ermanno Olmi's *The Tree of Wooden Clogs* (1978);

Peter Watkins' *Edvard Munch* (1976); Eric Rohmer's *Perceval* (1978), to name only a few—have owed their existence to the support of state-run television.

Even before television and the state stepped in, there were independent producers—such as Georges de Beauregard, who supported Godard and others of the New Wave in the sixties—willing to risk small gains on little-known filmmakers who would make unusual films. Throughout the history of European film, its makers found funding for experimental work and integrated their work with the rest of the imaginative work of the culture. In the teens and twenties, for example, the avant-garde played an active role in film, giving it, through the works of such as Abel Gance, Walter Ruttmann, Fernand Léger, Luis Buñuel and Salvador Dali, Eisenstein, Dziga Vertov, Jean Renoir, Jean Epstein, intellectual respectability. In fact most of the formal advances made in cinema originated in Europe and Russia. D. W. Griffith established the basic forms of film narrative that became the norm world wide; most of the experiments performed upon this structure, the challenges to it, the questions raised about it, came from abroad. And when they came, they were often absorbed back into the mother lode of American film. An entire history could be written about the influences of European styles and their originators on American film, a history that, depending on one's perspective, would show Hollywood as either enriching itself or perpetually homogenizing world cinema.

Thus, while European and American cinema both function on an economic base which determines what can and cannot be made, this base has been wider outside America, more ready to support financing on something other than a profit basis, thereby enabling films to be made that question or defy cinematic conventions. But in fact no direct split between filmmaking in America and elsewhere exists. There is rather an interplay in which the dominant style (or styles) of American movies are always present to be denied, expanded upon, embraced, and rejected, only to be embraced again. The presence of American cinema is a constant, and there is no filmmaker I know of, even the most revolutionary, who hates American film. Intellectual arguments are marshaled against it; the emotions always respond to it. It is an attitude I share, and it colors the arguments in this book. I have set up American cinema as a model, often an invidious one, always an overgeneralized one, in order to examine its relationship to the work of individuals in Europe and in Latin America and their reactions to it. Melodrama, for example, is a narrative form that I often contrast to the modernist endeavor. Melodrama demands a great emotional response from its audience, an identification with the central characters of a film (whose personal problems are foregrounded without being linked to a defined social context that may determine them), and insists that conventional attitudes and gestures be accepted as unique components of a character's psychology. Melodrama is a form of assurance and security; as a structuring device in American film and its European derivatives, it all but guarantees that what is experienced in one film will not be very different from what has been experienced in most others. Just such forms of repetition, emotional safety, and reinforcement are what the modernists oppose with forms of question and surprise. But without melodrama, the modernists would not have a form to react against or, in some cases, incorporate. Despite my affection and admiration for American film (at least through the mid-seventies), I sometimes portray it as a kind of monolith that various figures have done battle with and look at it with something of the attitude of the filmmakers who were trying to deal with it.

What gives the American tradition the appearance of a monolith is the structure of repetition that I just noted. Since the early teens, when it began organizing itself to reach the widest possible audience, American film began to adopt a number of conventions in content and form that it has repeated, albeit with many variations, to the present day, always proclaiming that these conventions fulfilled audience desires. But in fact popular film does not so much fulfill or reflect the desires of its audience as create them through a complicated ideological process in which cultural and social attitudes are enhanced, given form, and reinforced in a circuit of exchange between the producers and consumers of cultural artifacts. The decades-long attitude of

American film toward the role of women, the bliss of domesticity, the pleasures of poverty, the ability of the individual hero to effect changes in his world, American film's persistent attempts to reinforce the social and political status quo—all developed not so much out of what people believed but out of what filmmakers thought was believed. Their job was, and for the most part remains, to perpetuate conventions and not challenge them. Film became part of the ideological structure, feeding the audience images that were assumed to represent their beliefs and concerns. Audiences gave the images passive assent, and the images are repeated into what seems to be a cultural infinity.

So too with the forms those images took. The development of conventional patterns of composing and cutting images to create the chronologically continuous, spatially coherent, suspenseful, but finally resolved series of events that is the structure of most commercial narrative cinema did not just happen. These forms are no more the natural constituents of the filmmaking process than are the conventions of content. They had to be learned by both filmmakers and their audiences. Once learned (by the early thirties) they became standardized—with minor variations, and major individual exceptions—throughout the West. Once standardized, they were assumed to be the norm. And once that assumption was made, it was difficult to break out of. But breaks were always occurring, and they began very early. Erich von Stroheim, who started as D. W. Griffith's assistant, soon began making his own films, which directly challenged the rustic simplicity and Victorian melodrama of his predecessor. Sergei Eisenstein studied Griffith's films and turned what he learned on its head, changing the ameliorative, the melodramatic, and the romantic into the revolutionary. The German expressionists defied the conventions of "realism" developing in American cinema, turning the image into an artifice of madness. The French avant-garde in the twenties and early thirties continued the process of response to the conventions; and, with the appearance of *Citizen Kane* in 1941 and the development of *film noir* in the mid-forties, Hollywood created its own internal subversion of the dominant forms. But it was not until the end of World

War II that a national cinema emerged to create a concerted alternative to the American style.

Italian neo-realism was a loose collective movement whose aim was to change the form and function of commercial cinema. As a movement it lasted less than ten years, but its legacy offered a range of possibilities for challenge: new approaches to image-making, to cutting, to narrative structure, to audience response. The challenge was picked up by a diverse school of cine-modernists in the sixties. In Western and Eastern Europe and in parts of Latin America a cinema developed that in its questioning of conventions and its imaginative manipulation of form was in every way equal to the other arts in complexity and in the richness of its confrontation with the world. This movement climaxed with the May 1968 events in France and the great politicization of culture that occurred throughout Europe in the succeeding months. In the mid-seventies the movement began to wane, and a combination of the loss of creative energies and the reassertion of a profit-seeking market returned much commercial cinema to the old, and by this time somewhat discredited, forms. West Germany countered the decline, and through the system of government subsidies supported the work of some impressive new talent.

But if modernist filmmaking declined in the seventies, film criticism became revitalized. The fuse for the explosion of cinema in the sixties had been set by the criticism of André Bazin and his followers (Truffaut, Godard, Chabrol, Rivette, Rohmer) in the fifties. After 1968, film criticism began to revise the ideas of Bazin and inquire into the ways film interacts with its audience and the culture that contains both. Using the tools of semiology, of structuralism and Lacanian psychology, and most important, of ideological analysis, the new criticism, which originated in France as it had in the fifties, regarded film as a formal, cultural, political artifact, built out of a complex of conventions, ways of seeing, ways of interpreting what is seen. By conflating the ideas of Marx and Freud, of Roland Barthes, Umberto Eco, Jacques Lacan, and Louis Althusser, critics such as Christian Metz and the writers for the newly politicized *Cahiers du Cinéma* in Paris and *Screen* in England revised the *auteur* theory–the notion that the director is the main creative force of a film, fusing together its various parts. They regarded the work as the locus of many conflicting forces–financial, technical, generic, ideological–a place of contradictions and irresolution. They studied film through the phenomenon of narrative, discovering how and why stories are told cinematically, how and why we understand the telling. Finally, they investigated and revised the notion of realism, perhaps the oldest aesthetic of film and the one most tenaciously clung to.

Film criticism, in other words, began to catch up with what European filmmakers themselves had been doing in their work, redefining the notion of film as a reflection of reality, investigating more exciting and usable ideas that would enable the medium to create its own reality, its own way of speaking to and about the world. And this is an essential part of the complex phenomenon of modernism, the discovery by artist and critic that art is not a "natural" phenomenon or a container of great thoughts and universal values perceived and communicated by individual genius. It is rather a cultural artifact, speaking a specific language that is arbitrary and manipulable, able to articulate very specific formal and thematic concerns.

This book traces these discoveries. Although it concentrates on the period from the neo-realists on, digressions along the way will indicate how past movements and figures imposed upon and challenged the dominant modes of filmmaking. Within this progress another kind of response is examined, that of the viewer, the one who by perceiving the film completes it. That is, I will be questioning how such films are meant to be perceived, what role the viewer is asked to take in response to images and narrative. For another mark of modernism is its denial of traditional audience passivity: its demand that the viewer engage the work on an intellectual level, that the "work" of art be shared. This notion moves film away from its traditional status as entertainment, or perhaps redefines that status, offering entertainment as a participatory act. In any case it is responsible for the lack of commercial popularity of the films in question. That is a sad fact, because the majority of these works are accessible to any one who cares to confront them; very few of the filmmakers discussed here despise their audience or deliberately set out to confound them. Quite the contrary. Their films are invitations to thought and feeling, a denial of the obvious, an affirmation of possibilities. Defying the obvious, they defy convention while drawing from it, standing outside of it, requesting the audience to join them. This study is an attempt at a joining, an examination of convention and response, of cinema used as a probe and the viewer as a co-worker in the field of meaning. It is a study in aesthetic history, with a nod toward economics and an emphasis on influences and changes, on restlessness and a demand that cinema speak with its own voice.

Obviously a book covering such a wide field requires some restrictions and choices to make it manageable. I want to balance individual figures and their films with movements and ideas, the history of film with the works that make that history. I offer no complete overviews of any one filmmaker's work (in many cases these already exist), and figures will often reappear throughout the book in different contexts. The choices of figures and films are based on those works that are representative of movements and upon familiarity. This is a ticklish problem, for the discussion needs to be balanced between films that will be familiar to many readers, films that have already been discussed widely in print, and films that are important even though they may be largely unknown. Availability is the single greatest problem in the study of film in general and of contemporary European film in particular, and I have tried to limit this study to films which, even though they may not have been exhibited commercially, are at least available through non-theatrical distribution. Unhappily, because of these problems, no one will find all their favorite films included here, and some may take issue with what has been included and excluded. For example, much has already been written about the New Wave filmmakers, and Godard in particular, yet they are included because they are pivotal to my argument. Godard is the guiding force of all the experimentation in narrative cinema since the early sixties; to avoid him would have voided the project. Besides, I consider Godard the most exciting filmmaker in contemporary cinema.

Other choices of inclusion or omission are based on other factors. In discussing recent Eastern European cinema, I have chosen to concentrate on Hungary rather than Poland. Filmmaking in both countries is going well (or was in Poland at least until December 1981), but at the time of writing Hungarian films were more readily available for screening, and the works and place of Miklós Jancsó fit the direction of the book better than the somewhat more widely known films of Poland's Andrzej Wajda. Such choices reveal an unavoidable subjectivity. I give, for example, only summary treatment to the films of Ingmar Bergman, who many consider a major figure in the development of contemporary cinema. I do not. In fact I see his films standing in opposition to the movements central to this study. But Bergman has endured with a respectable audience that regards his work as the epitome of serious filmmaking, and I have no desire to attack that audience. Bergman will serve as a useful foil in the arguments that follow, a contrast to the filmmaking committed to formal, cultural, and political inquiry that I find more exciting and more revealing of the possibilities of the cinematic imagination.

For the sake of space and coherence, I do not speak much about Japanese cinema. Fortunately there exist two major critical works on the subject, Joan Mellen's *The Waves at Genji's Door* and Noël Burch's *To a Distant Observer*. Burch's book, which discusses in detail the development of a Japanese cinematic grammar, the ways those filmmakers structure their stories in comparison to American methods of filmic storytelling, is a particular influence on the methods I use here. There are other omissions (I regret, for example, that I have not sufficiently covered the new feminist filmmakers, particularly those now working in Germany), but rather than write a survey, I have chosen to trace some movements of the cinematic imagination through many countries over a period of some three decades.

Many countries indeed. This study deals with *foreign* films. Like most viewers foreign to the films, I must depend upon subtitles, which are, at their very best, rough approximations of what the characters are saying, and at their worst distortions. The dialogue, however, is at least approximated. Other material, like inserts of book pages, signs, posters, and extraneous verbal information from, for example, a television or radio, usually goes untranslated. This environmental material enriches the films of Godard, indeed is often central to them, and may be missed by subtitler and foreign audience. Much of the resonance of Fassbinder's *The Marriage of Maria Braun* (1978) is lost to a non-German audience because the continuous news broadcasts that punctuate the film and the significance of the soccer game broadcast that ends it go unsubtitled and unexplained. Such gaps, if unfilled, must at least be recognized.

This problem sometimes extends even to the titles of films. In most instances I have used the title by which a film is best known in the United States, occasionally putting the original title in parentheses when it is significantly different. Sometimes further explanations are needed. Godard's *Sauve qui peut* (*La Vie*) (1980) is called, after the idiomatic meaning of its first phrase, *Every Man for Himself,* which is not only sexist but almost the same as Werner Herzog's 1974 film *Every Man for Himself and God Against All* (which is itself also called *The Enigma of Kaspar Hauser*). Thus I have decided to use Godard's French title throughout. As far as dialogue is concerned, I have tried, where possible, to quote from the English translations of published screenplays. These often differ greatly from the subtitles in the film itself; but unless the change is major, I have trusted the translator rather than the subtitler. Otherwise, I have worked on faith and with the knowledge I have of foreign languages that occasionally permits recognition of a gross error in the subtitles. The problem becomes less acute in light of the fact that it is the image and the arrangement of images that make up a film's narrative in which I am most interested. The complexities offered by these elements more than make up for some subtleties lost by the subtitles.

One other aspect of "foreignness" is of particular concern to an American writing for an American audience. While the last section of the book is devoted to political film, the social-political nature of European and Latin American cinema is discussed throughout. The majority of the films I examine contain an implicit or explicit political discourse of a kind notably absent from American film and from

American culture in general, where art and politics are artificially separated. In form and content these films address themselves to the individual's place in society, to economic and social relationships, to class. Class consciousness is strong in most countries, where terms like "working class" and "bourgeois" have important political, cultural, and economic meanings. Furthermore there is a greater acceptance of left-wing political ideas in European culture and its cinema (and of course in the cinema of Cuba and Eastern Europe) than in the United States, and many important films since the war have been made either by left-wing intellectuals in Western Europe or revolutionary artists in the socialist countries. One important element of the neo-realist movement, for example, is that it politicized cinema, not for a particular party, but for a particular point of view, for the purpose of bringing an audience into closer proximity to a particular social and economic group. Most of the important cinema that followed, while not always concerned with the same class as the neo-realists, continued their concern with the political potentials of the image. It is impossible to understand these films without understanding these concerns and articulating them.

Finally, a word must be said about a troubling aspect of critical writing on film. A film critic does not share the literary critic's luxury of having a text always at hand for constant reference and to check quotations for accuracy. A great number of films were viewed and reviewed for this study—and then were gone, back to their distributors. Visual memory is untrustworthy; only notes provide the detailed information for analysis. There is a constant threat of small errors creeping in and remaining undiscovered. And as far as visual quotation is concerned, stills give only a rough approximation, and sometimes none at all.

Given the fact that the kind of filmmaking discussed here is no longer practiced to any great degree, and when practiced is rarely seen outside its own country, this book could be a lament, an act of nostalgia. I would like to believe, however, that imaginative filmmaking is not finished, but only in a recessive period. Therefore, instead of lamenting, this book will celebrate the past and future of engaged, progressive filmmaking, a communal act in which filmmaker and audience are involved in inquiry and speculation, in a desire, variously expressed, not for repetition, convention, exploitation, or the tedious reinforcement of the way we think we are, but for insight and change. Like the films of Godard–indeed, like the films of most of the people discussed in the following pages–this book is a celebration of cinema.

CHAPTER ONE
THE VALIDITY OF THE IMAGE

The cinema was born with neo-realism.
Giuseppe Bertolucci

THE WORD "realism" is the most problematic in any discussion of cinema. Because the first principle of filmmaking is the photographic reproduction of something that exists–a street, a room, a face–and the putting of that photograph into motion, the idea that film has a close relationship to the physically real world is inescapable. On top of this come the claims of widely different filmmakers that the narratives they construct out of these moving pictures are themselves "real," that they mirror, "the world," show us life, give us psychologically valid characters. But such statements are founded on unexamined assumptions. The photographic image is an image–physically and perceptually removed from its origins in the world. Film narratives and their characters may be based upon some aspects of actual behavior, but are in fact more strongly based on conventional film narrative behavior and our expectations of how characters in film ought to behave. They and their stories are no more real than any other fictions.

The term is, however, constantly evoked (and occasionally revoked, for a Hollywood filmmaker when threatened will claim that movies are only escapist entertainment). "Realism" formed the basis of André Bazin's criticism. Bazin, whose theoretical position was grounded in the belief that film could create images spatially and temporally faithful to the fullness and richness of the world, was the major critical influence on postwar European film culture and founder of the French New Wave. He drew his ideas from a variety of filmmakers, from Robert Flaherty and Eric von Stroheim to Jean Renoir, Orson Welles, and William Wyler. But the films he most admired, that seemed to authorize his theory, were those made in

Italy beginning just after the war, as part of a movement that took for itself the name of neo-realism.

This movement is our starting point, for here is where the past and future of European filmmaking fused and separated, and where modernism took hold. Neo-realism, by its title, reclaimed the territory of reality, and in that reclamation denied the claims of past filmmaking while announcing itself as a beginning for filmmaking to come. Every serious filmmaker to follow had first to understand what neo-realism was about before proceeding with his or her own approach. When Giuseppe Bertolucci (Bernardo's brother) said that "the cinema was born with neo-realism," he was not indulging in southern European hyperbole, but locating the origin of contemporary film.[1]

There are few terms in the language of film criticism that have such general use and recognition as "neo-realism," nor is there another so well defined, placed, and understood; for the critical term was used contemporaneously with the phenomenon it described, and by those involved in creating the works so described. While the origins of the term itself are not clear—David Overbey presumes the first time it appeared in print was in 1942, but in the context of an Italian critic's description of French cinema—what it defines is.[2] "Neo-realism" refers to an aesthetic movement that created a group of films in Italy between (approximately) 1945 and 1955. Its best-known representatives are Roberto Rossellini's *Rome, Open City* (1945), *Paisan* (1946), and *Germany, Year Zero* (1947); Luchino Visconti's *La Terra Trema* (1947); Vittorio De Sica's *Shoeshine* (1946), *Bicycle Thieves* (1948), *Miracle in Milan* (1950), and *Umberto D.* (1951); Fellini's *I Vitelloni* (1953) and possibly *La Strada* (1954) and *Nights of Cabiria* (1956). There are other films, less well known, and there are important antecedents, such as Visconti's *Ossessione* (1942), and even more important descendants. These films were shot on location; they used non- or semi-professional actors; they employed an unembellished narrative whose subject was the working or peasant class in a state of extreme poverty and deprivation (with a concentration upon children). There is an apparent reticence on the part of the neo-realist filmmaker to comment upon the images he is creating, and the narrative formed by the images seems to yield an objective, though certainly not documentary, perspective. This apparent objectivity is countered, however, by sentimentality, an almost melodramatic expression of love and sorrow toward the subjects of the film.

The visual elements of neo-realism are immediately recognizable in any of its representative films. The harsh grayness of the cinematography, the framing of the characters amidst barren urban or country squalor, in ruined tenements or desolate town squares, walking along a wall, the camera set or tracking at a diagonal to the character and background, are all visual codes that immediately signal a particular attitude and approach to the subject—that signal, more than anything else, "neo-realism." The desolation of the *mise-en-scène* (the structure and elements of the visual space, which both defines the characters and is defined by them) does not so much reflect as contain and surround the desolation of the characters. They are their surroundings: poor, ruined, and seemingly without hope. But always enduring. The suicide of the young boy, Edmund, in *Germany, Year Zero* is an unusual act for a neo-realist character, mitigated by the fact that Edmund comes to stand for Germany and the destruction it brought upon itself. In *Rome, Open City,* the deaths of Pina, Manfredi, and Don Pietro at the hands of the Germans are a sign of affirmation. Their humanity is transferred, within the film, to the children who carry on their struggle, and, outside the film, to the audience, whose understanding of their struggle validates it and their deaths.

The violence and death in Rossellini's war films are unusual and do not become a major part of neo-realist narrative structure. Rather, the violence that is most often committed on the characters is economic, and they are defined by their poverty. *Bicycle Thieves* exemplifies the pattern: the only way for the central character, Ricci, to work is to have a bicycle. When it is stolen by someone even poorer than he is, there is absolutely no recourse to anyone or anything. To get the bicycle out of hock in the first place, Ricci and his wife had to pawn their sheets. When the camera pans up the shelves and shelves of

The death of Pina (Anna Magnani). *Rome, Open City* (Museum of Modern Art Film Stills Archive).

sheets pawned by others out of similar need an almost universal condition is revealed. Ricci loses his bicycle and is lost. The film observes his wanderings with his little son Bruno in their attempt to find either the bicycle or the culprit, an attempt impossible from the start and ending with Ricci in his despair trying to steal a bike, getting caught, and walking off with Bruno, disappearing into the crowd.

This essentially passive losing and enduring of the poor provide an unalterable narrative structure for neo-realist filmmaking. Like the formal construction of the narratives of these films, the events of the narratives can be abstracted into immediately recognizable patterns—so much so that, from the vantage point of many years, neo-realism seems to be nothing more than a genre, with all the predictable conventions and responses that make up any other film genre.[3]

If it were only a film genre, one among so many others, the movement would not be as important as I have said. It would fall into place as a momentary coalescing of themes and structures, developed out of certain historical events by a group of filmmakers with similar ideas about what could be done with their medium, nurtured by a rather high degree of international success. It is true that, like other genres, neo-realism grew, peaked, and diminished. By the mid-fifties its practitioners had all gone on to other kinds of films; controversy continued in Italy over what they had done and why they were not doing it any more; and European cinema in general went into a short creative retreat. When the New Wave broke in the late fifties, little overt relationship to the Italian school was apparent. The new generation of filmmakers paid much homage to Rossellini (Godard had him co-write the script for *Les Carabiniers,* 1963). But the young French filmmakers seemed more concerned with Hollywood films than with European, and neo-realism seemed to assume a comfortable, esteemed place in film history, often referred to, but ignored as an influence.

Yet we have to look twice. There are two neo-realisms: one is the genre of films made in Italy in the decade between 1945 and 1955. The other is a concept, an aesthetics, a politics, a radical reorientation of cinema that changed the perspective on what had gone before and made possible a great deal of what came after. Occasionally concept and execution came close together in the films made by Rossellini, De Sica, Visconti, Fellini, and others during that decade, and I do not mean to imply that theory was more important than execution. But we can only fully understand what we see in neo-realism by looking at the images of its films through the theory, and the theory from a particular historical perspective. Neo-realism is a pivot, a "break," in the sense that Louis Althusser uses the term to express the point at which a new consciousness begins to appear, in this instance, a new consciousness of cinematic image-making and storytelling.[4]

In order to understand this "break," we need to examine something of the cinematic history that preceded neo-realism and something of the theory of that history as well. Within that context the ideas of the neo-realists will become clearer and their films can be examined not as an isolated phenomenon, but as a considered response to what had preceded them. In the brief survey that follows I wish to describe some alternate notions about film history and hook together the jagged edges of schools, movements, and the works of individuals who countered prevailing trends and rapidly solidifying traditions. After presenting a context that helps to clarify what the postwar Italians were doing as they (quite unconsciously) laid the ground for the great period of European filmmaking that followed them, I shall try to look at their ideas and films in the spirit in which these were expressed and made. Then it will be possible to look at them again from a more critical point of view and discover some things that went wrong, but which, in so doing, made possible a further response and further altered directions in cinema's aesthetic history.

Conventional histories of film would indicate a straight line of development. From Lumière and Méliès through the great figures and movements to the present day, neatly interlocking stages of filmmaking seem to move in orderly progression, with various apotheoses reached along the way. In this perspective, Lumière started it all in 1895. His little shot of a train pulling into a station so startled its first audience that they pulled back in fear. Méliès the magician followed, doing tricks on film; he invented optical effects and fantasy cinema. From these two sources developed the two major kinds of film: documentary and fiction.

The rest, in the conventional view, flowed almost naturally. Edwin S. Porter discovered the possibility of creating narrative structure by intercutting sequences, thereby allowing different elements of story to coexist in an illusion of simultaneity. D. W. Griffith further developed and refined the technique, "invented" the closeup, and perfected parallel montage, that fundamental element of film narrative construction in which two events separated in space but coexisting in time are paralleled to one another for contrast, suspense, and tension. In Weimar Germany, expressionist cinema formulated psychological structures through artificial, highly stylized sets that reflected characters' states of mind. In post-revolutionary Russia, Kuleshov, Pudovkin, and Eisenstein further developed Griffith montage into a primary formal device by means of which the audience was led toward meaning by the relationship or (in Eisenstein's case) the collision of images.

The thirties marked the ascendency of American film, the growing strength of the studios with a concomitant strengthening of studio styles, the star system, genres, moral structures and strictures, and, as important as all of these, economic markets. Although there were major figures abroad, with Jean Renoir foremost among them, European film was somewhat eclipsed in the thirties. Fascism and World War II put a halt to most creative filmmaking in Europe until the mid-forties and the rise of neo-realism. The fifties marked the beginning of the fall of the American studios and the rise of major European figures, Ingmar Bergman and Federico Fellini in the forefront. With the appearance of the New Wave in France and elsewhere, European film regained the ground it lost in the thirties and forties, reasserting its influence and its importance as the serious alternative to American film.

There is nothing wrong with this skeletal linearity. It plots out the major events and directions; it is, in fact, a plot of sorts for a historical narrative, which, when fleshed out with detail and analysis, provides the basic story of film. But the telling has itself become something of a genre, with the same figures and the same configurations recurring. In recent years some important variations and revisions to the tale have been made. Subjects have been rearranged and new ones introduced. Important questions have been raised about the primacy of certain figures and discoveries, particularly in the early days of film. The effects of technological developments on film form have been studied in an attempt to overcome separation of technical history from the aesthetic. The economics of the film business is no longer looked upon as a separate study, but as integrally involved with both technological and aesthetic developments.[5] Among the most important revisions in film history are those involving the place of the viewer in that history. Every change in the formal patterns of film narrative construction, and every change in the content and subject matter treated and created by that narrative construction, has meant changes in the way the viewer reacts to the narrative, changes in what is asked of and what is done to him or her, changes in the relationship of spectator to film being observed.

Like any narrative form, film is incomplete until perceived by a viewer. Therefore, to understand the movements and stages of film history is to understand how filmmakers wanted their cinema to be read. The creation and arrangement of images by a Russian in the twenties and a Frenchman in the sixties, or by F. W. Murnau in *Nosferatu* (1922) and Werner Herzog in *Nosferatu* (1978), are not only to be understood in terms of periods, movements, and subjective inclinations that dictate certain forms and approaches. A reverse perspective is possible. We may ask what is dictated *by* the form and content of a certain period or a certain filmmaker. How is the viewer expected to deal with the images and their narrative structure? I do not necessarily mean a specific spectator in 1908 or 1919, for that would demand a crude kind of guesswork and create the danger of false premises. Although films do give us clues as to what a culture was about at a given period of time–perhaps even indicate what people were thinking–my point here is to inquire how those images address the world, the viewer in the world, and most important, the cinematic conceptions and preconceptions of how the world can be addressed. Answers can be found in the films and the history that surrounds them. Further, by breaking into the linearity of history and counterpointing movements and figures, the hidden history of the spectator's role and the filmmaker's attitude toward it can be discovered.

With this in mind we can get a better notion of neo-realism's place and its demands. The conventional history tells us, quite accurately, that Rossellini, De Sica, and Visconti–all active in films during the fascist period–wanted, after the war, to break from the studio and the ideologically bound, middle-class cinema that had been prominent in Italy. It was called the "white telephone" school, a term that sums up the decor of a cinema of quasi-elegant bourgeois escapism that demanded little but that its audience yield itself up to an elegant world of love affairs and romantic intrigue. As a response to this kind of filmmaking, Rossellini, with scriptwriters Sergio Amidei and Federico Fellini, and De Sica, in close collaboration with screen-writer and movement theorist Cesare Zavattini, took to the streets and to the working class. Rossellini, writing a script as the Germans were fleeing Rome, begging raw film stock from American newsreel cameramen, filming without direct sound (a tradition still followed in the now technically sufficient world of Italian film production), created a film about the work and deaths of Italian Partisans almost on the spot. He followed *Rome, Open City* with two films that continued a kind of immediate history of war's end. De Sica and Zavattini concentrated on the refuse of the war, the adults and children on the streets, in jails and tenements. Visconti went a somewhat different route. A leftist nobleman, he received his film training with Jean Renoir in the late thirties. In 1942 he had made what is generally considered to be the first film with major neo-realist tendencies. *Ossessione* is of strange heritage. It is based on James M. Cain's novel *The Postman Always Rings Twice,* which had been filmed earlier in France and was again filmed in 1946 by Tay Garnett at MGM, with John Garfield and Lana Turner in the place of Massimo Girotti and Clara Calamai (and filmed yet again by Bob Rafelson in 1980 with Jack Nicholson and Jessica Lange).

Ossessione is a great sexual melodrama with wretched working-class characters who inhabit or wander through the poverty of the Po Valley. In it Visconti achieves a texture, almost an aroma, of sweat and lust that is simultaneously repellent and attractive, creating an intensity of image rarely seen in European film up to that time. But *Ossessione* was only a preparation for neo-realism. When Visconti made *La Terra Trema* in 1947, the first of a never-completed trilogy on the workers and peasants of Sicily, he used a non-professional cast and introduced the political element that only hovered on the periphery of *Ossessione. La Terra Trema* is not a film of sexual passion, but of a passion for liberation and independence.

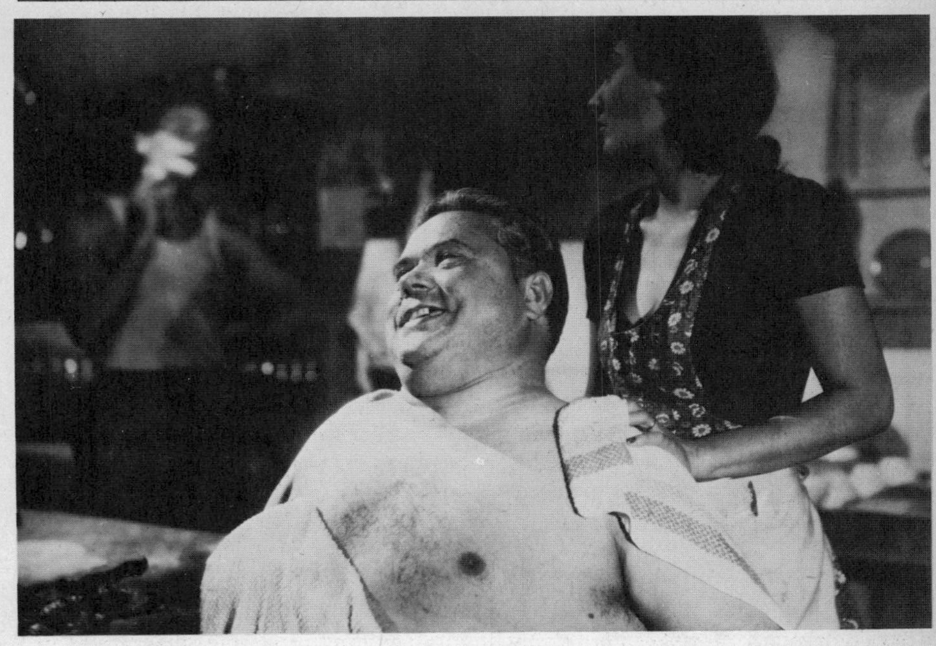

An aroma of sweat and lust. *Ossessione* (Museum of Modern Art Film Stills Archive).

In taking their cameras outside, using largely non-professional casts, and dealing with the working and peasant class in politically and economically determined situations, these filmmakers were indeed reacting against their own national cinematic tradition. But they were reacting as well to the larger tradition of Western cinema originated and perfected in Hollywood. They did battle against what they saw as a cinema of escape and evasion, uncommitted to exploring the world, seeking instead to palliate its audience, asking them to assent to comedic and melodramatic structures of love and innocence, of unhappy rich people and the joyful poor, of crime and revenge, the failure of the arrogant and success of the meek, played by stars of status and familiarity in roles of even greater familiarity. It was a tradition of cinema that asked little of the spectator besides assent and a willingness to be engaged by simple repetitions of basic themes, a tradition that located the spectator in fantasies that had the reality of convention.

The polemics of neo-realist theory actively attacked this tradition. In the early fifties, Cesare Zavattini wrote:

> This powerful desire of the [neo-realist] cinema to see and to analyze, this hunger for reality, for truth, is a kind of concrete homage to other people, that is, to all who exist. This, among other things, is what distinguishes neo-realism from the American cinema. In effect, the American position is diametrically opposed to our own: whereas we are attracted by the truth, by the reality which touches us and which we want to know and understand directly and thoroughly, the Americans continue to satisfy themselves with a sweetened version of truth produced through transpositions.[6]

"Produced through transpositions": the phrase captures precisely the problems the neo-realists had with the film that preceded them. Their concern was with the most fundamental process of narrative film, the methodology and ideology of representation, and the ways the spectator was asked to observe and partake in it. In the "transpositions" of reality into conventional images that occurred in American film and, by association, in Italian cinema of the thirties, they found only an evasion of reality and a diminishment of its complexity. Their response was to challenge those evasions and to reevaluate a history of cinema that ignored an entire class of people and denied its audience access to certain realities of existence. It is a cinema most familiar to most filmgoers, and while its origins and development are well documented, they bear some repetition and reevaluation in order to understand what the neo-realists and their followers were challenging.[7]

Films were made, originally, for working-class audiences. But the economic reality was that large amounts of money could not be made from peep shows in working-class neighborhoods; profit and respectability could come only from an audience with money and respectability. Two things were immediately needed to attract this group:

elegant exhibition and a film content that combined the blandest, seemingly most inoffensive morality with sexual titillation which could in turn be defended by a high moral tone. In American filmmaking (but by no means restricted to it) the result was an ideological leveling that began in the early teens and continued with various dips and curves into the early forties. The economic, political, and psychological complexities of the film audience's experience were largely transposed into images that sweetened life by simplifying it and denied economic inequality by denying that such inequality had any importance for happiness. It was a cinema of amelioration in which good characters achieved marriage and a middle-class life, where obedience and sacrifice were rewarded. The moral codes and dramatic constructions developed by D. W. Griffith in the teens set a pattern that popular cinema has embellished and continuously brought up to date. In the dominant cinema that America created and shared with the world, the dominant ideology was rarely questioned and a political context rarely recognized, analyzed, or criticized.

The transposition of social and moral complexities into melodramas of virtue rewarded and suffering transcended was accompanied by a transposition of another sort. Filmmakers developed a style that became as manageable as the content the style expressed. Narrative elements and their construction—the arranging of shots and sequences—were experimented with in the early part of the twentieth century, perfected by Griffith during his Biograph period (1908–13), and became a universal standard by the time sound was adopted. The mark of this style is continuity, an uninterrupted and unquestioned or unquestioning flow of events, a narrative construction so smooth and assured of its ability to promote its content that it becomes invisible. The flow of images on the screen assumes the reality of the given, as immediate and self-sufficient—*self-evident*—as the ideology it promotes.

The style grew out of trial and error, not complicity or conspiracy, and there were as many varieties of it as there were studios in various countries with filmmakers who attempted to impose some individuality on the work they did. What is more, it is a complex style, based on conventions that, because they were repeated so often and accepted so thoroughly, are looked upon by most viewers and filmmakers as the natural way to tell cinematic stories. Cutting from an establishing shot into various parts of the action; always completing actions by, for example, following a character in matched cuts from one place to another so that all action is accounted for; breaking up a dialogue into a series of over-the-shoulder shots, from one character to another, with eyelines perfectly matched—these and other small details of construction make up a pattern of storytelling that the neo-realists felt the need to reconsider. They realized that, whether practiced by MGM, Rank, Ufa, Gaumont, or the studios of Cinecittà, the classical style—the zero-degree style, as it has come to be called—was a complex of conventions, of formal and contextual choices, made, repeated, and naturalized: a transposition, to return to Zavattini's phrase, of the various realities of human experience and their expression into the simplified, expectation-fulfilling discourse of cinema.[8] National cinemas were dedicated to a comfortable situating of the spectator's gaze in a cinematic world where space was whole and enveloping (even though it was made up, particularly in American film, of short, fragmentary shots), time complete and completed in an easily apprehendable order. Within this small but complete world the passions of both character and spectator would be large but manageable, directed in assimilable curves and, above all, predictable and resolved.

The neo-realists were certainly aware that while this style was dominant, it was not all-inclusive. Small matters, such as the use of the over-the-shoulder shot—the so-called ping-pong method of dialogue construction—were not universally adopted by the European studios. More important, there were early reactions to the dominant form that prepared the ground for their work. The most significant is found in the films and critical theory of Sergei Eisenstein, who provided the first major alternative to the kind of cinema being developed by Griffith in America. He understood, more thoroughly than did Griffith himself, the possibilities of editing, regarded montage as the essential structuring principle of filmmaking, and sought to use it to transpose reality into a cinema that prodded consciousness, attacked traditional politics and morality, and stimulated thought as well as emotion. In the collision of images that made up the structure of his films, Eisenstein sought to create a dynamics that would impel the viewer to a recognition and understanding of revolution. His films were a structure of and for change, the opposite of Griffith's, which were a structure of and for rest and resolution. Discussing the classical closeup, Eisenstein wrote in his 1944 essay "Dickens, Griffith and the Film Today":

> The American says: *near,* or "close-up."
>
> We are speaking of the *qualitative* side of the phenomenon, linked with its meaning. . . .
>
> Among Americans the term is attached to *viewpoint.*
>
> Among us—to *the value of what is seen.* . . .
>
> In this comparison immediately the first thing to appear clearly relating to the principal function of the close-up in our cinema is—not only and not so much to *show* or to *present,* as to *signify,* to *give meaning,* to *designate.*

It is not the comfortable situating of the spectator's gaze that concerns Eisenstein, but the meaning of the gaze, the reason the spectator is seeing a particular structure of images at a particular time in the course of a film. On Griffith's cross-cutting he wrote:

> . . . this *quantitative accumulation* [of images] even in such "multiplying" situations was not enough: we sought for and found in juxtapositions more than that—*a qualitative leap.*
>
> The leap proved beyond the *limits of the possibilities* of the stage—a leap beyond the *limits of situation:* a leap into the field of montage *image,* montage *understanding,* montage as a means before all else of revealing the *ideological conception.*[9]

Where the American style creates suspense by multiplying incidents, provoking the viewer to experience tension with the promise that the tension will be eased with rescue and affirmation of security, Eisensteinian montage structure exposes the notion of security. The rhythm of images is the rhythm of historical analysis and revolutionary change. Rather than tension, Eisenstein's cutting provokes a movement through situations to a resolution that is itself further movement. Thus the people of Odessa celebrate the mutiny of the *Potemkin*'s crew; they are attacked by cossacks, who in turn are fired on by the ship; the ship's uprising is then joined by the rest of the fleet. And each sequence is formed by a dynamic, often violent, rhythm of images that provoke the spectator and demand an intellectual and emotional reaction to the events.

There was no doubt in Eisenstein's mind that Griffith's cinematic forms also revealed an ideology.

> In social attitudes Griffith was always a liberal, never departing far from the slightly sentimental humanism of the good old gentlemen and sweet old ladies of Victorian England. . . . His tender-hearted film morals go no higher than a level of Christian accusation of human injustice and nowhere in his films is there sounded a protest against social injustice. . . .
>
> But montage thinking is inseparable from the general content of thinking as a whole. The structure that is reflected in the concept of Griffith montage is the structure of bourgeois society. . . . In actuality (and this is no joke), he is woven of irreconcilably alternating layers of "white" and "red"–rich and poor. . . . And this society, perceived *only as a contrast between the haves and the have-nots,* is reflected in the consciousness of Griffith no deeper than the image of an intricate race between two parallel lines.[10]

Eisenstein appreciated Griffith for his ability to make the narrative elements of film into flexible, expressive structures. But he saw that these structures never moved beyond the self-satisfied repetition of middle-class social ideals. The close-up "showed" and punctuated emotional response. Cross-cutting, or parallel montage, manipulated cinematic space and time, creating a suspense that was resolved when the "space" of danger and "space" of rescue were finally joined and the hero rescued the heroine (or the reverse in the "Mother and the Law" section of *Intolerance*). Griffith's montage was sufficient to his ideology: pietistic, racist, conservative, closed off from most political and social concerns (only rarely, as in an early Biograph short, *A Corner in Wheat,* could Griffith break out of this enclosure, creating a montage of rich and poor in something like a political context. The pleas against injustice voiced in *Intolerance* are so broad and sentimental that they avoid any analysis or adequate understanding of history). The forms of his films were themselves manifestations of Griffith's social, political, and psychological attitudes, and Eisenstein was the first writer on film to understand that form is ideological. In response to American film, he promoted not only an explicit political content, but a political form and an alternative to the conventions of continuity begun by Griffith and advancing through the twenties. Against the pretenses of illusory realism—the form that hides itself so that content may appear to emerge effortlessly and without mediation—Eisenstein held out the possibility of a realism of the cinema itself, which spoke clearly in its own voice, not hiding its means, but using them to manifest and clarify political and social realities, transposing them into the dynamism of the image. "Absolute realism," he wrote, "is by no means the correct form of perception. It is simply the function of a certain form of social structure."[11] American film attempted to erect its "realism" as an absolute, as the universal way to tell cinematic stories. Against this attempt Eisenstein, and other major figures outside America (and a few inside), fought.

The neo-realists did not explicitly recognize Eisenstein as a cinematic forebear. (Few postwar filmmakers did.) His intrusive style, his insistence that the shot—the single unit of a recorded image—is only the raw material to be manipulated into the montage construction, went against their desire to use film as a disengaged observer of social existence. But if they did not explicitly recognize his importance to their own work, it is there nonetheless. If the style of neo-realism owes little to Eisenstein's means of expression, it owes a great deal to his desire to express a political alternative to the dominant cinema. That was what the neo-realists wanted to do, and Eisenstein's work made doing it easier for them, even if only as an unacknowledged model. So did other major attacks against the American style, less political than Eisenstein's and somewhat more in line with what the neo-realists would be doing; they provide further examples of the dialectics of perception and response that make up the history of cinema.

At first thought, German expressionism could not appear more dif-

The expressionist image. *The Cabinet of Dr. Caligari* (Museum of Modern Art Film Stills Archive).

ferent in intent and execution from postwar Italian cinema. Yet it is an important precursor. The opposite of Eisenstein's style, expressionism operated through the exaggeration of *mise-en-scène.* The shots made by Eisenstein and his cinematographer, Edward Tisse, though always put to the service of the larger montage structure, are carefully constructed and composed, dynamically calibrated reinventions of historical events—or events that should have occurred in history. Even in *Ivan the Terrible,* which reflects an expressionist influence, the images are at the service of history. But expressionism denied history, at least the history of external human events, and created instead closed and distorted images of psychological states. The exaggerated *mise-en-scène,* the use of painted sets to create distorted reflections of emotional stress and imbalance, provide a third term in the developing cinema of the twenties. To the growing strength of Hollywood melodrama and its obsessive continuity, to Eisenstein's clash of the images of history, expressionism opposed a cinema of legend and myth, presenting cultural archetypes and psychic struggle in the form of tableaux. In films like Robert Wiene's *The Cabinet of Dr. Caligari* (a nightmare fairground of the mind, originally intended to be a somewhat revolutionary statement about the madness of authority, but changed by its producer into simply a vision of madness); *Der Golem;* Fritz Lang's version of Nordic myth, *Siegfried* and *Kriemhild's Revenge,* and his myth of a proto-fascist future, *Metropolis;* Murnau's version of *Faust* and his *Nosferatu,* the first Dracula film, the world is expressed in gesture and design removed not only from familiar perception, but from the perceptual conventions emerging in film outside the expressionists' experiments. "The declared aim of the Expressionists," writes Lotte Eisner, "was to eliminate nature and attain absolute abstraction."[12]

This is of course an aim different from those of both American cinema and Eisenstein. For them "nature," the "real" world, were starting points, just as the neo-realists later claimed the real world to be their point of origin. But in their attempts to avoid the world as it was and instead build their own with the artifice of paint and light, the expressionists were concentrating attention on the image and inviting the spectator to examine and react to that image as a notion of a state of mind—an intent not totally different from Eisenstein's or the neo-realists', despite the different ways each pursued it. This requires some explanation, for Eisenstein's montages of revolution or the neo-realists' images of poverty and despair are rarely considered akin to the expressionist world of bizarre shapes and shadows. But the dependence upon the image in all three forms an important link. It is a peculiarity of perception that what one tends to recall from an Eisenstein film is a shot rather than a montage sequence: a face; the movement of the woman's long hair over the opening drawbridge in *October;* the boots of the cossacks stomping down the Odessa Steps, the falling baby carriage, and the woman's bleeding eye in *Potemkin.*[13] This may be because visual memory cannot store a montage, but only

The Eisenstein image. *October* (Museum of Modern Art Film Stills Archive).

continuous movement. More likely it is because of the power of Eisenstein's images. When one thinks of an expressionist film, one recalls a background (or more accurately a backdrop), the shape of a window painted on a wall or a frozen gesture. Expressionist film was the cinema of the designer; in it the formal organization of strained lines and figures is of predominating interest. It ran counter to all the other cinematic movements of the time. Even the French avant-garde of the twenties, who borrowed from expressionism, still based their images very much on the possibility of things actually seen. The images of expressionist film have little effect apart from themselves, apart from the fascination of the image itself. Expressionism was a short-circuited form, and as such has been reviled by most critics and filmmakers of a realist bent. Yet the expressionists' dependence upon the image actively counters the classical American style, which attempts to subordinate image to character and both to an unimpeded progress through narrative conflict to resolution.

The irony is that expressionism has had more of an influence on film than Eisenstein has. Eisensteinian montage became a debased form which was used in the thirties most often by Slavko Vorkapich in Hollywood to create "symbolic" episodes (like Jimmy Stewart's tour of Washington in *Mr. Smith Goes to Washington*), or for rather effective special effects (as in the earthquake sequence of *San Francisco*). While the internal dynamics of Eisenstein's cutting have taught many filmmakers a great deal, its political possibilities have been largely ignored. Expressionism, on the other hand, had an effect on the Hollywood style. Its major directors were brought to America, and their style influenced the Universal horror films of the thirties and was taken up by Orson Welles in *Citizen Kane,* which in turn influenced forties *film noir,* which in *its* turn influenced the New Wave filmmakers. When the German cinema was revitalized in the seventies, expressionism became more than an influence; it emerged as a problematic. Werner Herzog struggled with it, going so far as to remake Murnau's *Nosferatu,* imitating some of it and simultaneously removing many of its essential elements. Rainer Werner Fassbinder understood the expressionist urge. He never copied the style, but knew its intent, and created a *mise-en-scène* of observed entrapment that is in the expressionist tradition. However, Fassbinder, like his contemporary Wim Wenders, may have gotten his expressionist tendencies as much from American *film noir* as from his own cinematic tradition.

These criss-crossing influences will be examined in more detail as we proceed. Here it is important to note that in its emphasis on the function of the image, expressionism was one part of the response to the American tradition that touched neo-realism,* particularly as it modulated in the mid-twenties into a form called *Kammerspiel* (cham-

* "Response" is used figuratively here. German expressionist film is, of course, part of a large movement in that country's theater, literature, and painting.

berwork), a smaller, more open narrative structure that concerned itself less with aggravated psychological or mythic states and more with the immediate desperations of life in the Weimar Republic. (*Kammerspiel* was part of a larger artistic movement at the time called *Die Neue Sachlichkeit*—the "new objectivity," or "matter-of-factness.") In this form its potential influence on neo-realism became even greater.[14]

There were still other responses and influences, in particular two figures who were part of the movement leading toward neo-realism. The reactions to the Griffith tradition examined so far all came from outside the United States, but the approach to cinema he fostered did not go uncontested in America. Erich von Stroheim, who had been Griffith's assistant, provided a strong contrast to the work of his mentor. In his major films of the late teens and twenties—*Blind Husbands, Foolish Wives, The Merry Widow, The Wedding March,* and *Greed*—he responded to Griffith's pastoral landscapes, studio-set cities, and fanciful recreations of historical periods by creating two alternative worlds. The most predominant was a fantasy, late-nineteenth-century Middle Europe, a place of aristocratic decadence, the diabolical corner of the operetta kingdom—the dark capital of Ruritania, where noblemen drank blood and crippled girls were forced into marriage by pitiless fathers engaged in whorehouse orgies, and murdered bodies were deposited in sewers. Too grotesque for melodrama (though permitting just some sentimentality), smirking at the morbid moralism of Griffith and his followers, von Stroheim's lurid universe created a corrective dialectic. Cruelty takes the place of virtue, squalid death the place of rescued honor, perversity wins out over innocent passion.

In *Greed* the corrective has a different quality. Its world is contemporary, its characters working class, its physical detail built out of locations as well as sets. While too much ought not to be made of this—much of silent film was shot outdoors, on location—*Greed* goes further than most in turning locations into environments that detail the characters' social condition. The tenements, offices, bars, amusement parks they inhabit reflect their economic and social status as well as their diminished spirits. The inhabitants of *Greed* are among the meanest and most brutal in cinema, American or European, up to that time. They are perverse and obsessed, murderous in the extreme. The final shootout between the two male characters handcuffed together in the middle of Death Valley presents images grim in their expression of a willed, unsentimental destruction. Grim, but with a sense of von Stroheim's delight in the nastiness he portrays and his cold observation of aberrant behavior. Perhaps this emerges as a major legacy of von Stroheim's: a distance from the characters and their surroundings, an ability to observe with some humor and some horror the details and charms of perversity in a manner that cuts through the simplicities of melodrama that were developing under Griffith's tutelage. Von Stroheim's films ask of the viewer a willingness to observe the details of degeneracy with no hope offered for relief. The inhabitants of *Greed* are observed rather like insects under glass, and von Stroheim asks us to share with him the entomologist's pleasure at viewing his specimens. *Greed* and his other films are a prophecy of Luis Buñuel's unpitying exorcising of bourgeois pieties.

His ability to observe detail recommended von Stroheim to André Bazin, who in turn recommended him to a new generation of filmmakers: "But it is most of all Stroheim who rejects photographic expressionism and the tricks of montage. In his films reality lays itself bare like a suspect confessing under the relentless examination of the commissioner of police. He has one simple rule for direction. Take a close look at the world, keep on doing so, and in the end it will lay bare for you all its cruelty and its ugliness. One could easily imagine . . . a film by Stroheim composed of a single shot as long-lasting and as close-up as you like."[15] The last part of this statement may be truer to Bazin's conception of von Stroheim and where he fits into Bazin's aesthetic history of cinema than it is of the director's work. And as far as influence is concerned, von Stroheim's was almost as diffuse as Eisenstein's. Perhaps only Buñuel picked up directly the line of happy perversity that runs through von Stroheim's films. Otherwise, von Stroheim was a principal in the movement of anti-melodrama, the kind of filmmaking that turns away from conventions of easy emotional manipulation and the deployment of stereotypical characters with whom the viewer can "identify." But however indirect, his influence is apparent in the neo-realists' work. Like von Stroheim in *Greed,* they are attracted to working-class characters, though they come to these with a compassion von Stroheim would scorn. Even more important, the sense of detail, the environment that does not exaggerate the characters' state but defines it, the ability to make observation function in the place of editing are all qualities the neo-realists looked to adapt.

It must be noted in passing that von Stroheim played another major role for future filmmakers to observe, understand, and use to their benefit, that of Hollywood martyr. He was the first major figure to suffer from the growth of filmmaking into a heavy industry, with the capital-conservation, maximum-profit, minimum-expenditure mentality that goes with such growth. Von Stroheim was fired from both Universal Studios and MGM for his obsession with detail and his profligacy with time and money. *Greed* was originally forty-seven reels long. Von Stroheim himself cut it almost in half; then Goldwyn Studios, at the point of the merger which would create MGM, had it cut to ten reels, the only form in which it is available, the rest having presumably been destroyed. The few films he was able to direct after that were almost all re-cut by their studios.[16] With the coming of sound and the complete normalization of production, von Stroheim's directorial career was over. He was too slow, too meticulous, too arrogant for the line. What happened to him in Hollywood, as well as what happened to Eisenstein (his footage for *Que Viva Mexico* was stolen from him and his idea for a film of Dreiser's *American Tragedy* given by Paramount to the safely non-revolutionary Joseph von Sternberg) and then to Welles (who was removed from RKO for making extravagant, non-commercial films), did not go unheeded by European filmmakers, who attempted with some success to keep control over their work.

The economic and industrial aspects of filmmaking played as important a part in the emergence of a new cinema after the war as did the aesthetic movements and the work of major individual filmmakers. The neo-realists reacted as strongly against the methods of American film production as against the form and content of the films those methods produced. In turning away from studios to location shooting with non-professional players they joined economic necessity and aesthetic desire in an attack against the complex of events that made it difficult for a filmmaker like von Stroheim to work. And so his career had a double influence. Both what he did in his films and what was done to him and his films by the studios gave future filmmakers much to consider.

Von Stroheim's career directly converges with that of another formative figure who remains to be acknowledged along the way to neo-realism. Jean Renoir has stated that von Stroheim's *Foolish Wives* was a major influence on his early work, and his admiration was directly recognized when he gave von Stroheim an important role in *The Grand Illusion* (1937). But Renoir's work goes beyond von Stroheim. His career reflects the political, economic, and aesthetic shifts that have occurred in cinema over a great period of time—almost its entire history, from the silent era to the late sixties. Only the work of Hitchcock and Buñuel also spans so great a period, though their longevity is the only thing they have in common with Renoir.

Renoir's cinematic embrace of the world is more open and gentle than that of either his contemporaries or von Stroheim. Hitchcock's gaze discovers the terrors of seeing too much, revealing anarchy and irrationality; Buñuel and von Stroheim delight in these very things; but Renoir's look reveals a world in which the violence we see and do is at the service of a larger understanding of bourgeois frailty and proletarian need. "Everyone has his reasons," says Octave, the character played by Renoir in *The Rules of the Game* (1939)—one of the most quoted lines in any film—and it stands for Renoir's notion of human behavior, from the anti-bourgeois anarchy wrought by Michel Simon in *Boudu Saved from Drowning* (1932), to the justified murder of the odious boss Batala by his employee in the Popular Front film *Le Crime de M. Lange* (1935), to the elegies for a dying aristocracy in *The Grand Illusion* and *The Rules of the Game*. Renoir's is a cinema of understanding, of the embracing attempt to comprehend history and the function of men and women in it. The other movements and figures we have been observing are limited in comparison. He has ranged through a variety of stylistic approaches and subjects, through them all seeking ways to make the spectator's eye participate in the image, which embraces a large field, probes and elaborates, but does not close it off. The relationships of Renoir's characters to each other and to their environment are determined by a narrative and visual openness, a sensitivity to shifting attitudes and allegiances and the movements that indicate them. His use of camera movement and cutting creates a scope of activity, an interplay of face, gesture, and landscape that invite connection and enlargement. Bazin writes:

> Renoir . . . understands that the screen is not a simple rectangle. . . . It is the very opposite of a frame. The screen is a mask whose function is no less to hide reality than it is to reveal it. The significance of what the camera discloses is relative to what it leaves hidden. But this invisible witness is inevitably made to wear blinders; its ideal ubiquity is restrained by framing, just as tyranny is often restrained by assassination.[17]

The image, even Renoir's, cannot show everything, and in the dialectics of the seen and the not-seen lies an important part of his talent. In his use of deep focus, his persistent but gentle panning and tracking, the respect he shows to the spaces his camera organizes and to our orientation as spectators within those spaces, he indicates always an awareness of more. In his films of the thirties there is always something beyond what is immediately before the camera. But what is beyond is not a fearful otherness, but a *with*ness, a continuation and an expansion. Griffith enclosed his world within the melodrama of parallel montage, framing the heroine's face and the hero's, separated, but needing to come together, overcoming the world's opposition. Von Stroheim locked in on the details of sordidness. The expressionists denied an expansion into the world by ignoring it. For them reality was the space created within the frame; if not a stage space, certainly a staged one. Eisenstein was open to the realities of history, but his montage encouraged the viewer to create an intellectual, historically relevant space from the dialectical images juxtaposed on the screen. He provided the material and its initial structure; the viewer completed the design.

Renoir is, therefore, one of the first major filmmakers to open up screen and narrative space, to give his viewers room, to allow them active participation. Like Eisenstein, he requires the spectator to aid in the completion of the film's total design; but unlike Eisenstein's, his films have spatial continuity, and the spectator need only continue the connections Renoir provides. The viewer is somewhat more passive before a Renoir film than before one by Eisenstein, and the combination of this passivity and Renoir's openness leads often to a sense of ambiguity in his work. The elegiac attitude toward class structure in *The Grand Illusion,* the open embrace of the multitude of political and social perspectives in *The Rules of the Game,* do create problems of ascertaining point of view. But there is no uncertainty about the fact that Renoir introduces the important elements of trust and respect into his cinema. He is a director of movement and attitude, of characters who work through and are affected by historical as well as personal change. He is able to create formal structures expressing process, alignments and realignments, movements of characters and of the audience's responses to characters that are more open than melodrama permits. Renoir moved away from the rigid and determining structures of the figures and schools that preceded and surrounded him and replaced them with observed emergences of characters and situations that are fluid and changing. The closest formal analogy to *The Rules of the Game* is a symphony. As in a complex work of music, the inhabitants and events of this film work by statement and variation, through themes and characters taking dominant and recessive positions, through the crossing and re-crossing of lines of movements. (It is no accident that Octave is a would-be orchestra conductor.) Unlike music, of course, these movements are created by human figures acting with and reacting to each other in a precise narrative pattern. But in orchestrating their movements and actions rather than setting them on a trajectory within a predetermined space, Renoir is able to create an illusion of multiplicity and interdependence. The movements of the participants in the rabbit hunt, the interpenetration of servants and masters during the ball, the seemingly spontaneous series of decisions and mistaken identities that lead to the shooting of Jurieu, mark out a pattern of social imbalance, collapsing order, and characterological weakness that grows from no fixed point, but instead a number of points, moving, converging, departing. *The Rules of the Game* is a rich film; Renoir made no other as rich. Yet all of his best work creates to some extent this flow of chance and counter-chance and shares a generous visual and narrative field with the viewer.

Chance and counter-chance and the generosity of visual and narrative space became major elements of the new cinema of the sixties, and Renoir reigned as a guiding figure. Truffaut attempted to emulate him most directly, while Godard took his openness of form to its limits. All the major filmmakers of the sixties shared to some degree the respect Renoir had for his viewer. The neo-realists provided the bridge between him and them, and one film of Renoir's was of particular importance to their work. Although, as Raymond Durgnat points out, the subject of *Toni* (1934) is romantic passion and the *crime passionnel,* Renoir smuggles it through a quasi-objective study of working-class life in the manner the neo-realists were to favor.[18] He observes his characters' passions within, and determined by, a particular milieu and a particular class. The film is about a migrant worker in France, whose barren life in a quarry is mitigated by opportunities for love, ruined (and here Renoir cannot escape from thirties stereotypes) by a fickle woman. But more important than the story of the film is its treatment. Shot on location and creating a *mise-en-scène* that does not merely place its inhabitants within a landscape but implicates them in it, the film observes a physical detail of character and place that looks forward to Visconti's *Ossessione.* In fact Visconti is the only one of the neo-realist directors who knew of the film prior to 1950, and *Ossessione* may be a source for the transmission of Renoir's ideas to the neo-realists.[19]

But it is even more likely that Renoir came upon some notions of cinema which in theory and execution predated what the neo-realists came upon independently some ten years later. Twenty years *after* making *Toni,* Renoir himself spoke about it in the language of a neo-realist:

> Good photography . . . sees the world as it is, selects it, determines what merits being seen and seizes it as if by surprise, without change. . . . At the time of *Toni* . . . my ambition was to integrate the non-natural elements of my film, the elements not dependent on chance encounter, into a style as close as possible to everyday life. The same thing for the sets. There is no studio used in *Toni.* The landscapes, the houses are those we found. The human beings, whether interpreted by professional actors or the inhabitants of Martigues, tried to resemble people in the street. . . . No stone was left unturned to make our work as close as possible to a documentary. Our ambition was that the public would be able to imagine that an invisible camera had filmed the phases of a conflict without the characters unconsciously swept along by it being aware of its presence.[20]

Renoir expresses more of a documentary urge than the neo-realists would have cared for, and in reality *Toni* is nothing like a documentary, for its melodramatic content finally causes its attempted objectivity to collapse. Yet in Renoir's statement of intent—as well as in some aspects of the film—we can see parallels to the neo-realist desire. Here is Rossellini writing in 1953: "The subject of neo-realist film is the world; not story or narrative. It contains no preconceived thesis, because ideas are born *in* the film *from* the subject. It has no affinity with the superfluous and the merely spectacular, which it refuses, but is attracted to the concrete."[21] However, despite what Renoir says, the "concrete" in *Toni* is almost an afterthought, as if he had a story and sought an interesting way to present it. There is no sense of it being born "in" the film. Nevertheless neo-realism lies as a possibility in his work, as it does in expressionism and *Kammerspiel,* in Eisenstein, and even in the dominant melodramatic forms of American cinema. For in cinema, as in any art, the creation of any one form predicates the possibility of a response to that form. As each major movement or individual dealt with the notion of realism, interpreting film as a reflection of the "real" world or the creation of a new reality that would clarify experience, the function of the image changed; and each change represented another notion of what the image was capable of. The neo-realists wanted the image to deal so closely with the social realities of postwar Italy that it would throw off all the encumbrances of stylistic and contextual preconception and face that world as if without mediation. An impossible desire, but in it lay the potential for yet other assaults on cinema history, another modification of the role of filmmaker and spectator.

We are in a position now to look again at neo-realism proper. I have noted some of its basic elements—location shooting, poor working-class subjects played by non-professionals, use of the environment to define those subjects, an attitude of unmediated observation of events—and have examined some movements in cinema that preceded it. But something was needed to bring those various elements and the responses to earlier movements together, and that immediate cause was the end of World War II and the defeat of fascism. Only once before had a major historical event created a new cinema—when Eisenstein, Dziga Vertov, and their colleagues responded to the Russian Revolution with cinematic languages that spoke of changed perceptions of individual and social life. The end of the war in Italy did not signal major change, only devastation; years of repression were ended and an occupied country was suddenly on its own, free to look at itself and its past. The left and liberal sectors shifted their attention from the bourgeoisie and attempted to come to terms with the social and cultural conditions of those suffering most after the war. With the right momentarily in retreat and the center beginning to form, something of a Marxist position was able briefly to take hold. In film, that position was made manifest in the choice of the working class as subject and expressed formally in a desire to observe representatives of that class in day-to-day activities of survival without, as Rossellini says, the interference of the superfluous and the spectacular. Perhaps even without melodrama. At such a time misery could no more be embellished than it could be ignored. The poverty and neglect were real, and the ideology responsible for them was no longer operating to negate its responsibility and to transpose reality into a mockery of itself. Fascism is essentially a politics of melodrama and spectacle. In its political shows, its emotional excess, demand for sacrifice, and apotheosis of death as the most noble act of the hero, it manipulates emotion toward predetermined ends. The neo-realists wanted no ends predetermined; not even means. They wanted to observe the postwar world freed of the mediations and diversions that had helped create the war in the first place, and felt that if they allowed the movie camera to gaze at the world without interference, the lives of the poor would reveal themselves and their stories would grow from the simple act of observation.

Thus melodrama and any sort of formal demagoguery were to be avoided; they wished their new cinema to be non-directive in its attitude toward its subject and to allow its audience the freedom to respond to that subject with as little extraneous guidance as possible. Some neo-realist theory called for doing away with anything that might interfere with the raw material of raw life—even narrative itself. Zavattini wrote: ". . . the neo-realist movement recognized that the cinema should take as its subject the daily existence and condition of the Italian people, without introducing the coloration of the imagination, and thereby, force itself to analyze it for whatever human, historical, determining and definite factors it encompasses."[22] In 1948, an Italian Catholic critic, Felix A. Morlion, wrote:

> the Italian neo-realist director prefers simplicity. He is not eager to obtain effects through sensational editing in the manner of Eisenstein and Orson Welles. His goals are different: humble cinematography, seemingly unoriginal editing, simplicity in his choice of shots and his use of plastic material [the visual design of the film]: all go to give his interior vision substance. . . .
>
> The Italian neo-realist school is based on a single thesis diametrically opposed to that thesis which regards the cinema only in terms of lighting effects, words, and purely imaginary situations. Neo-realism's thesis is that the screen is a magic window which opens out onto the "real"; that cinematic art is the art of recreating, through the exercise of free choice upon the material world, the most intense vision possible of the invisible reality inherent in the movements of the mind.[23]

These words recall Bazin's remarks about Renoir, but go even further. Bazin recognized the dialectical play of revelation and withholding in Renoir, the image's ability to suggest reality by what it hides of it. The neo-realists theorized a deconstruction of all the formative elements of film and of the tensions between form and content that might manipulate the subject of the film or the spectator. Bazin picks up the call and, writing about *Bicycle Thieves* in 1949, says it "is one of the first examples of pure cinema. No more actors, no more story, no more sets, which is to say that in the perfect aesthetic illusion of reality there is no more cinema."[24]

Some twenty years later, Godard ended *Weekend* with the words "End of Story. End of Cinema." In 1967, the neo-realist urge to break down the narrative forms and conventions of the entertainment film was still being evoked, although by this time, at the close of a decade of modernist filmmaking, the call seemed more likely to be heeded than it had been in the mid-forties. For when we look at neo-realist film now, such statements as Morlion's or Bazin's seem more like wish-fulfillment than anything else. But to the Italian intellectuals of the time, and to Bazin in France who saw in their ideas not only a vindication of his own theories but a way to revitalize all of cinema, overstatement was necessary. It is the tradition of aesthetic manifestos to declare the death of the forms they challenge and to claim they begin the art anew. More important, the logic of the neo-realists' thinking was correct. If film was to become a tool, a way of getting at the lives of people whose lives never were the subject of cinema; if film was to be an eye, a way of looking at a world rarely seen clearly in cinema, then all the methods film had used to evade observation of this world had to be eschewed. Not merely must the white telephones go, and the entire class those telephones signified, but also the cinematic constructions that perpetuated their irrelevance must be repudiated.

"The basis of every good work of art," wrote Morlion, "is not what people *think* about reality, but what reality actually is."[25] The filmmaker must suppress his interpretive powers, his transpositional powers (to revert to Zavattini's term), and eliminate the conventions that make the transpositions of reality possible. The neo-realists would return to zero (another call repeated by Godard). They would start with the photographic origins of film, its ability to record images of the world "objectively." In 1945, Bazin wrote: "For the first time, between the originating object and its reproduction there intervenes only the instrumentality of a nonliving agent. For the first time an image of the world is formed automatically, without the creative intervention of man."[26] This insight would be scorned by most photographers and filmmakers. But its theoretical impact was enormous. Both Bazin and the neo-realists were looking at the cinematic medium as just that, a medium, a means of getting to the world and getting the world to us without intervening in it. "Reality is there, why change it?" De Sica said. The neo-realists believed that the cinematic image could be *depended upon* to reveal the world seen by the filmmaker if the filmmaker merely looked and kept his counsel, interfered as little as possible.

And so Bazin theorized about what he called the "image fact,"

> a fragment of concrete reality in itself multiple and full of ambiguity, whose meaning emerges only after the fact, thanks to other imposed facts between which the mind establishes certain relationships. Unquestionably, the director chose these "facts" carefully while at the same time respecting their factual integrity. . . . But the nature of the "image facts" is not only to maintain with the other image facts the relationships invented by the mind. These are in a sense the centrifugal properties of the images—those which make the narrative possible. Each image being on its own just a fragment of reality existing before any meanings, the entire surface of the scene should manifest an equally concrete density.[27]

The image is a kind of monad, a part of reality that incorporates within itself the fullness and complexity of the world from which it is taken. Its initial "meaning" is only that it *is,* and the spectator revels in this fact. Further meaning accrues to it when it becomes part of a narrative by being connected to other "image facts."

Bazin did not know—or would not recognize—that this is very close to Eisenstein's concept of the shot as a "montage cell" that achieves meaning only in relation to other shots.[28] However, the difference between their two concepts is telling. For Eisenstein the shot is only valuable in relation to the montage. For Bazin the phenomenon of narrative that occurs when one shot (and for the sake of simplicity I will equate "image" and "shot") is connected to others is almost secondary to the miracle of the shot's ability to be a precise rendering of reality. Neither Bazin nor the neo-realists regarded the image as being in service to a larger montage structure. "The assemblage of the film must never add anything to the existing reality," Bazin says.[29] The image may give of itself to other images so that a narrative can exist, but it must retain independence and its own validity. And in practice, the neo-realist film does not draw attention to its cutting. While not quite in the Hollywood zero-degree style, its editing is invisible, as Morlion said it must be. Rossellini and De Sica in particular cut mainly to reposition the gaze, center it on the major event in the sequence or the major participants in a dialogue. Their cutting rarely adds information, but is functional in the very best sense, guiding our concentration without manipulating it. Closeups and point-of-view shots (in which we see the character and what the character sees) are used sparingly, and whenever possible the environment figures as strongly as the individuals within it. The image generates all the meaning it can; commentary is inside it.

A fine example occurs in *Bicycle Thieves*. Ricci, the central character, is in his first morning on his new job, pasting up posters on walls. A co-worker is showing him how to do it. With significant irony, they are putting up a poster of Rita Hayworth—a premier sign of forties Hollywood with all the connotations of glamor, artificiality, and contrivance that De Sica was attempting to abjure.* The subject here is not glamor or contrivance, but an unassuming workman on his first job in a long time, learning his rather simple task. The sequence begins with the camera to the left of the characters, at a diagonal to them and the wall on which the poster is going up (neo-realist characters, as I noted earlier, are always observed by walls, the urban boundaries of their lives). As Ricci's co-worker shows him what to do the camera executes a simple dolly and pan toward him

* The concept of the sign is borrowed from semiology and indicates a unit of meaning made up of a physical expression (the poster in this instance) and its attendant denotations and connotations.

Ricci pastes up the Rita Hayworth poster. *Bicycle Thieves* (Museum of Modern Art Film Stills Archive).

as he pastes Rita to the wall. The shot is framed by two ladders. De Sica then cuts unobtrusively to a more distant shot from the other side, again diagonal to the characters and the wall. The camera is far enough from them so that we can see two little boys on the street (whom we had barely glimpsed previously), beggars, one of whom is playing an accordion. The accordion player moves toward the ladder, and Ricci's co-worker turns briefly to look at him. The little boy puts his foot up on the ladder and receives an unceremonious kick from the workman (who this time doesn't even turn around). As the boy walks away, another man walks into the frame from screen right, moving down the diagonal in front of the men at their work. He is well dressed, a tidy middle-aged bourgeois with a pipe. As he walks along the wall, the boys walk after him, and the camera, as if taking a casual interest in this event, pans away from Ricci and his colleague to follow the man with the two children in calm pursuit. But "follow" is not quite accurate, for the camera does not dolly toward them and there is no cut to a closer position. It merely pans away from its central concern to observe this seemingly peripheral event. The accordion player plays. The other little boy tugs at the well-to-do man's sleeve (a little further along the street we notice a man sitting in a chair by the curb). The well-to-do man ignores the boy, who turns and walks back to his friend. At this point there is a cut back to Ricci and his co-worker, who continues his instructions, the shot framing them in basically the same diagonal position as before. The two men then get on their bikes and the camera pans with Ricci as he heads off on his own, passing the two boys on the sidewalk.

The whole sequence lasts less than a minute. It gives us next to no information about "plot" and merely advances the narrative toward its first crisis, which occurs in the next sequence when Ricci's bike is stolen. If such a series of events occurred in a literary work, it might be called "descriptive" or "atmospheric." But there is more to it than that. Here, we might term the sequence *milieu gathering,* the expansion from direct concentration on the central character to his immediate world. It is an expansion of the frame, but not in the measured, almost choreographic style of Renoir's expansions of screen and

Ricci and Bruno walk the streets. *Bicycle Thieves* (Museum of Modern Art Film Stills Archive).

narrative space. De Sica's digressions are more casual; they assume the point of view of interested observer, concerned with the main character, but interested as well in the world that surrounds him. As observer, the camera attempts to be non-judgmental and non-provocative as well. Its movements do not provoke us or confront the characters, do not lead us on or compromise them through a prearranged strategy, a reframing meant to excite expectation or anxiety. We are asked only to share an interest in the commonplaces of this particular world, which become less common by the simple and unexpected attention given them.

This careful neutrality is not present throughout the film, and De Sica does play upon expectations when, for example, Ricci and his little son Bruno search for the stolen bicycle in the marketplace.

Anxiety is created when Ricci–and we–think Bruno may have drowned, and when father and son discover the thief and are surrounded by the people in his neighborhood. De Sica even indulges in a commentative montage. During their search, Ricci and Bruno stop at a restaurant. As Bruno eats his meager pizza he looks over his shoulder at the rich family at another table, and De Sica cuts between Bruno and that family's little boy stuffing himself with an enormous meal. Nor is the digression with the street urchins entirely innocent of narrative import and emotional preparation. It occurs at the high point of Ricci's life in the film: he has work. The beggars foreshadow his later situation, bicycle stolen, himself almost turned thief in desperation, walking the streets hopelessly.

In fact neither De Sica nor any of the neo-realists were pure in their execution, nor were they willing to take very great chances. Certainly not as great as, for example, Godard in *Sauve qui peut* (*La Vie*) (*Every Man for Himself*), where he pans or cuts from a central narrative event to anonymous people on the street. But this is not yet the moment for criticism. Godard could indulge in radical dislocations of attention precisely because De Sica had pointed the way. As I indicated, neo-realism was a delicate concatenation of theory and practice, and at this point I am more interested in ways in which the theory was successfully realized than in how it was compromised.

The beggars sequence in *Bicycle Thieves* summarizes the major goal of the movement for formal restraint: "During the projection of the film," Luigi Chiarini wrote about Rossellini's *Rome, Open City* in 1950, "the audience no longer sees the limits of the screen, does not sense a skillful artifice, and no exclamations are uttered about the virtuosity of the directors and actors. The images have become reality, not seen with lucid detachment as in a mirror, but grasped in their actuality and very substance. The formal presence of the filmmakers has dissolved in that reality."[30] What was happening *in* the frame was more important than what the filmmaker might do with the frame or to the frame. The Hollywood style of the thirties did not concentrate on the image, but on the way the image could present stock characters in excessive situations, knitting these images into a smooth continuity that made up the narrative. The neo-realists did not defy continuity, but neither did they sacrifice the image to it. They allowed the image to create a world, casually, and with as little embellishment as possible. Even when the "everyday" is extraordinary, as in *Rome, Open City,* there is an attempt not to make it more than it is. Rossellini tries to restrain the image, holding it to the observation of poor people doing heroic things—resisting and fighting the Nazi occupation—rather than making them appear heroic. The heroism emerges from their acts and their deaths. No comment is made upon it because no comment is needed.

If the word "realism" in film has any meaning at all it lies in this phenomenon: the refusal to make more of the image than is there, and an attempt to allow the fewest and simplest faces, gestures, and surroundings to speak what they have to say and then to move on. This is what neo-realism discovered and what was passed on to the next generation. Whether in the casual observation of the beggars in *Bicycle Thieves;* the brief look on Bruno's face of disbelief mingled with fear when he finds himself standing among clerics speaking German (a language with many connotations to a postwar Italian); the simple two-shots of Pina and her fiancé on the tenement staircase talking about their future in *Rome, Open City;* or the point-of-view shot from the fiancé being taken away in the German's truck, watching as Pina runs after him and is shot down, there is in the best of these films a *desire* not to embellish or do more to the characters or the viewer than is necessary. In Visconti's *La Terra Trema,* where great care is taken in composing images, where boats and harbor and the people who inhabit them are given an Eisensteinian grandeur, the visual care expresses Visconti's desire not for embellishment, but for honor. There is an admiration of these people and their struggle which does not make them more than they are; perhaps just what they are. Visconti is not dealing in the exaggerations of early socialist realism, the poster nobility of workers and peasants, but with a class of people in a particular geographical area (Sicily) to whom attention needed to be paid. The documentary urge inherent in much of the neo-realist aesthetic also leads him a step further; the rich images are accompanied by a voice-over commentary which, even though it often merely repeats or sums up what we have already seen or will soon see, also attempts to provide an extra objective perspective, a concerned voice to match the concerned eye that forms the images. But some contradictions begin to emerge. Within this documentary impulse, almost contrary to it, there is a desire to go beyond creation of an illusion of unmediated reality. Visconti will not drop all aesthetic pretense. He observes his world, coaxes it into being, frames and composes it, regards it in the light of his own admiration and compassion, honors it, and finally monumentalizes it. There are images in the film that call for an aesthetic response, an appreciation of the way they are lit and composed. And the manipulation of the narrative, like that of the images, is designed to move us in particular ways.

In the end, the calls to remove subjective contemplation and mediation and reduce aesthetic interference, while necessary to the moral work of the neo-realists, were recognized as impossible to follow. The outstanding fact about the movement is that they were committed to making fiction films, not documentaries, despite the impulse toward documentary in their theory and occasionally in their practice. The subjective urge was always present, and finally recognized. Chiarini wrote: "Facts speak through the suggestive force of neo-realism; not as brutal documentary, because absolute objectivity is impossible and is never 'purified' out from the subjective element represented by the director; rather, in the sense of the historical-social meaning of facts."[31] In their urge to purify cinema, they never gave serious thought to using documentary, as had John Grierson in England during the thirties, or Dziga Vertov, who wanted to chronicle post-revolutionary Russia with his kino eye in the twenties. There was nothing for the postwar Italians to chronicle with documentary. There was no revolution and they did not find lyricism in work or sponsorship by government and business to create such lyricism as Grierson and his followers had. Instead they chose to dramatize and give structure to postwar events and to a class of people rarely considered worthy of narrative in the cinema. They invented characters, but allowed them to be played by individuals who were close to those characters in their own lives. They told a story but at the same time attenuated it, subordinating conventional continuity and character development to the observation of detail. Bazin wrote: "The narrative unit is not the episode, the event, the sudden turn of events, or the character of its protagonists; it is the succession of concrete instants of life, no one of which can be said to be more important than another, for their ontological equality destroys drama at its very basis."[32] Just as the "image fact" achieves importance by the effect of its real presence, so "the concrete instants of life" contained by the image achieve importance beyond drama, beyond narrative even. Seeing an image of life itself is a dramatic event; it need not be manipulated into something greater than itself. The neo-realists sought a form that would attenuate the structures of fantasy in traditional film. The spectator would be offered small, unelaborated images built from the lives of a certain class of people at a certain moment and in a certain place. These images would, finally, request the viewer to recognize in them not "reality" but an attempt to evoke the concrete, the immediate; they would request an attention and a willingness to trust the image not to betray either its subject or the spectator.

In *Paisan,* the second of his three films on the war, Rossellini comes closest of all the major neo-realist filmmakers to making a fictional narrative that does not intrude upon subject and observer. The film integrates at least three approaches: it is a quasi-newsreel documenting the movement of American troops from Sicily northward to the Po; within this historical structure it presents six episodes, in specific geographical locations, sketching small dramas occurring between the soldiers and Resistance fighters and the people; and within these episodes it reveals, tersely and without embellishment, some attitudes, agonies, defeats, and victories, military and personal, that resulted from the deprivation of war and two foreign invasions, German and American.

The *mise-en-scène* throughout most of the episodes is one of catastrophic destruction and barrenness, of heaps of rubble or empty

"Joe" and the little boy on the rubble heap. *Paisan* (Museum of Modern Art Film Stills Archive).

streets through which individuals pursue each other or search for those who have become physically or emotionally lost. In the Naples episode a black American MP meets a small boy, another of those street beggars who populate the neo-realist universe. The episode is built out of a series of small ironies and understandings. When they first meet, at a street fair complete with fire-eater, the soldier is drunk, and a group of young children try to rob him. The boy follows the soldier and the two of them visit a puppet show, which depicts the white crusader Orlando battling a Moor. The black American liberator watches a display of ancient racism and in his drunkenness attacks the white puppet. The boy leads him away through the ruined streets to a rubble heap where the two sit. The soldier plays a harmonica and talks of his fantasy of a hero's welcome in New York, realizes it is a fantasy, and says he does not want to go home. He falls asleep, and the sequence ends in a manner typical of Rossellini's approach through the film. The little boy shakes him, tells him rather matter-of-factly, "If you go to sleep, I'll steal your shoes." The soldier sleeps. The image fades to black.[33]

The episode concludes with the soldier finding the little boy again (although at first he does not recognize him), yelling at him, taking him home to the cave where he and many other children live, war orphans left to their own squalor. The soldier comes to a quiet understanding of the poverty that makes thievery an ordinary childhood activity. He does not take the shoes offered him by the little boy (which are not the ones he stole from him anyway) and simply leaves. The last shots are a closeup of the boy's sad, scared face and a distant shot of the soldier driving off. Swelling music provides the only punctuation. Emotions are not wrung from us here, and the revelation of the city's hopeless poverty that we share with the black soldier, which ironically reverberates with his own situation as a black man, remains understated. Rossellini need only suggest the horror that often proceeds from understanding, or, in more precise neo-realist terms, permit revelation to occur through observation of the individuals in their environment, and allow both them and us the reactions appropriate at the moment and place of the revelation. He need not expand on these self-contained and self-expressive images: the poor children in primitive conditions who must steal to live; the black American soldier, hero, drunkard, understanding the poverty, unable to have any effect on it. Recognition passes in the exchange of glances within the film and across the film to the audience, who are then left between the look of the child and the soldier in the distant jeep.

The film's other episodes work in similar patterns. Some are a bit more melodramatic, such as the Roman episode, about an American soldier who spends the night with a prostitute he does not recognize as the woman he once loved. Or the Florence episode, in which an American nurse seeks her Partisan lover, only to discover he has been killed. But even here the personal drama is undercut by that essential neo-realist wonder at things observed. Again, Rossellini is most concerned with the way this piece of history looks, and the Florence episode is constructed primarily of scenes of the nurse moving through the streets of an open city. The urban landscape takes precedence over the woman's search, and her discovery of her own loss is undercut by Rossellini's re-creation of the physical emptiness and random violence of a wartime city, where a jug of wine is pulled across the street by a rope so the enemy will not spot the people, and a group of British soldiers sit on a hill viewing church architecture through binoculars.

In one episode, we are set up for melodrama and then denied it. The visit of a group of American chaplains—a Catholic, a Protestant, and a Jew—to a Franciscan monastery would ordinarily threaten (certainly in an American film) either a great deal of cuteness, choking sanctimoniousness, or a lesson in the virtues of brotherhood. But again, Rossellini refuses to extend significance or commentary beyond the demands of the moment. We learn that the Franciscans served the town during the war by caring for the peasants' animals. The Americans wonder at the age of the monastery and offer the friars cigarettes and chocolate, as well as more substantial provisions. The friars in return show hospitality and, among themselves, great consternation over the fact that one of the chaplains is Jewish and another Protestant. When the friars confront the Catholic chaplain with their concern over the souls of the Jew and the Protestant, he quietly acknowledges it without sharing it. At dinner, the friars fast, "because Divine Providence has sent to our refuge two souls on which the light of truth must descend." The Catholic chaplain appears to hesitate at their remarks and then gets up to speak. It is just at this point that our expectations are denied. Our training in Hollywood melodrama would lead us to expect the chaplain to give a fulsome defense of his colleagues and a plea for understanding. Rossellini's chaplain says: ". . . I want to talk to you. I want to tell you that what you've given me is such a great gift that I feel I'll always be in your debt. I've found here that peace of mind I'd lost in the horrors and the trials of the war, a beautiful, moving lesson of humility, simplicity, and pure faith. . . ."[34] Sanctimoniousness is replaced by understanding, conflict by acceptance, and embellishment is foregone.

Throughout the film the images create and then seem to recede behind a simple historical presence, the fictive record of a particular moment. Again, this is not the Hollywood style of invisible form; we are quite conscious of the effect of withholding and foreshortening. Artifice is present, recognized, *and* self-effacing simultaneously. As viewers, we are aware of the restraint and its results, a continuous blocking of our desire for conclusiveness, for emotional statement, for closure.

Paisan is a difficult film to evaluate fully. The acting—which is hardly acting at all in a conventional sense—is erratic and so against our expectations of professional performance that it appears amateurish. The cutting, even more than in other neo-realist films, is perfectly functional, getting the narrative from here to there in the swiftest way possible. The structure of the episodes is so truncated that it produces an off-handedness that elevates incompleteness to the status of a structural necessity. But the attenuation and lack of climax is thematic as well as structural. The history covered by the film goes just up to the complete liberation of the country and does not even permit a final satisfaction from that event. The last episode concerns the joining of American and Allied soldiers with Italian Partisans against the Germans in the Po Valley during the last weeks of the war. It opens with the image of a body in a life preserver floating down the river, carrying a sign reading "Partisan," placed there by the Germans. The episode ends with Germans shooting their captives on a boat, the bodies falling one after the other into the river. In between these events is a chronicle of terrors: the liberation army surrounded by Germans on the Po marshes, peasants attempting to gather eels for food, a weeping child on the river bank, a Partisan shooting himself in his despair. Within the war film genre, this episode negates completely the conventions of individual heroism and substitutes a barely cohesive group struggle that is itself apparently hopeless. It is bearable only because

A chronicle of war's terrors. *Paisan* (Museum of Modern Art Film Stills Archives).

we know that the Allies and the Partisans did win. The commentary over the floating bodies at the end tells us, "This happened in the winter of 1944. A few weeks later spring came to Italy and the war was declared over."[35] It is only within this context that the episode loses its connotations of futility and instead comes to express a grim persistence with a promise of victory emerging from loss.

Or more accurately, in neo-realist terms, it comes to represent itself, its images self-sufficient in their historical validity, demanding of us nothing more than an immediate comprehension of them. But when I say that *Paisan* or any other neo-realist film comes to represent itself, I am not suggesting that it is a self-referential form. The creation of a film narrative that comes to signify mainly the creation of a film narrative was the work of the modernist movement that followed neo-realism and was made possible by it. Such an operation could not have been further from Rossellini's or his colleagues' minds. What I am suggesting is that the foreshortened emotions created by the foreshortened structure of *Paisan,* their incompleteness and inconclusiveness, permit and indeed force the viewer to deal with them with a minimum of directorial assistance. Which may be why this film, more than any other of the period, is so unsatisfying within the context of our cinematic expectations, and most successful in the context of neo-realist theory. It refuses to do more than show, or demand more than that we understand what is shown. Beyond that there is the possibility for us to integrate the narrative with our understanding of the history its images reflect, a history of pain and loss, of deprivation and struggle, and of some kind of victory.

The players in this version of history have little personality or life beyond their presence in the narratives; what we see of them is as much as we ever learn about them. Rossellini gives us nothing in the way of past, future, or psychological background for his characters. The "Joe" of the first episode reminisces to an uncomprehending Italian girl of his home in America. The "Joe" of the second episode fantasizes a heroic homecoming for himself to an uncomprehending little boy. But in neither case do the thoughts and feelings of these characters provide the psychology or motivation we are used to finding in melodrama, and in neither case do their feelings lead anywhere. In the first instance, "Joe" is shot by the Germans when he lights a cigarette lighter to show Carmela pictures of his family. Carmela is herself killed when she tries to shoot the Germans. The drunken fantasies of the second "Joe" only lead to a realization of his unheroic life, and when he falls asleep his boots get stolen. Even the sentimentality latent in the Roman episode, in which a drunk American soldier doesn't recognize the prostitute he has picked up as a girl he met and fell in love with six months earlier, is undercut. The pathos threatened when the prostitute attempts to re-create the past by slipping away from the drunken soldier and leaving him her old address, hoping he will come to her and recognize her as his former love, is left unfinished. The next day the soldier looks at the address and throws it away without recognition. Francesca is left waiting; the soldier drives off. Nothing more is made of it.

The "psychological realism" missing in *Paisan* is a basic component of film melodrama, Hollywood or European, so basic that melodrama is partly defined by its presence. It is the means by which characters are given a "life" and personality that appear to bear some relationship to the lives of the film's viewers. The character talks, has memories, passes through events, indulges in introspection and confrontation, suffers, endures, triumphs, or dies, often triumphing in death. In short, the psychologically motivated character has experiences and memories which reveal a personality. But these are often exaggerated and stereotyped, mirroring not the concerns of real individuals in a real society, but the conventional attitudes and personalities of other "psychologically motivated" characters in the history of film. They may change from period to period and country to country, depending on changes and differences in reigning ideologies; they often reflect contemporary fantasies and change as the fantasies change. But despite what "psychological realism" may tell us about our fantasies and our ideology, it tells us nothing about the realities of the immediate world and immediate experience, which is why the neorealists tried to do away with it. For them situation takes the place of psychology, the type replaces the individual, the ordinary the heroic. What we know about a character is what we see of that character in action in his or her environment; no other motivation is needed.

Bazin, writing about the Florence episode in *Paisan,* says, "Attention is never artificially focused on the heroine. The camera makes no pretense at being psychologically subjective. . . . As if making an impartial report, [it] confines itself to following a woman searching for a man, leaving us the task of being alone with her, of understanding her, and of sharing her suffering."[36] If, Bazin might have added, we care to do so. This episode, like all the others in the film, gives us permission to move on and not be alone with the heroine, not identify with her. The spectator is not distanced from the characters as in a film by Resnais, Godard, or Fassbinder, filmmakers who want completely to cleanse their characters of psychological conventions and their audience of expectations. The neo-realists wanted only to avoid heaping upon the spectator clichéd emotion extraneous to what was needed to understand the character in his or her immediate situation, and rather to allow audience response to flow from the "image-facts" and not a preconceived notion of character. In his war trilogy Rossellini comes close to conventional character psychology in the figure of Edmund, the child of *Germany, Year Zero,* who commits suicide after following the advice of a Nazi to kill his ailing father. But here the enormity of the crime and of the act of a child's suicide goes well beyond the cinematic conventions of troubled children with troubled families in troubled times. Again the physical and political landscape merges with the individual and his actions in an almost allegorical interchange. The child is as ruined as his surroundings. When he is not in the tenement flat his family shares with others, he is walking the shattered streets of Berlin (an activity he shares with most neo-realist characters), as lost as the country he represents. His suicide becomes Germany's own and his actions are explained finally not by his own emotional nature, but by his function as a historical symbol. His life and death outrun their local narrative function and come to stand for a greater history. At one point in his wanderings, he is given a recording of a Hitler speech by his old Nazi teacher to sell on the black market. In the ruins of the Chancery building, Edmund plays the recording and Hitler's voice echoes. We see an old man and a young child listen in some bewilderment. The camera pans the ruined cityscape as Hitler boasts of bringing the country to its glory.

Meaning flows from the relationship of word and image and history, and the ironies of Edmund's life and his leap to death in a bombed-out building become, finally, more than can be contained within a mere psychological narrative. The "dailiness" the neo-realists sought expands in *Germany, Year Zero* not to some vague universal statement of innocence lost, but to a large and specific judgment about history. Zavattini wrote:

> Whereas in the past, cinema portrayed a situation from which a second was derived, and then a third from that, and so on, each scene being created only to be forgotten the next moment, today, when we imagine a scene, we feel the need to "stay" there

> inside it; we now know that it has within itself all the potential of being reborn and of having important effects. We can calmly say: give us an ordinary situation and from it we will make a spectacle. Centrifugal force which constituted (both from a technical and a moral point of view) the fundamental aspects of traditional cinema has now transformed itself into centripetal force.[37]

The melodramatic urge—shared by the conventional war film as by most genres—seeks to force the trials of its characters outward into large statements of suffering and transcendence that are greater than history, sometimes greater than the characters themselves. Rossellini reverses the melodramatic urge of the war genre, collapses it into the immediate images of ruin in *Germany, Year Zero,* or the particular struggles and defeats in *Rome, Open City* and *Paisan.* History is drawn, with the spectator's gaze, into the images, which then communicate back to the viewer the place of the character *in* history, often subjected *to* history. Most neo-realist cinema operates on this principle: characters inhabit a ruined, collapsed world; their fight against it is momentarily and minimally heroic, like that of the Partisans in *Rome, Open City,* or the fishermen in *La Terra Trema.* Their struggle is an external one; little psychological torment is involved. The despair of Ricci in *Bicycle Thieves* or the old man in *Umberto D.* is not so much personal as it is social, a despair at not being able to gain an economic self-sufficiency. All of these characters lose by the end of the film, but in their loss there is the attempt to express a wider gain. The whistling of the Partisan children gathered around the executed priest at the end of *Rome, Open City* is the most commanding sign of life coming out of destruction in any of the films, and the executions of the Partisans at the end of *Paisan* suggest not a dismal end of struggle, but the necessary conditions of its victory. No glory is given to the deaths, but nothing is taken away from their function in the wider fight. And besides they allow us to hate fascism even more.

But at this point, at the recognition that all neo-realist films end in images of loss, or at best endurance, we can discriminate some more between theoretical intentions and practical realizations. Let me repeat a statement by Zavattini: "It should . . . be clear, that contrary to what was done before the war, the neo-realist movement recognized that the cinema should take as its subject the daily existence and condition of the Italian people, without introducing the coloration of the imagination, and thereby, force itself to analyze it for whatever human, historical, determining, and definite factors it encompasses." Looking back on the movement when he wrote this, Zavattini announced clearly the shift from middle-class subjects and moralism to a more objective observation of the working class, "without introducing the coloration of the imagination." He is aware that it is only a bravura statement, and he admits that the narrative urge of the neo-realists is strong; "they tell stories and do not apply the documentary spirit simply and fully."[38] The essays from which these remarks came make up an apology. Neo-realism as a coherent movement was fading when Zavattini wrote them between 1952 and 1953, and there were many attacks upon it from both right and left. In his apology Zavattini's bad faith becomes apparent as he continues to support the theories of the movement against his own inability to see them through. As a practitioner, Zavattini the screenwriter, De Sica's collaborator, never shied from the coloration of the imagination or from attempts to use it to move the audience. And while he and the others were successful in breaking the "bourgeois synthesis" of traditional cinema, they were not successful in analyzing "whatever human, historical, determining and definite factors" were encompassed by "the daily existence and condition of the Italian people." They showed that existence and showed it well; they rarely analyzed it. While they went far in creating an "intensity of vision . . . [in] both the director and the audience" and "a dialogue in which one must give life, reality, its historical importance, which exists in each instant,"[39] they rarely dealt with history in such a way as to indicate that their characters might control it rather than only suffer it. They permitted the spectator to see a particular world, but never to see past it. They sometimes suggested, but never clearly presented, possibilities for change in that world.

Nor were their attempts to revise narrative structure complete. For all they did accomplish, they could not, or would not, move away from an essentially sentimental attachment to their subject. The desire for objective observation never replaced sympathy for the characters, a sympathy which manifested itself in the communication of the social-political despair the characters suffered. Images which in theory were meant to be intense observations of daily existence were, in fact, perhaps by the nature of that daily life, images of pathos. The wanderings of Ricci and little Bruno in *Bicycle Thieves,* their frustration at every turn, the sequence in which Ricci thinks his son has drowned after he has cuffed him in anger, the threats against Ricci by the crowd protecting the thief, Ricci's own attempt at stealing a bike, Bruno's reproach, and their final walk, hand in hand into the crowd, all constitute a pattern guaranteed to arouse our sadness and frustration and make our emotions echo the characters'. Melodrama is just barely avoided in *Bicycle Thieves,* as it is in *Rome, Open City,* by the refusal to allow the characters to suffer psychologically and by keeping the movement of the characters and their story simple, without predictable curves of passion, and anchored in the physical and historical environment the images create. Rossellini does make special demands on our reactions in the death of Pina, the torturing of Manfredi, and the execution of Don Pietro in *Rome, Open City.* In that film he is perhaps too close to the realities of fascism to be able to distance himself from its terrors, and not yet aware that an identification with and emotional reaction to viewed pain and suffering can preclude an understanding of it.[40] He learned this quickly, and *Paisan* attenuates direct emotion almost completely. De Sica and Visconti never learned it.

This structural difficulty, the inability to separate their own emotions and ours from the characters they create, is compounded by the neo-realists' insistence on using children as the fulcrum on which to turn these emotions. It is easy to understand the attraction, for children are the most visible and obvious sufferers in any political, economic, and social disaster. They are helpless and therefore wronged the most. To see these wrongs through them, from their perspective, or at least with them as central participants, is to perceive the scope of these wrongs most immediately. The problem—and it is unclear whether Rossellini and De Sica were aware of it—is that the use of children results in a special pleading which, at its worst, becomes cynicism, a vulgar way to assure audience response. The neo-realists fortunately missed being vulgar; they did not miss a certain cynicism and a great deal of naivete. Eric Rhode, one of the few historians not captivated by neo-realist children and able to see the faults of the movement as a whole, accuses the filmmakers of committing moral blackmail. His analysis is important enough to be quoted at length:

> Through his portrait of Peachum in *The Threepenny Opera,* [Bertolt] Brecht had implied that all claims to charity are a form of licensed thievery. He had recognized how in an unjust society the exploited can exploit the exploiters in a way that traps everyone into some form of guile. De Sica and Zavattini are not willing to accept responsibility for this conception of society. They reduce everyone to a childlike state, as though everyone were a child in the sight of God. Their childlike perception of the minutiae of daily life tends to be passive, for all its delicate precision. They cling to the surface of things, and in their clinging assume a perpetual complaint. Brecht had understood that once adults slip back into childlike states of mind and displace responsibility for the community elsewhere, they prefer to complain rather than take action when the community fails to satisfy their needs; and since these needs are seldom satisfied, they tend to imagine that their lives are ordained by some malignant power.[41]

Though De Sica and others used children to focus their view of society and our emotional reaction to it, I do not agree with Rhode that they assume a childlike perception themselves, nor do I think their perception to be passive. The passivity in their films exists elsewhere. I do agree, however, that the omnipresence of children is a way for them to avoid a certain responsibility. A child, by all the definitions of middle-class morality, is helpless and in need of constant protection by either parents or charity. The neo-realist child gets none from the latter and only as much from the former as the parents can spare in their own desperate attempts at survival. The desolation continually observed by the neo-realists' cameras is not only unabated, but seems unabatable, as does the poverty that is created by and inhabits the desolation. Within this desolation the children suffer mutely and serve as witnesses and as surrogates for our point of view. Here is where Rhode's perception is acute, for in attaching our point of view to the suffering child, the neo-realists put *us* in a state of passive and helpless contemplation. De Sica and Zavattini are the main offenders, but even Rossellini, whose children in *Rome, Open City* are active participants in the Partisans' fight, overplays his hand and our perception by giving them a greater role than they deserve and we need in order to understand the situation. None of these filmmakers acknowledged Brecht's principle of sustained, distanced analysis in the work of art, an analysis that disallows emotional identification and passive acceptance of events by the audience. And so their stated desire to see the world clearly and without conventional cinematic preconceptions came into conflict with their inability to withdraw themselves from a sometimes clichéd sympathy for the helpless. The result was that the neo-realists ultimately failed the people they portrayed by being unable or unwilling to create for them victory over their situation (even in Rossellini's war films the victory is only alluded to), and failed their audience by too often allowing them to sentimentalize rather than analyze character and situation.

Early in their careers, and perhaps only because of their anti-fascism, the neo-realists seem to have had leftist sympathies which drew their attention to the poor and abused. They were not, however, revolutionaries. Though they changed the aesthetics of Western cinema, they did not call for a change in the structure of Western society. What was more, the aesthetic they promoted countered the idea of change. It demanded they observe, but not alter what they saw; it constrained them from offering their characters much more than pity and sentiment. A notion of passivity is built into neo-realist theory, and as a result the filmmakers only allow their characters and their audience to reap the rewards of passivity: more pain, more poverty, softened somewhat by a notion of stoicism and endurance (on the part of the characters) and sadness, understanding, and not a little bit of superiority (on the part of the audience).

In the twenties, Eisenstein could create film that was revolutionary both in form and content; he had the force and support of a historical revolution behind him. There was no such support in postwar Italy, only the grimness of a ruined country with an uncertain future. Suffering overtook celebration, and the filmmakers who emerged to document this moment were more taken by the suffering than by anything else. After all, suffering of this stature had never before been documented on film, certainly not without softening and an artificial leap to a change in fortune. Committed to the retention of simple but eloquent details, to an unadorned but compassionate image, the neo-realist filmmaker was not free to alter them or to express anything more than what he saw. It was, finally, a self-defeating cycle, and it can be seen operating in a most troublesome way in Visconti's *La Terra Trema.* This film was to be the first part of a great neo-realist, revolutionary trilogy about the social and political struggles of fishermen, miners, and peasants living in the poverty-ridden south of Italy. The project was started with financing from the Communist Party, and in its original conception had a revolutionary thrust and a notion of the poor triumphing over their oppression that might have taken the film beyond the usual neo-realist observations of passive suffering. Visconti did not follow through on this original concept, partly because his ideas changed as he was shooting and partly because the project never worked out as intended.[42] Only the first part was made, and in its time suffered because of its pace, its length (over three hours), and, in Italy, its dialogue. Visconti used a non-professional Sicilian cast who spoke their own dialect, largely incomprehensible to the rest of the country (which is one reason a voice-over commentary was added). For some time after its initial screenings, the film was available only in a cut, greatly reduced version. But seen whole, and despite (or because of) its changed intentions, it can be taken as a *summa* of the movement. All the immediate textbook concerns of neo-realism are attended to. The film is shot on location and acted by the inhabitants of the location, who play roles close to their own lives. Visconti shows a careful eye for the rich but simple detail that defines these lives and renders movingly the looks and gestures, light and texture of their world.

His images are made with extreme care, and the use of deep focus and silhouette, the lights of boats at sea, the sweeping pans of land and ocean, all indicate an admiration, even a celebration of what is seen. It is not an idle formalism (this crept into Visconti's work soon enough), but, as I noted earlier, an attempt to draw attention, to honor the place and its inhabitants. This attitude can be glimpsed in some sequences of *Bicycle Thieves,* where De Sica honors his working men not with nobility, certainly, but with a sense of purpose and control, as in Ricci's first morning of work, when he and Bruno join other men in the streets just after dawn, going for their buses, dominating the landscape and the early light. Visconti goes much further than De Sica.

But in *La Terra Trema* visual splendor and the observation of novel detail begin to exercise more control over the narrative than does a sense of social and political revelation. Visconti succeeds in documenting the town and inhabitants of Aci-Trezza–more than documenting it, organizing the buildings, the coastline, the fishermen and their families in images that finally overwhelm them. "The documentary moment prevails over the ideological," Geoffrey Nowell-Smith writes, and the picturesque prevails over the documentary. Meanwhile the revolutionary intent that Nowell-Smith cites as the initial driving force of the film gets turned into a moving neo-realist affirmation of enduring humanity. The film at times approaches, in Nowell-Smith's words, "an anthropological cinema in which the anthropologist sets the scene and comments on its significance, but retires from the picture when it is actually being taken so that his presence is no longer felt."[43] And so a problem arises. Visconti tries to have things two ways: he attempts to make a visual record of a place and a way of life, unencumbered by an authorial presence; and he attempts to apply an authorial presence through the voice-over commentary and by forming this record into a narrative of rebellion and failure. His desire to document a people and their environment, his decision not to depict a successful revolution, his intrusion into the narrative to guide our emotions result in a powerful but conflicted work.

The film traces the fortunes of a poor fishing family who attempt to make themselves independent of the *padroni,* the omnipresent bosses, wholesalers in this instance, who take the results of the family's difficult labor, pay them poorly for it, and then sell it at a large profit. The early part of the film observes the Valastros' work at sea, their family life, their bitterness at being unable to sell their own catch. Visconti's commentary, spoken throughout the film, tells us of their poverty and anxiety and their few simple pleasures. We are presented with a cycle of work and domesticity interspersed with innocent flirtations, all of which is knitted together by a voice-over narrator who speaks for the people, asking how they could be content with their exploitation. One member of the family, the older brother 'Ntoni, is not. Against the protestations of his conservative grandfather, he leads a small rebellion. The fishermen gather after the catch; 'Ntoni throws the wholesalers' scales and baskets into the water and is promptly arrested by the police. The wholesalers realize that, without the fishermen to catch fish for them to sell, they will not make money. They have 'Ntoni released from jail.

At this point Visconti begins to evade the difficulties in the situation he has created. 'Ntoni, freed, persists in carrying out his struggle for liberation from the owners, and in so doing confronts the unwillingness of his fellow fishermen to join him. He takes the dangerous step of mortgaging his family's house to get the money he needs for his independence. Visconti observes the neighbors' suspicions and their playful mocking of the Valastros; he is sensitive to the shifts in class attitudes. In their momentary wealth, with money from their house and a good catch, the Valastros become the rich and are suspected by the other workers. Both 'Ntoni's girlfriend and his sister's boyfriend express an insecurity about this sudden wealth. It is just here that the "anthropologist" is at his most subtle, and here that the would-be revolutionary filmmaker withdraws and the melodramatist enters, leaving his characters, their situation, and the audience to fend for themselves against the intrusion of cinematic convention. The Valastros reach a high point of success. They have a good catch. They manage to get help from their neighbors in salting the fish. There is laughter and music. 'Ntoni and his lover run happily through the countryside to make love at the shore. Every message sent out by the activity on the screen begins to arouse a single melodramatic expectation: a disaster is inevitable. Visconti cannot help doubling the expectations set up by the images: the narrator emphasizes the couple's happiness, an emphasis that sets up an inevitable response. The happiness will not last.

Visconti dissolves from the couple to the windy dock. The men return to the sea. They go off in their boats and the screen fades to black. The image fades up on a pan of the harbor and town, ending on a bell ringer. The narrator tells us that the sound of the bell in Aci-Trezza makes hearts sink, for it means a storm is approaching. The pattern is obvious. The storm comes; the family at home are deeply worried. We are shown images of women in black, silhouetted against the shore, looking out expectantly to the turbulent sea. The Valastros survive physically, but their boat, and therefore their livelihood, is ruined. One of the wholesalers tells 'Ntoni he will pay for all this. In truth Visconti, the owner of the narrative, will make the family, and us, pay dearly. The decline in fortune from this moment is precipitous and direct. The wholesalers cheat the family, a brother leaves home with a stranger to work in the north, a sister takes up with a town official, 'Ntoni finds companionship with the town drunks because they are the only ones who will not laugh at him. The family's house is sold; they end up in rags. "All that is left of the Valastros," says the narrator in a remark that suggests Visconti may be luxuriating in the fall of his characters, "are their eyes with which to cry." 'Ntoni must humiliate himself before the wholesalers he once tried to beat, beg for work before a boss who sits beneath the fading but still clear imprint of Mussolini's name on the wall. The film ends with the Valastros settling into their broken-down new house and 'Ntoni returning to the sea, understanding that his failure was due to a lack of solidarity among the fishermen, but indentured to the *padroni* more thoroughly than before.

'Ntoni and his brothers in rags. *La Terra Trema* (Museum of Modern Art Film Stills Archive).

Mussolini's name on the wall above the wholesaler is an important emblem, meant as a contrast to the hammer and sickle seen on the wall outside the wholesalers' office and elsewhere. Visconti alludes to the two political orders, one indicating repression, cruel and arrogant power, the other a communal spirit, the strength of the fishermen together, working for themselves. But with the prominence of Mussolini's name over the boss's head, Visconti seems to suggest that the pull of the right is strongest, that repression will continue and a successful communal struggle is not about to occur. He does not say or indicate why he thinks this and allows the political substructure of the film to be diminished by the melodramatic curve that takes over the narrative. The characters are pulled away from the possibilities of political struggle and given over to that most simple and diverting of dramatic conventions, fate. Like so many of their cousins in other neo-realist films, the Valastros suffer and lose. Their spirits are unbroken, but save for 'Ntoni's important understanding that only in unity can the fishermen face the wholesalers, they are without direction or hope.

Though I have said that one of the most important elements of neo-realism was its attempt to counter melodrama–the fixed curves of loss and sacrifice and unearned emotional response that had become the supporting pattern of most commercial cinema–I have now to modify that argument and say that though Rossellini, De Sica, and Visconti would have liked to move into an anti-melodramatic mode, they succeeded only on occasion; the conflict between their desire to create an observed social-political reality and their attachment to old forms of sentimental storytelling was never resolved, for a variety of reasons. Predominant among them is that these filmmakers often confused one concept of "realism"–an attempt to explore the actual conditions of people, hoping, perhaps, that from the revelation of these conditions might arise a notion of how to change them–with a literary and cinematic *convention* of "realism" that holds a narrative to be "realistic" if it is sad and if its characters come to an unhappy or unresolved end. They also felt obliged, as I indicated earlier, to follow out the logic of their aesthetic. If neo-realism was to concern itself with the observation of existing conditions, and that observation revealed a seemingly insuperable and stagnant poverty, then that was what had to be shown.[44] To have dramatized change would have injected into the fiction a subjective impulse contrary to the dictates of observation.

The resulting conflict was often more than the films could bear. The neo-realists may have hoped their films would work dialectically, that their exposure of poverty, suffering, and endurance would suggest possibilities for change in the social structure. But this dialectic rarely operated successfully. For what is ultimately communicated in most of the films is not hope but, to apply Nowell-Smith's comments on Visconti, "a deeply rooted pessimistic fatalism" which pulls too strongly against "a more optimistic intellectual conception of the possibilities of human action" that the filmmakers might want to suggest.[45] No one and nothing helps Ricci when his bicycle is stolen. He goes to a community center after the event for help. On one side of the hall is what appears to be a Communist Party labor meeting, in which a speaker tells the gathering of the need for more jobs. Ricci's personal needs are rebuffed by the speaker. At the other end of the hall some people are rehearsing a show, making entertainment at this most serious point of Ricci's life. The Party will not help him, and only a friend, a garbage man who is rehearsing, steps forward with the promise of aid. The next day the garbage man and another friend briefly help Ricci look for his bicycle, but he is soon left alone with his son in a hopeless and humiliating venture which winds up only in a general affirmation of humanity—a powerful affirmation, to be sure, but also an easy one to make. Nothing specific is offered for the particular case of Ricci and his family or those like him. Similarly, at the end of *Umberto D.* De Sica and Zavattini's old man (abused old age here takes the place of abused childhood) who is unable to live on his government pension and has been thrown out of his lodgings, contemplates suicide, but finally, with his little dog, surrounded by children in the park, decides to go on. For what and how is not made clear. Again an affirmation of life takes the place of an analysis of how such a life can be affirmed. We are not permitted to despair, but neither are we given any concrete reason not to.

This notion of the need to endure hardship and despair with hope comes out of another conflicting strain in the neo-realist endeavor, the attempt to merge a leftist understanding of class and social structure with Catholic faith.[46] Behind the neo-realist aesthetic lay the belief that an openness to the world would lead to revelation; that the filmmaker need only gaze into the book of God's creatures to discover the truths of humanity. Bazin writes that De Sica's strength lies

> in not betraying the essence of things, in allowing them first of all to exist for their own sakes, freely; it is in loving them in their singular individuality. "My little sister reality," says De Sica, and she circles about him like the birds around Saint Francis. Others put her in a cage or teach her to talk, but De Sica talks with her and it is the true language of reality that we hear, the word that cannot be denied, that only love can utter.[47]

In two instances the religious simplicity that Bazin found in the neo-realist endeavor was literally expressed. Rossellini made a film about Saint Francis in 1950, and in 1964, after the movement was long over, Pier Paolo Pasolini filmed *The Gospel According to Saint Matthew.* In both instances the spectacle and exaggeration that are part of the American genre of biblical cinema are replaced by a simplicity and matter-of-factness (bordering on the childish in Rossellini's film) that subordinate awe to the ordinary and build significance from what the viewer may make of the events rather than how those events are made. The artfulness of Pasolini's film lies in the rigorousness of its adherence to neo-realist principles and its sense of documenting the biblical text with the simplest of black-and-white cinematic images.

But Bazin's meditation has nothing to do with films that have a religious subject matter per se. He is indeed attempting to find in neo-realism a Catholic openness to God's work in nature and a faith that faith itself will reveal the divinity in the world. It is a faith that simply will not work, for it turns insight away from the political and social nature of existence into quietism and into hope with no basis in reality. Anger is dissolved into sentimentality. The neo-realists politicized the image, made it reveal the sufferings of a class; at the same time they insisted that their revelations could not go beyond what was seen by the compassionate eye, which had to remain passive in the face of those sufferings. The strains became too much and the neo-realists became less and less able or willing to sustain the contradictions inherent in the form and content of their work. In 1950, Zavattini and De Sica made *Miracle in Milan,* in which one of the finest neo-realist environments, a squatters' city in an urban wasteland, generates a narrative of the triumph of naivete and wish-fulfillment. A young man, innocent and good to the point of simple-mindedness, leads his people out of poverty and the clutches of an industrialist who wants their oil-rich land only with the aid of ghosts and angels. The poor literally fly to heaven, "towards a kingdom where good morning really means good morning."[48] Neo-realism becomes neo-fantasy, "simply a fairy story and only intended as such," says De Sica.[49] His intentions may not be questioned; but his images may. They are, some of them, among the best-realized cityscapes in the movement. Early in the film there are renderings of gray buildings and streets (photographed by G. R. Aldo, who was cinematographer for *La Terra Trema*) that look forward to the style Antonioni would develop in the late fifties and early sixties. But by this point in his career De Sica seems unwilling to trust the validity of his images and needed to transcend them with optical effects and a narrative growing out of a childish fantasy that betrays extreme pessimism, as well as the reactionary belief that the poor will only find their reward in another life.

The rapid decay of its original impetus in the early fifties indicates that neo-realism was perhaps a genre after all, a specific concatenation of form and content that responded to historical and social events and was guided by theories fraught with contradictions. When the situation created by those events changed, disappeared, or was radically altered, and when the contradictions could no longer be contained, the genre changed. It had become repetitive or—in the case of *Miracle in Milan*—silly; its form and content simply used each other up, and the filmmakers wanted to go on to other things. Finally, too, the state had its word and censored what was left of the movement. In the late forties, the audience for Italian film was excellent abroad,

Gray buildings and streets. An anticipation of Antonioni's visual style in an early sequence of De Sica's *Miracle in Milan* (Museum of Modern Art Film Stills Archive).

but poor at home. The movement came under political attack—by the left for not providing a strong enough model for analysis and change, by the right for being too left, and by the center coalition government in power for keeping away Italian audiences and portraying Italy in a bad light abroad. The government won. Italy joined NATO and, as a recipient of aid from the Marshall Plan, was enjoined to control and if possible do away with any activity that might be taken for left-wing. In 1949 the Christian Democrats placed Giulio Andreotti in charge of the film industry with powers to subsidize only those films that were "suitable . . . to the best interests of Italy." Statements made by government ministers at the time indicate the direction being taken—the direction indicated in *Miracle in Milan*—toward a cinema of passivity and pacification:

> Film is merchandise. If the government has the right to control the export of vegetables and fruits to make sure that they are not rotten, it also has the right, and the duty, to prevent the circulation of films infected with the spirit of neo-realism.
>
> Film is escape, relaxation, forgetfulness for the poor. The people have need of bread and circuses.[50]

A Hollywood mogul could not have better expressed these reassertions of traditional cinema, the balm and embalmer of a society.

However, the fact remains that, as a collective movement, neo-realism was already on the decline as the government asserted its authority over it. Its three major practitioners were all anxious to move on, particularly into international production, where fame, profit, and escape from government restrictions might be better realized. Their films were already popular abroad, and Rossellini sealed this popularity by scandal—first with "The Miracle" (1948, one part of a film called *L'Amore*), which brought down the anger of the Catholic Church and various legions of decency in the United States, and then by an affair with Ingrid Bergman which resulted in a series of romantic and melodramatic films. One of them, *Voyage in Italy* (1953), was of major importance to the French New Wave and to Michelangelo Antonioni. I will return to it in the next chapter. Visconti, whose *Ossessione* could be said to have started the movement, moved the furthest beyond it. By the time he made *Senso* in 1954, his direction was clear: it is a large-scale, color costume drama, its English-language version co-written by Tennessee Williams and co-starring the American actor Farley Granger. His appearance is part of a peculiar phenomenon in fifties Italian film. The neo-realist imperative to use non-professional players went through a transmutation. Professional Italian actors began appearing in the Italians' post-forties films, but with them, and in major roles, came various actors from America, their voices dubbed into Italian and giving performances better than they ever managed at home. Anthony Quinn plays Zampanò and Richard Basehart plays the clown in Fellini's *La Strada* (1954); Basehart appears with Broderick Crawford in the same director's *Il Bidone* (1955). Steve Cochran, who usually played a gangster in American film, became one of Antonioni's first lost, wandering figures in *Il Grido* (1957). In the sixties and seventies American actors of greater stature appeared. Burt Lancaster became a sort of alter ego for Visconti, first in *The Leopard* (1963) and then in *Conversation Piece* (1975). In Bertolucci's *1900,* Lancaster was joined by Donald Sutherland and Robert De Niro. At its inception, this phenomenon seemed to offer those directors who were still working in the neo-realist mode a way of using unfamiliar faces while still having actors with some training. Also, by casting these Americans as Italians, the filmmakers created a conflict of styles and personality that offered rich material to manipulate.

But in Visconti's case, Granger's appearance in *Senso* may be the result of a desire for a pretty face rather than an unusual mix of acting styles, and the film makes clear Visconti's move into glossy international production. It would be an easy judgment to say that the rapidity with which Visconti left neo-realism indicates his small commitment to it. But that would be to misjudge the style of his forties films. The images of *Ossessione* and *La Terra Trema* demonstrate a greater desire for eloquence, for overstatement, than do those of his contemporaries. His is an essentially operatic spirit, dependent on large gestures, opulent design, and melodramatic movements.[51] In the forties these lay below the surface of his films; the subjects and forms of neo-realism did not permit them freedom. But when these forms broke down in the fifties, Visconti was freed. In *Senso,* a contessa meets her Austrian lover at the opera; indeed, they have their first confrontation with the opera stage in the background. This is a film of great passions, betrayals, and tear-stained faces; its only relationship to neo-realism occurs in the occasional exteriors where characters walk down barren wartime streets (the film is set in 1866 amidst the Italian fight against Austrian rule). Visconti was to deal with a variety of subjects in his work, but *Senso* established his approach—

his decadence, if you will–manifested in his need to pump up his *mise-en-scène* and stuff the cinematic space he creates with opulent detail that overwhelms the characters, who in turn overwhelm themselves with melodrama. I do not use the word "decadence" lightly. Visconti continually worked against his best political instinct–almost all his historical films deal with the rupture caused by the coming to power of the middle class in Italy–by an indulgence in spectacle which is never quite fulfilling enough for him. It is quite possible to reduce the structure of some of his later films, like *The Damned* (1969) and *Death in Venice* (1970), to a series of zoom shots among decaying characters and situations, zooms that neither select nor reveal, but only pile on non-signifying details in operatic proportions.

Others of the original neo-realists did not move quite so far beyond their original tenets. De Sica, however, pretty much let his sentimentality and a sense of sexual exploitation get the better of him. His 1960 film *Two Women,* written by Zavattini from an Alberto Moravia novel, attempts to recapture the wartime milieu and images of uprooted wanderers. But it is largely undone by the gratuitous exploitation of its star, Sophia Loren. It is a vindication of the original neo-realist desire to *avoid* star players, for rather than become part of the *mise-en-scène,* which is what the neo-realists wanted their players to do, Loren in this later film *is* the *mise-en-scène.* All space is organized around her, more accurately around her physical and vocal presence, and all other observations are dominated by her. Only Rossellini managed to keep close to the notion of observation, of allowing the camera to create the illusion that it was attentive to a given and ongoing situation. After his cycle of films with Ingrid Bergman in the fifties, Rossellini undertook a variety of projects, including a documentary on India, until in the mid-sixties he began a series of histories for Italian television: *The Rise to Power of Louis XIV* (a film which got commercial theatrical distribution outside Italy), films on St. Augustine, Socrates, Pascal, the Medici, the Apostles–a modern cinematic encyclopedia. These films pretend to be not so much re-creations of history (although that is of course what they are) as observations of the making of ideas, filmed in long, gentle shots, the zoom lens (a kind that is Rossellini's own invention) moving from person to person in each particular sequence with a casualness that is both spontaneous and ceremonial. The camera gazes and inquires, permits the characters to expound while locating them in an environment that indicates historical time and place without extravagance.

These films are, among other things, responses to Visconti's histories (as well as to Hollywood costume drama).[52] They present discourse—coherent, defined expression—rather than aria, a sense of possible location rather than grandiloquent decor, and above all display a calm distance from their subject. They do not have the passion of Rossellini's forties war trilogy, though their dramatic reserve is in a direct line from *Paisan*. Politically they are committed to a centrist position, accepting the "great ideas" and events of the past with very little analysis or question about their social genesis (again the neo-realist premise of observation overtakes the need for understanding what is observed). At the beginning of *The Rise to Power of Louis XIV,* Rossellini shows a group of "common" people working and chatting by the riverside as a group of court doctors ride by on their way to treat the ailing cardinal. The people talk about royalty, the difficulty they have in finding doctors for their own ills, and about the way life went on after the British chopped off their king's head. They represent the same kind of endurance and ongoing-ness shown by the poor in the forties films and demonstrate the same lack of inquiry about that condition on the part of the director. But although these films reveal the same uncertain commitment to political understanding that the neo-realists suffered at the peak of their movement, they remain the closest to the original neo-realist tenets, respecting the images they create and the audience who observes them.[53] Rossellini maintained a talent for being both withdrawn from and engaged with his material at the same time, creating the illusion that he is allowing events to play out freely before his camera.

One figure, Federico Fellini, who is closely associated with the neo-realists, has hardly been mentioned so far, even though he is the best known Italian filmmaker outside his country. There has been such a great deal written on him already (more than the complexity of his work will bear) that I want to make only a few remarks. Fellini belongs, like Antonioni, to the second wave of Italian filmmakers, who began their production in the fifties. However, he began his work with the forties group, collaborating with Rossellini on the scripts of *Rome, Open City* and *Paisan.* He co-directed his first film, *Variety Lights* (1950), with Alberto Lattuada, a minor neo-realist filmmaker not very well known outside Italy, who turned to and is still making comedies that are occasionally exported. Three of Fellini's fifties films–*I Vitelloni, La Strada,* and *Nights of Cabiria*–stand as signposts out of the movement proper and into ways of expanding and revising the genre so that it could ultimately spread its influence to other styles, other concepts of filmmaking. *I Vitelloni,* for example, is not concerned with the poor, but with a group of young men in a small town. Sons of lower-middle-class parents, they avoid work, avoid action, circling the town square and its streets, one of them marrying and learning painfully to be faithful to his wife, one finally leaving the town and its apathy. Visually, the film's exteriors are among the best examples of the hard-edged black and gray neo-realist style. The nighttime sequences show the influence of American *film noir* (examples of which were by this time just getting to Europe). Unlike his forties predecessors in Italy, however, Fellini does not define his characters exclusively by their environment. More than in Rossellini's *Germany, Year Zero,* it imposes on the characters, rather than reflecting their social and economic condition. It contains them, it even frightens them. The would-be writer of the group, Leopoldo, looks for support to a visiting *artiste,* one in a long line of Fellini masters of ceremony–cum-ringmasters-cum-fakers. Out in the dark, windy square, Leopoldo begs this man to help him be somebody, to take him out of this boring town where nothing ever happens. The old man, quiet, mysterious, non-committal, leads Leopoldo through the dark and down to the harbor. But the night, wind, and shadows are too much for Leopoldo, as are the promises of the unknown that they hold. He runs off, the old man laughing after him.

Environment begins to take on something of the symbolic here, and while there is only a hint of this in *I Vitelloni,* the symbolic snared Fellini in his later work, until finally environment became decor, smothering character without revealing it. But here restraint holds, and Fellini refrains from attempts to investigate psychology and turn memory into set design, willing still to observe behavior with graciousness and a certain distance. The episodic structure of *I Vitelloni* enables him to be flexible, to move into and away from his characters, collect incidents in the lives of his young men that are funny and poignant, but non-judgmental. At the end of the film, one of them gets up the courage to leave the town. Urged on by a young boy who works at the railroad station (Fellini modified the function of the neo-realist child; here and in later films the child or the child-like is a source of innocent understanding, often allowing an adult character insight into his own jaded life), Moraldo boards an early morning train. As it pulls out, shots of him are intercut with retreating traveling shots of his friends at home, in bed—an expressionist sequence of sorts, extrapolating Moraldo's state of mind and revealing the situation of all concerned. It compares the activity of one of the characters with the passivity of the others without eliciting from us any strong approval or disapproval. We are not forced into a confrontation with the characters, and the film ends with the railroad boy who, smiling, walks the rails back to town—an intermediary figure who diffuses our concentration and separates us from the action.

This is the last film in which Fellini permitted even this much distance to exist. A need for psychological investigation and for huge statements about large emotions overwhelms his later films. *La Strada* and *Nights of Cabiria* remain rooted in neo-realism, in the observation of the poor and disenfranchised wandering in a desolate landscape. But the landscape recedes as carefully premeditated characters in finely tuned melodramatic narratives move forward and demand emotional response. Bazin, attempting to defend *Nights of Cabiria,* writes, ". . . we . . . now . . . see the characters no longer *among* the objects but, as if these had become transparent, *through* them."[54] In fact, character begins to separate from objects, and soon the two will fight unsuccessfully for Fellini's—and the audience's—attention.

Fellini becomes concerned with *significance* which, in the films from *La Strada* through *8½* (1962), means probing desperate characters and insisting that the audience share their emotional turmoil. Unlike Ingmar Bergman (perhaps Fellini's only rival in international movie fame), Fellini does not permit his characters a fearful and obsessive introspection. He is close enough to his tradition to observe them from the outside in.[55] Gelsomina, in *La Strada,* is defined by Giulietta Masina's expressive face (full of ticks and reactions borrowed partly from Charlie Chaplin, partly from Jane Wyman's performance in the 1948 American film *Johnny Belinda*), by the character's poverty and physical isolation, by her association with children and animals, and of course in contrast to the brutish Zampanò, the itinerant strong man who treats her worse than an animal. But Fellini exaggerates his images, gives them a great deal of emotional force. He makes them plead with us for our attention and reaction. Gelsomina distracts us from her place in the landscape. The relentless cruelty of Zampanò turns him into an abstraction—and in fact it is the process of abstraction, the pull on the characters out of their situation into something of a lecture on brutishness and innocence, that constitutes both the success and failure of the film.

In *La Strada,* Fellini develops an important extension of neo-realist possibilities. By forcing his images and creating confrontations informed by ideas that reach for great significance—the transcendence of innocence in the face of lumpish brutality—he is giving character and landscape a connotative dimension and a moral structure. He is also personalizing his characters more than the forties neo-realists would have done, and with curious results. The neo-realist character is neither a stereotype nor an abstraction, but a representative, a figure of his or her class. While the characters in both *La Strada* and *Nights of Cabiria* have class attributes, the abstraction process is one of declassification, removal to the status of impassioned idea or, perhaps more accurately, of moral marker in a landscape of despair (a purple phrase adequate to Fellini's intentions). The political morality of the neo-realists was embedded in their choice and treatment of character and place; Fellini adds to this his abstract morality, and we are asked to make the tally. He wants moral perception and judgment where the neo-realists wanted observation and comprehension; on top of that he wants profound emotional reactions. The melodrama that always threatened neo-realist narrative is now indulged in without embarrassment. The lonely, abused Gelsomina befriends a clown, a man as foolish and innocent as she, but unlike her, willing to stand up to Zampanò. The strong man kills him. Gelsomina becomes more pitiable than before and is abandoned by Zampanò, though not before he shows some expression of guilt. After a passing of time, Zampanò wanders through the streets of a town and hears someone singing music associated with Gelsomina. A woman hanging wash on a line tells him Gelsomina is dead. A devastated Zampanò pretends not to be moved. He does his strong man act, but the camera itself refuses to participate. As a punishment, and to point up Zampanò's aloneness, it retreats to the exterior of the circus ring as he goes through the mechanics of his performance. But this retreat from proximity is not sufficient. The roaring, brawling animal must show some notion of humanity, some salvation. He returns to the sea at night (the persistent, if not terribly original, Fellinian "symbol" of rebirth), sits on the sand and begins to sob, then falls on the beach, clutching the sand the way the clown he killed clutched the ground in his death throes. The camera pulls back and up—this time not leaving him alone but exposing him fully to our gaze—music swells, and we are left wrung dry.

There is no denying the power of this; there is also no denying, on rational reflection, that we are being manipulated, that Fellini has rejoined an earlier and persistent cinematic tradition, the very one the neo-realists attempted to alter. Certainly he felt he was dealing with more important subjects than those undertaken by Hollywood melodrama, though in fact they are the same subjects—the struggles of good and evil, innocence and corruption, the place and worth of the self in a cruel world—presented in a more abstract, apparently more sophisticated form. But only apparently. The forms of melodrama and their demands for unmediated emotional response are largely the same regardless of the particular subject. Fellini finally abandoned the neo-realists' call for observation and a measure of disengagement, he closed up the spaces of engaged observation and reentered the arena of grand emotion and moral generalization. He continues in this area through *La Dolce Vita* (1959), where his concern is with a rich, middle-class urban milieu, which (like all such milieus examined by sixties European filmmakers) is without values, compassion, or direction. He flirts briefly with some modernist effects of memory and perception in *8½*, a film that marks the end of his creative period. In it he tries to give form to his own personality, erect a model of his own experience, and succeeds because here the film's spectacle, its fragmented structure of memory and desire, permit some distance, allow it to become more a reflection upon memory and desire than merely a story of a set-upon film director who can no longer get his projects off the ground. The film has the energy of discovery, of form being invented and images elaborated. But the self-indulgence intimated in the film was not held down. In his following works, Fellini moved into the artifice of spectacle, the fantasies of memory, which became more insular and repetitive as he proceeded.

Fellini's decline is not without its lessons about film history. Unlike many of the filmmakers who followed in the wake of neo-realism and extended its possibilities—directors such as Michelangelo Antonioni, Bernardo Bertolucci, Truffaut and Godard—Fellini slipped back to a melodramatic mode via expressionism, an autobiographical expressionism in which the structures of memory and fantasy are limned out with history relegated to a backdrop and nostalgia elevated above analysis. He returns to a romanticism that insists that the productions of the artist's life and imagination must be of interest simply because they are the productions of the artist. The images of such films as *Juliet of the Spirits, Satyricon, Amarcord, Roma, The City of Women* are meant to be valid simply because they are Fellini's images. But this redundancy, like all such, has a gap in its center. The demand for attention is based only on our supposed curiosity about the workings of a single, and not singular, imagination. Otherwise, these films respond to nothing. In his later films he wishes to create worlds that express some profound psychological truths, but manages to make images that only correspond to his own fantasies and—when the spectacle is stripped away—unexceptional memories. The endless movement of grotesque faces within the landscape of a world-cum-carnival must be taken on faith. Bad faith.

I risk here the accusation of being a "realist" of the most fundamental kind, somewhere close to Siegfried Kracauer, perhaps, whose *Theory of Film* promulgates the myth of an ideal cinema that passively records an "ongoing" world without changing what it sees.[56] But this is quite the opposite of what I am getting at. The film image does have a presence and immediacy and a perceptual status that seem to parallel the way we look at the world itself. But it *is* an image and not the "reality" of our day-to-day perception. ". . . The secret of film," writes Christian Metz, "is that it is able to leave a high degree of reality *in its images,* which are, nevertheless, still perceived as images."[57] Neo-realism never mistook the image of reality for reality itself, and in fact wished to make the image an eloquent device that would be valid *in the way* it communicated behavior, emotion, action and reaction, history and place. No matter what kind of film, image is artifice and there is never any confusion on the spectator's part about this fact. The question of major importance concerns the degree to which the image makes the spectator aware of its status as a made object. The neo-realists wanted their images to reveal a world ignored by conventional cinema and to present that world unmediated by cinematic stereotyping. They depended upon the artifice of the camera eye to transcend artifice and create a version of reality more stark, immediate, and accessible than that of the past. They questioned the "reality" of American and American-influenced film because it was a reality that did not examine its illusory nature and did not provoke the spectator to examine assumptions about the world or the methods of observing the world cinematically. Fellini is a filmmaker who forgot these questions and the answers. While he remains deeply committed to the artifice of the image, he forgets that this artifice is meant to generate meaning. A gap is created between his introspections and the viewer's desire for his images to communicate something. In the end nothing is revealed but commonplaces. In his later films, the neo-realist urge to reveal and question has disappeared beneath an irrelevant (and sometimes—as in *Orchestra Rehearsal* and *The City of Women*—reactionary) subjectivity.

The complexities of artifice, the extent to which the filmmaker requires the spectator to be aware that the image is a construct—a special and specially perceived version of reality—will concern us in some detail in the next chapter. Here I wish to indicate some of the immediate results and influences of the neo-realist movement and the effects it had on various cinemas, including American. Partly by coincidence, and partly by direct influence, a movement toward "documentary realism" started in American film in the mid-forties. Filmmakers began shooting on location, and in such works as Elia Kazan's *Boomerang!* (1947), Abraham Polonsky's *Force of Evil,* and Jules Dassin's *The Naked City* (both 1948) the expressionism of *film noir* is modified by a more subdued relationship of character and surroundings. Place is established as a defining presence. None of these films were anything like what the Italians were doing at the same time; they share only the desire to get out of the studio. But in the hothouse world of Hollywood filmmaking, where any exterior shot in closer proximity to a character than the knees up was done in the studio against a rear-screen projection of a background, this desire to look at the world was of great importance—short-lived importance, for American filmmakers retreated back into the studio in the fifties. But when the studios ceased operating as self-sufficient entities, filmmakers returned to the streets, and the look of American cinema changed. The neo-realist influence was in the far distance, filtered through the influence of the French New Wave, but a link was present.

Neo-realism's influence in Europe was more complete and impressive. In England, the tentative and short-lived beginnings of cinema independent of Hollywood, dealing with the cultural and social concerns of the country, were patterned after the work of the postwar Italians. The so-called kitchen sink school, including such films as Jack Clayton's *Room at the Top* (1958), Karel Reisz's *Saturday Night and Sunday Morning* (1960), Tony Richardson's *Look Back in Anger* (1959) and *The Loneliness of the Long Distance Runner*

(1962), Lindsay Anderson's *This Sporting Life* (1963), turned, like the Italians before them, from middle-class subjects to the working class; they observed characters in relation to their environment in hard gray tones, and through their images attempted to get their audience to examine a part of the culture that their cinema had hitherto ignored or treated with moral condescension. The English version of neo-realism ran into similar thematic and formal problems as had the Italian. The films were unable to get either close enough to or far away enough from their characters to effect a radical change in the conventional ways characters were understood. They tended toward the melodramatic, even the hysterical, in their evocation of the pain and frustration of stagnant lives, and more often than not took that stagnation as so much of a given that frustration was played upon as an emotional asset. The British neo-realist characters are rarely permitted even those signs of endurance and reintegration into the sad flow of life allowed the Italian. The British filmmakers, working largely from scripts drawn from novels or plays, could not, it seems, break out of the individualist tradition of psychological realism. Their films are largely character studies, and in attempting to join the tradition of the motivated, introspective, suffering hero with the neo-realist urge to create characters who must be understood from a social rather than a subjective perspective, they set up a tension that was finally unresolvable. Their working-class characters, set within the environment of the industrial midlands of England, are frozen by that environment and by their class. They rail against it, fight against it, pretend to stand over and against it, but cannot or will not overcome it. (Let us stand back from the fiction: they cannot or will not be *allowed* to overcome it, for as in traditional melodrama, audience reaction is earned by their failure rather than by victory or assertion.) The characters' joys are minimal, their suffering intense.

Albert Finney's Arthur Seaton in *Saturday Night and Sunday Morning* is obsessive in his attempts to impress his vitality onto a monotonous factory life and to negate any preconceptions people may have of him. But in the end he stands with his girlfriend on a hill overlooking a new housing development, on the brink of slipping into the moribund life he has fought. The vitality of these working-class heros is always denied, not merely because of the impossibly oppressive economical and social system that surrounds them, but because of their psychological make-up, or rather the psychology made up for them by their creators, which denies them any possibility for change or escape. Frank Machin, the Richard Harris character in Anderson's *This Sporting Life* (a film which mixes a flashback time structure influenced by Alain Resnais with an operatic style of gesture and delivery borrowed from Visconti), endures and perpetuates a masochism and self-hatred figured in the brutality of the slow-motion soccer game that ends the film and encapsulates his life. In those instances when self-hatred should turn into defiance, it is turned inward rather than imposed upon the world that created it. In *The Loneliness of the Long Distance Runner,* the Tom Courtenay character, imprisoned in reform school, given special treatment because of his athletic ability, stops just short of winning a race because it would mean yielding to the wishes of the authorities. It is a powerful and frustrating ending for the film, and perfectly enigmatic. No reason is offered for the character's self-defeat other than some vague motivations of pride, stubbornness, and, again, masochism. The "realism" attained by such frustration is created only in its opposition to a conventionally happy ending; social realities are presented not in an attempt to understand them, but as a narrative device. In British neo-realism, class is made a background to the study of unusual characters.

It may be unfair to single out British cinema for special criticism. It has carried on a decades-long struggle with American influence and American money without, to this day, being able to discover a successful means of independent production.* Its "neo-realist" movement was just one of many false starts toward the establishment of an independent, national cinema. That it adopted to a greater extent than did the Italians a melodramatic, psychological approach can,

* Although, with the government now providing some assistance through the National Film Finance Corporation and the British Film Institute Production Board, there is an opportunity for independent production to gain a foothold at least.

perhaps, be explained by the direct influence of American cinema as well as the confusions suffered by the middle-class intellectual writers and directors approaching what was for them a new subject matter. But while the films are not complete successes, they are important as documents of the spread of the neo-realist influence: a "new" cinema in England presented itself in a neo-realist mode.[58]

The same happened in India, whose first internationally recognized film (from a country whose internal film production was the highest in the world) was a neo-realist work. Satyajit Ray's *Pather Panchali* (1955) brings to bear on its local subject a feeling for country landscape worthy of Griffith and Renoir, and an observation of a family struggling with poverty constructed with less sentimentality but with all the intensity of De Sica, who was a direct influence.[59] Like De Sica, Ray works through the point of view of children, though without De Sica's special pleading. *Pather Panchali* and the films that follow it and make up a trilogy—*Aparajito* and *The World of Apu*—are concerned most of all with building images of faces and landscape, of faces in a landscape, and with detail, textures, and spatial relationships that define events more quietly than sentimentality and melodrama. The films have the value of anthropology for viewers unfamiliar with the rural Indian landscape and its inhabitants, and Ray observes with something of the anthropologist's eye the detail and the intricacies and painfulness of family relationships.

In a sense, Ray's early films make use of neo-realist technique in a "purer" form than did those who originally developed it, a phenomenon that may be explained by the fact that he had a chance to contemplate the form as those in the heat of its development could not. We see this "purity" again in another film that is part of the beginning of a new movement. Nelson Pereira dos Santos's *Vidas Secas* (*Barren Lives*), made at the beginning of the Cinema Novo movement in Brazil in 1963, is a grim and unelaborated fictional documentation of a family living, desperately, on the *sertão,* the dead plain of northeast Brazil. Once again we see a response to the elaborate fictions of American cinema in a simple, unadorned study of the progress of wretchedness and poverty, images that do not yield to the softening of cliché and, like the best works of neo-realism, offer hope only through the revelation of intolerable lives—revelation that might be a prod to action. Dos Santos wrote: "Neo-realism understood that within a capitalist society it is possible to practice, through cinema, a humanistic, transforming mode of thought. That was the great lesson of neo-realism. . . . And Cinema Novo is the application of the method in Brazil."[60] *Vidas Secas,* along with works like Ruy Guerra's *Os Fuzis* (1963), was a major statement of the need for aesthetic and political change, as were the Italian films of the forties. Brazil in the sixties, like Italy in the forties or Britain in the late fifties, was unaccustomed to having film image a despairing poverty, a family's endless and hopeless wandering of an endlessly inhospitable landscape. As in Italy, the new movement met political opposition. Unlike that in Italy, it developed into a highly experimental and deeply political mode, particularly in the films of Glauber Rocha, whose experiments extended the limits of neo-realism, but remained rooted in it.

Within the genesis of contemporary international cinema, probably the most unexpected and hilarious influence of neo-realism is on Luis Buñuel, who (at this writing) is the world's oldest working filmmaker and whose career all but encompasses the history of film. Buñuel began in the French avant-garde with *Un Chien andalou,* a surreal short film made with Salvador Dali in 1928. After the outrage over *L'Age d'or* (1930)—his lunatic fantasy of obsessive love, the history of the church, and the biology of the scorpion—he made one short film, a "documentary," *Las Hurdes* (1932), about a region in Spain so poor and primitive that its inhabitants are presented as being beyond compassion as well as help. (No foreshadowing of neo-realism here, only the expression of a sensibility never moved to pity by the outrageous.) There followed eighteen years of silence. Not even Buñuel's biographers are certain of the details of what he did or where he was during that period. According to his own testimony he worked in Europe as dubbing adviser for Paramount Pictures and supervisor of coproductions for Warner Brothers. He did some producing; he represented the Spanish Republic in Hollywood until the end of the Spanish Civil War and then worked for the film department of the Museum of Modern Art in New York until it was discovered that he was the director of *L'Age d'or* and he resigned. He then went back to Hollywood and may possibly have worked as an assistant director (one rumor is that he was assistant to Robert Florey on a film called *The Beast with Five Fingers,* 1947, about a disembodied hand, which turns–or crawls–up again in Buñuel's own film *The Exterminating Angel,* 1962).[61] In 1946 he moved to Mexico, where he was once again able to make his own films, although at first only a few local potboilers. He reports that his producer, Oscar Dancigers, asked him "to put up an idea for a children's film. I gingerly suggested the scenario for *Los Olvidados.* . . ."[62]

Gingerly indeed! *Los Olvidados* (1950) is Buñuel's reemergence into international filmmaking, and a film as violent, anarchic, and funny as those with which he ended the first part of his career in the early thirties. But with some major differences. *Los Olvidados* is more subdued than *Un Chien andalou,* which contains probably the single most notorious image in the history of cinema: a man slicing open a woman's eye with a straight razor. *Un Chien andalou* is an antinarrative, a series of surreal images whose chronology and spatial relationships are purposefully dislocated to dislodge the viewer from the complacency of continuity. *L'Age d'or,* the film that followed, has a narrative of sorts: a man obsessively pursues a woman through a series of overwhelming obstacles and outrageous hindrances. Buñuel's eye is on the obstacles and hindrances; he is more interested in observing a huge cow on a bed, a peasant and his cart in an upper-class drawing room, or a man hurling a burning tree, a bishop, and a stuffed giraffe out the window than he is in his story. More accurately, such incidents, as well as the interruptions that allow him to pursue a history of imperial Rome or a history of the scorpion, become the narrative Buñuel is most interested in, the history of madness induced by repression. It is a history still spoken in the language of Dada and the surrealists, a language Buñuel never forgot, but modified and modulated, used as a subversive tool.

Los Olvidados does not fight narrative but embraces it, and by doing so subverts it. The form Buñuel chooses to embrace is directly connected to the Italian neo-realists, for he tells the story of poor children in the slums of Mexico City, uses some non-professional players, and opens the film as if he were going to document the dreadful conditions of the breeding ground of delinquents in a major city. The narrative parameters of *Los Olvidados* offer excellent proof of how well neo-realism had established itself as a major cinematic genre whose conventions were immediately usable, recognizable, and finally able to be turned inside out. This film is no document of poverty and delinquency, no objectively observed gathering of details of daily life among Mexico City's poor. Neither is it merely a sad gaze at the suffering of innocent and guiltless children in an oppressive world. Buñuel's children are no more innocent than his adults, perhaps less so. His adults are merely dulled into insensibility by the brutality of their world. The children take an active and gleeful part in promoting that brutality.

Buñuel uses neo-realism to reassert himself into the mainstream of narrative filmmaking and to rearrange and revalidate his own methods of narrative construction. Like the neo-realists' films, *Los Olvidados* tells its story in a linear and logical order. However, every opportunity to disturb that order is taken. Like neo-realism, the film carefully observes the characters and their squalid environment, but Buñuel insists on intruding upon the observation and capturing not merely the exterior of everyday life, but its ludicrous and perverse interior and the events that make the interior visible—a blind man flailing at his young tormentors with a stick that has a nail protruding from one end or stroking the back of an ailing woman with a live dove; a gang of toughs robbing a legless man, lifting him out of his begging cart and leaving him flailing on the sidewalk; a young girl in a barn pouring milk over her thighs.

He wishes to describe the unconscious of his subjects with the same observed detail as the neo-realists used to describe their external lives. Indeed Buñuel is the neo-realist of the unconscious, and his camera, searching and tracking around faces and events with an apparent objectivity, is in fact seeking entrance not into their souls but

into their terrors and perversity. A boy, Pedro, has a dream about his mother and Jaibo, another tough, who will sleep with Pedro's mother and eventually beat him to death. The dream begins with a tinkling of bells and the crowing of cocks. A chicken descends in slow motion. In a flurry of feathers, Pedro sees the grinning corpse of one of Jaibo's victims under his bed. Thunder crashes; the mother, with a manic grin, comes to Pedro, holding a chunk of raw meat in her hands. Her slow-motion movements make her ominous and threatening, an angel of death. The wind blows inside the room, the mother advances to Pedro; but before he can get the meat, Jaibo reaches out from under the bed and grabs it from the mother's hand. Every opportunity is offered in this dream sequence for old-fashioned Freudian analysis. But Buñuel, unlike all other dream-makers in the history of

The perversity of the Buñuelian world. *Los Olvidados* (Museum of Modern Art Film Stills Archive).

film, only tantalizes us with meaning, while overwhelming us with image. It would be safe to say that the dreams of Buñuel's characters, here and throughout his work, have the effect of our own dreams; they have latent meaning, but their primary effect is to awe and discomfort the viewer—as dreams do the sleeper. The unconscious of Buñuel's characters intrudes upon their conscious and upon ours, and their conscious life intrudes upon their unconscious. To Buñuel's eyes, both lives are lived simultaneously and are open to observation without comment. He invests the neo-realist image—the hard, deep-focused, black-and-white world of poverty—with a concern for the unspoken and the unspeakable, with a subjectivity that is always present and never explained.

Buñuel's success lies in his ability to merge the dreams the characters have in the narrative with the narrative itself and to evoke out of the images he creates a range of disturbing realities. Early in the film the blind man is knocked down by a gang of toughs. He lies in the mud, and the camera, accompanied by a crash of music, pulls back to reveal a chicken staring into the man's blind eyes. The image is unexplained, unmotivated, and although it is followed by a shot of Pedro sitting in a chicken coop (the boy–like Buñuel himself–is obsessed with chickens), neither the staring bird nor the boy's chicken fetish is ever accounted for.

Ultimately, the perverse linkage of perverse images disturbs the viewer so thoroughly that Buñuel is able to provoke a classic reaction of pity and fear growing from a state of disbelief and horror like that which might accompany a dream. Jaibo kills Pedro and is himself killed by the police. Over his dying face is superimposed the image of a stray dog padding down a rain-slicked road in slow motion as voices on the sound track call: "Look out, Jaibo. The mangy dog. It's coming. . . . No . . . no . . . I'm falling into a black hole. I'm alone. . . . As always my son. As always. Good night."[63] Pedro's body is discovered by some people who do not want to be discovered with it. They carry it in a sack on the back of a donkey, through the shanty town in the night. Pedro's mother, who is looking for her son and unaware he is dead, passes them. She does not even ask if they have seen him; she merely passes in the dark and says "Good evening." She goes off one way and they another, finally dumping her son's body in a rubbish heap.

The "realism" of *Los Olvidados* is so severe in its manifestation of depravity, the grotesque, and the dreamlike that it prevents any sentimental attachment, and creates instead a withdrawal into contemplation. The final sequence of the film is moving, but also terrifying in its coldbloodedness. Through it, Buñuel almost manages what the neorealists wanted to attain–a precise rendering, without comment, of everyday occurrences–but could not attain because sentimentality or unfocused belief in human endurance stayed their hand. Buñuel's "everyday" life is a carefully contrived series of evils whose motivations are never explained. Poverty and brutality coexist, though one does not necessarily account for or explain the other.

There are moments in the film when Buñuel does attempt to give conventional motivations to his characters. Pedro suffers from a lack of maternal affection. Well-meaning prison officials attempt to rehabilitate him by showing trust. But these interludes of the ordinary only point up a larger structure in which the unconscious is given an image (something the neo-realists would never have dreamed of doing) and commonplace motivations are subordinated to a more revealing design. The weaving of the conventional, the inexplicable, and the perverse forces attention to the images themselves along with their disturbing content and does not permit retreat into the comfort of the already known. "I wanted to introduce mad, completely incongruous elements in the most realistic scenes. For instance, when Jaibo fights and kills the other boy, the camera movement reveals the framework of a large eleven-story building under construction in the distance; I would have liked to put a big orchestra of a hundred musicians on it. One would have seen it just in passing, indistinctly. I wanted to put in a lot of things of that kind, but it was totally forbidden."[64]

His producer may have forbidden some obvious surreal imagery, but more important, the repression imposed by the need to work in a commercially viable form forced Buñuel to play the disturbing, the questioning, the perverse with and against "the realistic scenes" until they fed off and counterpointed each other. The result is a neo-realism of assault and disturbance and, most important, an indication of the directions in which the movement could lead. After *Los Olvidados* Buñuel left neo-realism far behind, though what he learned of the possibilities of using and altering its images has stayed with him throughout his career.

The Italians in the late forties provided a source of revitalized image-making that was picked up from country to country, by filmmaker after filmmaker. What started as a national movement came to alter the history of film. Some of that history will be examined in the chapters that follow. But here I want to make a leap of some thirty years and examine three Italian films of the late seventies, by filmmakers of differing temperaments and points of view, working under different circumstances and conditions, yet each reaching directly back to his cinematic roots and showing them still to be vital. In making this leap I will be dealing with changes in cinematic attitudes and styles that I have not yet detailed; however, by bringing neo-realism proper up to date, I will be able then to fill in some of the intervening ground in elaborating the development of contemporary cinema.

The films in question are Bernardo Bertolucci's *1900,* Ermanno Olmi's *The Tree of Wooden Clogs,* and Paolo and Vittorio Taviani's *Padre Padrone,* all released between 1976 and 1978. While *Padre Padrone* and *The Tree of Wooden Clogs* are small-budget films, made for Italian television but distributed commercially, *1900* is a major production with an international cast, distributed by Paramount, which enforced upon it a successive whittling-down. The film originally ran about five and a half hours. Bertolucci cut it to four, and Paramount cut about another fifteen minutes when they finally gave it a limited release in the United States. As it is now distributed the film is only a notion of Bertolucci's work and, as I have not seen Bertolucci's original cut, much of my commentary will of necessity be an extrapolation, working from the film as it is available in the United States to a supposition of its original form. Despite this problem, *1900* is a major film and Bertolucci, of course, a major figure in contemporary cinema. A second-generation postwar Italian filmmaker, heir to the neo-realists, follower of Godard, he created three films—*The Spider's Stratagem, The Conformist* (both in 1970), and *Last Tango in Paris* (1972)—in the modernist tradition (they will be examined in detail later on) which sum up some of the major movements in contemporary cinema.

The element that links these three films is their subject matter, the peasantry—a social-economic class that could hardly be more distant from most Western filmgoers. Indeed, it is as distant from contemporary film as was the working class in the forties. The peasantry is only an idea to most people, though it still exists in Italy—indeed in any country where a rural, agricultural working class attempts to make a living working farms. For the narrative imagination, from the nineteenth century on, the peasantry is made up either of lumpish boors, proto-revolutionaries, or sturdy men and women who suffer or accept their lot. They are often given mythic status, looked upon with pity and reverence, with romantic awe as the repository of natural wisdom, or with political hope as the procrustean bed of revolution. Each of the three films deals with, or partakes of, one or another of these literary myths and attempts to construct from it a narrative that explains history or defines humanity through the peasant class. In *1900* Bertolucci attempts a familial epic of revolution, of socialism growing and flowering through one area of Italy during the twentieth century, embodied in the friendship and struggle between the peasant Olmo and the *padrone* Alfredo. In the short version, the struggle centers around the rise of fascism, the event that informs contemporary history and, in one way or another, lies at the core of much important European cinema. In *Padre Padrone,* the Taviani brothers examine the contemporary peasantry through the growing consciousness of one individual, a man who was literally indentured by and to his father as a shepherd (the title of the film means "father-master") and attempts a painful and incomplete escape to become an intellectual who can study the world that held him prisoner as a child. Olmi's *The Tree of Wooden Clogs* appears to be the most neutrally observant, demythified film of the group, examining life on a particular farm in Lombardy at the end of the nineteenth century.

Of the three, it is the closest to the neo-realist aesthetic. Olmi is the oldest filmmaker of the group. He began his work in the late fifties and his best-known film before *The Tree of Wooden Clogs, Il Posto* (1961), is a gentle, almost off-handed series of episodic sequences focusing on a young man and his first job, with all the neo-realist elements of unobtrusiveness and detailed observation of people in an urban environment (though the environment here is one of bustling renewal, rather than the grim poverty of fifteen years earlier). *The Tree of Wooden Clogs,* though taking place at another time and with an entirely different subject, retains many of the elements of that earlier film. Olmi makes use of a non-professional cast who take part in activities—some of which must still be part of the peasant farming tradition—observed in almost documentary detail. He retains the neo-realist notion of attention to the "image fact," the particulars of daily

routine and of place worked into sequences that impose no apparent point of view except that of engaged observation.

What is particularly remarkable about his use of this part of the neo-realist tradition is that he builds his images out of small bits and pieces of the observed whole. In his commentaries on the neo-realists, Bazin stressed again and again their refusal to interfere with what they saw by cutting unnecessarily into the image. Olmi cuts incessantly and his shots are very short. We see what he wants us to see, at the moment he wants us to see it. But despite this, he manages to seem as non-directive as possible. The fragmentation becomes cumulative, each piece expanding and altering our observation of the activity, resulting in a kind of fugal counterpoint (Olmi in fact uses Bach for the film's musical accompaniment) of daily activity and per-

Families in groups. *Opposite, La Terra Trema* (Museum of Modern Art Film Stills Archive); *above, The Tree of Wooden Clogs* (Gaumont/Sacis/New Yorker Films).

sonal drama—many dramas—intricately woven one with the other. The result is a rhythm that unites and propels all the parts. The warmly colored images and restrained, self-contained activities of the characters emerge from their editorial construction not merely whole, but with the illusion of integral continuity to which the audience is made delighted and sympathetic subject.

The illusion operates on many levels. The formal continuity expresses Olmi's notion of the quiet persistence of these people who, in the best neo-realist tradition, endure and persevere, despite the most difficult constraints of personal deprivation, oppression, and of history itself, which seems (according to the film) to go by them with no effect. Their isolation and insulation are so severe that a kind of self-defeat becomes apparent. The tight, almost clockwork construction of the film traps its inhabitants, closes them off from the world around them, and tries to convince us that the events shown are unassailable and unalterable, particularly by the inhabitants of the film itself. Like many of the neo-realists, Olmi is content to see his characters as uncomplaining recipients of economic oppression; he will show the oppression, reveal the poverty, indicate the small ways the community help each other out. In the end, however, there emerges the sense of realism-as-pessimism that he shares with his tradition. Worse than pessimism, worse than the illusion of reality as passive suffering, Olmi seems to preach quietism in the face of disaster. He is aware of the disaster. A brief epigraph near the beginning of the film locates it in time and place and succinctly sums up the peasants' state: "Two thirds of the harvest were the landlord's due." But within the film this grim reality is not dwelt upon; it remains as a given, as something which must be endured. We see the landlord, the *padrone,* at a few points in the film, a fat little man, supercilious and lazy, but with no real personality other than meanness. Olmi is uninterested in him, except as a contrast to the warm vitality of the peasants and as instigator of the evil deed that ends their community. The economic and historical facts of his existence and the feudal structure he and his peasants are part of can only be understood through the poverty and grueling work the peasants endure, which offer the viewer some opportunity to perceive the reality of their condition in a way the peasants themselves never seem to do.

Olmi wants to be within the sphere of their labor, rather than outside analyzing it. Therefore, he concentrates upon the daily activities of his people, who are innately good and hopeful. The core narrative events of the film concern a father who, upon the urging of the local priest, sends his son to school. Unlike the father in *Padre Padrone,* this one expresses hope and amazement over the possibilities of schooling, rather than viciously denying it. Even though he has small means and a large family, including a baby who is born in the course of the film, he urges the boy on. When the child breaks a shoe on his way home from school, the father quietly goes out, cuts down one of the *padrone*'s trees, and fashions a new clog for his son. In the course of time, the cut tree is discovered and the *padrone* orders his bailliff to throw the offending family off the farm. This is done quickly, unceremoniously, and with no support whatsoever for the family from the other members of the community, who peer out at the scene from behind their windows, or the priest (who does not even make an appearance when the family is removed). It is important to emphasize that these events, while a central part of the film, are interwoven with many other events and characters. Through the film's contrapuntal structure, Olmi avoids any excess of attachment to the characters on the audience's part and any undue sentiment created by the events.

But he also indicates that these events were inevitable, and that no thought of changing them ever occurred to those who suffered them; nor does he indicate that the peasants have any alternatives to passive obedience. At a village fair, a socialist–well dressed, bearded–makes a speech. His appearance is calculated to separate him from the peasants he addresses with words on citizens' rights and the abolishment of privilege. The camera looks at the crowd, but is particularly interested in one peasant whose eyes wander from the speaker to a gold coin lying at his feet. The sequence proceeds by giving full attention to this individual and his pains to step on, pick up, and carry off the coin to the farm, eventually hiding it under a horse's shoe. This leads to great comedy later on when the man cannot find the coin and proceeds to spit on and beat up the horse, accusing it of having stolen it; the horse has to be saved by the other members of the community. What is troublesome in all this is the ease with which Olmi removes us from political reality; how easily he indicates that greed is more important to the character than ideas.

Later in the film a newly married couple leave the farm for a honeymoon barge trip to Milan. As they pass through a town, the smoke of a battle is seen. A priest gives the couple (and the audience) some minimal information about the fighting taking place between police and demonstrators and begins moralizing about lack of faith and respect for one's neighbors. In Milan, the couple pass by some demonstrators being herded off by the police. But their attention is on themselves and their goal, a convent where they spend their wedding night and are given an orphan child to take back with them to the farm. In their simplicity, the couple accept another burden, their familial and religious duty permitting little hesitation when the child is offered. One must accept on faith—and the film is so loving in its detail that it is difficult to accuse it of bad faith—that these people were oblivious to what was going on about them.

Yet it is clear that Olmi purposely separates the consciousness of the peasants from an understanding of their world, that he attenuates that consciousness, directs it toward their work and their continuing attempts at survival and encloses it within tradition. As I said, it is possible to read the film dialectically—as we can the films of the original neo-realists—to discover in the hermetic, hopeless world of these people the extent of their oppression and the need for change. But, if the neo-realists squelched the dialectic through sentiment, Olmi does the same by embracing the peasants' lives with such warmth and detail that we may well forget about political response and indulge, with him, in a kind of warm appreciation of their strength in the face of hardship.

Finally, the film inherits the best and the worst of the neo-realist legacy. It asks us to embrace the strength and fatalism of its beleaguered characters and indulges in a non-judgmental attitude in the face of events that the filmmaker feels must be observed without overt manipulation. It recalls the arguments about the illusion of objectivity, the "reality" of observed events and individuals that goes on without the intervention of the filmmaker's consciousness. The historical validity of *The Tree of Wooden Clogs* is beyond question. There were peasants, as there were (and are) other groups, who did not respond to their condition except with passive endurance. In that light the film operates in the good faith of the neo-realist desire to present the world in its dailiness, unencumbered by preconceptions. But because its objectivity is only an illusion created by Olmi's skill—he *chooses* to create an insular, unreflective peasant world whose inhabitants seem to be untouched by the events around them—the spectator is actually being manipulated by its form and content into the position of acceptance and sad contemplation—is offered, like the film's inhabitants, the opportunity to accept rather than judge.

Earlier I noted Bazin's revelation of the ideal neo-realist moment: "No more actors, no more story, no more sets, which is to say that in the perfect aesthetic illusion of reality there is no more cinema." *The Tree of Wooden Clogs* attempts to achieve this ideal, to make cinema vanish in the act of perfect observation. But in his less enthusiastic moments Bazin knew better: ". . . Every realism in art was first profoundly aesthetic," he wrote. ". . . Realism in art can only be achieved in one way—through artifice."[65] And with this recognition a turn away from the neo-realist aesthetic occurred. The filmmakers who followed the movement understood that accepting without question the illusion of an unmediated observation of the world is a trap that can result in diminished responsibility on the filmmaker's part. They understood that the arguments about an objective versus a manipulative cinema can be circular and endless unless such arguments are turned into a dialectic. Reality, finally, is not "out there," and there is no hope for the image to be true to such an abstract, idealist notion. The image can be true only to a filmmaker's reading of "reality" and his or her ability to give such a reading a voice, imply a point of view or interpretation, to make images that direct and comment while permitting the spectator room to join the act of interpretation. The neo-realists themselves knew this, and Olmi chose an artifice that created the illusion of observed activity. The history of film after neo-realism is the history of how much overt recognition was given by the filmmaker, by the film itself, to the artifice that created it, that made it appear "real" or as a commentary about "reality."

The two other films in our peasant trilogy demonstrate an awareness of forcing the image, of forming and directing it to specific ends, of exercising an obvious control far greater than the Italian filmmakers of the forties would have wanted. Like *The Tree of Wooden Clogs, 1900* is set in a farm in northern Italy, and it concerns the activities of peasants and owners; yet it foregoes any illusion of objectivity. Bertolucci breaks a number of major neo-realist premises. The cast is professional, and almost anything but Italian: Robert De Niro and Gérard Depardieu play the *padrone* Alfredo and peasant Olmo; Dominique Sanda is Alfredo's wife; Burt Lancaster and Sterling Hayden are the owner and worker of an earlier generation; Donald Sutherland plays a fascist. In its construction, the film actively avoids the convention of unmediated observation and instead creates large, striking images of figures in interiors and landscapes that are each composed not to capture small, off-handed activities, but to render large and purposive gestures. In the tradition of Visconti, Bertolucci bases his work in operatic conventions—political opera, for the movements, the recitatives, the arias of *1900* are all in the cause of socialism and the triumph of the left. Where Olmi is content to observe an enduring quietism, restricted in place and time, Bertolucci examines the possibilities of long-term struggle between landowner and peasant, with fascism providing the pivot around which the struggle turns. The lines are drawn clearly and broadly: the peasantry are good folk and much more aware of their state than in *The Tree of Wooden Clogs* because they know who they are and what their social and economic position is; they know, too, that it must change. They are close to the soil, close to history, and politically astute. The fascists are portrayed without mitigation as mindlessly and murderously evil. The owners are trapped in between, liberal, indecisive, jealous, desirous of protecting the workers, unable to give up privilege, caught in a *status quo* that no longer exists; that never existed, because (as Bertolucci understands it) the peasants were aware of the system and acted against it as best they could.

Early in the film, in a sequence that takes place after the turn of the century, the *padrone* calls out the peasants to announce that, because of a crop failure, they will have to work for half pay. "We don't get double pay for a double crop," is one response. Another response is made by a worker who quietly slices off his ear as a mark of protest. It is a dramatic gesture, indicative both of the anger Bertolucci allows his peasants to express at the situation and also of their momentary misdirection of that anger. It is only a temporary misdirection, however, for they strike, and even though the *padrone* brings in scabs, and the police circle the fields, organization has begun. The strikers march with a red banner and, in a Punch and Judy show, the puppets play out the peasants' side against the police. In response, the actual police beat down the puppets. The peasants attain some degree of political organization; but it is diverted as World War I ensues and the fascists rise to power in the twenties. Alfredo, the new *padrone,* becomes embroiled first in the decadent upper-middle-class life of Rome and then in a marriage that fails because of his refusal both to confront the fascists at home and to side with his childhood friend, Olmo, who represents the forefront of the peasants' struggle. After establishing the lineage of the ruling and working families, their personal and political struggles, the American version of the film focuses on the conflict among four characters: Olmo and Alfredo, personal childhood friends and class enemies; Alfredo's wife, who perceives more clearly than her husband the threat of the fascists, whom he attempts to placate, even at the risk of Olmo's life; and Attila, the local fascist leader.

Alfredo, his wife, and Olmo are traditionally "well-drawn" characters. They exist with full "personalities," struggle with and suffer internal conflicts of conscience, duty, friendship, and loyalties—conflicts which eventually pull the film off course. Attila, on the other hand, is a straightforward, two-dimensional, almost allegorical figure of political and moral evil. His character is molded to fit perfectly the historical design of the film. He is an idea of fascism pure and unadorned, a figure who takes equal pleasure in smashing a cat (which he pretends is a communist and ties to a post) with his head, bashing out the brains of a child by whipping it around the walls of a room, or crushing an old woman behind a door. Attila's is not a banal evil, but an active, calculated one. His evil is so great that his rise and fall structure the movement of the American version of the film.

When Italy is liberated on April 25, 1945, nature blooms and the peasants take to the fields with pitchforks to destroy Attila and his wife. (In the first American version of the film, this sequence opened the action, so that the body of the film explained the peasants' act of revenge and set up Attila as a powerful force of reaction against which Bertolucci could match the progressiveness of the peasantry.)

The peasants' revenge against Attila (Donald Sutherland). *1900* (Museum of Modern Art Film Stills Archive).

After the war, with Attila dead, Alfredo is tried by a peasants' court, in the middle of the farmyard, under a red patchwork canopy the peasants have been making for years. Good dialecticians to the end, they declare the *padrone* dead, but allow Alfredo to survive as living proof that the concept of ownership is dead. But their victory over history is incomplete. Italian soldiers representing the postwar government take their guns away. The crowd disperses, leaving Alfredo, Olmo, and a young boy whose name is also Olmo. Alfredo asserts his survival and the survival of his class. He proclaims "The *padrone* lives!" and engages his old friend in a wrestling match that extends forward and backward in time: through old age and back to when they were children, daring each other to lie between the rails while a train passed over them. An old Olmo watches an old Alfredo lying crosswise on the rails. There is a cut to a shot of a mole emerging from the ground, then to a train going over a young Alfredo lying between the rails. The shot is held on him, lying with his hands over his eyes, and the film ends.

This sequence attempts to sum up the film and with it the political movements in rural Italy throughout the century. Its montage of time, friendship, opposition is Bertolucci's key statement about the continuing struggle between classes and the individuals who represent them. By emulating some Eisensteinian techniques (the sequence is a homage to Eisenstein) he hopes to indicate that the dialectics of film history also continue. The neo-realist premise of *1900*–its embracing of a poor and struggling class of people–is encompassed by the Eisensteinian urge to manipulate and arrange events toward a didactic end. But Bertolucci is so far away from the Eisensteinian tradition that he can only allude to it and strain toward a symbolic gesture.

Eisenstein could joke with his montage, as in *Strike,* when company spies are compared to animals, or be deadly serious, as when, in the same film, a sequence of workers being shot down by the police is intercut with shots of animals felled in a slaughterhouse. He could use montage within a sequence to expand time, stretching and repeating gestures to emphasize the moment, as in the plate-breaking sequence of *Potemkin* or the bridge raising in *October*. In the final sequence of *1900* these great effects are reduced. The struggle between worker and owner is ongoing; history moves like a train, running over both; consciousness emerges like a mole from the ground. The end of *1900* (and I am only supposing that it is the ending originally intended by Bertolucci) shows something of a problem inherited from the film's neo-realist origins. Because there was no revolution in Italy after the war, the neo-realists were unable (and, for reasons already discussed, unwilling) to allow their characters to triumph. Bertolucci is able to provide a fantasy of triumph that is modified by history and character. He wants a victory for the left, but knows a clear-cut victory is unlikely; he loves his two struggling characters and does not want either one to triumph to the other's detriment. Alfredo's indecisiveness is meant to manifest a kind of liberal-centrist position and sensibility, one which gives all sides their due without a defined moral or political commitment. Olmo, the strong and politically sophisticated peasant, struggles with his own emotional attachments to Alfredo, with whom he grew up. The conflicts between friendship, political necessity, and history become too strong. Bertolucci knows that, historically, neither Alfredo's nor Olmo's side triumphed. Like Visconti's *La Terra Trema,* Bertolucci's revolutionary project is thwarted by the realities of Italian society. While he feels free to posit the rise of a radical consciousness through the middle of the century, he does not feel free to speculate on the direction of that consciousness after the second World War. Finally, the Eisensteinian techniques appear almost as parodies, for the kind of historical conflicts Eisenstein reflected and developed in his films are not available to Bertolucci. Character is substituted for history; attention becomes focused on two attractive individuals; and finally, everything gets stuck in the glamor of international filmmaking.

There is no better way to understand the appropriateness of the neo-realists' use of non-professional or little-known players than by watching in *1900* well-known American actors and a French movie star impersonating Italian peasants and landowners. (It is almost as if Bertolucci seriously considered the possibilities, if not the ramifications, of the legend surrounding *Bicycle Thieves*—that De Sica was offered American backing for the film if he would use Cary Grant in the role of Ricci.) The conflict between personality and character and history permits neither closeness to nor distance from the narrative, but rather requires a constant attempt on the part of the audience to integrate the actor into the role and the character into the historical events going on. Bertolucci created what was to be an epic history but was cut down by the exigencies of distribution, by his own desire to mimic the grand style of Hollywood production, and by his inability to draw a satisfying conclusion.

The film is, finally, a hybrid—a conscious mixture of Eisenstein, of *La Terra Trema* (but with the workers offered some possibility for victory rather than melodramatic defeat); *The Leopard,* Visconti's ornate spectacle in which Burt Lancaster plays an aristocrat caught in the last stages of the Italian *Risorgimento;* and *Gone with the*

Wind. While rooted in neo-realism, *1900* branches through the history of film; style and direction, form and content clash, and despite all its exuberance the film fails to cohere. This cannot be blamed solely on the cuts made in the original version. The film attempts too much and its images are both trivial and portentous, wanting to communicate both the scope of history and some discrete elements of ordinary life with a grandeur that is often at odds with the speculative and inquiring nature of the narrative. In the end Bertolucci leaves his main characters in a state of uncertainty and his audience in a state of dissatisfaction.

The Tree of Wooden Clogs and *1900* seem to move in opposite directions, the one celebrating the stoical endurance of the peasantry, the other examining their revolutionary fervor. Both, however, suffer an identical problem of perspective. They romanticize their subject. Bertolucci's is a revolutionary romanticism, an expression of great historical consciousness and action among the peasant class. There were revolutionary outbreaks such as those depicted in the film, but Bertolucci's celebration is too unquestioning, unanalytical, and inconclusive. When the film tries to come to terms with the inconclusiveness of the revolution its ambiguities damage the narrative movement that has already occurred. Olmi's is a more serious and detrimental romanticism. His admiration of the peasantry as a suffering but uncomplaining class, caught up in their toil, blissfully innocent of the trap they are in, runs the risk of sanctification, of creating a myth of heroic, holy passivity.

There are alternatives to the approach of Olmi and Bertolucci. *Red Psalm* (1971), a film by the Hungarian director Miklós Jancsó, offers one of the best responses to the neo-realist endeavor and dilemma, and it will be examined in some detail in the last chapter. Another alternative appears in *Padre Padrone,* the third film of the unintended peasant trilogy that appeared in the late seventies. Of the three it is the most removed from its neo-realist origins, and therefore the most successful. By taking a neo-realist subject and then severing it from a neo-realist treatment, the film manages to reflect back upon its origins as well as upon the legacy of the movement.

The immediate structural difference between *Padre Padrone* and the forties tradition is its point of view. It concentrates on a single figure and uses that figure as a perceptual locus, observing and judging events from the perspective of the central character. This would seem not to be very different from the methods of Rossellini in *Germany, Year Zero* (a film admired by the Tavianis and alluded to in *Il Prato,* a film made for Italian television after *Padre Padrone* but not commercially released in the United States) or De Sica in *Bicycle Thieves* and *Umberto D.* Each of these narratives focuses on a central character and observes the world if not through that character's point of view, then certainly parallel to it. But the neo-realists used this direct or indirect first-person point of view not to analyze a character's feelings or even perceptions, but to place that character in a situation and observe actions and reactions. In *Padre Padrone* the Taviani brothers partake as well as observe; they "report" on the phenomenon of the contemporary peasantry–in this case the shepherds of Sardinia in Italy's wretchedly poor south–through the eyes and developing personality of Gavino Ledda, the individual upon whose life the film is based. The result is a film about growth and change, about learning and development in a situation where it is difficult for an individual to grow, learn, or change. It is also about the violent interaction of a son and father–not the innocent suffering of a child struggling in the misery of his father's world (a favorite theme of the neo-realists), but the struggle of a child against a father whose brutality is a reflection of their world. The film focuses objective social-economic reality through a subjective conflict. Whereas the neo-realists wanted the viewer to supply the subjective response to what they hoped would be an objective rendering of character and events, the Tavianis rework this methodology–in light of the thirty years of narrative experimentation that separates *Padre Padrone* from the neo-realist tradition–into a complex of subjective, sometimes almost expressionist, inquiry into states of mind, first- and third-person commentary on events, and subdued objective observation of the world inhabited by their characters.

The complex is achieved by locking the narrative off from most authorized conventions of "realism," neo or other. The film begins

The father takes Gavino out of school. *Padre Padrone* (Museum of Modern Art Film Stills Archive).

and ends with the "actual" Gavino, who first introduces and then sums up his experience; not in the form of a separate introduction and conclusion, but rather as part of the film's *mise-en-scène.* He is introduced to us documentary fashion, through a voice-over commentary, as he stands in the school building that will be the setting of the film's first sequence. He is whittling a stick for his "father"—that is, for the actor playing his father—who is waiting to enter the classroom to take the young Gavino (a child playing Gavino as a little boy) out of school and put him to work in the fields. At the end of the film, we see the "actual" Gavino again, bringing up to date the recent events of his life, addressing the camera as he points out the activity in town due to the presence of the film crew. The camera pans to a window and we see the town square with people gathered around the film equipment truck. There is a cut back to Gavino and a zip pan (a quick, rushing movement) back to the schoolroom, back to the opening of the film, the father again leading the young Gavino out to work, repeating his warning to the other children, who are mocking Gavino, that it will soon be their turn. As at the beginning, the camera holds on the frightened children, their teacher looking away helplessly; there is a cut to the town square as the sound of the wind that plays over the fields is heard, and a dissolve to the "actual" Gavino, this time sitting in the meadow, the place that held him captive as a child. The film ends with a closeup of his back, rocking as he did in his childhood insecurity, then stopping as the wind blows and the clarinet concerto that was Gavino's solace as an adult comes up on the sound track.

Contained in the opening and closing of this film is an element of construction that was of major importance in the development of European and Latin American cinema in the sixties. We, as audience, are made to recognize the film as an artifact, as something consciously constructed, with actors impersonating characters, and with its own specific ways of showing reality. The beginning and end of the film joke with its status as documentary, its basis in "fact," and the ease with which fact elides with fiction. The Taviani brothers take such care in manipulating their film into this status of self-consciousness that there is no possibility of looking at it as the observation of ordinary life. It announces itself as the conscious creation of an extraordinary life; not only do the subject and the narrative continually comment upon each other, but the presence of a controlling narrative "voice," separate from both, shapes and controls the whole. In 1977, there was nothing unusual about this, and the complexity of these multiple points of view is not very great when compared to what had been done by filmmakers in the sixties and early seventies. However, in comparison to neo-realism, the complexity is extreme. In the body of the film we are shown many events with a force and immediacy that tend to break down the provocative distance created by its opening and closing. Gavino's attempts to endure and escape his father's brutality and his isolated shepherd's life tend to absorb our perception and response completely, particularly early in the film where the father's violence against the child reaches appalling heights. But even here, the filmmakers intrude in such a way as to remove us from the action when our sympathy threatens to overtake us, them, and the material. At one point, after beating Gavino senseless for leaving his fold to speak with a friend, the father holds him and sings. The camera frames the two in a perfect image of a pietà, and the father's singing is joined by other voices on the sound track as the camera drifts away from the two figures to the countryside. The viewer is permitted to experience revulsion at the beating, relief at the father's show of concern. But a break in identification with the events occurs with the ironic allusion to Catholic iconography, and separation is created as the camera moves away and the other voices are heard. The viewer is reminded again of the father's threat as a closeup of him is suddenly inserted, followed by a fade to black.

The Tavianis refuse to allow a single attitude or mood to predominate for too long. The bleakness of poverty is not as unrelenting in this film as it was for the neo-realists, and is the source less of pity and compassion than of frustration and anger. It can even yield images that are (or can be made) ludicrous and amusing. Immediately after the fade to black on the father, we see Gavino, his face swollen from his beating, milking a goat. For all his efforts, he cannot keep the goat from defecating in the milk. His frustrations are spoken offscreen in threats to the animal, to which the animal itself responds, "speaking" to Gavino through his imagination, threatening to continue its unpleasant activities so the father will beat Gavino some more. In despair, Gavino attempts to drown the goat in its own fouled milk. Then a chain of association begins that the Tavianis find irresistible. In the midst of his altercation with the goat, Gavino sees two other animals copulating. He notes this and begins stroking the goat; there is a cut to Gavino's young friend in the neighboring field fornicating with a mule. We hear heavy breathing on the sound track. We see other children masturbating with chickens. A chorus of heavy breathing builds. Gavino's father sees the children, gets excited, rides off to his wife, and leaps upon her. Other adults proceed to the same occupation as the chorus of heavy breathing reaches a crescendo and the camera pans the town.

There is much good humor in this, and at no one's expense, except perhaps the goat and the chickens. The scatology and sexuality are not exploitative as they are, for example, in Ettore Scola's neo-realist parody *Down and Dirty* (1977). They are one of the means the Tavianis use to alter the narrative tone and structure and diminish reliance on conventional chronology or spatial continuity. Such digressions and shifts in point of view provide as well a means to approach, with discretion, the psychology of the characters, or at least their emotional and physical reactions, without presuming to reveal them entirely or to reduce them to stereotypes.

Later in the film, an older Gavino sits in his meadow, learning to play a broken accordion he bought for two goats from some wanderers. He has slit his lip with a knife so his father will think he was robbed and beaten. The camera pans the awful, rocky place he inhabits and moves back to Gavino as these words appear on the screen: "I am Gavino, son of the shepherd Efisio, who is the son of the shepherd, Luca. The cold has filled our pens with fleas. The fattest ones are under my armpits. . . . I am Eligio, son of the shepherd, Giovanni, who was the son of the Carabinere, Enrico. I had to eat cheese that was too fresh. When I blow on my tongue, it burns." The camera continues to pan the meadow as sounds of sobbing are heard on the sound track and a boy on a donkey rides past, crying. More words appear: "Angels of paradise who play so sweetly, I'm Matteo, and I beg you: let a basin of boiling water appear that I can put my feet in, for I'm dying of cold." Sobbing and sad music are intermixed with the waltz associated with Gavino's accordion, and the sequence ends with a closeup of the crying rider and the words, "Mine is a prayer."

This sequence is immediately followed by a shot of the father walking along, worrying that Gavino is slipping away from him, worrying that he must keep his mind nimble, which he does by reciting the multiplication table to himself. In the opposite direction rides Sebastiano, a shepherd who smokes his cigar with the lit end in his mouth, so his enemies will not see him in the dark. As the camera follows him, he decides to make peace with them. He meets with them; they make up and proceed to slaughter their sheep together until one of the enemies turns and bashes Sebastiano, kills him, and steals his sheep.

No one mood is permitted to wear itself out, and no opportunity is missed to manipulate the viewer's perspective and the tone of particular events, and to comment upon them in the imagery or on the sound track in a manner that is not quite psychological, sociological, or directly political, yet manages to combine these three modes of inquiry. Sympathy, outrage, awe, concern are all elicited without any one reaction predominating. *Padre Padrone* is a didactic film in the best sense. We are engaged and yet asked to keep our distance, and we learn with some force of an exotic and appalling way of life through a film that is itself somewhat exotic in its mixture of styles and levels of discourse. But the various levels are never foreign to the subject of the film. Gavino is a peasant who became an intellectual, who went from barren fields to a somewhat less barren life in the army, and finally to a university where he became a linguist and studied the dialect of his region. Throughout he kept returning to his home and the shadow of his father. The conflicts of this process are realized in the conflicting perspectives of the film. Just as Gavino learns language that will help him to understand and control his world, the film learns the narrative language that best describes him and his past and best speaks to us of the character, his surroundings, and his history.

The Italian filmmakers and theorists of the forties discovered alternatives to the artificial language of commercial cinema. They allowed the image to record and reveal a historically viable world, a "real" world, stories of which would be more eloquent and moving than the middle-class melodramatics of conventional film. In so doing, they made available to the filmmakers who followed them a starting point from which to build new languages of the image, new narrative forms. The "break" in film history that neo-realism created led to many experiments in restructuring and revitalizing cinematic storytelling, renewing inquiry into the cinematic possibilities of telling these stories and different ways of engaging the audience in their telling. Having considered the new models of image-making the neo-realists provided, we can proceed to examine the structures that were built by the filmmakers who followed them.

CHAPTER TWO
THE SUBSTANCE OF FORM

Of course it's been said about my work that the search for style has often resulted in a want of feeling. . . . However, I'd put it another way. I'd say that style is *feeling in its most elegant and economic expression. . . .*

Clive Langham
in Alain Resnais's *Providence*

Reality changes; in order to represent it, modes of representation must change.

Bertolt Brecht[1]

THE LONG-TERM result of neo-realism was an explosion of form. It was as if the act of changing the subject matter of commercial cinema and altering the ways in which the audience was requested to look at the new subject released possibilities of expression dormant in cinema throughout the thirties. It is true that there had been experimentation in narrative form since the beginning of film history, and that the new energy of expression following neo-realism spread and developed slowly throughout the fifties and all across Europe, climaxing in the sixties. But "explosion" is still a fair term; for within a fairly short period of time, film caught up with what the other arts had been doing since the turn of the century: expanding, reflecting upon, and defining its own formal nature, subordinating content to the expression of content, the story to its telling.

By the late twenties, film world wide had established a sophisticated and flexible means of telling stories through images that was diminished with the coming of sound, when the image was put to the service of dialogue.[2] The standardization of narrative technique and narrative content proceeded apace as industrialized filmmaking in the West continued to move toward easily and universally comprehensible form and content: a homogeneous set of conventions of spatial and temporal continuity and a uniformity of moral content that made cinema accessible to the greatest number of people with the least possible effort. But while filmmaking was normalizing production and standardizing form and content, the older arts were completing a process of breaking down the old codes and conventions of representation. The human figure and recognizable landscapes began to disappear from painting in the post-impressionist movements. In post-revolutionary Russia, artists, dramatists, poets, and filmmakers sought new and wider audiences and new ways of addressing them. Weimar Germany saw the fruition of the expressionist movement and new forms of architecture, music, and the graphic arts. Between the wars, poets and novelists were examining not only what could be said with language, but what the nature of that saying was. Fiction became its own subject; form was recognized as the essential content of the work of art.

It is a marvelous irony that some of the modernist forms in fiction and painting came from the developing forms of film. Cubism is a kind of spatially simultaneous montage.[3] In the novel, "the discontinuity of plot and the scenic development, the sudden emersion of the thoughts and moods, the relativity and the inconsistency of the time standards, are what remind us in the works of Proust and Joyce, Dos Passos, and Virginia Woolf of the cuttings, dissolves and interpolations of the film. . . ."[4] (Later, the New Novelists of France, among them Alain Robbe-Grillet and Marguerite Duras, employed the methods of cinematic description in their prose writing, and in turn wrote and directed films, attempting something of a cross-disciplinary style.) The modernists were challenging tradition, particularly the tradition of art as comforter—the locus of satisfaction and harmony, the guide to transcendent visions of nature, or the place of ideological reconciliation. Painters would not compete with photography, and rather than represent images of the world created images that reflected the properties of line and color and volume. Poets, continuing the work of the *symbolistes,* considered not only the thought and feeling that might be expressed by language, but the language itself that creates thought and feeling. Novelists and composers sought to redirect attention away from narrative meaning in the novel or emotional expression in music to the structures of narrative and of musical expression themselves. Across the arts modernism involved a movement away from "meaning" as an abstraction, an entity separable from the forms that make it. Grand emotions, philosophies of life, depictions of nature were no longer the sole purpose of art; the *work* of art and how it was perceived became the focus of attention. Content, of course, never disappeared, particularly in the narrative arts. All stories, no matter how much attention is directed toward the telling, have meaning.

Different artists followed the modernist impulse in different directions. The movement was no more monolithic than the forms of classicism and romanticism that both preceded and coexisted with it. It had many schools and many practitioners and many contradictions. While radical in its formal complexity and unconventional in the demands it placed on its audience, much of the modernist endeavor was in service to traditional social-political ideology. The work of Pound and Eliot, while busily reconsidering and restructuring poetic forms, used those forms to discuss conventional, even reactionary, notions of history and human worth. Others used new forms for new ends. Bertolt Brecht directed his dramatic theory and practice to social and political change, seeking a revolutionary art that would lead to a revolutionary culture. For the Russians in the late teens and early twenties the interaction of art and politics went unquestioned. Eisenstein developed his theory and practice of montage to construct dynamic images of revolution and create for the spectator a way of looking at history dialectically. Dziga Vertov wanted to use film as a place of inscription, a way of "writing" the work of the revolution for and with the viewer, giving new eyes with which to see a new world.

The split in the modernist movement between those who were interested only in the formal possibilities of their art and those who would use those possibilities to turn both the art and its audience toward a confrontation with social-political realities continued into the sixties when commercial narrative film finally caught up with the movement. Another split, potentially more serious, involved–and still involves–not factions within the movement, but two overriding factions, artist and audience. Modernism threatened to create a gulf between them wider than had ever existed before. It demanded an extraordinary reorientation of imaginative intent and response, and insisted that the way the work exists, and the relationship of that mode of existence to those who perceive it, are as important–more important–than any other "meaning" the work might have. The demands thus made on audience attention, the call for work on the part of the spectator, the refusal to communicate meaning and feeling instantly could only cause resistance and even resentment among the majority of people too busy or simply unwilling to meet these demands. A new artistic elitism threatened—a separation of the work of art from a broad and engaged audience.

The response to the threat came in many forms, some of them severe. In Russia, where much of the formal experimentation occurred, the government, worried that attention to form was denying the needs of the audience and threatening the dominant socialist ideology, repressed the modernist movement. The state feared a return to a kind of art for art's sake where the artist would presumably satisfy his or her own imaginative needs without responsibility to a larger group or purpose. The result of this fear was a call for a return to "realism," a simple and direct communication of social and political phenomena through conventional forms of expression. "Socialist realism" grew out of ideological turmoil, out of a concern that artists be in touch with their audience, and out of fear; it became a reactionary stance that chose to forget or repress the fact that revolutionary content can only be created by revolutionary form, that perception precedes action, and that content is determined by the way content is made. It took many years for the socialist countries to realize that "realism" meant something other than simple access to simple meaning (too many years, in the course of which Soviet cinema lost its vitality). By contrast the Italian neo-realists, who, like the socialist realists, chose the working class as subjects, were aware that straightforward glorification of the figure of the worker in simple narratives of triumph could not open perception and would be counterproductive to their cause. Theirs was a response both to socialist realism *and* to literary modernism and it made cinema modernism possible.

The fascists took care of the threat of elitism by simply destroying anything that smacked of imagination and threat to the status quo. "When I hear the word 'culture' I reach for my gun," Goebbels is supposed to have said. The comment is parodied by Godard in his film *Contempt* (1963), when Jeremy Prokosch, the American film producer (played by Jack Palance), a man of cultured boorishness, says "Whenever I hear the word 'culture' I bring out my checkbook."[5] Godard has an ironic understanding of Goebbels's comment—a statement of the philistine's fear of that which is different, perhaps even threatening. "Culture" for Goebbels was irrelevant and dangerous to the needs of the state, and as a fascist he wanted to annihilate it completely. For Godard's producer, "culture" is a distraction from commercial viability, and as a capitalist he wants to buy it off. But beneath the brutal mindlessness of Goebbels's comment is a perception that Godard gets at in a less brutal way.

Fascism, of any variety, despises difference and would destroy it. But within the concept of "culture" there is often a notion of difference that is itself destructive if it proposes to remove "art" from direct contact with ordinary experience and intellectual or emotional need. The concept of culture often carries the connotative burden of elitism, of snobbery and arrogance (a fact that makes Goebbels's statement ludicrous, since fascism is arrogant and elitist at its ideological core). The extreme reactions of the right and the conservative left toward the modernist movement point up its subversion of conventional and safe artistic attitudes and expectations. Yet the fact is that its subversion *can* be seen to support the connotations of elitism and snobbery inherent in "culture." If the writer, painter, musician, or filmmaker desires to concentrate on the formal properties of his or her art, demanding we learn its language and then struggle for meaning within it, the risk of alienation, of the audience refusing the struggle, is great. Most people do not want to work for their aesthetic satisfaction. When the demands become too great, the work is simply ignored. Such seems to be the case with contemporary "serious" music, which has lost its audience and is of interest, in the main, to its own practitioners and theorists. Such is the danger whenever a work appears to be emotionally inaccessible.

The initial modernist movement was over by the late thirties—politically squelched, ignored by the public at large. The second World War offered little room for aesthetic contemplation, and the movement lay more or less dormant until the mid forties. The relationship of film to this first part of the modernist movement was tangential.

Commercial narrative cinema was busy consolidating itself economically and aesthetically. There were major experimental figures, like Eisenstein, who were part of the avant-garde movement in Russia, and there was a substantial avant-garde movement centered in France. In the twenties and thirties, people like Abel Gance, Jean Epstein, Louis Delluc, Marcel L'Herbier, René Clair, Joris Ivens (from Holland); Walter Ruttmann (Germany); and, of course, Buñuel were actively engaged in exploring cinema's formal possibilities.[6] Few of them had direct influence on commercial film, however. Buñuel endured a cinematic exile and then had to reemerge through the forms of neorealism before reestablishing himself as a key figure (and still had to wait many years before he saw himself having any direct influence, notably in the work of the New Wave and the Germans). The expressionist movement in Germany was rather quickly routed into mainstream American production. F. W. Murnau, Fritz Lang, E. A. Dupont, cinematographer Karl Freund (to name only a few of the German emigrés) came to America to work.

In the end the Hollywood style was able to absorb and level all others, reprocess them, and return the mixture to Europe where it in turn influenced the styles of various national cinemas. Individual figures like Renoir, Jean Cocteau, and Orson Welles pushed and probed at the boundaries of what was essentially an international style. In *Citizen Kane,* Welles rerouted the expressionist style once again, initiating a change in *mise-en-scène* and narrative content that developed into *film noir,* the dark, paranoid cinema that altered the look of American film and had a lasting influence abroad. (Even Ingmar Bergman admits to its influence on his forties films.)[7] But the fact that *film noir* involved a radical change in form and content went unrecognized until the French began commenting on it in the fifties. Given its status as a mass art, narrative filmmaking in America could not admit to any experimentation and change even when these were occurring. Hollywood suppressed the initiators of change—Welles, like von Stroheim before him, was not permitted to work—and absorbed the changes themselves into its basic methods. One reason the *noir* style became such a constant in forties filmmaking may well be that repetition is always easier than exploration, and American filmmakers simply reproduced the style rather than attempting to understand it. That had always been their method, for it was and is neither aesthetically or economically feasible to allow the Hollywood style to begin questioning itself or its audience's response. The economic apparatus of commercial cinema is so large and complex that everyone, from investor to spectator, is involved in maintaining an illusion of a status quo. Arnold Hauser writes that "in order to amortise the invested capital, the cinema-goers of the whole world have to contribute to the financing of a big film."[8] And to get such global financing there must be global assent, to a style and a subject matter that please and do not threaten. So another irony occurs. If the early modernist movement borrowed from cinema, cinema itself—popular, commercial cinema—protected its audience from modernism. Roy Armes writes: "In fact the cinema established itself as a refutation of modernism, becoming the new refuge of story, character and spectacle, and it is to this that it owed its vast popularity."[9] The continuity of the Hollywood style offered security to an audience who might find the demands made by the experiments in the other arts a chore.

None of this resolves the finally unresolvable arguments about the validity and value of mass or popular culture versus high art; "entertainment" for the largest number of people versus subjective expressions of inquiry in painting, literature, music, or film created for those few with the education and time to understand them. The arguments are unresolvable partly because they are based on the false premise (itself often elitist) that the public gets what it wants—or worse, what it deserves. But the "public" is not a real entity as much as it is an ideological construct, a set of attitudes and responses created over a period of time by people who have gathered to themselves the apparatus necessary to supply a culture with its goods and services—in this case the service of entertainment. The problem is not that a large public is incapable or unwilling to accept new forms. Film itself was a new form of expression only a relatively short time ago; its narrative methods had to be learned by both its audience and its creators over a period of years. The fact that specific methods of continuity construction, specific contents, and specific ideological biases emerged and controlled the film product was largely the result of convenience and fear on the part of filmmakers, not the film audience. The studios created that audience and were reluctant to change their creation by changing the other creations, the films they made. In a short time the creation took on a life of its own and the filmmakers believed that what they made was what the audience wanted; the audience was made to believe the same. This self-fulfilling process exists today in American television production and has become even more aggravated in film production, where the films themselves are of less interest to the executives who execute them than is the deal that can be made to maximize profits on the venture.

Given all this, it is not surprising that mainstream theatrical film by and large resisted the kind of experimentation that was going on in other narrative forms–and even in other branches of film–in the twenties and thirties, or, if it did not resist, absorbed the experiments into its own development. Nor is it surprising that today cinematic experimentation and inquiry are avoided in many countries even more than before. What is surprising is that they showed up at all in that period from the late fifties to the early seventies. A number of factors account for the phenomenon. Certainly the excitement created by neo-realism and its commercial acceptance was a primary catalyst. Also, the old, established forms of cinema were simply no longer terribly interesting (except to critical investigation of their nature and the reasons for their longevity). The work of the postwar Italian filmmakers provided a response to the old forms that was accessible, not overwhelmingly threatening, and profound enough to provoke some reevaluations of cinematic possibilities. The commercial and critical acceptance of Bergman and Fellini in the mid and late fifties spurred producers and distributors to allow a certain amount of individual expression in the films they handled, and this served as another important opening into commercial distribution for films that began to explore their limits rather than repeat what had always been done within them.

Neo-realism was a response not only to the history of cinema, but to the war, which created cultural and political upheaval throughout Europe. The cinema of each country responded to it in different ways and at different times. It took over twenty years for the West German cinema to reemerge and reexamine itself and its culture. It took the French about ten years to channel the political and philosophical excitement of the postwar years into a renewal of their cinema, which in turn became the renewal of cinema the world over.[10] In East Europe, the renewals were sporadic. In the fifties, Poland's Andrzej Wajda, in *Ashes and Diamonds,* enlarged upon the political subjects developed by the neo-realists and in so doing advanced the ability of film to create committed political drama. In the sixties Yugoslavia, Hungary, and Czechoslovakia each produced major figures, and in the late sixties filmmakers in Cuba, Brazil, and elsewhere in Latin America seized upon the narrative devices being developed in Europe and pushed them further, picking up where Eisenstein had left off, mixing his methodology with Godard's, allowing film to function as part of their society's political structure. In all, it was a period when the major threads of film history were picked up and rewoven, when film was rediscovered as a means of expressing the individual imagination, an analytical tool able to explore self and culture. It was a time as well when filmmakers believed the audience able and willing to join the task.

2

In the last chapter I pointed out that one of the main conventions cast aside by the neo-realists was psychological realism, the explaining and analyzing of character motivation through conventions of guilt, love, jealousy, revenge, nobility of spirit, and various other emotions that in melodrama are substituted for specific investigations of human behavior, conventions satisfying and convincing only because of repetition, acceptable only for want of alternatives. Alternatives were needed both to conventional melodrama and to neo-realism itself. Filmmakers could not be restricted to observation of the social conditions of the working class; what was more, as middle-class artists, they were compelled by tradition to seek methods of exploring and analyzing individual consciousness (of all the traditions broken by modernist cinema, this was the most difficult and resistant). So, among the first endeavors of the post–neo-realists was an attempt to reinvestigate the middle-class soul, to avoid the conventions and clichés of romance and comedy, and to discover how to use narrative images to establish subjective states rather than merely allude to pre-existing stereotypes.

Two Italian films, Rossellini's *Voyage in Italy* (1953) and Michelangelo Antonioni's *Il Grido* (1957), signal some early moves in the reinvestigation process. *Voyage in Italy* is among the group of melodramas, also including *Stromboli* and *Europa 51,* that Rossellini made with Ingrid Bergman. Its subject could not be more mundane: a wealthy, middle-class, middle-aged couple, Catherine and Alex Joyce (Ingrid Bergman and George Sanders), discover on a trip to Naples that they are bored with each other. Alex goes off in search of other women; Catherine wanders and sees the sights of the town. In the end they are reconciled. The banality of the subject is overwhelming, and Rossellini attempts to diffuse it by focusing not only on the characters but on the landscape that surrounds them, a landscape to which he makes them subject. The film becomes a three-way dialogue between Catherine, her inarticulate grief, and the world that surrounds her and provides her voice. She is subject to that world and made, along with the audience, silently to respond to it.

Rossellini performs some important operations upon the neo-realist aesthetic he helped develop. He is, obviously, concentrating on a social class the neo-realists scorned; but he is still observing his characters as part of an environment and allowing that environment to speak as much about them as they do about themselves. More so, for in neo-realist cinema the characters and their environment reflect one another. Here they are at odds. Alex, to be sure, seeks out places in which he is comfortable: nighttime city streets, parties in Capri. But Catherine tours the streets and the antiquities of the city, all of which are alien to her, surround and trouble her, and finally to some degree enlighten her. The characters are not so much defined by the landscape as they are set against it and changed by it, along with our perceptions of them. In the forties, Rossellini and his colleagues tended to look at both character and environment whole, to observe the character within the place. In *Germany, Year Zero* Edmund is within and part of the ruined streets of Berlin; they reflect each other and a greater condition of cultural ruin. In *Voyage in Italy,* Catherine and her surroundings are at odds, so much so that rather than portray the character within the place, Rossellini intercuts them, giving us Catherine gazing at things and showing us the things she looks at—statues in a museum, flaming lava pits, the bones in a catacomb, the Naples streets filled with pregnant women, a passionate and vital past and present.

This editing defines both the film's narrative direction and the character, a woman isolated from experience and history. Her troubled gaze is played against statuary in a museum which in turn is rapturously embraced by Rossellini's camera, panning and tracking heroic figures while a tour guide drones a banal monologue. A three-way perceptual split occurs. We are shown wondrous, exciting sights, passionately observed by Rossellini; we gaze as well at Catherine's mute and troubled face; and we hear the clichés tumbling from the mouths of the various tour guides, for whom the city's treasures are a way to earn a living. They annoy us and frighten Catherine (at one point a guide forces her to pose like a prisoner in the caves; another shows her the lava pits that burst into smoke at the touch of a lit cigarette). The voyage becomes, finally, the spectator's as well as hers as our perceptions are linked to and severed from Catherine's continually. Point of view is set and broken from point to point. The climax of this counterpointing of seer and seen occurs when Alex and Catherine visit the ruins of Pompeii and observe the castings of body shapes that were formed by the ancient eruption. We watch Alex and Catherine as the forms of a couple appear. It is an astounding sequence of juxtaposition: an emotionally dead couple sees the reincarnation of a physically dead couple, a resurrection before their eyes and ours. It has an effect. Although they are still considering divorce, Catherine and Alex move off through a Pompeian street in a series of shots that show both of them together within a defined space, rather than separate from each other and their surroundings. They drive to Milan and their car is stopped by a religious procession. Catherine is moved by the faith of the people and their childlike innocence. She gets, literally, carried away by the crowd. Alex catches up with her and they both look at supplicants who have been cured by faith. They proclaim their love and embrace. The camera pulls away from them and cuts to the crowd of people going by.

The problem with *Voyage in Italy* is evident from the verbal transcription of its end, for it finally yields to the banality of its subject more than it tries to compensate for it. But in the attempt, it pushes forward the possibilities for the cinematic gaze to create meaning out of the way characters react to what they look at. The film realizes the possibility inherent in the neo-realist image to reveal states of mind; its images permit the spectator to fill in the silences that exist between the character and the landscape. The film advances upon the traditional Hollywood shot/reaction shot technique (look at character/look at what character sees/look at character reacting) by allowing a disjuncture of gaze rather than simply a suturing of the space between the character who looks, the thing looked at, and the audience who watches both.[11] By keeping Catherine's reactions separate from our reactions to the wonders we and she see, Rossellini opens a space in which we can come to an understanding of her character, her sorrow, and her anxieties, though none of these are verbally articulated as they would be in a more conventional melodrama.* Rossellini asks the viewer to construct a response out of the dislocations that exist between the character and the environment before he fills in the spaces with a conventional reconciliation. When this occurs he again attempts to suggest an emotional response by means of what the characters and the audience observe, and attention is directed to that pri-

* Some circumspection is needed here: the American release version is about thirty-five minutes shorter than Rossellini's original cut. Much more dialogue may be present in the original. There is also some comparison to be made between the point of view structure developed in this film and the methods Hitchcock was developing. (Hitchcock had also used Ingrid Bergman as an actress in *Spellbound,* 1945, *Notorious,* 1946, and *Under Capricorn,* 1949.)

mary neo-realist image, the street and its people. The surge of humanity in religious celebration is meant to release the anger and anxieties of the couple and return their faith and hope. Unfortunately the viewer's perception of their emotional turmoil is not easily displaced by the sudden reconciliation and reaffirmation of the strength and faith of the ordinary people. The film betrays, like many of the neo-realist works before it, a readiness to accept sentiment in the place of understanding. But that is somewhat beside the point. The importance of *Voyage in Italy* lies not in the resolution of its plot, but in the ways it investigates its characters through its images, and its request to the viewer to participate in that investigation by participating in the play of perspectives and points of view. Bazin says that the film creates "a mental landscape at once as objective as a straight photograph and as subjective as pure personal consciousness."[12] In recognizing this shift in the neo-realist act of observation he predicts the coming of a new cinema in which the objective world will not merely reflect, but become a constituent part of the consciousness of character and audience.

There is another element of importance in the film. It introduces a major thematic concern of sixties European cinema: the isolated and alienated hero and heroine. Ingmar Bergman had already been flirting with this subject in the forties, and it is difficult to trace direct lines of development, although there is a clear relation to the existentialist philosophy and literature that developed in pre- and postwar Europe, which itself has roots in the Marxist concerns with the alienation of labor and the reification of human activity. Alienation and disengagement had long been a subject of the modernist novel and can be seen in much of twentieth-century art, where connection, harmony, continuity are refused in both form and content. In film this theme is not only associated with these aesthetic and philosophic traditions but can also be seen as a negative inheritance of neo-realism. The inability of the neo-realist filmmakers to reach an understanding of the poverty and despair that was their subject and the pity and sentiment that became their essential reactions turned easily into expressions of impotence, especially when the subject of the modernist filmmaker was the middle class. In this case, the experience of filmmaker and character merged; the sense of removal from the world—figuring itself finally in a general neurasthenia, a numbness and fragmentation of the spirit—became a major character trait, and in some cases, a world view.

The despair arising from historical catastrophe that Rossellini presented in *Germany, Year Zero* becomes, in *Voyage in Italy,* the despair of individuals who are cut off from history. The separation of Catherine's perceptions from the things she perceives, her coldness and inwardness, the supercilious behavior of her husband work to create a withdrawal and silence between the couple and between Catherine and everything else. But, as I have indicated, the strength of the images is greater than the film's thematic commonplaces, and the structure of their juxtapositions tells us more, non-discursively, than does Catherine's voiced opinion of her condition (at one point she says she is sad because she is childless) or the religious yearnings that creep in at the end. Even more expressive are the disjunctures of which the film is made, the breaks in reactions and responses that enforce upon the spectator the need to make connections where the characters cannot. As a result, an interesting dialectic occurs that functioned through many of the films about alienation in the fifties and sixties. While the characters of the films are subjected to anxiety, ennui, despair, and rootlessness, the construction of the films demands that the viewer be actively engaged in finding his or her way among the very spaces in which the characters are lost. We are engaged in an act of discovery which the characters themselves are incapable of.

Voyage in Italy is an important but incomplete film. Four years later Antonioni advanced the elements that Rossellini had just begun to consider. *Il Grido* ("The Cry") is not the best-known work of this filmmaker, who with *L'Avventura, La Notte,* and *L'Eclisse* in the early sixties entered the front ranks of international directors, his films articulating inarticulateness and the collapse of passion and engagement in the post-industrial West. His subjects of alienation, of anger and paralysis of the spirit, rapidly became a convention. But his formal achievements added considerably to contemporary film's ability to structure meaning with and through the image. Antonioni came indirectly out of the neo-realist tradition, and early in his career he demonstrated a desire to move away from the minimal formativeness of that tradition and its need to make the observed more prominent than the act of observing. In *Chronicle of a Love Affair* (1950), a sort of middle-class version of Visconti's *Ossessione,* he is already concerned with expanding the possibilities of expressive framing and composition. His shots are unusually long and often complicated. The urban landscape occasionally overpowers the figures, diminishing them and making them one component in a larger structure. But unlike his later films, *Chronicle of a Love Affair* retains a concern with subject matter and plot (a woman wants her lower-middle-class lover to kill her rich husband) that Antonioni will eventually subordinate to a visual concentration, a desire to communicate information exclusively through *mise-en-scène,* the structuring of the space within the shot.

Il Grido is a measure of his early achievement of this aim. The film shares with the neo-realist tradition an observation of physical barrenness and a concern about disenfranchised people in a forbidding landscape. Unlike neo-realism, the poverty portrayed is not economic or even social, but emotional, spiritual (to use a desperately overworked term). The landscape, not quite urban, nor rural, is made up of the towns, roads, and flatlands of the Po Valley, an area of attraction for Italian filmmakers that figures in *Ossessione,* the last episode of *Paisan,* and an early documentary made by Antonioni. But the film is not about the Po Valley itself, nor its people. Antonioni uses both as material out of which to construct a series of observations of one individual drained of personality, energy, and desire. The narrative is in the form of an anti-journey. Aldo (played by Steve Cochran, dubbed with an Italian voice) wanders with his daughter from place to place, discovering nothing, learning nothing, eventually returning to the place from which he started and committing suicide.

This plot description is liable to confirm the worst suspicions people have about "foreign" films, that they are aimless and overwhelmingly depressing. That *Il Grido* is in fact neither aimless nor depressing points out precisely what Antonioni is up to, which is a relocation of the narrative away from events and meanings the film may refer to, to those which reside in the images themselves and are largely inseparable from the images. It is true that *Il Grido* is "about" a character who wanders aimlessly and commits suicide; it is not an abstract film, lacking paraphrasable content. However, that content is brief, spare, and neither very satisfying nor important. The meanings *seen*—the meanings of the images, the ways the characters are placed opposite each other, in a landscape, in the frame that composes them and the landscape—are the meanings of greatest importance.

In *Il Grido,* and Antonioni's subsequent films, paraphrasable content is diminished. It is difficult to detach a verbal summary from them; if detached, the summaries become clichés. Looking at the films' construction with an interpretive eye creates an understanding that is available only from visual engagement. The films are closed forms, operating within the circuit created by their projection and the audience's observation, with an effect similar to painting or photography. They do not subscribe to the "realistic" conventions of American film (though Antonioni's methods have an interesting relationship to American *film noir*), nor do they evoke an open, ongoing environment as does the cinema of Jean Renoir. Their connection to the world of ordinary experience is subordinated to the world created in and by their imagery.[13] In fact it is possible to accuse Antonioni of having more a photographer's imagination than a filmmaker's (he explores the possibilities and ambiguities inherent in the revelatory powers of the photographic image in *Blow Up,* 1966). But it would be more accurate to state that while he begins with the image and with the photographer's knowledge that the image formulates bits of the given world into precise, imaginative expressions of that world, he has the filmmaker's understanding of movement, of changing spatial coordinates, and of the ability of events to build on each other incrementally. He fully understands the possibilities of dramatic confrontation; but he is uninterested in the kind of confrontation that isolates the participants from their surroundings. Like many contem-

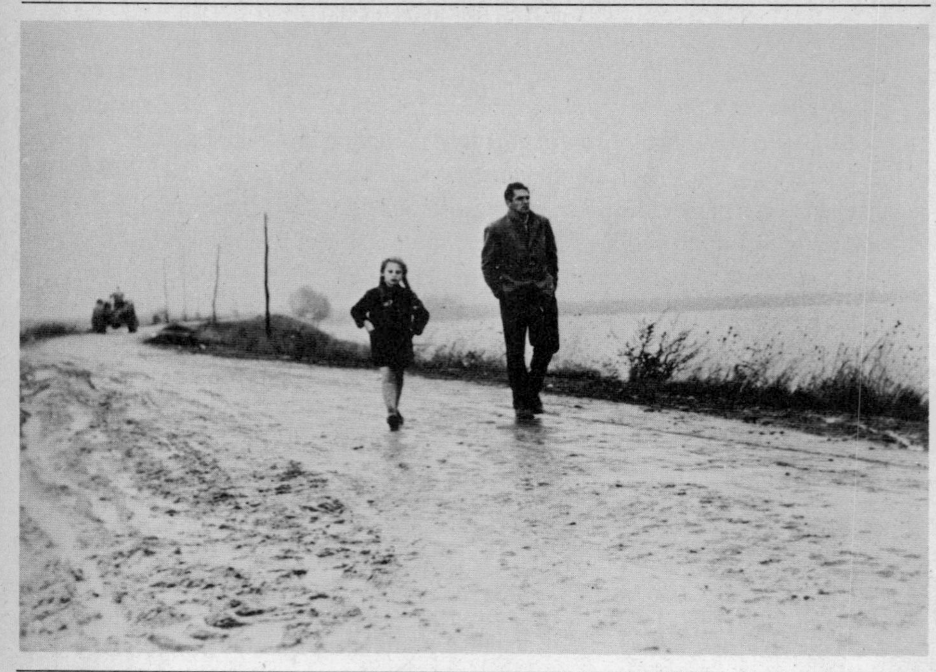

Aldo (Steve Cochran) and his daughter wander the flatlands of the Po. *Il Grido* (Museum of Modern Art Film Stills Archive).

porary European filmmakers, he finds the closeup, in theory, of limited value (in other words, he and his colleagues use closeups from time to time, but in a very precise and calculated way, seldom at the expense of the environment of which the faces are a part). The characters inhabit a place, which is as important, perhaps more so, than the characters alone.

The habitation of *Il Grido* is determined by barely graded gray tones. Mists and barren trees or a flat, gray horizon predominates in the exteriors. The interiors are composed so that people move behind doors or furniture, or are marked off from one another by objects in the frame. And the characters will often leave the frame before a shot is over, removing their presence, emptying the shot, which nevertheless remains before us, demanding our attention. *Il Grido* follows the path of a gray, obstructed character, a working man spurned by his lover, the mother of his child; he moves through various landscapes, from woman to woman, drained further of self with each step he takes. The landscapes measure his emptiness. At one point Aldo and a woman he has met are seen on a flat, featureless marsh. The only objects present, beside the two figures, are a rowboat and some decoy ducks. The woman examines one of the decoys as Aldo, walking forward and dominating the frame, talks of what he considers was a better time, his life in Ferrara with his lover, Irma. The woman walks forward and joins him in the frame as she asks what kind of story this is, a story that seems to have no end. They turn and there is a cut to a reverse shot of the two, the landscape the same as it was, surrounding them with stretches of gray. The camera pans with Aldo as he moves away, isolating him as he continues his reminiscences. There is then a cut to the woman, herself isolated, telling of a miscarriage and a hoped-for marriage that never happened. The sequence ends with a distant shot of both, small in the frame, their backs turned to the camera, walking off into the distance.

In description, the events seem schematized, forced, and symbolic. The decoy ducks, the empty spools of telephone cable among which Aldo and another woman attempt to make love, a gray field full of mute old men among whom Aldo's little daughter wanders—these objects and movements sound contrived outside their visual and narrative context. Within that context, however, they express Aldo's emotional states, obviating any other analysis or means of understanding him. It is just here that Antonioni's advancement of the neo-realist premise can be seen most clearly. The neo-realists politicized the image, articulating the simple and sad relationship of poor people in a poor environment, concentrating on their attempts to carry on a life within it. Antonioni psychologizes the image. The characters' environment in *Il Grido* is no longer the location of their social-economic reality, it is the reflection, or better, the correlative of their emotional reality. More than that, it actually creates the characters, because we know them only by the way we see them in their surroundings. Thus a curious thing happens within the dialectics of film history. It is as if Antonioni reached through the neo-realist frame back to the expressionist movement of the late teens and early twenties, merging both in an unusual hybrid. The neo-realists disallowed the use of studio sets; the expressionists depended on them. Theirs was a set designer's world of painted backdrops, painted shadows, and plaster trees. The distortions of environment they created to reflect the emotional distortions or mythological worlds of their characters were made to order, static and staged. Antonioni begins with a place that exists and so arranges his characters in it and his camera's approach to it, so treats it with lights and lens, that he molds the "real"–the preexistent material he finds–into a *mise-en-scène* that affects, explains, amplifies, and corroborates the characters. The "real" world is given an expressive form (and here is where the relationship with *film noir* occurs, although the intentions of those who created the American form were different from Antonioni's).

When, with *Red Desert* (1964), Antonioni began filming in color, he did not hesitate to interfere with his locations in more drastic ways, using paint when the existing colors were not expressive enough. In *Blow Up,* a photographer photographs two lovers in a park. Enlarging his pictures, he discovers what appears to be a murder. Late in the film, he returns to the park to look for the body, which of course is not there. The story goes that Antonioni filmed the sequences in chronological order; when he and his crew returned to the park for this sequence, the season had changed, so he had the grass and trees sprayed to match the color of the earlier sequence and enhance the mood.* This tinkering has no relation to the expressionists' construction of

* Many years ago, when I was more deeply impressed with *Blow Up* than I am now, I visited Maryon Park near Greenwich in London where these sequences were filmed. In the film, it is an isolated, empty, eerie place, with the wind blowing the trees and a strange, indecipherable neon sign hanging over it in the distance. In fact, the park is in the middle of a residential area and not far from the docks, which can be seen from it. There is no neon sign. Except for the addition of the sign and the wind–and the proper green of the foliage–Antonioni tinkered very little with the physical state of this location. He made the place a reflection of his photographer's state of mind essentially through the way he chose to compose the image and angle his camera.

visual design in a studio. Antonioni expresses emotion and situation out of the given world and in so doing opens out the neo-realist image—or better, opens it in, makes it not only reflective of the state of the characters, but responsive and profoundly related to them. And the audience, to a greater degree than in the work of the neo-realists, is asked to read the image and work out the complex relationships between character and landscape.

But is this expression of emotion through the environment in addition to, or in place of, the political component of the neo-realist image? At the end of *Il Grido,* Aldo returns to the town he left at the beginning. There is political turmoil as the people of the area fight the government's desire to build a military airport. The town is blocked off by the police, and Aldo has to run their barricades to get in. A parallel is set up. The town is blocked by political action and Aldo is blocked by emotional inaction; the political activity is of no interest to him. In fact Aldo's physical movements are set against those of the townspeople, who move in the opposite direction. After he sees his former lover with her newborn baby through a window, he walks to a refinery tower, an enormous structure that dominates the town, climbs it, and falls or jumps. The film ends with a high shot of the townspeople running in the distance as the camera pans over Aldo's body, his lover kneeling over it.

This is a gambit the neo-realists avoided in their various attempts to integrate the lives of their characters with larger political or social realities. Antonioni, working in the tradition of the middle-class narrative, is more concerned with the individual and particularly with the ways in which the individual is so overwhelmed by his or her despair that collective action, political action, is rendered impossible. The "politics" of Antonioni's work is, like all its elements, contained within the complex imagery and the movement—or lack of it—of the characters. That Aldo is oblivious to the militancy of the townspeople, that his physical movement is contrary to theirs do not constitute an ignoring of political activity on Antonioni's part—no more than the infamous sequence in *Red Desert* where a man addressing a group of concerned workers is interrupted as the camera—assuming the man's distracted gaze—drifts away from the group to follow a blue line up a wall. In both cases the statement is in the contrast, in the inability of Antonioni's characters to get out of themselves enough to take part in communal activity. The often-discussed "alienation" of Antonioni's characters is a result of the way they are blocked by their inability to confront and understand themselves and their environment; they bend and collapse under the weight of their own anxiety, which corresponds to a cold and obdurate physical and social landscape that the characters *might* change were they not rendered impotent by it. When Antonioni moves from the exurban setting of *Il Grido* to the urban and industrial characters and environments of the later films the blockage and collapse of the individual become extreme. The characters are part of, and undone by, architecture and its sterile lines. The monumental forms of the contemporary world are the signs of their entrapment and isolation; they become reduced figures amid landscapes made barren by the artifacts of cities and heavy industries. Despair and impotence replace communal activity entirely, and emotion collapses into entropy.

At the end of *L'Eclisse* ("The Eclipse," 1962), the last and best film of the early sixties trilogy, the characters disappear altogether. The final sequence serves as a coda to a large-scale work on dessicated love and the dehumanization of the stock exchange, a work which is really about the human figure being displaced by the architectural and economic forms it has created. Near the end of the narrative proper, a woman (Monica Vitti, Antonioni's archetype of the upper-middle-class woman immobilized by things, status, boredom, and depression) and her lover, a young stockbroker (Alain Delon), part, promising to meet that evening. They have been making love in his office, and when she leaves, he hangs up all the telephones he has taken off their hooks. One by one they start ringing. His papers begin blowing. He becomes inundated by the material of his work. Antonioni observes the woman downstairs, her figure, as so often in the course of the film, blocked by a piece of her environment, a scaffold in this instance, then an iron grating as she goes out on the street. Throughout, Antonioni's camera has subordinated her to the things that sur-

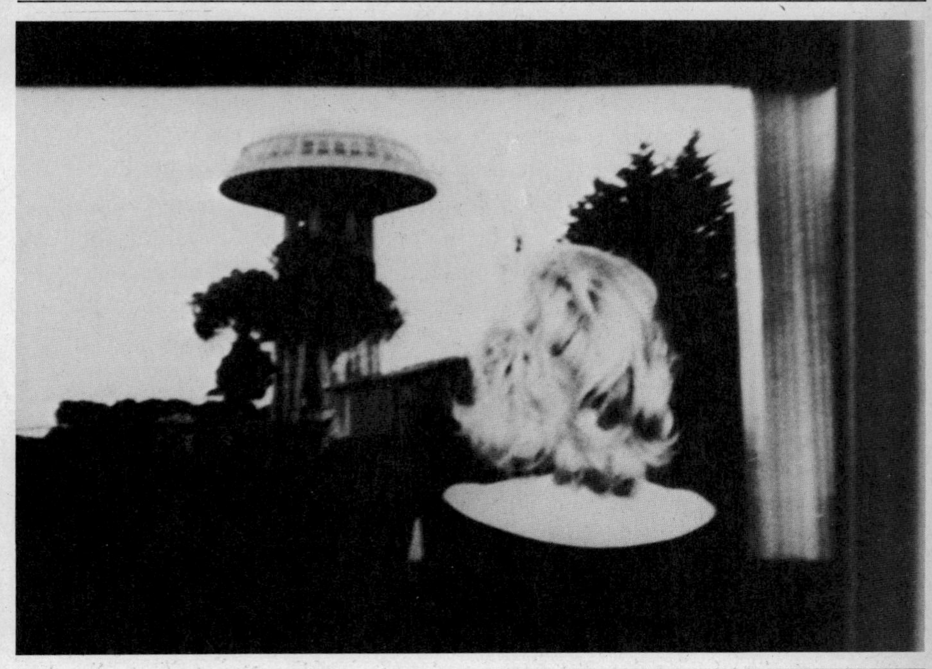

Monica Vitti at a window. The figure dominated by urban structures. *L'Eclisse* (frame enlargement).

round her. Now it succeeds in getting rid of her completely. It moves away from her to the trees over the street, seen through iron fencing. The camera returns to her standing beneath the trees, low in the frame; she looks around and then walks out of the shot. The camera again holds on the trees. There is a cut to a long wide shot of the street where she and her lover promised to meet, a street we have seen often in the film, but which is now more desolate than usual. A nurse pushing a baby in a pram walks by. The camera pans left to observe, in the distance, an enormous tower that was first seen earlier in the film, when its mass blocked the view from an apartment window. We see a building under construction, covered with massive bamboo mats. A water sprinkler is playing. In the shots that follow, various parts of this landscape are picked out, each new angle revealing another aspect of the intractable or unaccountable: the shell of the building covered with mats returns again and again; rainwater collects in a barrel and pours over into the street; a man rides by in a horse-drawn sulky, a mysterious figure, yet in context no more strange than the nurse and pram (which cross his path), or the buildings and light towers he passes, or the featureless people waiting for, or alighting from, a bus. Another building appears, white and angular, like an abstract painting, except that, in a closer shot, we can make out the heads of two people on the building's roof, pointing to something in the distance. The water flowing out of the collection barrel (into which, earlier in the film, the man had thrown a matchbook, which we can now see, in various shots, sinking to the bottom) forms an abstract pattern on the street. There is a tight closeup of the side of an old man's face, showing his jowl, part of an ear, and his neck; then a cut to the top part of his head–eyes and temple; and then a three-quarter profile as the camera slowly arcs around his face. Finally there is a cut to a low angle, below the man's waist, continuing the arc until he walks off, out of the frame, out of consciousness. The camera picks up the corner of the covered building. The montage continues as twilight approaches. In the dark, people get off a bus. Streetlamps go on. We see the covered building in the dark, and the sequence ends with a closeup of a street lamp, blinding in its brightness.

This montage lasts about six minutes and contains about forty-three shots. It has the effect of an anatomy of oppressive objects, human and inanimate; the structures and faces that make up an upper-middle-class urban sensibility, and which are, like that sensibility, indecipherable and inflexible. It is a montage of anxiety (in case we do not quite get it, Antonioni shows us a man getting off a bus and reading a newspaper with the headline "Atomic War," permitting a verbal message to permeate the images and play a wider and known anxiety off the bits of material that are anxiety-provoking in themselves). The things that surround us are made strange, visually detached from the context in which they would ordinarily go undetected and rendered impermeable to perception and understanding, their parts rearranged, in a linear version of cubist painting (though without the humor of cubism).[14] The montage is a phenomenological act, a bracketing of material objects that does not reveal an essence but provokes in us an essential unease and dislocation in our attempt to make sense of them. What Antonioni does here is the opposite of the montage that the Japanese director Yasujiro Ozu often employs. Ozu interrupts his narrative with shots of trees, gardens, a railroad station. But for him, they are images of continuity, of peace and stillness, meant to integrate viewer and characters into a structure of harmony. The montage that ends *L'Eclisse* is disruptive and discordant. Like the atonal sounds that accompany it on the music track, it forces us into a recognition of the oppressive weight of things that do not relate.

Within the film, and for Antonioni's work as a whole, the end of *L'Eclisse* is a summary statement of fragmentation and separation of self and world. Through no fault of his, the statement became a cliché of the early sixties, modified into a catchphrase, "the inability to communicate." Antonioni communicates very well, however, and his view is more complex than the cliché. He has been able to translate the cultural phenomenon of urban, upper-middle-class depression into the visual signs—the "image facts," to use Bazin's phrase—of that phenomenon. In his best work, emotional and intellectual attenuation and obstruction are given their objective terms. Unfortunately for Antonioni, he has been unable to move very far from this strategy. In *Zabriskie Point,* an underrated film made in America in 1969, he attempted to overcome the blockage through a montage in which bourgeois encumbrances—a house, food, appliances, books—were blown to bits, at length and in slow motion. However, the montage is only a fantasy sequence. He attempted to update the sensibility of the paralyzed self in *The Passenger* (1975), a film about an identity crisis so severe (a newspaper reporter, played by Jack Nicholson—a seventies figure of tortured identity—borrows the persona of a gunrunner in Africa) that, at its end, the camera literally uproots itself from the character, denies his very presence as it drifts through his room, out the window, into the street, leaving him out of sight as he is killed.

Though Antonioni was unable to move far beyond his initial insights, his expression of those insights helped build a foundation for the development of European film in the sixties. The fragmentation of the *mise-en-scène* into small, intractable bits of an obdurate city-scape at the end of *L'Eclisse* is a definitive statement of the modernist sensibility and a reevaluation of the neo-realist style. It is, technically, a montage: a juxtaposition of images whose ultimate meaning is greater than any of the individual shots that make it up. But montage was a technique in some disrepute at the time, indeed ever since the neo-realists called for an unobtrusive and unbroken look at character and place. A further understanding of the controversy surrounding montage will help us understand the aesthetic concerns that went into forming the new cinema.

The question of montage had been of crucial importance since Eisenstein, who saw it as the structuring principle of film, allowing the filmmaker to create dynamic movement out of the raw material of the shot. In American cinema, non-dialectical montage—editing to create a strict continuity of space and time—did become a structuring principle. This was not the Eisensteinian principle of the collision of shots that would enhance and mold a revolutionary perception, but a harmony of shots that would lead the spectator through a simple and closed world. From the early thirties, however, Renoir and other European filmmakers were working against both the Eisensteinian and American principles of cutting in favor of the long take. The neo-realists extended the actual length of shots to some degree, and extended further the earlier reactions against cutting as a manipulative force, a means of directing the spectator to specific items in the *mise-en-scène,* preferring rather that the wholeness of a given space (as opposed to the preordained *completeness* inherent in American continuity cutting, which is a different matter) be observed by the filmmaker and communicated to the viewer.

André Bazin emerges again as a key figure here, for his appreciation and analysis of neo-realism was part of his general aesthetic, which upheld the virtue of the long, deep-focus shot against the fragmentation and manipulation he felt was inherent in editing. His ideas were crucial, for as editor of *Cahiers du Cinéma,* as guardian and guide of a group of young critics in the fifties, he laid the groundwork for the films of the sixties. I have emphasized that what the neo-realists developed and passed on to their followers was a reliance on the image itself, a faith that the image, uninterrupted and barely tampered with, would reveal the world the filmmaker wanted observed. Neo-realist theory fell directly in line with Bazin's belief in the analogue nature of the film image, "analogue" in the sense that it seems to correspond to the way we ordinarily perceive the world it records. "The camera cannot see everything at once but it makes sure not to lose any part of what it chooses to see."[15] The camera, the tool of the filmmaker, is the somewhat reluctant intermediary between the "real" world and the "real" image of that world. Any interference in its mediation must be done with thought and care lest the status of the image it records be damaged. Montage is the great threat to this status and may operate in the nature of a " 'transformer' " diverting meaning so that it "is not in the image . . . , [but] in the shadow of the image projected by montage onto the field of consciousness of the spectator."[16] The image and the meaning it holds create, communicate, and must not be tampered with. Montage, by violating the image's completeness, displaces meaning, makes it come from an ordering of images rather than from an unmediated perception of the barely mediated reflection of the world in the image itself.

To preserve the analogue state, Bazin would have the image imitate certain ways the eye perceives the world. He favors the use of the long take to permit an uninterrupted, undirected gaze at the figures and objects that are, first, before the camera and then before the spectator on the screen. Within the shot he favors deep focus, so that objects near and far are clear to the observer, thereby bringing "the spectator into a relation with the image closer to that which he enjoys with reality."[17] By aligning the image with the phenomenon of unmediated perception and forbidding the filmmaker to engage in anything but the most necessary manipulation of it, Bazin hopes it will capture all the richness and "ambiguity" of reality. By "ambiguity" he implies a multivalence, a range of possibilities in what is seen and interpreted in a film, a freedom for the filmmaker, and especially for the spectator, to elicit meaning.[18]

Bazin's theory has an ideological bias. Implicit is a notion that manipulative cinema—the cinema of montage—is authoritarian, while that of the long take is inherently democratic. While Bazin admired Eisenstein, he distrusted what he took to be the manipulative structure of his montage. He failed to note that what Eisenstein was doing was in theory not far from what he himself was looking for: " 'involving the spectator in the course of a process productive of meaning.' "[19] Bazin did not extend his theory of the image very far into a theory of narrative and of the way the spectator perceives the cluster of images (and sounds) that tell a story in film.[20] If he had, he might have seen more clearly that meaning is not transferred from "reality" through the image, but produced by images in a narrative structure and perceived by a viewer who is always directed in some way by that structure.[21] This is a most important point, and transcends the shaky alliance of the cinematic image with the "real world." When we pare away the ideological and occasional religious effluvia from Bazin's thought, and go beyond the oversimplified call for the realism of analogy, we discover in his aesthetic two major events: an attack on the editing structure of American cinema, in which a spatial and temporal whole is built up from carefully selected pieces of the image which are edited to create the illusion of completeness, and a call to the filmmaker to create images that invite the spectator's active participation in comprehending them. The latter presents a healthy paradox. The film image must be true to the wholeness of "objective reality," but reality is not given to us by its analogue image, certainly not merely reproduced; it must be worked for, produced in, and read from the image.

If we look again at what Antonioni was doing in the late fifties and early sixties, we can see the importance of Bazin's insights. In *Il Grido,* all commentary is contained within the images themselves. The editing is almost entirely functional, moving us from event to event, advancing the hopeless chronology of the narrative. Occasionally Antonioni will cut for effect, as when the comparatively violent action of a speedboat race is used as a contrast to Aldo's becalmed spirit and moribund demeanor. But whenever possible, the commentary is kept within the frame. Aldo hears the noise of a prizefight going in a local club. When he goes to investigate it, we see the fight in the background, Aldo in the foreground; his stillness contrasts to the physical activity and, through the dynamics of the frame, drains its energy by diverting our attention from it to him. When Aldo's girlfriend picks up the decoy duck on the marshes, Antonioni does not leap to a closeup and thereby does not force significance into the object or the action. Character and landscape work as internal complements to each other, commenting and reflecting. But there is no "realism" here. We see objects, tonalities, and relationships in these images that we would be unable to see in ordinary experience. Antonioni is creating the objective correlative of an interior world, and whatever reality exists here and in his later films is the reality of the experience of his characters, whose anxieties are reflected in and reflections of their physical, social, and economic environment. Even more, they are reflections of the filmmaker's desire to create the visual manifestation of those anxieties.

In short, Antonioni is a formalist, a filmmaker as concerned with the act of cinematic seeing as with using his vision to comment upon larger social and political phenomena. He invents images rather than records them. Even though he films on location and uses long takes, what the camera eye sees is not the physical reflection of a "real world," but a world perceived as the psychological and social manifestation of an individual state of mind and the emotional status of a class of contemporary Europeans. In the montage that ends *L'Eclisse* he does not deny Bazinian principles, but finds a way of breaking down objects and figures that allows us to see the whole of an environment that is forbidding and deadening. The montage does not analyze any of the causes of that deadening or offer an explanation as to why the environment should be forbidding. The fragments do not resonate widely into the cultural milieu the way Godard's images will do. But even though they are the analyzed parts of a larger whole, they are not reductive. Each bears the weight of its own strangeness and oppressiveness and is as such complete. And so, too, is the entire section, for each shot is an increment of the last and a preparation for the next. The images are part of the narrative whole as well: they are both the presentation of and an answer to an enigma, to the question posed by the narrative at this point. What has happened to the two major characters of the film who promised each other to meet at the place whose physical parts make up the montage?[22]

The montage responds to the question in dialectical fashion: they are the images. Throughout the film, Monica Vitti's Vittoria has been observed dominated by the structures around her, caught off center in compositions that are dominated by a wall or a column or tower; she is composed against or behind a partition or door or grating. Now she and her stockbroker are displaced, eclipsed, by things which, curiously, become more expressive than Vittoria herself ever was. Like Eisenstein's, Antonioni's images counterpoint each other and our perception, analyzing and building a structure of structures, an architectonics. And that, finally, is what the film is "about." Not the difficulties in communicating, not a woman drained of vitality and emotion, not even the inhumanities of capitalism, but a particular way of seeing the human figure dispossessed by the structures it has created. The film is "about" the way cinema can show us figure and landscape and comment upon their interrelation. In *Il Grido* Antonioni psychologized the image. By the time he gets to *L'Eclisse,* he has gone a step beyond the political and psychological expressiveness of the image to a point where the image, while constructing a narrative, contemplates itself and its powers of creating forms, attitudes, states of mind and being.

Bazin never quite made the leap from a consideration of images that reflect the ambiguities of the "real world" to those that reflect the ambiguities of their own existence as images. But this was, in retrospect, an inevitable movement for the post–neo-realist filmmakers to make. Freed from conventional editing, committed to acts of extensive cinematic observation, they could begin calling attention not only to the world they observed, but to the act of observation itself. Bazin believed that the long take could create a film image that would be analogous to the spatial and temporal continuity of the world as directly perceived. He chose not to be aware of the fact that the longer we gaze at an image the more we become aware that we are gazing at an image and not a replica. Anyone familiar with that archetype of the long take, the kitchen sequence in Welles's *The Magnificent Ambersons,* where Georgie Minafer stuffs himself with strawberry shortcake while teasing his aunt to hysterics, knows the effect. As the sequence builds, the camera staring impassively and at length, we get caught not only in its drama, but in its very presence as an image of considerable duration. The image communicates both the building drama within it and its own existence as communicator of the drama. Or consider Jacques Tati's *Playtime* (1967), a film that seems to be built directly on the Bazinian model. Here complex, multi-faceted comic episodes–based on tourists set loose in a modern and sterile Paris–are created in takes that are long in duration and wide and deep enough to include many details. They invite us to pursue every bit of the image, searching and re-searching the shots, which are never exhausted even on repeated viewings. Few films in contemporary cinema demand (so genially) so much of our gaze, and few films have so little direct relationship to a preexisting "reality." For one thing, nothing in the film is "real." The sets were built specifically for the film, and Tati emphasizes their artificial reality to the point of using cardboard figures in the background of many shots. More important, the effect of the component shots, as well as of the film itself, is gained by the most careful manipulation of spatial and dynamic coordinates, so that finally it is the cinematic design that forms our perception. *Playtime* is not about tourists and sterile architecture as much as the effects of line, arc, and circle on movement, perception, and community; it is a film about reflections and images and the cinematic creation of space.[23]

What is missing in Bazin's notion of cinematic perception, but present for the filmmakers who followed his ideas, is the recognition of another term in the process of perception, the "digital" term or mode.[24] We see the content of the image in a way that seems analogous to our perception of such events "in real life." But we also see the image, or the chronology of images that make up the narrative, and may (depending on the film or our perceptual alertness) become aware that they are not "real life," but discrete constructions, made up of elements specific to cinema—lighting, angle, composition, movement, gesture, sound, and cutting, even elements of theme and character that exist only in film—which combine in ways that suggest a reality we are familiar with, but are certainly not that reality. We "read" and translate these elements, and in fact the perceptual process in film usually moves from analogue to digital and back to analogue again, from the immediate association of the image with a "reality," to a recognition of discrete cinematic elements that construct that image, then back to a reintegration of the construction with the elements of our world that we recognize in the image. The perceptual process is never clear cut and most often we are not aware of the "digital" mode of our perception. In fact traditional cinema tries its best to erase it and succeeds by using that element most indigenous to its means of construction, cutting. In other words, by fragmenting its images in a way that can be executed only by the methods of cinematic construction and never in ordinary perception (notwithstanding some old and silly arguments that cutting is analogous to blinking), it creates an illusion of continuous, "analogical" perception. By calling for the removal of that illusion, Bazin, perhaps unwittingly, freed cinema to reveal its nature as mediator, as something that might speak from, of, and to our realities, but in so doing change them into its own structures. In forcing recognition of formal properties, placing them into the foreground so that the spectator must confront the methods of producing meaning as well as the meaning produced, Bazin's theories helped generate the modernist phase of narrative cinema.

There is one film that stands as the model of the modernist endeavor in its foregrounding of the "digital" mode, a film that teases, provokes, circles, fragments, bores (in both senses), promises, integrates, and leaves us, despairing of meaning, with nothing but its own images. Alain Resnais and Alain Robbe-Grillet's *Last Year at Marienbad* (1961) created on its appearance an enormous amount of discussion that continues to this day. It was the first film to bring together many elements of cinema modernism and place them, defiantly, in commercial distribution. On this level alone, *Marienbad* is a wonderful joke and an act of cinematic aggression. Posing as a film for a large (though not mass) audience, distributed through the ordinary channels for "art films" of the time, it thereby offered itself to the usual critical scrutiny, which meant endless discussions of what it was about. Did a man meet a woman at a fancy spa the year before, as he keeps insisting to her and to us he did? Were they lovers or did he rape her? Is she married to someone? Do the man and woman leave together at the end? What is the meaning of the match game played by the woman's husband (if he is the husband) that only he can win? Which events in the film are flashbacks? Flash forwards? Fantasies? If they are such, what is the measure of their continuity with the "present" time of the narrative? These speculations about meaning abound whenever the film is projected. If plot and story are the thing, if psychological motivations are thought to be what best explains character, then *Marienbad* in a minefield, offering the viewer many spaces to transgress and threatening disaster at every step taken. *Marienbad* is a subversive film, and its first act of sabotage was to present itself in a manner that would engender discussion of its story when in fact the "story" is not what the film is "about."

What *Last Year at Marienbad* is "about" is the way we look at film and the way film regards its subjects, the characters in it and the characters who watch it. It is about the creation of cinematic narrative and the conventions that have developed through the history of that creation. Rather than posing and answering the usual narrative questions, such as, Who are these people? What are they doing? What are their reasons for doing it? it poses new questions altogether: Why are these people? Why are they here in this spa, or elsewhere, or anywhere? What are our reasons for observing them observe each other? When one person in a film looks at another, why does that imply spatial or temporal connection between them? Who is in charge here, anyway? The film has a narrator, the man who tries to convince the woman that they met last year. He is perfectly unreliable. The words he speaks and the actions that occur–seem to occur–are related only in a realm of possibilities. At one point, during one of the camera's many slow drifts through the labyrinthine corridors of the hotel where most of the action occurs, the narrator comments:

> . . . and silence too. I have never heard anyone raise his voice in this hotel—no one . . . The conversations developed in the void, as if the sentences meant nothing, were intended to mean nothing in any case. And a sentence, once begun, suddenly remained in suspension, as though frozen by the frost . . . But starting over afterwards, no doubt, at the same point, or elsewhere. It didn't matter. It was always the same conversations that recurred, the same absent voices. The servants were mute. The games were silent, of course. It was a place for relaxation, no business was discussed, no projects were undertaken, no one ever talked about anything that might arouse the passions. Everywhere there were signs: Silence, Quiet.[25]

This could be an allegorical description of conventional cinema—the same conversations, the same absent voices, a place for relaxation where passion (as opposed to manufactured emotion) is never raised. It is not such an allegorical statement, but no matter; it does speak to the deadness of the imagination that must be resuscitated, perhaps by violent dislocation, which is the theme of *Marienbad,* if the film can be said to have any theme at all.

Spatial and temporal coordinates, so carefully organized and made continuous in traditional cinema, are exploded in *Marienbad.* Every shot and every cut constitutes an enigma, makes us question where we are and why. Instead of the formal organization of material disappearing behind the story created by that organization, the reverse happens and the "story" becomes that formal organization which, like the narrator's harangue, will not leave us alone. The film becomes a sort of terrorist attack against the concept of the gaze, the relationship of looks from character to character within the fictive space, and from the observer to that space. In *Marienbad* the trustworthiness of the eyeline match and the comfortable situating of the spectator has been done away with. There is a great deal of play in this (as there is in much terrorist activity). Resnais and Robbe-Grillet are fully aware of their provocations and acts of discomfiture.

They prod us to expect the conventional, and relish making us squirm when they overturn the expectation at every instant.[26]

Early in the film, in a shot of one of the corridors, we can just make out on the right of the frame, in shadow, hovering with its feet above the ground, looking in the direction of some guests, a life-size cutout of Alfred Hitchcock! Resnais shows his hand. One thing he is making is an abstract critique of the ideal Hitchcock film. *Marienbad* is a thriller, or at least the idea of a thriller. All sorts of extraordinary deeds are suggested (though never shown or proved). Like a good Hitchcock film, this one has a MacGuffin, that item which concerns the characters, but is of no real importance to what is going on. In this case it is the answer to the question of whether the man and woman met last year at Marienbad. Like Hitchcock's masterpiece, *Vertigo, Marienbad* concerns a man who attempts to make over a woman into his own ideal image of her, who creates her and a setting for her. Like *Stagefright* it has a flashback–many flashbacks, though they may not be flashbacks–that lie. Possibly. Most important, like any good Hitchcock film, *Marienbad* is about perception, about the way characters look at each other and concoct versions of each other from what they see. Like Hitchcock, the author and *auteur* of *Marienbad* play with the spectator's look, fooling, confusing, disorienting us.*

What delighted the French about Hitchcock (and they were the first to articulate the complexities of his work) was his ability to indulge in complex inquiries about perception and to toy with character and audience, thereby subverting the basically conventional models of cinematic storytelling within which he worked. Rather than undermine traditional structures from within like Hitchcock, Robbe-Grillet and Resnais create an unconventional structure while embedding fragments of the conventional one within it. Whenever the man and woman in *Marienbad* exchange glances, whenever there is a shift in time or space, the old codes, the promises of conventional continuity,

* Robbe-Grillet's introduction to his screenplay is the best indication of the closeness of collaboration in this work, which is closely related to Robbe-Grillet's novelistic practice. But as Robbe-Grillet says, the image-making and cutting were Resnais's; it is his film. So is the Hitchcock reference.

rumble beneath the glance and gestures, but are repressed. In the next instant, we are again reminded that our expectations about narrative continuity are based only upon what movies have told us to expect. When character A, on screen right, looks with eyes directed outward, and in the next shot character B, on screen left, looks with eyes directed inward, only two things assure us they are together, talking to each other: the fact that we may have first seen them together in a two-shot and the fact that in previous films such a cutting structure has always indicated two characters speaking to each other. When a character refers to a time past and we then see a new place—a room or street we have not seen before—we assume this is the place the character has referred to. Film after film has convinced us of this, usually with the guiding sign of a dissolve from the character to the place. In *Marienbad,* such assumptions are taken precisely as assumptions and their validity is always questioned.

Also questioned is the convention of explanation, the convention that says all enigmas will be solved by film's end, all characters and all motivations will be understood and given meaning. Robbe-Grillet, perverse as always, says about the characters in the film, "We know absolutely nothing about them, nothing about their lives. They are nothing but what we see them as. . . . Elsewhere, they don't exist. . . . [The] past, too, has no reality beyond the moment it is evoked with sufficient force; and when it finally triumphs, it has merely become the present, as if it had never ceased to be so."[27] Perverse and perversely literal. The fact is that in any film (any narrative fiction for that matter) the only thing the characters are is what we see them as when we see them. Especially in film, which is poor in grammatical past tense, the past has no reality beyond or before the moment it is evoked. What is seen on the screen *is,* now. That is why flashbacks have traditionally needed to be introduced verbally by a character and by specific devices, like the dissolve, and in particular the "de-focus dissolve," as if the past were emerging from the haze of memory. But in *Marienbad* time and place are undifferentiated; they are all present and all partake of the specificity of the cinematic image, whose space and time are only *there,* only in the image itself.

The static cinematic memory, with and without shadows. *Last Year at Marienbad* (Museum of Modern Art Film Stills Archive).

To a greater degree than *L'Eclisse, Last Year at Marienbad* is a film about film, about its nature and its narrative conventions. It is also about the imagination, ordering up its creations to do this or that, with the proof of their activities only within the imagination itself. The film's narrator is in fact a voice of the imagination, questioning its own creations, attempting to determine the reality of their actions, the solidity of their being. The audience too, even more than the characters and their activities, becomes the subject of the narrative. We are subjected to it and act in it. Our reactions, our psychology, our past and future are more important to the narrative than those of the characters, for the film asks us to aid in its creation, while questioning the validity of that creation at the same time.

All of this makes it a film greatly to be admired, but not loved. It is an exercise of importance, but its insularity, its absolute removal from any world but that of its own making, its denial of emotional response and its continual frustrating of intellectual response greatly reduce its significance. It was Resnais's job in the films he made after *Marienbad* to expand upon the significance of his images. In his next film, *Muriel* (1963), the complex play of time and memory that goes nowhere in *Marienbad* is rooted in the destructive recollections of war, the Algerian war in particular, which injured the French the way the Vietnam war injured Americans. *La Guerre est finie* (1966) turns memory inside out, studying the perceptions of a Spanish radical who confronts his role as an aging revolutionary suffering persistent failures and attempting to deal with the work of the New Left. With *Providence* (1977), a film written by the British playwright David Mercer, Resnais returned to the ideas of *Marienbad,* this time explicitly and literally focusing on a writer who keeps creating a narrative landscape, shifting time, place, and characters to suit his needs and his disposition. But here there is a warmth and humor absent from the earlier works, *Marienbad* in particular. The operations of the imagination in *Providence* reflect a soul, a personality that is alive, angry, and troubled; the film reflects upon the politics of imagination, the way it exercises power. *Providence* humanizes the inquiry of *Marienbad,* its meditations on narrative tyranny, the tyranny of convention, and the ways that tyranny can be subverted. In most of his films after *Marienbad* Resnais attempts to focus his political concerns while keeping his narrative forms open, responsive, and challenging.*

Marienbad is as important a work for sixties cinema as *Rome, Open City* was for the forties and fifties, not only for its formal experimentation but for the unyielding nature of that experimentation. In isolating itself from connotation it frees itself to examine its own forms. In frustrating its viewers it permits, out of that frustration, an

* This, however, cannot be said for *Mon oncle d'Amerique* (1980), Resnais's most recent film as of this writing. While genial and provoking, this film seems to accept a notion of behavioral predetermination that reduces the imaginative inquiry of *Providence* and the earlier films, confirming the reality of conventional responses instead of, as in *Last Year at Marienbad,* challenging them.

awareness of the perfectly arbitrary nature of film form. What Robbe-Grillet and Resnais did in *Marienbad,* along with Antonioni's work in the early sixties, effected a profound change in cinema. "After 1960," writes James Monaco, "every film made, whether its director intended it or not, had to be seen with this dual vision: it was at once a story and a comment on storytelling. . . ."[28] Resnais and Antonioni foregrounded the digital aspect of the filmmaking process; they demonstrated that narrative filmmaking *is* a process—a transposition, in Zavattini's phrase; and they wished to examine the transpositional act rather than, or as well as, its results. As a result the whole concept of realism was turned around. Instead of the image revealing the world, it revealed itself; instead of narrative being faithful only to the richness of experience in the story it conveyed, narrative became faithful to the richness of its own construction, to the way in which the story was conveyed.

Much more than neo-realism before it, modernist cinema attempts to prevent the spectator from slipping easily through the structures of presentation into an emotional world of character and action. Traditional cinema generates desire in the spectator and assures its satisfaction. The longings and sufferings of hero and heroine and the narrative that takes them and the viewer through the stages of emotion guide the viewer through an uninterrupted and unquestioning trajectory of cause and effect, while making certain that she or he will want and be able to follow the developing emotions. The modernist undertaking interrupts and questions narrative movement and the completeness of the fictive world it creates. It demands that the viewer account for what is being seen and felt.[29]

This foregrounding of cinematic construction and the demand for active engagement on the part of the viewer opened two possible directions for narrative film. One, which allowed for the richest movement in contemporary cinema, was instigated by the French New Wave, moved throughout Europe and into Latin America, and has continued through the works of the new German cinema. These are the films that will concern us the most. The other direction is somewhat less influential, concerned only with the formal possibilities of narrative, often at the expense of what these possibilities can offer for our understanding of the experience encompassed or created by film, the experience of the contemporary world that film must embrace. I said that *Last Year at Marienbad,* for all its interest and importance, is insular, even arid in its refusal to contemplate the significance of its images outside their immediate context. The images, while addressing the history of narrative film structure, do so with an obliqueness and opaqueness that threatens to close the structure down, render it unimportant. *Marienbad* is an irritating film. Its questions about the validity of narrative are posed through figures and gestures of such little relevance and concern that we finally have to struggle not merely with questions and analysis of spatial and temporal illusions presented by the filmmakers, but with why we should concern ourselves with such questions and analysis in the first place. Possibly Resnais hoped that, apart from the formal investigations, other meaning would emerge from the film, a meditation on the hermetic, ritualized world of the European upper class. But because the world created in the film is so thoroughly isolated and self-sufficient, we have little if anything with which to compare it in order to comprehend its deathlike state. Obviously I am asking the film to offer a coherent, paraphrasable content, something I said earlier must not be demanded. That original notion must stand. As much as the viewer desires *Last Year at Marienbad* to yield up conventional content, that much must it deny the desire.

But the denial can sometimes be counterproductive. Robbe-Grillet directed his own scripts in the sixties. One of these films, *Trans-Europe Express* (1967), demonstrates the modernist dead end. The body of the film is a rather conventional European thriller, with Jean-Louis Trintignant (an icon of sixties European film, the featureless mask upon which a director could impress any character he desired)[30] as a slightly bumbling dope runner. Robbe-Grillet interrupts the narrative with his own attempts to discuss and create it. He and two colleagues sit aboard the train in which their hero travels, making up the story that the character takes part in. Of course the story tends to get away from them, complicate itself, and perhaps even backfire on the tellers' intentions. Pirandello does it better in *Six Characters in Search of an Author,* and the film stands as an example of the poverty of experiment when neither the narrative proper nor its self-examination reveals an intelligent or enlightening discourse.

Marguerite Duras, like Robbe-Grillet, is a novelist as well as a filmmaker. She too is part of the *nouveau roman* movement (which might very roughly and generally be defined as a phenomenological approach to the novel, narrating through description and ellipsis as opposed to character analysis—an essentially cinematic approach that enables its practitioners to move between novel and filmmaking with a fair amount of ease). Like Robbe-Grillet, she wrote a film for Resnais, his first feature, *Hiroshima, Mon Amour* (1959), a meditation on history and sexuality, the effects of time, politics, and national conscience on two lovers. Duras's own films are not easy to find in the United States. One that is available demonstrates both the power and the failure of this particular branch of modernism. *Nathalie Granger* (1974) is a study of violence in which the only violent act is a child's pushing her doll's carriage into a tree. It approaches its subject—and only approaches, never confronts it—from its reverse side. Violence is only alluded to; quietness and immobility are the film's structuring principles. The child, Nathalie, is said by her teacher to be more violent than is normal for her age, and is, presumably, taken out of school. However, all that we are permitted to see of the child reveals nothing to bear out the reports of her. On the radio, throughout the film, are other reports, of a pair of young killers on the loose in the area in which Nathalie and her mother, Isabelle, live with another child and her mother, played by Jeanne Moreau.

The body of the film is concerned not with Nathalie, nor with the killers, but with long takes in which we observe Isabelle and the Moreau character at home, doing housework, sitting, burning leaves, looking at each other, passing a few words, and, in one extended sequence, staring at a washing machine salesman (played against type by Gérard Depardieu) who with increasing despair tries to sell them his product, only to discover (they never bother to tell him) that they already own one. He leaves to go on other fruitless calls (we observe him through the window going from house to house), returns to their house, wanders through its garden and its rooms, and leaves again. (His presence this time is threatening, but the threat never reaches fruition.) In one long final shot through a window, we see him get into his truck. A bicyclist rides by. A man with a dog walks in front of the house. The dog suddenly lurches back in fear. The salesman's truck pulls away. The man with the dog turns and walks in the direction opposite to the one in which the dog saw something frightening. The film ends.

Like *Marienbad, Nathalie Granger* is most concerned with the possibilities of the gaze. It is made up almost entirely of point-of-view shots of one of the women looking at the other, or of third-person points of view, where the camera assumes a position outside the perspective of any of the characters, or, at one point, a cat's point of view, staring out the window at birds. In this relay of points of view, nothing is revealed. Faces and objects, carefully composed in hard gray tones by cinematographer Ghislain Cloquet, are studied and abandoned, or returned to in ritual fashion: a pile of smoldering leaves, power lines in an open field—symbolic content suggested but never commented upon or expanded. William F. Van Wert writes of Duras's approach:

> In such extremely long takes with such static frames, the unattentive viewer goes to sleep or leaves the film. The attentive viewer looks at the directional gazes of the characters, the pauses in their speeches, the gestures of the eyes and hands and the music or found sound or other characters' speeches on the sound track. Ironically, the camera immobility, in conjunction with the . . . sound and voices, creates an intensified *viewing* experience, often approximating through point of view and reaction shots the complete destruction of the shot/reaction shot . . . format traditionally used for conversations in film.[31]

As in *Marienbad,* the method of structure outstrips the meaning of what is structured, and there is an all but unyielding demand for attention to the structure at the expense of what could be, perhaps ought to be, happening in the frame. I may seem here to be prescribing what the filmmaker might have done instead of describing and analyzing what he or she has done. But in this instance I think it is fair to do. Inherent in the modernist endeavor is the call for the traditionally passive observer to assume a new role, to open a dialogue with the work, engage it intellectually, and help complete it. A film like *Nathalie Granger* calls out for completion, for an extension of the meaning of its images–explanations of why the dog in the last shot pulls away in fear, what the deadening boredom expressed by the two women is all about. Likewise it calls upon the viewer to request something more from its images. Their insistent inexpressiveness finally expresses a certain arrogance. The filmmaker's desire to place the viewer at a distance and refuse all comfort of emotional involvement–a comfort too easily won in traditional film narrative–risks removing desire. As Van Wert says, the viewer has the option of going to sleep or leaving the film, and if on some level the film removes the viewer's desire to become engaged with it, the act of distancing could become a severing of all ties between film and viewer. This is a severe threat, but a conceivable response to conventional cinema's threat to overwhelm us with irrelevant emotion.*

The work of the French New Wave turned the threat of modernist cinema into a provocative and energetic examination of the myriad ways in which film, world, and audience interact. Before looking at that work, however, I want very briefly to discuss Ingmar Bergman, the most famous of international filmmakers. His films of the mid and late sixties–including *The Silence, Persona, Hour of the Wolf, Shame,* and *A Passion* (*The Passion of Anna*)–incorporate various modernist devices, but cannot quite come to terms with them. Bergman is

* An interesting companion piece to *Nathalie Granger* is Peter Handke's delicate feminist film *The Left Handed Woman* (1978). Handke is a novelist who has written scripts for the German director Wim Wenders. This is the first film he has directed and, like Duras, he constructs his work in long, carefully composed takes, in which the placement of the figures is crucial. But space in this film is not as enigmatic or as stagnant as in Duras's film. In homage to the Japanese director Ozu, Handke makes his space an explanatory extension of his main character and her quest for her self. The film's compositions give, in fact, significance to the tired cliché of "finding one's space."

the great melodramatist of contemporary European cinema, concerned with individuals in the cinematic throes of personal crisis, of doubt and loathing and sickness unto death. He has fitted out his characters' agonies in a variety of forms: in the forties, he confesses, he was influenced by American *film noir* and neo-realism;[32] Eisensteinian composition appears in *The Naked Night* (*Sawdust and Tinsel,* 1953); and gothic expressionism infiltrates much of his work, aligning it with some aspects of the horror film (consider the dream sequences in *Wild Strawberries,* 1957, and *Face to Face,* 1976; the castle and its leering faces in *Hour of the Wolf,* 1968; the rising of the dead in *Cries and Whispers,* 1972; and the mad scientist in *The Serpent's Egg,* 1977).

In the sixties, Bergman's formal eclecticism drew him to consider the possibilities of reflexive forms that would distance the spectator from his melodrama and offer some perspective. *Persona* (1966) opens and closes with images of the cinematic apparatus, the carbon arc of a projector: at the beginning we see film running through the projection mechanism and fragmented images of a silent film, of a slaughtered sheep, of a hand with a nail driven through it. In an unlocalized space we see a boy on what appears to be a morgue slab; he rises and sees as if on a screen the merged images of the two women who will be the major characters of the narrative proper. Within that narrative, Bergman interrupts the action to bring us back to consciousness of its filmic reality. At one point the film burns and tears; at another he has a character deliver the same monologue twice. The first time the camera observes the person to whom she speaks, the second time it gazes over that person's shoulder, looking at the speaker. The construction of the narrative itself is full of ellipses (more accurately, empty with ellipses); it lurches along the paths of its mystery–the bizarre relationship of two women, one an actress who refuses to speak, the other her nurse who speaks too much, allowing the actress to drain away her personality. The modernist elements here work toward mystifying the narrative; they are an effective gambit, but only a gambit. In any given sequence, once Bergman begins to concentrate on the interaction of the two women, the devices used to create distance disappear, and we are invited to partake of immediate emotion and psychological mysteries. The characters' fears and agonies and Bergman's fascination with them overtake any desire he might have to examine the way they are created. His desire to communicate the perverse pleasures of emotional confrontation outweighs his need to confront the intellect by denying narrative desire and its fulfillment.

Despite the fact that his themes of suffering and the need for love are obvious, Bergman's modernism belongs to the obscurantist wing of the movement. Much more than Resnais or Duras he wishes to create mysteries rather than solve them. He wants to tinker with form rather than explore it; manipulate his characters and our emotions, and too often cloak psychological clichés and truisms in the guise of metaphysics. His commitment to the forms of inquiry that enlighten the viewer about how a film creates meaning was small. By the early seventies his narrative style had returned to the straightforward presentation of overwrought emotions.

3

The French New Wave avoided mystification and questioned melodrama. Their work is the culmination of the movement against traditional cinematic forms that began with neo-realism, and the core of creative energy in the films of the sixties and early seventies. François Truffaut, Claude Chabrol, Eric Rohmer, Jacques Rivette, and Jean-Luc Godard came to intellectual maturity under the tutelage of André Bazin in the fifties and began making full-length films in 1959. Their work was the result of profound engagement with cinema and its history, a point that cannot be stressed too strongly. Whenever a film critic talks about a figure or a movement prior to the New Wave, and whatever qualities of insight and analysis are attributed to that figure or movement, one must keep in mind that—with the rarest of exceptions (such as Eisenstein, Renoir, Carl-Theodor Dreyer, Jean Cocteau, Robert Bresson)—the figures who most affected film form and content did so intuitively. Most of them, unless they came from a wider circle of artists and writers—as did Buñuel, for example, or Eisenstein—received their training and formed their ideas while working "in the business." As I pointed out, the neo-realists' movement was a convergence of theory and practice; but even here the theoreticians and the practioners were different people. Rossellini, Visconti, De Sica were actively engaged in theater and film before and during the war. They did not step back from their trade and give it prolonged study before coming up with a radicalization of its means and ends. Neo-realism was the result of many social, political, aesthetic, and intellectual forces at work at a fortuitous time. The effort was concerted, not premeditated.

The work of the New Wave, on the other hand, began outside the film business, free of the commercial pressures and rapid compromises that business, even in Europe, demands. Which is not to say that these filmmakers were outside film. They were inside it; they developed their intellects with it; they viewed film for hours and days and weeks at a time in Bazin's cinema clubs and Henri Langlois's Cinémathèque. When they weren't viewing, they argued and wrote about film. They learned about film from studying it rather than creating it, and therein lies the importance of their education. Rather than learning to make images and narratives in the heat of production, under the aegis of a given tradition, the demands of convention, the unquestioning attitudes of well-used, easily executed and comprehended forms, they first observed these forms. They analyzed and judged. And their judgments were a surprise. Except for some isolated figures—Renoir, of course, Bresson, Jean Rouch, Jean-Pierre Melville, Jacques Tati, Jean Cocteau, and, outside France, Dreyer, Bergman, and the neo-realists—they had little but scorn for the filmmaking of Europe, and of their own country in particular.

In April 1959, on the occasion of the selection of Truffaut's *The 400 Blows* as the film to represent France at the Cannes festival, Godard wrote:

> In attacking over the last five years in these columns the false technique of Gilles Grangier, Ralph Habib, Yves Allégret, Claude Autant-Lara, Pierre Chenal, Jean Stelli, Jean Delannoy, André Hunebelle, Julien Duvivier, Maurice Labro, Yves Ciampi,

> Marcel Carné, Michel Boisrond, Raoul André, Louis Daquin, André Berthomieu, Henri Decoin, Jean Laviron, Yves Robert, Edmond Gréville, Robert Darène . . . what we were getting at was simply this: your camera movements are ugly because your subjects are bad, your casts act badly because your dialogue is worthless; in a word, you don't know how to create cinema because you no longer even know what it is. . . .
>
> We won the day in having it acknowledged in principle that a film by Hitchcock, for example, is as important as a book by Aragon. Film *auteurs,* thanks to us, have finally entered the history of art. But you whom we attack have automatically benefited from this success. And we attack you for your betrayal, because we have opened your eyes and you continue to keep them closed. Each time we see your films we find them so bad, so far aesthetically and morally from what we had hoped, that we are almost ashamed of our love for the cinema.
>
> We cannot forgive you for never having filmed girls as we love them, boys as we see them every day, parents as we despise or admire them, children as they astonish us or leave us indifferent; in other words, things as they are. Today victory is ours. It is our films which will go to Cannes to show that France is looking good, cinematographically speaking. Next year it will be the same again, you may be sure of that. Fifteen new, courageous, sincere, lucid, beautiful films will once again bar the way to conventional productions. For although we have won a battle, the war is not yet over.[33]

Godard sums up years of thought applied by his colleagues and himself to their own cinematic tradition. That the filmmakers he condemns are largely unknown to us now is a tribute to these perceptions of their banality, and even more to the films he and his colleagues made in the sixties, which all but eclipsed the works of their predecessors. The core of Godard's statement, however, is not the attack on established commercial filmmaking in France (*le cinéma du papa*) but the approval of one commercial filmmaker in America. The comment about Hitchcock comprises an essential element of the New Wave's discovery of cinema and their desire to elevate it to the status of individual expression, beyond convention, beyond the commercial demands of a studio, to make it the reflection of a personality. In their immersion in film and their attempt to discover how it exists as a unique narrative form, they came to a startling conclusion. The essential ability of cinema to tell stories through its images was to be found not in the "quality" productions, based on literary texts, that were the foundation of French cinema, but in the genre films of Hollywood—the foundation of world cinema. That cinema—the movies—scorned by American intellectuals, indeed not very highly thought of by the Americans who made it, that cinema which had been, since the twenties, a kind of colonial power, dominating and influencing audiences and filmmakers all over the world, was now being held up by a few young French intellectuals as the response to the high-minded, carefully made productions of their own country's film industry. It was an act of perversity, of perception, and of need.

The need was to find a place of authority, a frame of reference, something to point to and say, "This is what I mean when I talk about cinema." The European figures of authority—Renoir, Bresson, the neo-realists—were self-evident; they had control over their films, which were investigations as much as statements, examinations of the world they observed more than reconstructions of pre-fabricated ideas and forms. But this pre-fabrication is what Hollywood has always been accused of, indeed what I accuse it of; it is the very thing the neo-realists fought against. Why then did the young French critics turn to it for inspiration and a weapon? For one thing, they were able to see in the work of a number of American filmmakers an ability to overcome the pre-fabrications, the generic conventions, the givens of a reactionary morality and zero-degree narrative style, to burrow in like termites (to use Manny Farber's analogy) and discover in these forms new modes of expression.[34] The perversity of the French was their ability to perceive these triumphs not in the big productions of the major studios—for these were no better than the "Tradition of Quality," the quasi-literary, studio-bound, convention-ridden films of France—but in Howard Hawks's and Jerry Lewis's comedies, John Ford's westerns, Raoul Walsh's action films, and Alfred Hitchcock's "thrillers."

In such films they discovered two important things. The first was a continuity of content in the body of the work of one director. Recognizable characters, themes, situations kept reappearing no matter what studio the film was made for, no matter who might have collaborated on the script. The second, more difficult matter was a discovery of form. To find individual marks, traces in many instances, that demonstrated alterations in the uniform narrative construction of American cinema took and still takes a careful and dedicated eye. The formal strategies of the more assertive American filmmakers did stand out clearly. Bazin had already used Welles as a major example of long-take, deep-focus composition. John Ford's organization of groups in a western landscape, his ability to turn image and narrative movement into a moral statement about community and individual obligation were clear to many people (to Welles himself, who studied Ford's style). Not so clear (to return to Godard's example) was Hitchcock's particular place within the American structure. He was regarded by most as a "master of technique," able to build suspense and surprise an audience, and it took a considerable effort to demonstrate that Hitchcock was more than just clever, that he was profoundly involved in discovering, through the way he structured his films, the way film structured audience response and how that response revealed as much about an audience as about the characters in the fiction.[35]

In the course of making such discoveries about Hitchcock and others, the French worked out a theory of personality and subjectivity. In response to what they saw as the pompous blandness of traditional French cinema, they described a vigorous plurality in American film. In the face of the assembly-line, producer-dominated, crowd-pleasing aspect of that film, they traced the features of individuals, directors who inscribed their own ideas and spoke individual variations of the common cinematic language. The French were particularly delighted with the inherent dialectic: anonymous studio production no longer anonymous due to the emergence of individuals able to use the system for their own ends; these ends in turn pulled back into the anonymous assembly line, altering and redirecting conventions. The tension between the individual and the line kept American cinema and the individuals responsible for it vital and thriving.

There is a certain bad faith in some of these arguments and analyses. John Hess has pointed out that the attacks on the French Tradition of Quality, particularly those made by Truffaut, were reactionary, condemning the films not only for their pomposity, verbal orientation, and deadness of style, but for their anti-bourgeois attitudes. In his 1954 *Cahiers* essay "A Certain Tendency of the French Cinema," Truffaut condemns these films not only for their inability to overcome their literary bias, but for their anti-clericalism and anti-militarism as well. Truffaut blamed the films' impersonality not only on their dependence upon carefully worked scripts, but on their engagement in the political sphere as well.[36] To be fair to Truffaut, he does take care to point out that the filmmakers and the films' general attitude are themselves bourgeois. He pointedly asks, *"What then is the value of an anti-bourgeois cinema made by the bourgeois for the bourgeois?* Workers, you know very well, do not appreciate this form of cinema at all even when it aims at relating to them."[37] Certainly these films do not have the working-class orientation of neo-realism.* Still, this early statement of displeasure at film concerned with issues beyond the personal boded ill, particularly for Truffaut, whose own work suffers from his refusal to place his characters in the world and observe them as social and political as well as individual and emotional beings. It is a problem that becomes severe in films like *Jules and Jim* (1961) and *The Last Metro* (1980), both of which attempt to recreate a specific historical setting (the first World War and the Nazi occupation of France, respectively) and then forget the setting to focus on the romantic preoccupations of the characters.

Another difficulty inherent in the argument of the New Wave emerges from its very perversity. The Hollywood film they admired, the struggle between individual creativity and studio control they celebrated, were phenomena that could only be admired and celebrated from afar. Critically, the French *created* American film. They gave it status, a taxonomy, a pantheon of individual talent. They discovered

* Here I must admit to a certain bad faith myself. Like many American critics, I take the condemnations of the Tradition of Quality on face value, being unfamiliar with more than a handful of its films, though this handful tends to bear out the criticism. The Tradition requires a closer examination.

its thematic and formal structures and set up the models of analysis we are still using. Had they done nothing else their influence on film history would have been enormous. But when they turned to filmmaking they neither would nor could duplicate the American production process. Not only was the French studio system operating on a different and much smaller scale than the American, but the New Wave did not want to engage it. They did not admire the American production system as much as they admired the heroic endeavor of individual filmmakers in overcoming it. There was a great deal of romanticism in their attitudes toward Hollywood. Their desire was to emulate the individuals and not the system; but they had the historical sense to know that the individuals could not have survived without the system. When they turned to making their own films, they separated out the various components of the Hollywood phenomenon, choosing what they wanted and discarding what they did not need. The financial system of big-studio filmmaking was out. Large budgets to assure large profits meant large compromises. The French received limited funds from backers who were interested at least as much in the film made as in the money made from it and allowed the filmmaker all the control. Filmmaking for the New Wave, in contradistinction to both the French and American traditions, was a personal and independent effort. While the concept of the *auteur* (the director as guiding, creative force) had to be wrung from the production line of Hollywood, for Truffaut, Godard, and company it was a given, and each assumed the mantle with ease. Their rallying point was the words written by the filmmaker Alexandre Astruc in 1948:

> . . . the scriptwriter directs his own scripts; or rather . . . the scriptwriter ceases to exist, for in this kind of film-making the distinction between author and director loses all meaning. Direction is no longer a means of illustrating or presenting a scene, but a true act of writing. The film-maker/author writes with his camera as a writer writes with his pen. In an art in which a length of film and sound-track is put in motion and proceeds, by means of a certain form and a certain story (there can even be no story at all–it matters little), to evolve a philosophy of

> life, how can one possibly distinguish between the man who conceives the work and the man who writes it?[38]

"A true act of writing!" This statement, along with their discovery of American cinema, was the most powerful impetus for the French critics to enter production. Having given authorial recognition to American directors, they wanted now to assume that burden themselves and *write* in film, inscribing their personality and perceptions of the world directly into images and sounds, into narratives told by them with film, *in* film.[39] Even more, this personal cinematic voice would speak, as Godard says, of "things as they are." Again, though, this statement conflicts with their admiration of Hollywood. American film can hardly be accused of speaking of or showing "things as they are." American film alludes to, transforms, modulates historical realities, but rarely confronts them, rarely observes them "as they are." This was the major argument of the neo-realists, and Godard's call parallels theirs, though his romantic sighs for "girls as we love them, boys as we see them every day" bears little apparent relation to what the Italians were looking for in the forties. The neo-realists called for filmmakers to allow the world as it is to inscribe itself on film; some Hollywood filmmakers attempted to inscribe their personalities upon, or within, preexisting conventions; the New Wave filmmakers wanted to inscribe their subjective views of the world directly on film.

In working out the conflicts, they made wise choices and interesting combinations. As excited as they were by the promise of "writing" with film, of giving direct voice to their perceptions in a cinematic discourse, they were aware of the theoretical nature of their premise. The physical apparatus of cinema makes such direct inscription a concept only. A pleasant room with typewriter or pen will suffice for the writer. But the filmmaker faces an array of technical equipment, much activity, and the necessity of dealing with (indeed, directing) other people. Beyond this, like the writer, the filmmaker does not create from nothing. He or she must confront tradition, the multitude of conventions, the many discourses of the works that came before. The personality the filmmaker would inscribe on film must be informed by experience, insight, and analysis; it must be manifested in characters who are involved in dramatic situations.

Their recognition of these problems and demands brought them back to the Hollywood *auteurs*. For Hitchcock, Ford, Hawks, Lang, and the rest it was, as I said, a question not merely of overcoming the studio's pressure to conform and compromise, but of understanding the cinematic language being used by the studios and forcing it to respond to their own voices. When they began directing, the New Wave filmmakers were not ready or able to confront tradition with a commitment to observe a specific economic class and its concerns, as were the neo-realists; but because they needed a base out of which to work, and because the experience they had to draw upon for making their films came largely from film itself, American film again provided them with assistance. They discovered in its generic richness parameters loose enough to permit movement and expansion but tight enough to offer them codes and conventions they could use and re-speak, or break if they wanted to. One wide, encompassing genre appealed to them the most: the gangster film–*film noir*–romantic thriller, that complex of statements, gestures, attitudes, characters, and camera placements that epitomized the high forties and early fifties in Hollywood. It was to this genre that most of the members of the New Wave turned when they began their work. After an autobiographical statement, a study of small childhood moments in *The 400 Blows,* Truffaut turned to it in *Shoot the Piano Player;* after a false start in *Le Beau Serge,* Chabrol began his elegant Hitchcockian arabesques around the genre with *Les Cousins, Leda* (*A double tour*), and *Les Bonnes Femmes* (all made in 1959); Jacques Rivette worked for three years on his two-hour-and-twenty-minute version of the genre, *Paris Belongs to Us* (1961). Godard confronted it head on with *Breathless* in 1959. Only Eric Rohmer seemed immune, although the urban peregrinations of the destitute hero in his first feature film, *The Sign of Leo* (1959), are linked to some *film noir* and gangster traditions.

I am not suggesting that these films bear any immediate similarity to *Notorious* or *Lady from Shanghai,* to *Mildred Pierce, Pickup on South Street, Johnny Eager,* or, to go back to the thirties, to *Scarface.* (". . . I do like *A Bout de Souffle* [*Breathless*] very much," Godard once said in an interview, "but now I see where it belongs—along with *Alice in Wonderland.* I thought it was *Scarface.*")[40] They are not imitations. They share some important elements with neo-realism that divorces them instantly from the Hollywood tradition: they are shot on location; although they do not use non-professionals, they do employ players not well known at the time; they indulge, though in a somewhat different way, in the neo-realists' desire to use the camera as objective observer, allowing the action to play out before us rather than carefully composing and editing our point of view. Unlike the neo-realists, they seriously challenge the Hollywood conventions of continuity cutting. In this one area the New Wave filmmakers' love of American film turned into a confrontation. Their awe at its facility, its smooth and direct action, became a desire to question those qualities and seek alternative methods of narrative construction and, in turn, audience response to that construction.

Godard, as always, led the way. In his initial infatuation with American film as a critic in the early fifties, he questioned his mentor, Bazin, about the efficacy of the long take. He was taken by the affective power of the closeup, by the ability of American filmmakers to play upon emotions by tightening space through cutting, enforcing the viewer's proximity to the image. In an essay entitled "Defence and Illustration of Classical Construction," he wrote: ". . . The simplest close-up is also the most moving. Here our art reveals its transcendence most strongly, making the beauty of the object signified burst forth in the sign."[41] Like so many of Godard's early statements, this is somewhat prophetic. Although he is addressing himself particularly to the emotive power of the face on the screen, his recognition of the semiological fact of the screen image, the ability of that image to collect a large amount of emotional and cultural information and release it when placed in a specific narrative context, will be of great importance to his later development as a filmmaker. But at this point he was still struggling with some conflicting reactions. He admires the ease with which American film creates and directs feelings through montage. Yet elsewhere he also gives his intellectual assent to Bazin's principle that the best cinema is that which allows the unmanipulated gaze of the spectator free access to the image. Later in the fifties, when he was already shooting short films, he pursued this problem further. "If direction is a look," he wrote in an essay entitled "Montage, My Fine Care [*mon beau souci*]," "montage is a heart beat. . . . What one seeks to foresee in space, the other seeks in time."[42] This is not a new insight on Godard's part, but it is a major attempt to seek an understanding of image organization that would take into consideration Eisenstein's subordination of the image to montage, Bazin's subordination of montage to the image, and American cinema's subordination of both to the unobtrusive construction of a story. Again in an anticipation of his approach to filmmaking, Godard works out the problem dialectically: "Knowing just how long one can make a scene last is already montage, just as thinking about transitions is part of the problem of shooting. . . . The montage, consequently, both denies and prepares the way for the *mise en scène* [the spatial organization of the image or of the entire film]: the two are interdependent."[43]

Not a breathtaking conclusion, but at least indicative of the attempt to understand the interrelatedness of the two major components of cinematic construction, the shot and the cut. When these reevaluations were put into practice, yet another dialectical struggle occurred, between the American genres the French were adopting and adapting and the new attitudes toward the formal construction of these genres. Godard and his colleagues sought a multiple confrontation with, and revision of, cinematic practice. The construction of a film is determined by the way it is shot and cut. These in turn are determined by the choice of the genre, which dictates content and the way content is created. Choosing a genre, like the gangster film, and then structuring it in a radically new way changes the genre, its character, and our characteristic reactions. In *Breathless,* Godard announces fundamental changes from the very first shot. The film opens on a newspaper—a newspaper advertisement showing a woman clad in lingerie to be exact—and by so doing denies us the immediate access promised by American film, which usually opens with a long shot of a place that establishes the area that will subsequently be investigated and analyzed through the cutting of the film. Instead our attention is instantly diverted, even though it is not yet diverted from anything. In the subsequent shots of the opening sequence, Godard gives us the signs of the gangster film in rapid succession. The newspaper falls, revealing a man smoking a cigarette, hat slouched over his eyes, standing before a gate on a city street. He is the perfect image of a movie tough, and in case we miss the codes of dress and stance, he removes the cigarette from his mouth and rubs his lip with his thumb, a gesture that Bogart occasionally used, thereby signaling to us the forties and one of its premier tough guys. The man exchanges glances with a woman on the street. She points out a car. He hot-wires it and drives off. There is a dissolve, the classic cinematic transition of time and place, and we observe the road passing in a shot whose continuity is cut into so that the movement is erratic, changing abruptly. There are various shots outside and inside the car. Our gangster sings and talks to himself; he addresses us as well. He is stopped by a policeman, whom he shoots. But the shooting is shown us in small, discontinuous bits. The camera pans down the gangster's arm. The pan is interrupted by a cut to a shot further along the arm to the gun itself. It is cocked. There is a shot of the gun barrel. Then a cut to the policeman falling and the sound of the gun. Then a shot of the gangster running across a field.

In the course of a few minutes of screen time, Godard has abstracted and broken down the signs of the genre and questioned the preeminence of our gaze into the fiction. He has brought the fiction and its method to the foreground by first scattering before us the basic things to look at—the gangster, his girlfriend, car, and gun—and at the same time not cutting those images into the patterns we expect to see. By refusing to allow an opening establishing shot he does not comfort us with an inviting overview of place. By surprising us with Michel Poiccard's (alias Laszlo Kovacs, played by Jean-Paul Belmondo) direct address to the camera—he invites us to go to hell if we disagree with him—Godard impolitely reveals the presence of screen and audience. American filmmakers feared that if a character looked directly at the camera he or she would break the inviolability of the fictional space, the safety of the spectator's anonymity, and reveal the gulf between the spectator and the illusory figure on the screen. But Godard goes even further than this when he ruptures continuity by means of the "jump cuts" that persistently remove chunks of time and space from the action. He insists that the viewer look at the images and their arrangement and comprehend them, rather than pass immediately through them in search of a story.

Breathless performs disruptions similar to those in *Last Year at Marienbad* (and, of course, precedes it), but performs them with more ease and grace, with less arrogance as well. Godard does not defy us to come to terms with his film; he is as seductive as any of the American filmmakers he so admired, playing his formal investigations and experimentations against movement and adventure, within the comfortable confines of a gangster film. He does not deny content. Even though he redefines the generic confines—creating a gangster self-conscious of his role and its cinematic antecedents, relishing it but anxious about it, suffering for love, betrayed by the woman he loves—the redefinitions remain within recognizable bounds. The recognition factor, however, is deceptive. *Breathless* is not zero-degree filmmaking, though it is an attempt to return to zero. All aspects of its style and its formal innovation are planned to attack preconceptions of generic movie-making, part of the plan shared in different degrees by all the members of Godard's group (it must be recalled that Truffaut wrote the original story upon which *Breathless* is based and Chabrol gave technical and financial assistance to the filming). They were out to make a new cinema. "What I wanted was to take a conventional story," Godard said about *Breathless,* "and remake, but differently, everything the cinema had done. I also wanted to give the feeling that the techniques of film-making had just been discovered or experienced for the first time."[44] The Godard of the early sixties was never given to understatement; but he should have added one important point. *Breathless* not only gives the feeling of cinematic techniques being invented, but also allows the experience of viewing to be rediscovered. There is a tension created by the generic expectations of the gangster film set against the discontinuity of the shooting. The dislocations of the opening; the long tracks of Michel and Patricia (Jean Seberg) on the street or talking in bed; the abrupt jumps within some shots as time is condensed while space remains the same; the jumps between shots, the ellipses that reduce the normal continuity between actions, all force the spectator to consciousness of a cinematic act being performed. The neo-realists had made the viewer look at the image content, at people and events we had rarely seen on the screen before. Godard makes us look at things we were very used to seeing in cinema—a young hood, his contacts and his reluctant girlfriend, the police—and asks us to examine how these things are being looked at. Later he will ask why.

Each of the other New Wave filmmakers enforced this new consciousness of the look. Rivette worked in an opposite manner from Godard. Instead of foreshortening events as Godard had done, he extended narrative detail and in *Paris Belongs to Us* built an enormous, labyrinthine structure of paranoia, murder, the search for a worldwide conspiracy. Rivette turns narrative into a practical joke: the more detail we see, the more clues and threats and possibilities that are laid out, the less we and the characters know. Here and in later films—*L'Amour fou* (four hours and twelve minutes), *Céline et Julie vont en bateau* (three hours and twelve minutes), the first version of *Out One* (twelve hours and forty minutes—screened only once at that length)—the magnitude of time expended on the characters is in inverse proportion to what we learn about them. Rivette expands emotional and physical detail the way Godard conflates cultural and generic detail; the experience of his films is like that of the fairy-tale children who drop crumbs along their path to find their way back home, only to have the crumbs eaten by birds. The analogy is particularly apt for *Céline et Julie* (1974), which *is* a fairy tale about two young women who discover a haunted house. By sucking pieces of candy given to them after each visit (a latter-day version of Proust's *madeleine*) they can sit at home and relive their adventures, "seeing"

The Godardian gangster (Jean-Paul Belmondo with Jean Seberg). *Breathless* (Museum of Modern Art Film Stills Archive).

them as if they were watching a movie. We learn nothing about the house or its inhabitants, except that they play an endless melodrama of love and violence; nothing about the young women, other than that they enjoy their game immensely and that the magic they dabble in may or may not have something to do with their experiences. We do learn a great amount about our own capacity to fit narrative pieces together and our desire for the pieces to be put into place. We learn that desire can create patience, and it is a mark of Rivette's talent at arranging and timing his shots and of his direction of actors within the shot that he is able to keep our attention and desire, to delight us with the game even when no end to it is in sight.

Although that desire is threatened by other modernist filmmakers, the New Wave directors insist upon maintaining it. In the counterpoint between familiar genres and the commentary they make on them and on the way we look at film in general, an active engagement between film and viewer is maintained that comes from a forthright wish to please. In Truffaut's films, for example, the influence of Renoir manifests itself in an enveloping care for all the characters and the audience's attitude toward them. In the films of Claude Chabrol the pleasure is derived from the exercise of a delighted malignity. He is perhaps formally the most conventional of his colleagues, somewhat less concerned with restructuring narrative means than with narrative ends. In the best of his work he entertains Hitchcockian concerns for the violence that erupts in the most unsuspecting and unprepared of bourgeois circumstances. Chabrol is not concerned with the gangster side of the Hollywood thriller, as is Godard in *Breathless* and Truffaut in *Shoot the Piano Player,* nor is he much interested in the Parisian subculture, at least not after *Les Cousins* and *Les Bonnes Femmes.* More than the others, Chabrol's eye is on the propertied bourgeoisie of the provinces or the Parisian suburbs, a class he is able to delineate by their gestures, clothing, and surroundings, by the visual design of their world. Chabrol has the finest eye for production design of any of his peers. While Godard has the best eye for cultural design, for abstracting the sign (in a literal and figurative sense) that sums up a social or political attitude, Chabrol can surround his characters with a habitation that defines them, or with an instrument—a pair of ice-cube tongs, a cigarette lighter, or something larger, like a dinner party—that announces their status and class inclinations.

Like Hitchcock, Chabrol delights in the precarious situation of these inclinations, the ease with which they are toppled and the tenaciousness with which they are still grasped when the toppling seems complete. He is less concerned about the motivations for an act of violence than he is with his characters' reaction to it and—like Hitchcock—with the way he can tune his audience's reaction to the characters. In that cross-testing of reactions lies a great deal of play. Chabrol is not interested in winning over his audience, like Truffaut, or probing and challenging its ideas, like Godard, and certainly not with testing its endurance for narrative like Rivette. Rather, he is interested in testing the viewer's and his own commitment to and endurance for melodrama. Most of his films concern overwhelming emotions in highly pressured situations. A psychotic killer, son of a proper and hateful bourgeois family in *Leda,* is attracted to and murders their lovely bohemian next-door neighbor. A lesbian relationship between a well-to-do lady and a street artist in *Les Biches* (1968) becomes a game of domination and submission as the lady takes a male lover. Murder ends these films as it begins others. In *Just Before Nightfall* (1971), an advertising executive accidentally kills his mistress (who is his best friend's wife) in a fit of sexual violence. The film then proceeds to examine his attempts to work out his guilt, a guilt only he feels, for he goes unblamed by his wife and the friend when they learn about his deed (however, it is suggested that the wife poisons him at the end). The pattern of *Violette* (1978) is woven about the acts of a young woman who kills her father and attempts to kill her mother. Its characters are working class, but Chabrol is not terribly interested in social-economic problems. The Nozière family are not only cramped in their economic and physical existence, but cramped emotionally. No explanation is offered for Violette's anti-domestic behavior, though clearly her desire to escape the confines of little rooms and her parents' mean life and live the pretense of being an upper-class courtesan is a contributing cause. But contributing causes are not the main concern. Violette's movements through her life of sexual assignations, her preparation and administration of poison to her mother and father, and the details of her trial and imprisonment are the items of interest and delight.

These plot descriptions sound properly gruesome and ridiculous, and those are the exact qualities that appeal to Chabrol. He understands what happens when melodrama is extended to its limits. When he can begin a film, as he does *La Rupture* (1970), with a father smashing his small son against a wall, continue it with the wife being blamed as instigator of the act by the husband's crude, arrogant, and

Domestic upheaval. *La Rupture* (Museum of Modern Art Film Stills Archive).

rich parents, allow those parents to hire someone to blackmail the wife as the sexual temptress of a retarded girl, and end the film with the looney inhabitants of the wife's boarding house coming to her rescue as she hallucinates on drugs administered by the blackmailer (who then kills the wife's husband)—when such an increment of absurdities occurs, melodrama reveals its other face, which is parody, of itself and of our acceptance of such absurdities. Because Chabrol details each element with equal care and gazes upon the characters with a visual embrace that zooms, tracks, exchanges points of view, and defines each character, everything and everyone takes on moment and portent. Quite unlike Godard, and the early Truffaut, Chabrol does not attenuate his narrative, nor does he accumulate material in a linear fashion, as does Rivette. Rather he builds out each sequence with sufficient dramatic detail and a more than sufficient attention to spatial relationships among the characters. Within these dynamics, exaggerated just beyond the necessities of convention, melodrama turns on itself and the ludicrous is visible within the serious.

Rivette's is a hooking effect, a linking of sequence to sequence to sequence until an enormous interlocking linear pattern is achieved. *L'Amour fou* contains extended sequences of a play rehearsal. A documentary film unit is recording the rehearsals, and Rivette intercuts "our" view of the work with what the sixteen-millimeter camera sees. The effect is to send us back and forth, in and out. When these intercut and interlocking sequences are linked with scenes of emotional conflict between the major characters (the play's director and his wife), the result is prolonged diffusion, the weaving of our reactions into a loose pattern that threatens to unravel with each ensuing narrative stitch. Chabrol, on the contrary, knits very tightly, and instead of threatening an unraveling of our emotional attention, he induces a break. Like Hitchcock, he lures us further and further inside the narrative until we come out the other side and see it in all its moral intricacy and melodramatic foolishness. Excess forces a distancing and provokes that consciousness of means that is a primary effect of modernist cinema.

In *La Rupture* Chabrol creates a contemporary fairy tale of Beauty surrounded by any number of beasts. Their machinations against her and the madness of their blackmail schemes are so appalling that a point is reached in which our own sado-masochism takes over and we begin to enjoy their scheming, trusting that the film will be true to its genre and the woman will triumph in the end. When the triumph comes and the dotty women Hélène has been living with suddenly come to her aid, any guilt the viewer may feel over the perverse enjoyment of her trials is diminished by the joy at a new-found community of women aiding one another. Certainly a rare joy for Chabrol, and he attempts to mitigate it by ending the film with more violence and murder. In the process, he manages to address and expose some of our patriarchal attitudes toward women, indicate through exaggerating them the repulsiveness of those attitudes, and provide some fitting revenge. In his other work, he is more likely to end in an impasse, disallowing any resolution for characters or viewer. The combination track and zoom shot that ends *La Femme infidèle* (1968) is typical. A subjective point-of-view shot from a man being led off from wife and home by the police (he killed his wife's lover), it suggests fear and longing: he is drawn to his wife as he is being pulled away. Since it is a point-of-view shot, we share the visual frustration and uncertainty—and more. We share Chabrol's refusal to permit a resolution.

The acts of meanness, violence, and emotional terrorism committed by Chabrol's bourgeoisie, combined with their guilt and desire for pity, demand big emotions. Chabrol provides these, but makes them foolish, with the result that one melodramatic requirement goes unfulfilled: spectator identification with the central characters. They are usually too cruel, ridiculous, simple, mean, or self-pitying to elicit an attachment of spectator feelings. Even Hélène in *La Rupture* (the female lead of a Chabrol film is almost always named Hélène and almost always played by Chabrol's wife, Stéphane Audran) is too put upon, her victory too outrageous to allow the viewer to feel more than amused horror and then bemused elation. Besides, spectator identification, by permitting the viewer entry into the fictive space that Chabrol creates and examines, would reduce the ability to understand that space and its inhabitants. Therefore, the big melodramatic emotions the films create are not allowed to connect satisfactorily to anything within the films and any attempt by the viewer to identify with a character is frustrated. We are permitted to view the conflict, not partake in it or resolve it. Contemplation ultimately replaces emotional participation. Chabrol exercises neither the intellectual rigor nor the intense ideological analyses of Godard. Like Hitchcock, his is the joyful rigor of making us understand how emotions are manipulated by film at the same time the emotions are being played out and played upon.

Of all of the New Wave filmmakers, Chabrol is most consistent in this cat-and-mouse game he plays with traditional melodramatic forms; he set a pattern that was embellished in a different manner by

Rainer Werner Fassbinder. Truffaut never could get quite far enough away from his love for Hollywood to avoid the melodrama or turn it into a game. He understates it, but does not distance himself from it. Godard confronts it and analyzes it. Eric Rohmer is the most successful of the group in simply avoiding it. His formal experiments are less openly radical than his colleagues', and he is the least enamored of the Hollywood style. The six *Moral Tales,* of which three–*My Night at Maud's* (1968), *Claire's Knee* (1970), and *Chloe in the Afternoon* (1972)–received wide distribution and popular response, are films that suspend emotional action and reaction in a pattern of talk and introspection.* Rohmer is perhaps the only filmmaker successfully to make subjectivity its own subject, without allowing it to expand into a form of expressionism. His characters move through persisting states of self-examination, acted out in their relationships with others but always contained, never hysterical or destructive, abusive or hurtful. The *Moral Tales* are an astringent response to Bergman's confessionals, for although introspective and centered on dialogue, they are calm and they never ignore *mise-en-scène* the way Bergman so often does by concentrating on the face and neglecting the spatial context that gives that face meaning. The characters' surroundings and the way they are situated in them are of subtle and central importance. In fact the environment generates the situations.[45] The gray, black, and white December of Clermont in *My Night at Maud's;* the bright summer by Lake Geneva in *Claire's Knee;* the glassy suburbs and downtown Parisian offices and streets of *Chloe in the Afternoon* create the situations in which their inhabitants talk out concerns of will and freedom, the morality of making choices and staying with choices made. But the environment never imposes on the characters, never directly or symbolically reflects their intellectual and emotional state. Everything remains in balance, especially the

* Rohmer was the late starter of the original group. He did a number of short films in the fifties, and in the great year of 1959 a feature, *The Sign of Leo,* about a man down and out in Paris. The *Moral Tales* began with two short sixteen-millimeter films, *La Boulangère de Monceau* and *La Carrière de Suzanne;* then came *La Collectionneuse* in 1966, which is really the fourth *Moral Tale,* though filmed before *My Night at Maud's.*

position of the viewer in relationship to the characters in the fiction.

Rohmer offers no invitation to emotional involvement and asks of the viewer only disinterested observation and understanding. But there is not the modernist's defiance of the audience, nor any of Truffaut's pleasantries and charm (at least not until *Chloe in the Afternoon,* where Rohmer's control begins to slip), and none of Godard's obsessive analysis of the image and the reaction to it. But neither is there impartiality and coldness. Except for characters in *La Collectionneuse* Rohmer has great affection for all his creations, but it is affection examined rather than indulged; he observes the way his characters tend to observe themselves, commenting by discreet use of camera placement, gesture, expression, and the spatial relationships between them. In the central episode of *My Night at Maud's,* Vidal takes his friend, the subject of the film (unnamed throughout and played by Jean-Louis Trintignant), to visit Maud, a self-contained, wise, and ironic doctor and divorcée. She used to be Vidal's lover, and Vidal is taking his friend to meet her, partly just to see what will happen. The Trintignant character is an engineer and a devout, practicing Catholic, who has seen in church, followed, but not yet spoken to a young woman whom he has decided he will marry. The long sequence that takes place between the Trintignant character, Vidal, and Maud is played out in one room and is divided between the dinner table and the bed on which Maud lies while she talks to the two men.

It is a perfect triangle, and Rohmer shoots it as such, isolating the characters, often putting Maud and Vidal in a two-shot, while the Trintignant character is alone. Rohmer will observe at length the face of one of the characters who is listening to another (a favorite device of his, in direct violation of the "rule," current since the beginning of sound, that visual attention must be paid to the person speaking). Most of the talk revolves around the Trintignant character's moral choices, his belief in the Pascalian leap of faith, and—given the company he is in (Vidal is a Marxist, Maud not very religious)—his defense of his religion. None of the conversation becomes pompous, no one treats the other with cruelty, least of all Rohmer, and the sequence, like the film as a whole, is a study of people dealing with ideas and experiences informed by understated emotion.

In the course of the sequence, Vidal leaves. Maud has gotten into bed, and Trintignant sits in a chair at some distance from her. A lamp at the side of the bed accents the distance between them because its brightness focuses our attention in every shot in which it can be seen. Rohmer separates the characters further by isolating them in one-shots, and further still by having Trintignant get up from his chair and move to the opposite wall, where there is another lamp and a painting of a perfect circle. As he stands by the wall, he and Maud talk about the difficulties he has with women, his inability to separate the moral and physical aspects of love. He moves in front of the lamp, and its light surrounds him from behind; the painting of the circle is seen to one side. She thinks that it is a trick of the devil not to be able to separate the moral and the physical, and he says he would be a saint if he could. The quiet irony of the illumination and the painting in this shot is indicative of how Rohmer integrates dialogue, gesture, and setting. His character is the perfect *homme moyen sensuel,* not a saint and certainly not of the devil's party (the halo-like circle is off to one side and the illumination behind him is only a lamp and not the fires of hell). Instead of moralizing his morality or condemning it as priggish, Rohmer regards it from a slightly ironical distance and comments upon it visually. At no time does Rohmer attempt to absent himself. His control is absolute, and in a film that concerns problems of choice, will, and probability, that control offers the capping irony. It is the director's will the characters follow.

The Trintignant character spends the night with Maud, but does not make love to her (and she is angered not by his refusal, but by his indecision). Later in the day, he accidentally meets his "blonde," Françoise, the woman he saw at church. Eventually he marries her. In a coda to the film, the character, with his wife and child, meets Maud in another of the coincidental encounters that mark the events of the narrative, and he learns that his wife, before they were married, had an affair with Maud's husband, before Maud was divorced. In his quest for moral perfection, he has tripped himself up. Earlier on, his fiancée confessed to him that she had had an affair (with whom she did not say) and he lied in order to comfort her, saying that he had slept with Maud (he does not mention her name and in fact only partly lies—he did spend the night in her bed). This final revelation about his wife's affair therefore throws into question the moral and theological models he has constructed for his life. His lie to comfort his fiancée put the lie to his moral rectitude. Because of that lie and Françoise's indiscretion, he is embarrassed and forced to lie further when he and Françoise meet Maud. His wager with himself that marriage to Françoise would be better than having affairs with others is made at the cost of embarrassment for him and pain for Maud, who recognizes Françoise. But it is a cost he is willing to pay. He does, after all, make a choice and stay with it. The carefully engineered revelation at the end of the film does not emotionally undo him, but merely points up the ironies of chance he had been unwilling to consider.

No one is undone in the *Moral Tales,* and because of this they are in a curious way the most "realistic" of contemporary films—realistic, that is, to the temperament and sensibilities of middle-class, intelligent French people whose passions are internalized and who structure their world with talk. Rohmer does not lay siege to his characters nor allow them to attack us emotionally. His particular use of the long take allows us to be comfortable with them, aware of the way their reactions and gestures comment on their words and the way their environment supports them or ironically sets them off.

In *Claire's Knee,* the male character, Jérôme (Jean-Claude Brialy), is on a vacation before his marriage. He allows his friend Aurora, a novelist—in fact an actual novelist (Aurora Cornù) playing a novelist—to use him as if he were a character in a story, tinker with his passions, see how he reacts to different women. They chat in her room in front of a mural of Don Quixote, blindfolded on a wooden horse. "The heroes of a story are always blindfolded," says Aurora. "Otherwise they wouldn't do anything. It doesn't matter, because everyone has a blindfold, or at least blinders." Jérôme is blind, but certainly no picaresque hero, not even a would-be hero like Don

Quixote. The callow young woman whose knee attracts him and whom he would save from her equally callow boyfriend is uninterested in his attentions, but he persists in his game and his vacation becomes enriched by a series of false emotions and thoughtless tamperings with the emotions of others. In the end Jérôme succeeds only in blindfolding himself further and sharing with Aurora the illusion of being able to affect another person's life. He is left as solitary as he was in the beginning. But as in *Maud,* what we learn about him, and perhaps he about himself, is not shattering. This is not a film about loneliness and the inability to communicate. Quite the contrary. If Rohmer's characters suffer a gap between what they say and what they are able to do, it is a gap filled not with pain, but with understanding. The closest they get to being Quixotic is to be a little silly and somewhat removed from the realities of others' feelings; but they are never crippled by what they learn of themselves, or do not learn. Rohmer guides us and his characters through a moment in their lives that is not terribly important to anyone in the long run, yet important enough in his demonstration that cinematic storytelling can be engaging merely through the observation of small gestures and details and the accumulation of good talk.

In the films following the *Moral Tales,* Rohmer tries different ways to counter melodrama through manipulation of *mise-en-scène* and adoption of a painterly style. In *The Marquise of O.* (1976), a film based on a Heinrich von Kleist story, the carefully composed lines and color of neo-classical painting structure the compositions, giving a context and a distance to the exaggerated gestures and domestic hysterics that inform the narrative.[46] The *mise-en-scène* of *Perceval* (1978), a French-German-Italian television co-production, reaches further back in time to medieval painting and design, eschewing location work for a studio cyclorama and flat, painted sets. *Perceval* is a celebration of Catholic mythology and ritual, and as such presents itself in ritual form, with singing, direct and indirect address, and animation mixed with live action. It seemed possible that Rohmer's cinematic engagement with the contemporary world was over until in 1981 he released a contemporary comedy, *The Aviator's Wife.* In the *Moral Tales* Rohmer demonstrated better than any of his colleagues how small, unobtrusive films could be made. He modified conventional narrative structure so that action and intensity are replaced by the observation of subjectivity. Rohmer has proven that the intensity of event and emotion that most filmmakers believe necessary to gain and hold audience attention can easily be modulated to draw attention to detailed thought, to a discourse of the passions, in which passion is placed at the service of the discourse. For Rohmer, what we think about feelings is as important as the feelings themselves. His characters create themselves not by what they do or feel, but by what they say.

Unlike Godard, Rohmer's influence on other filmmakers is small, and he himself seems unable to extend his insights much further than where they were in the mid-sixties. He is the most conservative of the New Wave filmmakers, yet for all this, his denial of melodrama was crucial to the collective endeavor of the group (if, after 1959, their endeavor can in any way be called collective). It is a denial crucial to the work of most major European filmmakers of the sixties and seventies as well, for no matter what their individual concerns or their particular formal strategies, their central problem—which we saw developing in the theory and practice of the neo-realists—was an analysis of why American film transposed reality into conventional narrative patterns and of the ways the audience was asked to accept the reality of those transpositions. The modernist movement in cinema, in all its various forms, was directed to the redefinition of narrative form and viewer response. The questioning of the phenomenon of melodrama was central to its work.

4

Of all the experiments, the searching for alternative narrative forms, the almost obsessive desire to discover the ways that cinema can communicate and engage the spectator's mind, the work of Godard has been the most persistent, inquisitive, and influential. His influence can be seen in the films of Jean-Marie Straub and Danièle Huillet,

Bertolucci, Pasolini, Miklós Jancsó, the sixties films of Bergman, the later films of Buñuel, all of the major Latin American political filmmakers, and the new German filmmakers, Wim Wenders and Fassbinder especially. In America too his influence has been strong, particularly in the films of Martin Scorsese and Robert Altman. But Godard's is an influence that extends beyond individuals. The basic structures of commercial narrative film world wide since the mid-sixties—the treatment of locations, use of color, styles of cutting and shot composition—have their foundations in his work. If American cinema had colonized the world through the late fifties, the French, and Godard in particular, started a guerrilla war in the sixties, a war on the colonizer that took on special meaning as the decade wore on and the struggle of the new filmmakers could be seen in very rough parallel to the struggles of the Vietnamese against another form of American colonialism. In the fall of 1972, Godard spoke directly to this point in discussing his and Jean-Pierre Gorin's film-essay on a news photograph of Jane Fonda in North Vietnam, *Letter to Jane:* "We can deal with the million dollar picture by making a film with two stills. The North Vietnamese, the Vietcong, invented a two-still war against the million dollar picture war of the Hollywood Pentagon."[47] The political turmoil of the sixties was both catalyst and companion to the aesthetic turmoil in film, and Godard was aware of the parallels more clearly than anyone. The acuteness of his insight makes the contrast between the 1980s and the 1960s all the more ironic. In 1980, Godard was signing production and distribution deals with Francis Ford Coppola, who had in fact made the (thirty) million-dollar picture war of the Hollywood Pentagon (it was called *Apocalypse Now*). After spending the seventies in isolated experiments in political filmmaking and work with video, Godard returned from the front with an inoffensive, acceptably cynical thirty-five-millimeter theatrical film, *Sauve qui peut* (*La Vie*), which Coppola liked. These two new and unlikely partners are not going to make revolutionary films. (Since forming this strange partnership, Godard has made a film in France—*Passion* (1981)—and it is not clear what his association with the American neo-mogul will be.) But though Godard in his middle age may no longer want to carry on the good fight, the legacy he has left is still influencing filmmakers and filmgoers. The struggle he carried forward from 1959 through 1972 produced some of the great works of the modern imagination.

To understand Godard's accomplishment and influence, we need to retrace some history and look at the ideas of a figure who influenced him and some other major practitioners of modernism. The cinema guerrilla war of the sixties and early seventies was fought on the most difficult of fronts: where aesthetics and politics joined to re-evaluate the work of the past, bring it to account, and change the attitudes of and toward cinema that had been all but unshakable since its inception. The theory for the struggle came from the modernist movement, with its literary and painterly roots in the twenties and thirties and its political roots in the work of Bertolt Brecht, who was carrying on struggles in the theater similar to those carried on by the filmmakers who concern us here. Poet, playwright, political and aesthetic theorist, Brecht attempted to change certain fundamental concepts of art that had been part of western culture since Aristotle.

That is an enormous statement, but it was in fact an enormous tradition that Brecht fought against, persistently, persuasively, often ironically, in his plays and his theoretical writings. Central to it was the notion of art as imitation, as *mimesis,* the idea that the work of art re-presents the world, in a condensed and abstract way, but recognizably as a reflection. This concept of art as illusory representation of the world is a constant throughout history and it forms the basis of Bazin's theories of cinema. But it is essentially an ideal, a fantasy. E. H. Gombrich (among others) has demonstrated that the representation of reality in any period (and in any form of imaginative expression) is in fact the representation of the *idea* of reality current at any given time, using the formal conventions of representation operating at that time.[48] The persistence of the desire for representation, however, is stronger than the need to acknowledge that reality is always mediated by the codes and conventions of a particular art at a particular time, the digital mode I spoke of earlier. The urge for "realism"—for an apparently unmediated representation of the real world—is found at its most obsessive in popular theater and cinema, and we have seen this obsession operating in the zero-degree style, which embraces the spectator, brings him or her into the spectacle of the work, and presents it in a forward-moving continuity of time with all the conventions of proximity and transition and the exaggeration of motivation and event that create, through constant repetition, an illusion of unmediated substance and the absence of form.

For Brecht, who was a Marxist committed to a materialist understanding of the world and our perception of it, the illusory aspect of the realist tradition was more delusion than illusion and not entertainment but a snare. Rather than dealing with the world, as the tradition claimed it did, it evaded the world. The images that are said to reflect our lives turn out to deflect us from understanding our lives precisely because they concentrate our attention on something else: a reflection rather than an investigation. Middle-class art, of which theater and cinema (and now television) are important components, adds the most complicating element. It is meant to be entertainment, a means of allowing us to remove ourselves for a while from the debilitating, often brutalizing sphere of work and the pressures of day-to-day life. But remove ourselves to what? If theater and film are meant to be realistic, how can they also claim to offer us an escape from our reality? They cannot, and of course do not, do both. Instead of reality they present "reality," a set of conventions in form and content that divert the viewer from a confrontation with his or her world to a sympathy with the lives of "recognizable" characters suffering problems that appear to be possible but are in fact a fantasy of problems and a fantasy of solutions which are not merely improbable, but impossible.

But not irrelevant. The form and content of popular (and serious) "realist" art is profoundly tied to the various cultures of the West and it may not be dismissed. Novel and theater, film and television are inseparable from those cultures, and merely to condemn them is to evade the responsibilities that they themselves evade. The imaginative expression of any culture–high or low, elitist or popular–represents that culture and its ideology. Criticizing the form and content of a culture's art is implicitly to criticize the culture, just as analysis of that art explains the culture's attitudes. In calling for an alternative form of imaginative expression, the artist-critic is expressing a hope for change throughout the culture. Brecht's examination of the realist tradition and his theories about its demolition were part of a larger notion of social reorganization. Roland Barthes writes:

> Basically, Brecht's greatness, and his solitude, is that he keeps inventing Marxism. The ideological theme, in Brecht, could be precisely defined as a dynamic of events which combines observation and explanation, ethics and politics: according to the profoundest Marxist teaching, each theme is at once the expression of what men want to be and of what things are, at once a protest (because it unmasks) and a reconciliation (because it explains).[49]

Brecht saw the work of art as part of society's work as a whole. Such a work might reflect the dominant ideology, working from the top down, helping to mold people to the will of those in power, and therefore needing to be unmasked. Or it might work for the needs of the people and reconcile, because it explains and reveals the culture to its members and the members of the culture to each other. The work of art could combine the acts of unmasking and reconciliation by constantly making the spectator aware of what it was saying and how, whose voices were speaking in it, making the spectator privy to its methods, function, and purpose.

A truly popular art might be created, one that did not condescend to its audience or attempt to fool, satiate, or divert them. Brecht had a revolutionary optimism that an audience was there and ready for an expression of its realities:

> With the people struggling and changing reality before our eyes, we must not cling to "tried" rules of narrative, venerable literary models, eternal aesthetic laws. We must not derive realism as such from particular existing works, but we shall use every

> means, old and new, tried and untried, derived from art and derived elsewhere, to render reality to men in a form they can master. . . .
>
> Realistic means: discovering the causal complexes of society/unmasking the prevailing view of things as the view of those who rule it/writing from the standpoint of the class which offers the broadest solutions for the pressing difficulties in which human society is caught/emphasizing the element of development/making possible the concrete, and making possible abstraction from it.[50]

In the dialectical movement of this statement lies the method of Brecht's attack against the traditions of art that promote passive reaction instead of active engagement, sympathy instead of anger, assent rather than dissent. That method was to understand the thing in light of its opposite, to deconstruct every element that laid claim to being "realistic," every convention that invited from the spectator that willing suspension of disbelief that is the paradoxical, central premise of the realist tradition. What Brecht demanded was that the disbelief be reconstituted. If drama—or novel, or film—is to be in touch with reality then it must shed any pretense toward itself being a form, a representation, or a reflection of reality and clearly announce itself as a kind of speculum, an instrument to allow us to probe the world. It must probe, not reflect; move forward, not preserve outmoded ideas and relationships; make reality, or catch up with it, not perpetuate worn-out forms that claim to be real. It must be not a way of being, but a way of seeing.

This ought to sound familiar, for it is in fact the kind of thinking that led to the modernism of the early Resnais, of Robbe-Grillet and Marguerite Duras. But there is a major difference. Their works do not manifest a need to go any further than themselves. The foregrounding of form in *Last Year at Marienbad,* the narrative and visual dislocations in Antonioni's films, can act on their own behalf, promoting in the spectator a desire to investigate the dislocations and intrigues of form. The Brechtian notion of the work as speculum-spectacle-speculation had a different end. By forcing the spectator to examine the structure of a work, alienating him or her from direct contact with its content and from any assumption that content can exist without the intervention of form, Brecht hoped that the work would be able to act as a tool by which the spectator could learn more not only about the workings of art, but about the self in relation to the social and psychological realities that surround and create that self. Rather than an end in itself, a consumer article purchased, enjoyed, and forgotten, the work would be an active arbitrator between the spectator and his or her communal experience; at the same time it would be subject to the spectator rather than the other way around. Instead of reinforcing the dominant ideology (which is the primary role of popular entertainment), the Brechtian work would first challenge it by challenging its presumptions about imaginative expression ("realism," identification with the main character, emotional catharsis or gratification) and then challenge the spectator by asking her or him to *think* about what is being shown instead of indulging in easily got emotions. The spectator might then *use* the work as a means for understanding his or her role in society and history.

With this, Brecht obviates the romantic urge of art, which since the late eighteenth century has demanded on the part of creator and observer an excess of emotion at the expense of reason. "We murder to dissect," Wordsworth cried, announcing an anti-intellectualism in art, a domination of feeling over analysis, that has tended to remove art from social-political responsibility. Brecht would return the responsibility by making the work deny itself as an emotional way station, refuge from the turmoil of the everyday, and instead turn itself into an instrument to clarify history and return the spectator to history.

Brecht set out the basic methodology in a little dialectical table that he included in his essay "The Modern Theatre Is the Epic Theatre," "epic" being his term for the new work that would open the world to the viewer's active participation. On the left are the conventional elements of theater (and film), on the right Brecht's negation of and response to them:[51]

DRAMATIC THEATRE	EPIC THEATRE
plot	narrative
implicates the spectator in a stage situation	turns the spectator into an observer, but
wears down his capacity for action	arouses his capacity for action
provides him with sensations	forces him to take decisions
experience	picture of the world
the spectator is involved in something	he is made to face something
suggestion	argument
instinctive feelings are preserved	brought to the point of recognition
the spectator is in the thick of it, shares the experience	the spectator stands outside, studies
the human being is taken for granted	the human being is the object of the inquiry
he is unalterable	he is alterable and able to alter
eyes on the finish	eyes on the course
one scene makes another	each scene for itself
growth	montage
linear development	in curves
evolutionary determinism	jumps
man as a fixed point	man as a process
thought determines being	social being determines thought
feeling	reason

The precise method of achieving these "shifts of accent," as Brecht modestly calls them, involves breaking emotional continuity and realist representation throughout any given work. He would, for example, employ a non-realist acting style. "In order to produce A[lienation]-effects the actor has to discard whatever means he has learnt of getting the audience to identify itself with the characters which he plays. Aiming not to put his audience into a trance, he must not go into a trance himself."[52] Brecht (developing techniques from the radical Berlin theater of Erwin Piscator) would break dramatic continuity by having the character address the audience, go into a song, step out of the role and out of the narrative movement. The *mise-en-scène* of the work would be disruptive; no illusion of real space would be allowed. In theatrical presentation, the notion of the privileged view through an absent fourth wall would be disallowed, and all manner of verbal, graphic, and cinematic intrusions into the stage space would be called upon to identify it as a place where specific theatrical activity was going on. This is not the place to examine how Brecht specifically worked out his theories in his own productions. Nor can a great deal be said about his own direct experience with film, which was not very happy. He was never completely comfortable or successful with film as a narrative form, and could not come to terms with the commercial nature of the medium. He sued the production company of G. W. Pabst's version of *The Threepenny Opera* (1931) for changes made in his play, and lost (writing, as a result, a long economic and political analysis of the film business). The one film in which he did have a direct hand, *Kuhle Wampe* (1932, directed by Slatan Dudow), was cut by the German censors. Given the fact that it was the first and last Communist film made before the Nazis took power, it is remarkable that it survived at all. The film employs, sporadically, some Brechtian techniques, and an early sequence foreshadows some neorealist approaches: a montage of bicyclists desperately seeking work bears comparison to the ride *to* work of the cyclists in *Bicycle Thieves.*[53] In Hollywood, the writing Brecht did for Fritz Lang's *Hangmen Also Die* (1943) was greatly altered.

Though Brecht's own success in film was limited, his posthumous influence on its later development was enormous, greater than it was on the theater, and for a number of reasons. In those rare instances when the filmmaker has independence and control, film is the best form in which to make aesthetic principles clear and sure. The filmmaker does not have to worry about other productions of the work and can achieve through images and dialogue a clear and permanent presentation of methods and ideas. More important, film offers the perfect arena for the testing of Brechtian ideas. Through its short history, film has built up conventions of realism more profound and harder to crack than those of theater, and when they are broken, the effect is even more extraordinary than it is on the stage. When in 1962 Godard introduced a version of Brechtian devices, the effect, though not unprepared for (there had already been *Last Year at Marienbad,* and the New Wave filmmakers were busy experimenting with traditional narrative) was thrilling and conclusive. *Marienbad* might have been a sport, and certainly was in part a joke. But Godard's fourth full-length film, *My Life to Live* (*Vivre sa vie*) was neither sport nor joke; it announced more clearly than had *Breathless,* or any of the early works of the New Wave, a departure from traditional modes of narrative filmmaking and film viewing. More gently and firmly than *Marienbad,* it projected the fact that film was a form that could investigate and analyze its function as a language that addressed people in their lives.

My Life to Live is a "woman's picture"; its tradition is the thirties and forties MGM and Warner Brothers genre of the woman misused and abandoned by her man, the woman too free with her sexuality, too ready to look for happiness outside normal domestic circumstances, who must suffer for those desires and perhaps even die. The film is an odd combination of *Camille* and *Marked Woman,* or rather a reflection upon such films and the way we read them. Nana (Anna Karina) is one of many Godard women who turn to prostitution to live, who allow themselves to be an object, a commodity, in order to discover, economically and emotionally, their own subjectivity. Its structure turns the film into an object as well—though not a commodity—something to be contemplated and understood before it can be felt. As if he had Brecht's table of oppositions before him, Godard arranges an orderly deconstruction of classical narrative principles and replaces them with the structures of inquiry. There is no continuous plot development, but rather twelve episodes, each numbered and introduced with a title. There is no linear development of character or action; we see only fragments, "each scene for itself." And rather than requesting our involvement in emotional turmoil, the film turns us into observers and makes us face something, many things, the most important of which is the way we look at the film and understand its meaning. Brecht writes,

> As we cannot invite the audience to fling itself into the story as if it were a river and let itself be carried vaguely hither and thither, the individual episodes have to be knotted together in such a way that the knots are easily noticed. The episodes must not succeed one another indistinguishably but must give us a chance to interpose our judgment. . . . The parts of the story have to be carefully set off one against another by giving each its own structure as a play within the play. To this end it is best to agree to use titles. . . . Shown thus, the particular and unrepeatable incident acquires a disconcerting look, because it appears as something general, something that has become a principle. As soon as we ask whether in fact it should have become such, or what about it should have done so, we are alienating the incident. . . . In short: there are many conceivable ways of telling a story, some of them known and some still to be discovered.[54]

In the first shot of the first episode, Godard denies us what every other film has always promised and delivered: the face. While low-lit, almost silhouette closeups of Nana begin the film, in the first narrative sequence we watch two characters, Nana and Paul, sitting and talking at a bar. Their backs are to the camera. Each is presented alone in alternating shots, and each shot is played out without camera movement and with only a slight movement of their heads. Their faces are present, but reflected in the mirror in front of them, and because of that literally disembodied. A double screen is created: the one on which the image is projected and the mirror in that image on which is projected the faces that we should be seeing on the primary screen. If we did see them there, if Godard had begun his film with a conventional two-shot and then proceeded to intercut the two faces singly, we would have no perception of a screen at all. Our own look would have been untroubled. But because he doubles the image, giving us in the secondary screen (the mirror) what he denies in the primary, we are disrupted and disengaged. The image is made object and the viewer made to confront it as such. Later in the film, in another conversation, in another café, Nana sits with her pimp. When he first joins her, the camera picks them up in profile and then arcs around so we see them face each other, the back of the man's head covering the front of Nana's. Behind them is a window looking out at the traffic below. Only the traffic is not moving. It takes a moment or two to realize that it is an enormous photograph of the street. Faces that we should see, but once again are not permitted to see; a street that is not a street, but a frozen process shot (films, especially American films, had always used a rear-screen projection of the outside world placed behind the characters when the concentration was meant to be on the characters with the world acting only as a backdrop). But the camera begins to move again, awkwardly tracking around the two characters as if looking for the best way to look at them. There is a cut to a profile of the man and, as the conversation continues, the camera pans back and forth, from one profile to the other. The film is filled with such tryings-out of points of view, of distance and proximity. Godard searches throughout for alternative ways of seeing, of directing our gaze without falling into standard patterns of cutting or creating simple spatial relationships. He discovers new ways of telling a story.

Earlier in the film there is another investigation of the problem of the face. Nana goes to the movies to see Dreyer's *Joan of Arc,* and she cries. Dreyer's great, passionate closeups of a suffering woman reach Nana's heart and we see her on the screen, and Dreyer's Joan on the screen within the screen, both in closeup, in tears. "The simplest close-up is also the most moving," Godard had written. But he is now ready to try to understand what this ease of emotional reaction means. His fictional character understands her sadness only through the cinematic image of another fictional character's sadness, and there is something wrong about that. An image is just an image. Yet with these images we are led to experience stronger emotions than we ordinarily experience in our day-to-day lives. Godard is seeking a way to short the emotional circuitry, the analogue circuitry that conveys the notion that films are like life, even better than life, and replace it with another structure that will assure us that films are only like films. They will discuss life and investigate it, but not reproduce it or allow us to think they are a substitute for it. That is why he keeps tinkering with something as apparently simple as the closeup, precisely because it seems to be a simple element of the language that allows us access to the emotions of the fictional characters. Once looked at objectively, its simplicity vanishes and it emerges as a major element of complexity and confusion.

But not the only one. In *My Life to Live* Godard begins another process of breaking down. He begins analyzing the modes of discourse used by film—that is, the way the narrative is told, by whom and to whom. The traditional film assumes the perspective of an omniscient point of view, a neutral telling in which all the elements—character, *mise-en-scène,* music, narrative construction, and viewer position—are integrated, assured, and controlled. We have already established that this narrative is not neutral, that the integration and control are carefully worked out and drilled to assurance by repetition, that our secure place in the narrative is based only on our acceptance of the conventional forms and their ability to make us forget the formative means. Godard, like Brecht, wishes to separate out the homogeneous discourse into its component parts and allow us to hear the various voices that are speaking the film to us. For example *My Life to Live* presents itself as simultaneously a fiction about a prostitute and a documentary about prostitution.

The discourse of fiction and the discourse of documentary have always been allowed a convenient separation in the history of film. Lumière and Méliès are posited as the progenitors of two separate modes of cinematic expression, the one photographing things existing in the world, the other creating fantasies in the studio. But film always documents something. As long as a camera is used to record an image, taking a picture of something that preexists the photographing of it ("pro-filmic reality" is the term Christian Metz uses),[55] an act of documentation has occurred. This is not merely playing games with words. As I pointed out earlier, the neo-realists, in taking their cameras out of doors and into the lives of working-class characters, were documenting people and events, even though they were making fictions. Godard is very much aware of this element of neo-realism and all his films play with the dialectic of fiction and documentary, making the viewer aware of how each mode borrows from the other. ". . . I saw a film at the Cinémathèque, a film on Lumière . . . ," says Guillaume, the Jean-Pierre Léaud character in *La Chinoise* (1967):

> This film proves that Lumière was a painter, by that I mean . . . he filmed exactly the same things that the artists of that period were painting—people like Pissarro, Manet, or even Renoir. . . . He filmed . . . parks . . . He filmed . . . public gardens . . . He filmed the gates to factories . . . He filmed people playing cards . . . He filmed the tramways. . . . What was Méliès doing at the time? Méliès was filming *Le Voyage sur la lune*. Méliès was filming *La visite du roi de Yougoslavie au president Fallières*. And now, from the vantage point of our distance in time, we realize that these were really the current events of that epoch. . . . [Méliès] was making documentaries. They may have been reconstituted documentaries, but they were real documentaries. And I'll go even further than that. I would say that Méliès was Brechtian. . . .[56]

Perhaps. But Méliès was in any case documenting some fantasies of *fin-de-siècle* France while Lumière was rendering portraits of the way some of France looked at the time. The point is that a film documents fantasies and fantasies document a culture's ideology and its dreams. The "voice" of fact and the "voice" of fiction always intermingle. In *My Life to Live,* Anna Karina is not a prostitute, but an actress playing that role. We are not, in viewing the film, looking at prostitution—though one of the episodes mimics a conventional documentary on prostitution, with facts and figures read off on the sound track as the camera tracks down and pans the red-light districts of Paris. What the film is doing is documenting Anna Karina playing the role of a prostitute as well as documenting, for us, the various ways we observe this particular societal role. And in the fragmenting of the narrative, in the analysis of the closeup and of the role of frontality (the straightforward look at the character), Godard is also documenting his questions about the ways film addresses its audience

LAFOND
AU
IC 62
MARS
HORAIRE SPECIAL
le SAMEDI
EVA-MARIE SAINT
DUS
N COULEURS
LE ZO
VAU. 29.47
du 7 au LUNDI 12
RECORD D
DANNY
DOU
DU G
EN SCOPE
du MERCRE
LES PL
ARTISTE
AM
CEL
EN SCOPE
VARIETES
PAUL NEWMAN
L'ARNAQUEUR
EN CINEMASCOPE
SEUR
5
ONS
rue de
GIRARD

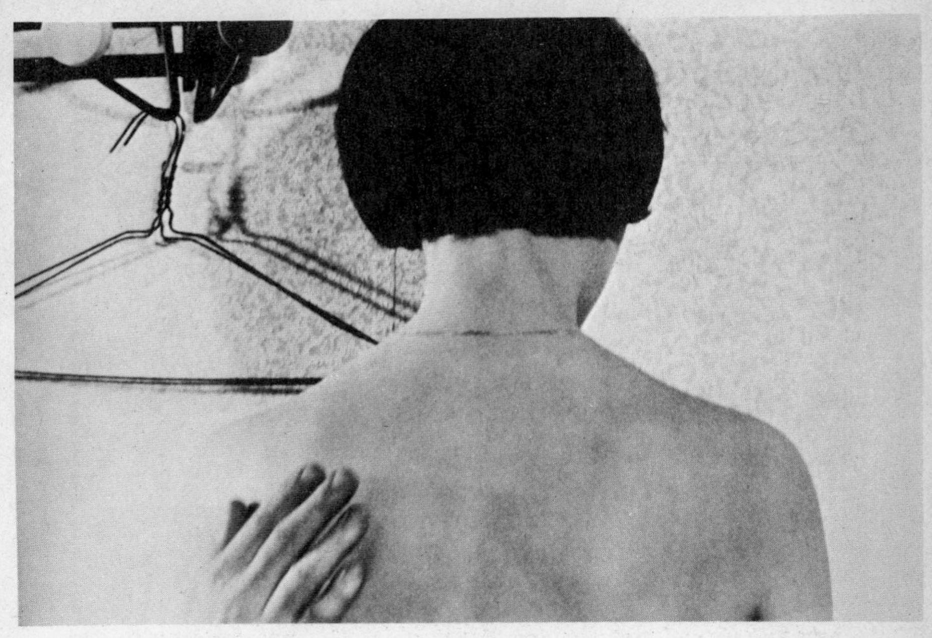

The signs of work. Anna Karina in *My Life to Live* (Museum of Modern Art Film Stills Archive).

and the way the audience responds. The film–like most of Godard's work–is a documentation of the filmmaker's and the spectator's response.

Particularly Godard's. The last sequences of the film introduce material that breaks open whatever narrative seams have been left intact. Nana sits (again) in a café, where she has a conversation with a philosopher. Not an actor playing a philosopher, but Brice Parain, a French linguist. They talk about words and meaning and the betrayal of them, about thinking and action, about how, to understand life, one must go through the death of not talking, about concerns seemingly beyond this story of a prostitute (and beyond the character of Nana), yet central to Godard and everything he does. The obsession with language–with the way things are said, the proper relationship between things and words and images, the appropriateness of any kind of discourse–inhabits all his work. If Parain's discourse breaks the narrative of *My Life to Live,* it advances the discourse that works its way throughout Godard's films, the discussion of why and how words and images mean, where that meaning lies, who controls it, and how it is perceived.

Part of the discourse involves the meaning of the filmmaking act itself. After the sequence with the philosopher, Nana's lover reads to her from Poe's story "The Oval Portrait," about an artist who sucks the spirit from his wife by painting her. The lover reads, but it is Godard's voice dubbed over him pronouncing the words (Baudelaire's words, of course, Poe's French translator). As he reads, Godard makes cinematic portraits of Nana-Anna (who was, at the time, Godard's wife; at one point his voice says, "It's our story: a painter who does a portrait of his wife"). Just before and right after the reading, the film goes silent: Nana and her lover talk to each other, but we only see their words in subtitles. Spoken language runs out for the moment and only the visual remains. Spoken dialogue is momentarily given up, the image dominates. The film attempts to regress to an "innocent" time when the image was silent (the characters themselves are trying to regress into an "innocent" love, to separate themselves from Nana's world). Perhaps Godard is experimenting with Brice

Parain's idea of understanding life by going through the death of not talking (understanding the image by silencing its verbal component). Perhaps he is merely withdrawing another conventional element of film to test the viewer's reaction. Certainly he is reflecting upon Poe's story: the artist uses up his material, saps its life, saps spoken language, in this instance. He reflects on the story in other ways as well. As a commodity Nana is used and not loved; she falls to the domination of her pimp. Anna, the actress, has been used by her director, who forces her to give up her personality and become an object, the way a prostitute must.[57] For the moment it becomes impossible for language to express the complexity of all this. The characters talk again, but the ending—at this point in Godard's career—is the impasse of silence and death. Nana is shot by her pimp. It is a conventional end, or a parody of conventional endings, for Nana dies just when she decides to give up prostitution and live with her true love. Godard allows the climax that takes care of the character and her story and our emotions, but he still leaves all the other discourses intact. For while the story may end, the process of storytelling goes on, not only in this film whenever it is seen, but in the subsequent films Godard makes. As Brecht suggests, Godard's eyes are on the course rather than the finish. His voice is persistent and his look continues to gather the fragments of the world.

My Life to Live is not Godard's most complex film. In each succeeding work more levels of discourse are added, more connections made among the apparently disjointed images of the world. The social-political connections of these images are examined more and more closely as the Marxist discourse, Brecht's substrate, forms as the base of Godard's own thinking and seeing. The concern of his films is always the same, the attempt to make sense of the human figure in the environment of contemporary history and culture. Following Brecht, he attempts to see the ways that figure is alterable; his characters and his viewers are asked to be part of a process of breaking down passivity and alienation. By alienating the viewer from a simple emotional reaction and from unquestioned involvement in a film's story, Godardian cinema integrates the viewer in an active engagement with the meaning-making process. In so doing it can create alterations in the way we see and understand. It can teach. If we learn that the stories we see on the screen are not simple reflections of reality—complete, closed, satisfying—but meditations on reality, *mediations* of reality, even intrusions upon reality, then we may come to understand that reality is not an absolute, but something malleable and, in the end, created. Alterable.

With the exception of a brief period in the late sixties and early seventies when he turned to a politically rigorous, agit-prop style (the "Dziga Vertov" films, which I will look at later), Godard's work is enormously accessible. He is able to fuse wit and irony, intellect and passion into narratives any one of which covers a large area of subjective, social, political, and cultural experience and has a vitality that invites any viewer willing to engage and meet its demands. The same cannot be said about the work of a filmmaking team who follow in the Godardian-Brechtian mode. Jean-Marie Straub and Danièle Huillet are French, but have done their work in Germany and Italy—work so demanding, films so unwilling to yield anything to the viewer's comfort and solace that they have remained on the radical end of the modernist movement, noted by many but seen by few.

Viewing a film by Straub and Huillet, be it *Not Reconciled* (1965), *Chronicle of Anna Magdalena Bach* (1968), *Othon* (1970), *History Lessons* (1972), or even their spectacular (for them) version of Arnold Schoenberg's opera *Moses and Aaron* (1975), is essentially an act of watching oneself watch a film. More than other modernist filmmakers, they call acute attention to the process that occurs between the viewer and the screen, rather than the events that are going on within the images on the screen. Theirs is the work of paring down, of removing every unessential link, transition, reference point, continuity cut, internal explanation; ours is the work of putting all of these back, of demanding of ourselves an attention so committed, a desire for engagement and understanding so strong that we are willing to take the little they give us as a starting point from which to elaborate a film.

Not Reconciled is "based" on Heinrich Böll's novel *Billiards at*

Half Past Nine, about the effects of Nazism on a family and a number of individuals whose lives intertwine before, during, and after the war. The film eschews all novelistic and cinematic conventions of chronology, character identification, character motivation, and historical explanation; the settings, while concrete, are highly allusive and disconnected. The filmmakers provide us with no *locus* and assume we will either be familiar with the novel or be willing to work through the film (which is only fifty minutes long) a number of times until the characters' faces become familiar to us and the relations between them begin to emerge.

In *Last Year at Marienbad,* the narrative—more accurately, the reverie about the making of narratives—is complete within itself at the moment we realize that its only external referents are the structures of cinema and the ways people have told stories with it. But *Not Reconciled* has a referent; it is about history and the inability to overcome it or fully understand it. And its success lies just here, in creating a narrative form that first forces the viewer to understand how intractable history is, how difficult it is to make sense of it, and second requests that the viewer try to make sense of it in a way the characters themselves cannot; the way, perhaps, Germany and the West willfully cannot make sense of it. The fragments of images that make up this film, the skewed, off-centered compositions, the bland non-acting of the non-professional cast who talk rather than perform their lines (an epigraph from Brecht at the beginning of the film says that actors must demonstrate that they do not make up lines but only quote them) are all not reconciled, and it is finally less important to comprehend entirely what goes on within the film than it is to understand *how* the film is going on. Its unreconciled pieces are analogous to the pieces of historical memory which, if put together in the ways of conventional filmic storytelling, would hide reality under melodrama (think, for example, of the television film *Holocaust*). The refusal to put them together avoids the threat of an emotional detour and instead makes us aware of the difficulties of memory (as do most of Resnais's films) and our inability to reconcile ourselves to a past that is, relatively, only a few years old. If, no matter how often we view

Not Reconciled, we cannot separate its strands, cannot clearly identify the various characters, their relationships, the events alluded to, partly acted out, never fully begun or concluded, then we still have been successful with the film—at least as successful as Straub and Huillet in reflecting upon Nazism as a series of disconnected acts committed by banal people who could make no clear connection between themselves and those acts.

But finally the film errs in so completely refusing analysis, in leaving all judgment to the viewer and placing upon him or her the entire burden of continuity and comprehension. As a response to melodrama, it is a lesson of restraint, an example of film as blueprint, with the spectator given the task of building the structure. But as a work that might create in us the desire to investigate, to inquire further into a way of looking at history and its participants, it fails. Its radically elliptical structure risks provoking anger as much as the wish to make it yield meaning; it threatens merely to alienate rather than using alienation as a device to permit an understanding of its form.

Understanding the films of Straub and Huillet demands an acutely dialectical perception. The viewer has to work as much, perhaps more, from what is not given by the film as from what is. The first act in the confrontation (and it is confrontation, not observation, that the films require) is to discover the idea out of which the images emerge, or upon which the film's structure is built. From the idea, the viewer must return to the images and work out the fit. It is film viewing as struggle. Even their most accessible work, *The Chronicle of Anna Magdalena Bach,* requires great patience, as well as knowledge of the conventional film biography of an artist, a wish to deny the validity of that convention, and a willingness to accept a visual and narrative structure as rigorous as that of Bach's music. Straub and Huillet are uninterested in creating any passion out of Bach's life and work, at least not the passion of the struggling artist we are used to seeing in film biographies. The only biographical problem they are curious about is financial, and the voice-over narration given us by Anna Magdalena (who wrote no chronicle) is concerned mainly with the various positions Bach held, the financial arrangements made, the occasional intrigues with various employers, and the family's perpetual concern about money. Conventional action and emotional expression are held to a minimum. In a moment of high drama, Bach is physically removed from his place of work in the middle of a rehearsal. He is led out and down a staircase. But lest we become too involved in this excess of movement, the camera holds on the empty staircase for a very long time, forcing us to consider the events, withdraw from them, recompose ourselves, reorient ourselves back to the image and away from the extra-musical events that heretofore were restricted mostly to the voice-over commentary. For the body of the film is the music, performed by actual players, recorded directly, in ornate period locations. But we are not permitted to become comfortable with the "authenticity" of these locations. Bach gives an evening concert out of doors. He stands at a harpsichord, framed to the right of the screen. To the left is a burning torch. This part of the composition is photographed almost, but not quite, at eye level. Behind is a rear-screen projection of a building which is shot at a tilt greater than that of the foreground figure. The result is a composition of disorienting artificiality that finally emphasizes not the contrasting realism of the other shots, but their own relative artificiality.

Straub and Huillet are obsessively concerned that the viewer not be comfortable with what is being shown. Most of the shots in the film are extremely long. The camera is set at a diagonal to the figures and often, in the course of the shot, will track, briefly, along that diagonal. The performers are rarely in the foreground. Quite the contrary. Soloists often have their backs turned to the camera, or are in the rear or off to one side of the composition. The result is to make the viewer search the image and integrate it with the music emanating from it. The shots are so long that we begin to perform with them a kind of visual and aural counterpoint. The visual composition works both with and against the composition of the music, and every detail, every architectural nuance, every grouping of the musicians contributes to a visual-musical "movement." Richard Roud describes it:

> . . . for once the word counterpoint is not metaphorical. Given the contrapuntal nature of Bach's music, what more natural than for Straub to have found, not an illustration, but an equiv-

> alent to it? Throughout the film he plays with binary symmetry, left-right polarity, and the changing direction of his diagonals both in the camera set-ups and in the camera movements. In fact, one could comfortably claim that there is never an eye-level, straight-on shot in the film: the camera is always a little above or a little below the actors, either to the left or right.[58]

These performance-compositions are punctuated by shots of an engraved title page of a piece of music, or a score sheet, on one occasion by a shot of the sun over the ocean, on another by a tree and a cloudy sky. We occasionally see Anna Magdalena at home, ill in bed in one instance, sometimes with children, and at the end there is a shot of Bach by himself looking out a window, as Anna Magdalena tells us of his failing health, blindness, regaining of eyesight, and death. We see no death. We do not even see him age.

The work of Straub and Huillet is a cinema of withholding. It is not "minimalist," a term often applied to them. That implies abstraction. In fact their images are very concrete, full of material. In their film of Corneille's play *Othon* (titled by them *Eyes Do Not Want to Close at All Times, or Perhaps One Day Rome Will Permit Herself to Choose in her Turn*), characters go about in togas, reciting Corneille's alexandrines in an impossible sing-song, while, through the first part of the film, we see and hear the traffic of modern Rome move in the distance. The images are packed with the contradictions of the world, insisting we read them as part of history and through the material of our lives. They insist so much that they become annoying in their demands. *Othon* is one of the most irritating films ever made. It does not permit us to enjoy Corneille's poetry, the complexities of the court intrigue presented by the poetry, the pleasures of period re-creation. Instead it demands an accounting for all of these, an accounting so defiantly on Straub and Huillet's own terms that, were it not for the calmness, indeed the recessiveness, of this film and the others, we would feel bullied. Certainly we feel put upon, for they ask of us more than do other filmmakers and they make their demands with the least promise of returns. There is no humor, no clear and clever didacticism, certainly no conventional passion (except that contained in the music that is part of *Chronicle* and *Moses and Aaron,* though

Bach and the late Schoenberg are not composers noted for overt passion).

Somewhere between spectacle and aphorism, withholding at all times the fullness of the former and the incisiveness of the latter, treating the viewer with a respect that appears to be arrogance, the films of Straub and Huillet endanger the complex relationship between viewer and film. But here is, in fact, where their importance lies. By endangering that relationship they force the viewer to question it, and that questioning satisfies the first part of the Brechtian endeavor—to make the relationship between work and spectator a primary area of concern. Straub and Huillet may not be able to go beyond the first part; their work does not exhibit Godard's vital, inquisitive embrace of and ironic quest through the images and myths of contemporary culture. Their films are much more subdued and limited, but they are equally concerned with the how and why of cinematic seeing.

The Brechtian mode of the modernist movement, especially as it was worked out by Godard in the course of his sixties films—culminating in *Tout va bien,* where romance, politics, the factory, unions, the media, and feminism are mixed in a counterpoint of comedy, drama, and didacticism—had a wide-ranging influence, particularly (and not surprisingly) among those filmmakers searching for means of political expression in their work. I will be returning to that influence a number of times in the course of examining the films of Fassbinder and, especially, the revolutionary filmmakers in Latin America. Before that, however, I want to look briefly at the influence of the New Wave on some other figures, in particular two filmmakers who began their work well before Godard and his colleagues appeared, but picked up their influence in the course of the decade. While neither is within the Brechtian tradition, they both practiced, even before their contact with the New Wave, modes of cinematic inquiry that demanded responses from an audience different from those required by conventional cinema. After contact with the New Wave these demands took on a new form.

In 1966, Buñuel made *Belle de jour,* his second film in color (the first was his hilarious version of *Robinson Crusoe* in 1952). *Los Olvidados* had marked Buñuel's return to commercial filmmaking and a revision of his style and approach based on the influence of neo-realism; *Belle de jour* marks another revision. Its subject—a moral investigation into the cultural psychosis of the middle class—was hardly new for him, but its style and approach was. The subjects of repression are no longer the various religious *idiots-savants* or the Mexican or Spanish bourgeoisie that had populated most of his films in the fifties and early sixties. No matter what the historical period of these films, they always appear to be somehow out of time; they create a closed world of perversity and obsession. In *Belle de jour* Buñuel announced his modernity. The main character is a contemporary young Parisienne (Catherine Deneuve), a doctor's wife, who takes up prostitution to relieve her sexual frustration and repression.

The images (made by Resnais's cinematographer, Sacha Vierny) have a clarity strongly influenced by the photographic style that Raoul Coutard developed with and for Godard. The film's narrative structure and cutting style, an easy, unexplained slipping into different modes of consciousness, was influenced by the New Wave experiments in shifting narrative modalities. As we saw, Buñuel was not a newcomer to these modes; indeed the crazed structure of *Un Chien andalou* and *L'Age d'or* had helped prepare the young French filmmakers for their own experiments, and Buñuel's films of the fifties and early sixties had always intermingled dream and fantasy, distortion and disruption into narratives that never quite settled down into an easily acceptable "realistic" mode. Thus Buñuel did not copy Godard or Chabrol; he recognized that their methods of inquiry offered him ways of getting to the contemporary world he had not thought of before. He was so pleased with what they had to offer that he acknowledged it openly. In *Belle de jour* he introduces a gangster, a tough with steel caps on his teeth, dressed in a leather coat (played by one of the fine contemporary European toughs, Pierre Clementi, who might have come from *Breathless,* Truffaut's *Shoot the Piano Player,* or from a film of Jean-Pierre Melville—one of the godfathers of the New Wave to whom Godard gave a guest role in *Breathless*). The gangster first appears on a Paris street where someone is selling the *New York Herald Tribune* like Michel Poiccard's girlfriend in *Breathless;* and when he is finally shot down, Buñuel films the sequence as a homage to Poiccard's death.[59] (Godard returned the great compliment by entitling a section of *Weekend* "The Exterminating Angel" after Buñuel's 1962 film about a group of Mexican *hauts bourgeois* who find themselves unable to leave a dinner party and slowly decay to a primitive, deranged state.) The references to *Breathless* in Buñuel's film are more than a homage by an old filmmaker to a younger one. They are a sign of rejuvenation, an indication that the old man who taught so much could still learn. The New Wave offered Buñuel a way of altering his *mise-en-scène* and his editing rhythms, of introducing a contemporaneousness, observing the perversities of his characters in a modern French bourgeois environment, somewhat after the manner of Chabrol and the Godard of *A Married Woman, Pierrot le fou,* and *Weekend.*

Belle de jour not only shows the ability of an established filmmaker to modify his style, to be both teacher and student; it validates Godard's statement that the work of the young French filmmakers was a reinvention of cinema, a reexamination of its form so thorough that any intelligent director would have to take notice of what was happening. European film in the sixties became a great network of cross-references and influences—something, in fact, like a Buñuel narrative in which everyone's cinematic dreams keep interfering with everyone else's. Each filmmaker's work seemed to give aesthetic support to the others' and a communal energy developed. Buñuel was not the only member of an older guard who partook of this energy. Robert Bresson, whose filmmaking career began in the thirties, is among the most uncompromising of directors. He is not locatable in any one tradition, though the demands he puts on his audience can be seen in the modernist context.

Bresson is interested not so much in making the audience aware of the formal patterns in his work as in withdrawing as much as possible from the audience (a methodology that greatly influenced Straub and Huillet).[60] He not only denies melodrama, he attempts to deny

The Bressonian face (Guillaume des Forêts). *Four Nights of a Dreamer* (Museum of Modern Art Film Stills Archive).

all emotional contact between viewer and character. His players exhibit no facial expression (save perhaps a small, brief smile at a moment of perverse or ironic triumph); they are the blank slate upon which the viewer may write or not, develop emotions for the character, or simply view that character as part of a pattern, moving through—or, more accurately, being moved through—a network of events. Working in opposition to Bazin's notions of the long take and the open frame which give the viewer room to look and make connections between character and environment, Bresson frames closely and edits sharply. His shots are mostly short and highly analytical, directing and redirecting our gaze to parts of his characters' anatomy or sections of their environment: a hand or foot, the wall of a room, the top of a staircase, objects and gestures that cohere spatially because they are clearly related to each other, yet at the same time are disconnected and refused wholeness by Bresson's fragmenting of them. The result is a recessiveness of *mise-en-scène* and an elliptical quality that have the effect of intensifying each image and forcing the viewer to complete the space and the narrative. Every Bresson film is built upon a continuous series of withdrawals and absences in which character and surroundings contribute spasmodically to an account of failure and destruction and (at least until the films of the late sixties) redemption.

In the sixties, Bresson's images take on an even greater substance and immediacy than they previously had, while at the same time removing the grace his characters usually enjoyed. As with Buñuel, Bresson's contact with sixties cinema brought him closer to the contemporary world; but in his case, the contact turned his insights darker. In earlier films like *A Man Escaped* (1956), about a prisoner of war who silently, meticulously plans and executes an escape from a Nazi jail, and *Pickpocket* (1959), which documents, through the disconnected movements of hands and arms in train stations, streets, and barren rooms, the career of a small-time Parisian thief, the world of the characters is out of time. The individuals and places are dreary, isolated, expressionless, offering no information about themselves except through their dreariness. The characters are saved by love, or by the grace of God, or perhaps by our own understanding of their sufferings. In his observation, his disengagement, Bresson is able to discover in his characters a plenitude, the grace of salvation not so much expressed in the films as offered through that disengagement and the character's persistence, teased from the narrative in spite of its sparseness, or because of it.

In the sixties, Bresson's slivered perceptions became much grimmer, while the *mise-en-scène* of his films became brighter and richer. After two films (*Au hazard, Balthazar,* 1966, and *Mouchette,* 1967) set in rural France, in which the characters are young women who fall victim to despair and a spiritual claustrophobia so extreme it destroys them, Bresson began working in color and, with the exception of *Lancelot du lac* (1974), setting his films in contemporary Paris.

In *Une Femme douce* (1969) and *Four Nights of a Dreamer* (1971) his characters are young and urban. The streets and rooms they inhabit have a brightness and modernity not apparent in the earlier work. But while the production design changes, the basic approach does not. The fragmentation of action into its smallest parts continues and, if anything, is exaggerated, serving to break down the sense of wholeness and movement that the New Wave directors sought. Where Godard and Truffaut embraced their urban environment in the early films, comfortably situating their characters in it, Bresson takes the streets and bridges, the rooms and traffic of the city and makes them the image of his characters' despair. The effect is not the same one Antonioni achieves by enveloping his characters in large, oppressive, or mysterious objects. Bresson has no expressionist tendencies (and the montage at the end of *L'Eclisse* is an overstatement in comparison to Bresson's methods). Rather, by accentuating parts of the figure and the surroundings, by rarely allowing the viewer to see things whole, he creates a subdued montage of repressed characters and disconnected personalities. The sounds of the city become overwhelming. Traffic noise predominates and imposes a kind of external continuity on an otherwise fragmented world. Everything else in the two films either reflects or objectifies an unyielding immobility and insularity. *Une Femme douce* begins with the suicide of the central character. More accurately, it offers partial glimpses of a suicide: a table falling over on a balcony; the sound of a screeching car below; a shot of a white scarf falling from the window; feet gathering around a body. The film pretends to piece together, in flashbacks, the life that led to this act. What is exposed is an old story of a husband who is possessive and jealous, a wife who is restless and desirous of more than she has.

But the power of the film lies in what is not exposed, in the silent exchanges of looks and the unchanging expressions of faces, movements in a movie theater or at a performance of *Hamlet*. The jealous husband stalks his wife; he drives her to illness. And all we learn about this couple is that obstructed passion fragments the soul, and that we, as observers of this fragmentation, can only see the pieces from the outside. Personality is never revealed. In this film, and in *Four Nights of a Dreamer,* the lively urban milieu mocks the hopeless breakdown of the characters, who are neither comforted by it (as they are in Truffaut's work) or molded by it (as in Godard's). City and character defy each other and both break down into pieces. Bresson's characters are pathetic and moving. The gentle creature of *Une Femme douce* is unable to articulate her stifled emotions, and the young artist of *Four Nights of a Dreamer* walks around the city with a tape recorder on which his own voice repeats the name of his love over and over. They cannot unburden themselves or us, and the result of our contact with them is an impasse, but an impasse that is charged with feeling and a desire to understand.[61]

"Accustom the public," Bresson wrote, "to divining the whole of which they are given only a part. Make people diviners. Make them desire it."[62] Like other modernists, Bresson demands that the audience work at the film. Like the filmmakers of the New Wave, who are something of his children as he in turn is something of their follower, he perceives cinema as the object of desire. This object is more obscure for Bresson than for the younger French filmmakers, and much more hermetically sealed. Like many a modernist, Bresson is a romantic who defies his romanticism by paring away all excess, breaking up the core of yearning in the work, making the viewer search out its parts.* A filmmaker like Godard will engage his characters, audience, and his own self at every level and moment of this search, actively seeking with them a place where some connections might be made. Bresson absents himself from the work and leaves in his place a broken discourse made up of glances, expressionless faces, and rooms, all finally bespeaking a terrible sadness and incapacity.

This incapacity and sadness is a major theme of the modernist endeavor. The struggle with despair in life and in art is continual and

* The defiance goes even deeper. Both *Une Femme douce* and *Four Nights of a Dreamer* (as well as the earlier *Pickpocket,* which is a rough analogue to *Crime and Punishment*) are based on stories by Dostoievski. Bresson removes all the eloquence and embellishment (though not the irony) from Dostoievski's talkative and self-analyzing characters.

unavoidable in cultures where individualism is promoted as an essential personal, social, and economic quality but then denied because the social and economic structures will not allow the individual to function with the freedom that is supposed to belong to her or him. Contemporary middle-class art responds to this ideological dilemma by depicting the sufferings of the individual whose expression of self is thwarted. Ingmar Bergman's films stand almost as archetypes of the expression of the frenzied and tormented self, speaking its despair to an empty world, hoping, after it has torn itself apart, that love will heal it again. Brecht and his followers responded to the theme of self-diminishment by asking for an examination of the causes rather than the expression of the despair and by disallowing the spectator's taking part in it, for that would only communicate it like a disease rather than examine it for a possible cure. Bresson caught the despair when he moved away from the Christian grace that provided something of a cure in his pre-sixties films. Rather than seek out other curative forms, he sought to place the despair at a greater distance, to empty its expression of all but the most essential parts. He makes his cinematic form echo quietly the fragmentation and despair of the soul.

Despair and disconnection—the alienated personality—is at the center of so much twentieth-century art that the subject would quickly lose interest through repetition were it not for the many forms of expression it is given. The vitality of form and the excitement of discovering life through cinema saved most of the New Wave filmmakers and many of their followers from yielding to it as subject, the way Antonioni and Bresson do. Two post–New Wave British filmmakers, Nicolas Roeg and Ken Russell, attack the subject with sometimes interesting results. Roeg works with alienated subjects quite literally, with strangers in strange lands; Russell takes despair and fills it to overflowing, purging it by choking the audience with its excess.

Like Resnais, Roeg is fascinated by the cinematic possibilities of manipulating time, not so much fracturing its continuum but playing with his characters' perceptions of it against the spectators'. To achieve this he uses the intrinsic formal textures of his medium—color, movement, shape, and sound—to build montages in which space is put at the service of time and time at the service of the mysteries of subjective perception and the coincidences of association. The science fiction genre offers the best room for such speculation, and both Roeg and Resnais have tried their hand at it. In *Je t'aime, je t'aime* (1968) Resnais uses the hoary old convention of the time machine to allow his subject to suffer a kaleidoscope of jarring memories, snatches of images of lost love and bad decisions built into an agony of discontinuity. In *The Man Who Fell to Earth* (1976), Roeg does something more interesting. He begins with the equally hoary convention of a visitor from space and then alters it, creating a narrative from the visitor's perspective, so that the events of the film are seen two ways at once: from the point of view of the naïf, the man who fell to earth, who can barely discriminate "reality" from the television images of it and cannot separate the nostalgia for his lost home from the betrayals he suffers in his new one; and from our own point of view, in which we see what is happening, attempt to supply the continuity the visitor cannot, and end up as frustrated and lost as he. By the end of the film, when everyone has aged but the visitor, trapped in his own timelessness, the audience comes to share his perspective and even go beyond it, so alienated from a comprehension of the film's obdurate chronology that we become aliens, wandering outside the fiction while the visitor is imprisoned within it.

Roeg was especially adept at making this kind of twice-told tale in which two perceptions of events–from within the film and from the outside–conflict and deform one another. *Don't Look Now* (1973), is, on the level of plot, a not too interesting story of the occult, of a man who is given presentiments of the future and is lured to a deadly confrontation with a homicidal dwarf in Venice, whom he takes to be the incarnation of his drowned daughter. On the level of perception, however, the film *is* what it is about–seeing. Colors and shapes, places and figures, keep appearing and reappearing. Space and its possible configurations become as important as time, and the configurations of both give the film a rhythm of the seen and possibly seen, of images associated on the level of form only, their content based on little more than the fact of their being seen. The main character is an architect who has written a book called *Beyond the Fragile Geometry of Space,* and it is just this fragile geometry that Roeg explores. Although he blunts his findings by resolving them with a bloody and silly ending, the structure he sets up is larger than the resolution and indicates how well film can play with a discoordination of its images, replacing an inevitable continuity with an ineffable revery about images and the possible ways of seeing and interpreting them.

Roeg belongs at a peculiar intersection of contemporary filmmaking. Too commercially oriented and too politically evasive to fit well with modernism or the Brechtian tradition, his films are created to be money-making entertainments, which is no condemnation, given the fact that within this context he is willing and able to position his audience into a perceptually active role, counteracting the simple contours of melodrama with more complex functions, allowing the audience to piece together attenuated bits of information, probing the relationships between them. It is unclear where he is going with these inquiries. His most recent film (as of this writing), *Bad Timing* (1980), is a nasty bit of business about sexual degradation in which the formal excitement of his previous work is reduced to its most banal components. The deracinated character, searching for self and for feelings, is still present, but now reduced to a moral squalor that is unenlightening and uninteresting. The respect he once showed for his audience and their ability to be engaged by his film's formal intricacies has vanished. Roeg, like too many other adventurous filmmakers, may have fallen victim to the economic pressures of the business, reducing his imagination to gain distribution. Or he may, in *Bad Timing,* merely have run out of imagination.

The work of Ken Russell offers a different response to the subject of the despairing, alienated individual and the problem of audience engagement and melodramatic continuity. His work is based more in the dramatic theory of Antonin Artaud than in that of Brecht. Rather than stand back and analyze events, Russell would overwhelm the spectator with them, present melodramatic gesture so enormous that it goes beyond parody to a point of self-recognition. Near the end of *The Music Lovers* (1971), Russell's biography of Tchaikovsky, the composer contemplates the title of his last symphony. He will call it "Tragic," as that best defines his life. No, no, says his brother Modeste, "that's too pompous." Call it the "Pathetic," he suggests, that's a much better description of your life. With this kind of deflation effected by one character upon the other, sometimes verbally, but most often in the images and their juxtaposition, Russell attempts to join sympathy with the ridiculous, understanding of suffering with the stupidity of suffering brought on by false perceptions and miscalculation. Deflation occurs through plenitude rather than scarcity: shots are filled with violent action and dynamically edited so that they extend the action or ironically comment upon it. Russell attempts to deal with romantic mythologies by undercutting them with their own absurd excesses: for example, Tchaikovsky lies in a stupor while his passionate patron, Madam von Meck, moves about the room licking the fruit her genius composer has eaten, while the strains of his *Romeo and Juliet* play on the soundtrack. Again, Tchaikovsky attempts to commit suicide by leaping into a canal. The water, unfortunately, only comes up to his knees, and he stands foolishly as a well-dressed woman walks by with her dog and smiles at him.

The important part of the Russell canon consists of the films he made for the BBC, "lives" of Frederick Delius, Isadora Duncan, Dante Gabriel Rossetti, and Richard Strauss (among others), and feature films, the most important of which are *The Music Lovers* and *The Devils* (1971), and to a lesser degree, *Savage Messiah* (1972) and *Mahler* (1974). In each, a historical figure or artist is scrutinized in the light of a number of mythologies: the popular myth generated by the figure during and after her or his life and the larger myths created by the genre of film biographies in which the artist (or scientist) struggles for recognition against his or her ignorant peers, dies in the attempt or, more frequently, achieves transcendent recognition. When Russell takes up a biography, the myths are shown to be inadequate or destructive, and the inadequacies–particularly those of the central figure–are not treated gently. Russell puts his figures through a series of cruel, mocking ceremonies of humiliation visited on them by themselves and by the people who surround them. The train sequence in

The Music Lovers, in which Nina (Glenda Jackson) attempts to seduce Tchaikovsky (Richard Chamberlain), her homosexual husband, is as savage a moment of hysteria and self-abasement as exists in contemporary film. The participants are drunk and half crazed, the car rocks, the lamp in the compartment swings back and forth creating a mad pattern of light and dark, disguising the cutting and further deranging our senses. In this violence of movement, champagne spills over Nina's body and Tchaikovsky cringes in terror, the camera alternately looking at the scene from above, regarding his face, then taking his point of view and moving up the hoops of Nina's skirts, creating a monstrous parody of sexual fear. It is a sequence worthy of the combined cinematic perversions of von Stroheim and Buñuel, and is not the least of the horrors and humiliations Russell heaps upon his characters. Though he is far removed from the quiet analysis of a Bresson or Godard, his challenge to the conventional pieties of film biographies and the hagiography of artists in general gives him an important place in contemporary cinema.

Russell has spawned no followers, though his influence can be seen in Peter Watkins's *Edvard Munch* (1976), whose atemporal kaleidoscope of images and sounds that make up the biography of one particularly distraught artist is more complex than anything Russell has attempted. As for Russell himself, the energy of his early seventies films dissipated rather quickly. In 1980 he moved to Hollywood and made a film called *Altered States* in which the ironic perspectives and mocking deflations of pomposity that humanized the characters of the earlier films is gone. Instead of putting his characters through an excess of emotion that might clarify their situation for the audience, he puts his audience through an excess of stimuli that clarifies only one thing, that an option for filmmakers with nothing more to say is to assault their audience with image and sound in an attempt to make them believe they have something to say.

There has always been a great deal of the showman and faker in Russell, and looking back upon the films of the early seventies one can see that he loves the very melodramatic gestures he seems to want to get some distance from. He shares with a more important figure, the Italian filmmaker Pier Paolo Pasolini, an inability to secure a consistent point of view. It is true that Pasolini was a much more intelligent filmmaker than Russell is, and films like *Teorema* (1968) and *Pigsty* (1969) stand as major Brechtian documents (I shall speak about *Pigsty* in more detail in the next chapter). But like Russell, Pasolini was capable of losing himself–in pornography, for example–and films like *The Decameron* (1971) and *The Canterbury Tales* (1972) are as scrambled in their exploitative sexuality as is Russell's *Lisztomania* (1975). In *Salò, or the 120 Days of Sodom* (1975), the last film he made before he was murdered, Pasolini attempted an intriguing social-political-sexual spectacle. He elided Sade's mathematical epic of sexual cruelty with the late fascist period in Italy, and by so doing moved Sade's work from the area of quasi-philosophy and speculation into a political arena where it more appropriately belongs. *Salò* is a huge allegorical fantasy of power and male domination in which the human figure is turned into an object to be exploited, hurt, and destroyed.

But the events of *Salò,* despite Pasolini's attempts to treat them as tableaux, to observe them coldly and distantly, as if they were on some far stage, to make them into a Brechtian spectacle, create as much perverse attraction as they do repulsion. Its final sequence, in which prisoners are literally taken apart and dismembered, is photographed from the point of view of one of the captors observing the scene through binoculars. Even so it is not far enough away, and the viewer is put in the peculiar position of wanting to look at the horrors and being unable to keep from averting his or her eyes at the same time. While the political perspective is never lost in *Salò* (it is not present at all in Russell's films), the proper analytical perspective is never quite found. The film hovers between profound anti-fascist statement and crude pornographic horror show, much as–on a considerably lower level–Russell's films hover between a healthy anti–romanticism and crude pornographic spectacle.

5

Inconsistency, unevenness, a fallible point of view ought not to be condemned out of hand. The urge to experiment does not guarantee success; it demonstrates the desire to investigate the limits of commercial filmmaking. The investigations of the sixties and early seventies created as many false starts and dead ends as influential successes. Some figures who began with ingenuity and energy ended in complacency, working within the very forms they once had questioned and abjured. What I have tried to outline here are some of the major paths of inquiry about the nature of narrative cinema. In the following chapter I will re-cover some of this ground from a slightly different perspective, exploring further the influence of Brecht and examining the areas of subjectivity and political response contained within the formal experimentation. But here we need to move away from Italy, France, and England to Germany, where the influence of the movements of the sixties was somewhat delayed. When it appeared, however, the phenomenon that occurred in France in the late fifties was duplicated. Filmmakers such as Alexander Kluge, Wim Wenders, Rainer Werner Fassbinder, and Werner Herzog, among others, began to work, like the French New Wave before them, as if they were reinventing cinema. In the early seventies, when the rest of European production seemed to be retreating to those commercial norms that had been under attack in the sixties, the country whose cinema had been in retreat since the late twenties came alive.

It was hardly a spontaneous generation or a virgin birth. There had been some active and engaged probing of cinematic possibilities in Germany in the sixties, producing films that went against the chaotic, reactionary, and basically American-dominated production and distribution methods of the forties and fifties, which had included the re-release by German distributors of "scores of Nazi entertainment films from the Thirties and Forties . . . at rates with which new films could not compete."[63] Alexander Kluge, whose works are rarely seen in America, began, in *Yesterday Girl* (1966) and *Artists under the Big Top: Disoriented* (1967), to experiment with some Godardian and Brechtian methods of narrative deconstruction. Volker Schlöndorff, whose *Tin Drum* in 1980 marked the popular acceptance of German film when it won an Academy Award, made some small movements toward an examination of his country's history in his 1966 film *Young Törless*. Jean-Marie Straub and Danièle Huillet, although French by birth, made their early films in Germany and served as an important model for the younger filmmakers. In 1962, a group of filmmakers, Kluge among them, issued a manifesto at the Oberhausen film festival. It summarizes attitudes now familiar to us. We have seen versions of them in the statements about neo-realism and in the proclamations of Godard and Truffaut in the fifties. They are the attitudes that always precede a fundamental alteration of a nation's cinema:

> The collapse of the commercial German film industry finally removes the economic basis for a mode of filmmaking whose attitude and practice we reject. With it, the new film has a chance to come to life. The success of German shorts at international festivals demonstrates that the future of the German cinema lies with those who have shown that they speak the international language of the cinema. This new cinema needs new forms of freedom: from the conventions and habits of the established industry, from intervention by commercial partners, and finally freedom from the tutelage of other vested interests. We have specific plans for the artistic, formal and economic realisation of this new German cinema. We are collectively prepared to take the economic risks. The old cinema is dead. We believe in the new.[64]

The difference in emphasis between this proclamation and some others is interesting. It assumes that a new "international" language of cinema exists and certainly could not help but assume this, since the filmmakers involved were following closely the work that was going on in the rest of Europe. The focus of the statement, therefore, is on the financial means of getting that language spoken in Germany. The French could find independent producers willing to take risks. Few people took risks in the German film community, dominated as it was by political fears and American capital. It was not until the state moved in with a complex and never very satisfactory financing program, providing subsidies (often through state-run television), and a group of filmmakers joined to form a distribution collective (*Filmverlag der Autoren*) that the financing and distribution problems began to be resolved.[65] With that resolution, as complicated and incomplete as it was, a blossoming of talent occurred that recapitulated and consummated the movements in European cinema begun in the forties, and German cinema finally emerged in the late seventies as the most advanced form of commercial narrative cinema in the West.

The new German filmmakers carry an aesthetic-political burden heavier than that borne by their European predecessors. German expressionism, German fascism, American occupation, the "economic miracle" (the explosive growth of postwar capitalist endeavor), and a recent wave of political oppression that threatens to cut off the state financing that originally enabled these filmmakers to work, if the work they do strikes the state as being too far to the left, constitute both material for and a danger to their films.[66] They have had to confront a past more complicated than that of any of their European colleagues, and out of the confrontation has come a cinema more informed by its past than any other (with, perhaps, the exception of the Italian) and more able to speak to the present because of this—though apparently unable to speak to its own people, for the "New German Cinema" has been celebrated more widely abroad than in its own country. Germans still prefer American films. But this is hardly a unique situation.

Wim Wenders, Rainer Werner Fassbinder, and Werner Herzog, the three best-known figures of the movement, and the ones with the largest body of work available in the United States, demonstrate three distinct methods of approach, with equally distinct concerns for formal and contextual matters. Wenders, to a greater extent than the others, is taken by America and American cinema. Even more than the young Godard, he is obsessed by American things, American rock music, the American landscape, both physical and moral, and its interaction with the German. "The Yanks have colonized our subconscious," says one of the characters in *Kings of the Road* (*Im Lauf der Zeit,* 1976). And they have colonized Wenders's films, which are all meditations on movement, on travel without direction or clear goal, in and out of Germany, in and out of the United States, with cities traversed and borders crossed to the sound of rock and amid the desolate emptiness of characters who barely react to or comprehend their own incessant motion. In his major films—*The Goalie's Anxiety at the Penalty Kick* (1971), *Alice in the Cities* (1973), *The Wrong Move* (1974), *Kings of the Road* (1976), and *The American Friend* (1977)—Wenders seems to be trying to make and remake, to make sense out of, Peter Fonda and Dennis Hopper's *Easy Rider* (in fact, Dennis Hopper plays the title role in *The American Friend*). *Easy Rider* was a dirge to late-sixties America. Its two characters cross the country on motorcycles, carrying dope, seeking to free their spirits and the spirits of those around them, and at the end are killed by rednecks. *Easy Rider* is a smug film, full of self-congratulation; Hopper and Fonda project a quasi-innocence on the central characters; almost everyone else is either uncomprehending or full of hate. But it is also a summation of the image of the road, a motif that has run through American film since the thirties.

The road is more than physical presence in American film; it is a sign—a communicative cultural presence connoting freedom of movement, adventure, discovery, danger, escape. A catalogue of various images of the car on the highway would be a structural index to our ideology of individual freedom and the conflicts, bad dreams, and disappointments that ideology leads to.[67] Wenders is in awe of the ideology, conscious of its built-in disappointments, and, in his desire to work some of its images into his own cultural and political milieu, able only to deal with the dark, conflicted end of it. For Wenders, the obsessive recurrence of the road and car and their alternates—trains, subways, airplanes, trucks—proves only one thing: that his characters cannot go anywhere. Whether they are German or American, *in* Germany or America, despair and anxiety are the only results of their movements and in turn the only things that make them want to move again. Although, as we have seen, despair and anxiety are common themes (and in fact Wenders owes much to Antonioni for subject matter and for the setting of his characters in a landscape), Wenders is able to overcome the commonplace by the way he constructs his central metaphor, sets off external movement against internal stasis, and elides European and American sensibilities.

Wenders's visual and narrative perspectives present some impor-

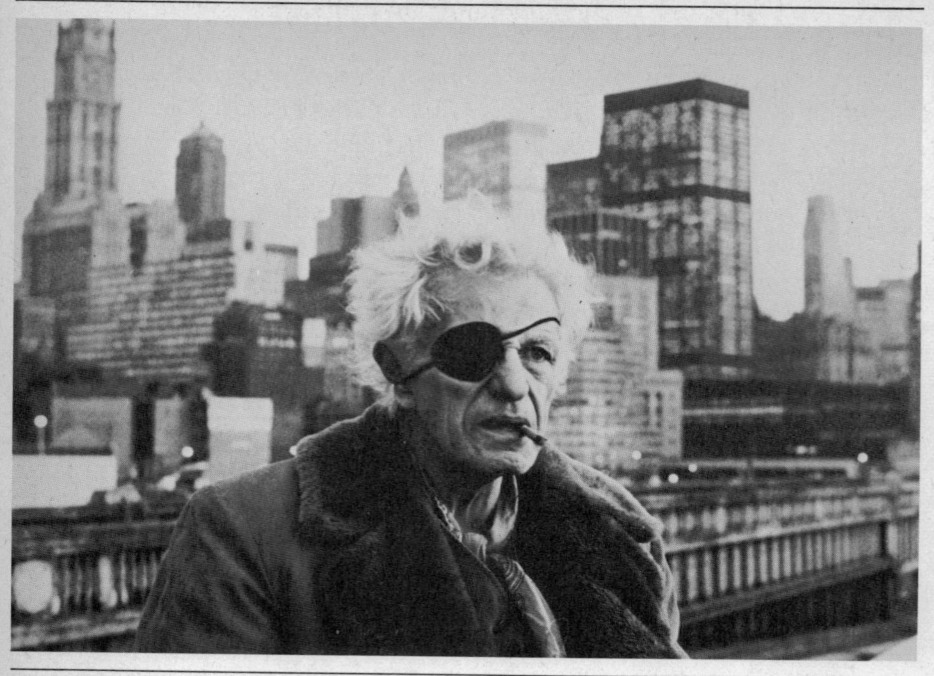

tant variations on the cinematic developments of the sixties. He tends to build his films in brief, almost episodic accretions. His suppression of transitional material is as extreme as Godard's, though not as radical as Straub and Huillet's, but unlike either he does not care to distance or alienate his audience from the narrative events–only his characters. Their life in transition has no transitions. In some respects he employs Truffaut's technique of "privileged moments," observations of instances when small actions unaccountably occur that enlighten all the participants and give pleasure or surprise, if not revelation. However, unlike what occurs in Truffaut's work, the enlightenment that occasionally befalls Wenders's characters is only transitory. They never learn anything and only rarely change. The spectator learns of

A meeting of cultures, a meeting of cinemas. Nicholas Ray (*opposite*); Bruno Ganz and Dennis Hopper (*above*) in *The American Friend* (*opposite,* Museum of Modern Art Film Stills Archive; *above,* New Yorker Films).

them; we see them alone in the frame, often surrounded by the things that mark their occupations or preoccupations, traveling in a car or train. Ripley, the Dennis Hopper character in *The American Friend,* wears a cowboy hat ("What's wrong with a cowboy in Hamburg?" he asks), and drives a white Thunderbird through the Hamburg streets. He lives in a dilapidated mansion that looks like the White House, in a dark room dominated by a pool table covered in plastic, on which is a box of cornflakes. A Coke machine and jukebox stand in the corner (the jukebox–the gaudy American house of pop–figures in the environment of many Wenders films, and often in Fassbinder's) and a neon "Canada Dry" sign hangs from the ceiling. Jonathan (played by Bruno Ganz, who has become the most recognizable face in the new German cinema), a picture restorer and frame-maker used by the "mob" to kill various people, who is befriended by Ripley and betrays him, is found either in his shop, where Wenders composes him with his picture frames, punning on the fact that he is indeed "framed," or with his wife and child in his old flat in an isolated tenement on the Hamburg waterfront. The flat is filled with static images of movement: a model funicular railroad in his son's room, on which Jonathan always bumps his head; a zoetrope, that proto–motion picture machine in which one can see figures endlessly repeat the same small physical action; a lampshade with a steam locomotive painted on it that appears to blow smoke from its chimney.*

When not in one of these two places, Jonathan is on the move between Hamburg and Paris, in trains, on the metro, on escalators, pursued or in pursuit. The movement gets him nowhere but deeper into trouble, betrayed, and finally betraying. Because it is so much a reflection of the *film noir* thriller (Wenders even deals with the *noir* theme of the man wrenched from domestic circumstances by corrupt characters), there is more physical action in *The American Friend* than in most of the European cinema we are examining here. But it is action meditated upon more than engaged in. In every sequence, even the most violent, Wenders will pause to observe, or add an extra shot so slightly peripheral to the central action of the sequence that it serves as a kind of punctuation and redirects our attention away from the sequence's center. This is a formal strategy common to most of his work, in which the gaze at the character and his situation (it is usually the male who is given greatest attention) becomes more important than what the character is doing precisely at the time. The neo-realist tradition again pokes through. Wenders is fascinated by the way people can be seen manipulating and being manipulated by their environment. But unlike the neo-realist environment, the one Wenders

* This picture is similar to a painting Ripley gives Jonathan to restore. The painting is by an artist in New York—played by the late filmmaker, Nicholas Ray—who is supposed to be dead and who forges his own work. *The American Friend,* which is based on a novel by Patricia Highsmith (who also wrote the novel upon which Hitchcock based *Strangers on a Train*), has a plot as complicated as any in American *film noir,* from which it draws its inspiration.

creates does not so much define as set them off, characterize them negatively sometimes, even abstractly by presenting a few key elements. The determinant spaces in Wenders's films cross the line of neo-realism to its opposite, an expressionist tendency that forms those spaces to reflect states of being. Thus Ripley's room in *The American Friend* is designed as an *idea* of the alienated American abroad, who brings with him garish bits of his culture. Elsewhere, there is a sequence in which Jonathan is in an airport. He rides a moving walkway and sees a man fall down in front of him. The shots are cut in such a way as to create the momentary impression that he is seeing himself stumble and fall. We see him walking through the terminal, the camera tracking before him. He suddenly looks around and Wenders cuts from that movement to a dolly in toward him sleeping in the waiting room in front of an enormous complex of escalators. Making the cut on his looking about creates the expectation that the next shot will be of something he sees. Instead we see him, by means of the portentous dolly, in front of an overwhelming impersonal structure of people in movement. The result is disorienting, threatening—the very qualities of the character's state of mind.

Wenders is one of the few German filmmakers who feel comfortable with their expressionist inheritance. Fassbinder alludes to it; Herzog, even though he remade F. W. Murnau's *Nosferatu,* keeps reacting in one way or another against it. Wenders, perhaps because he has managed both to absorb and be critical of American cinema, feels less intimidated by his own heritage. Although his films are about anxiety and irresolution, their form is secure and resolved. The dialogue he carries on with American film is much more at ease than is, for example, the dialogue that Godard carried on with it early in his career. The New Wave wanted to make American film by not making American film; they wanted to discover its essence and recenter it within a subjective context, a process that results in the conflict the films manifest between genre and personality. When the American filmmaker Samuel Fuller appears in Godard's *Pierrot le fou,* it is at a party where, playing himself, he answers Ferdinand's (Jean-Paul Belmondo) question "What is cinema?" Fuller responds (each word translated into French by another guest): "The film is like a battleground . . . Love . . . Hate . . . Action . . . Violence . . . Death . . . In one word . . . Emotion."[68] These are the qualities Godard examines in his films, analyzes (*Pierrot* is in fact a glossary of them), but never creates directly without mediation and meditation.

When Samuel Fuller appears in *The American Friend* (which pays homage to *Pierrot le fou* in many ways), it is as a character who is part of the story, a mafia porno king. He is implanted in the action; but because he is Sam Fuller, he also glosses it, his very presence, like that of Nicholas Ray, addressing Wenders's relationship to American film. Thus Wenders's examination of the American tradition is absorbed into the fiction itself. More than Godard, he makes his narratives self-sufficient, though still allusive and meditative, though to a lesser extent than Godard's. His work reflects the second generation after the New Wave, which is more ready to accept what Godard and his generation had to confront. This acceptance seems to make it easier for Wenders to deal with his own tradition. After all, American film had no trouble absorbing German expressionism, and it is reasonable to suppose that Wenders came to his own tradition via its American forties manifestation in *film noir*.* The landscapes and rooms he finds or creates for his characters extend their psychological state; they do not overwhelm them, as did the artificial sets of the Germans in the twenties. The characters exist comfortably in them, for there is no hysteria in Wenders's work, as there was in the expressionists' and even in American *film noir*. His is a comfortable and lyrical despair. And what is finally most remarkable about him is his ability to give a new visual and narrative power to the convention of the despairing, alienated hero, to examine it in the light of his country's own cultural tensions. No other filmmaker has dealt with the American presence in the European subconscious so directly.

* *Kings of the Road* is dedicated to Fritz Lang, who was a major part of the expressionist movement in Germany and made some major *noir* films in America. A character in the film clips a photo of Lang from a film magazine; the picture reminds him of his father. The photo itself is a production still from Godard's *Contempt*, where Lang plays a very fatherly film director. This intricate complex of allusions is typical of the layers of references in much of Wenders's work.

Unfortunately, Wenders runs the risk of yielding to it. Like so many of the German directors of the twenties (though not for their political reasons), he left his country to work in America, for the new doyen of international filmmakers, Francis Ford Coppola. He directed the film *Hammett* (a project Nicolas Roeg was once interested in), which he completed in 1982 despite conflicts with his producers.[69]

Like Wenders, Rainer Werner Fassbinder was concerned with the American presence. But for him it was not an obsessive concern, rather one of many determinants of modern German culture, and one way for him to work out some formal problems. Fassbinder found in the forms of fifties American melodrama stylistic methods that he could refashion and bring to bear on his own cultural and political insights. His movement back to and out of the fifties was as curious and enlightening a use of influence as any we have come across so far, and must be examined in the larger context of his work. The most prolific of filmmakers, he directed and usually wrote some thirty-nine full-length films between 1969 and 1982, including multi-episode series for television (which count as one film on his filmography). He began work in the theater and gathered around him a group of players, many of whom remained with him, appearing in one guise or another in film after film. Unlike the repertory companies of other European filmmakers (Bergman in particular), the individuals of this group rarely settled into fixed roles. Though they are instantly recognizable, they continually change types. In each Fassbinder film a Brechtian split is always present between the player we recognize and the character being created. "At no moment," wrote Brecht, "must [the actor] go so far as to be wholly transformed into the character played."[70] Along with this anti-realist, anti-illusionary device goes one other element. With the exception of Hanna Schygulla (whose "star" performance in *The Marriage of Maria Braun,* 1978, may have helped make that film Fassbinder's most popular with Americans, who still tend to separate a character from the total narrative the character is part of), most of Fassbinder's company, including Fassbinder himself, who often played a role in a film, are uniquely and wonderfully ugly, particularly in contrast to the kind of face we expect to see in an American film.[71] They are not ugly in the manner of

A gallery of Fassbinder faces: Günter Lamprecht, Gisela Uhlen, Gottfried John, Anton Schirsner, Hanna Schygulla, Elisabeth Trissenaar. *The Marriage of Maria Braun* (New Yorker Films).

the grotesques that populate Fellini's films. Fellini calls our attention to them, using them to create awe or amusement. The ugly faces in Fassbinder's films do not attract attention, but rather divert it, out of the fiction to a consideration of the face in film. They so work against the kind of attractiveness we are used to that they make us conscious of its absence.

From the very beginning of his career, then, Fassbinder forced the viewer to look at something that was, in the context of normal viewing experience, unappealing: players who were not beautiful, in roles that did not exploit the conventions of psychological realism because the player always stood back somewhat from the role itself. In the early films, this standing back is very pronounced. In *Katzelmacher* and *Gods of the Plague* (1969), *The American Soldier*

(1970; the latter two are variations of the American gangster film), *Beware of a Holy Whore* (also 1970, an enervated homage to Godard's lyrical film about filmmaking, *Contempt*), the pace of acting and cutting is slowed to a monotonous crawl. The camera is essentially frontal and static, and the players do little more than recite their words. *Katzelmacher,* which signals a favorite Fassbinder subject, the foreigner entering a German working-class milieu—here a Greek immigrant worker who boards with a couple and creates enormous racial and sexual tensions among the neighborhood layabouts—is made up of a number of scenes, each taking up the length of one shot. The neighborhood group lounges by a wall, observed frontally, from a medium distance, in carefully posed and unchanging positions, intoning their discontents. Some of the characters have various sexual escapades in a room. Every once in a while, two characters are seen walking down an alley between two buildings, the camera tracking before them and a melody heard on the sound track (the only times in the film that camera movement and music are allowed). *Katzelmacher* is an important (if barely watchable) exercise in which Fassbinder brings to bear on his work its major initial influences, Godard, Straub, and Brecht. The energies of Godard's (and Brecht's) analyses of class and character are countered by the recessiveness of Straub and Huillet's method of giving the viewer only the barest essentials, forcing him or her to construct the film from small amounts of information on the screen.

But Fassbinder recognized the dangers of the Straubian method. To cut off the spectator from *wanting* the film and the film from wanting the spectator, allowing the confrontation of both to create only a space between, filled with denial on the filmmaker's part and resistance on the spectator's, is counterproductive, and counter to Brecht's desire that the work should clarify thought rather than obscure it. Fassbinder's ultimate rejection of Straub was due to a desire on his part to speak to an audience intellectually and emotionally. "Films from the brain are all right, but if they don't reach the audience, it's no good. . . . [Straub] tried to be revolutionary and human in an inhuman way."[72] This strong response to the extremities of modernism is indicative not only of Fassbinder's, but of most of the new German filmmakers' concern that they not become another splinter movement, another critically respected but commercially ignored group of "independent" filmmakers. Independent, that is, of an audience and without an outlet for the distribution of their work. They were aware that the sources of financing as well as the audience in the early seventies were less open to cinematic experiment than in the early sixties. They were aware too that the government money they depended upon at the beginning of their careers would probably not be forthcoming for films that seemed arrogantly to defy their audience. To use cinema to investigate the way the world looked, they would have to make cinema that invited viewers to look at its investigations.

The first move in this direction was, for Fassbinder, a false one. In 1969, in the middle of his cold and distanced *anti-teater* films, he co-directed with Michael Fengler *Why Does Herr R. Run Amok?** The film contains the seeds of Fassbinder's thematics—a dull and passive petit bourgeois, with a boring office job, boring wife, and boring self, kills his family and hangs himself in the office toilet. But the film is created in a style that proved extremely uncomfortable for Fassbinder. Filmed in grainy, sixteen-millimeter color, mostly with a hand-held camera and available light, in long takes, it summarizes most of the *cinéma vérité* conventions of the time used in the service of a fictional subject. In other words, the film assumes the anxious gaze of a clinical observer of the events, curious but uninvolved, needful of seeing, but uncertain as to what to do with what is seen. It contains some fine sequences, such as a drawn-out act of humiliation in a record shop as Herr R. (played by Kurt Raab, one of Fassbinder's major ugly actors) tries to describe to the shopgirls an inane tune he wants to buy for his wife. But the series of humiliations and the inarticulate despair suffered by the character remain undefined and unanalyzed. We see them but do not understand them,

* *Anti-teater* was the name of Fassbinder's early theater group and production company. Substitute "cinema" or "theater" and it also defines the intent of the early films to counter cinematic conventions.

and the question posed by the film's title is only partially explored and never adequately answered.

Mock realism was not to be the answer to Straubian rigor. Fassbinder had to go back to an unexpected American source in order to rediscover the usefulness of his European influences. Godard's influence upon the *anti-teater* films is noticeable in the camera's head-on, ninety-degree gaze at the characters, and in the concentration on their endless talk. What is missing is Godard's ability to engage us in the talk and to fracture and layer the discourse of the films, so that many "voices" can be heard at once. Also missing is the analysis of the characters and their social/political situation that the multiple discourse can supply. Unlike Godard's characters, Fassbinder's appear separated from their environment. He needed a way to bring the characters forward without denying the information supplied by their surroundings, while at the same time preventing the audience from identifying with them.

Godard had applied Brecht, in various measures, to the genres of American film. The result was a series of essays and reveries on the musical (*A Woman Is a Woman*), the "woman's picture," (*My Life to Live*), the war film (*Les Carabiniers*), the science fiction film (*Alphaville*), the romantic thriller (*Pierrot le fou*), each an attempt to come to an intellectual understanding of its genre, analyze its elements, and speak to, rather than merely absorb and evade, its points of political and social contact. Fassbinder went through some of the genres, and chose one, the one that encompasses all of them (and has been our central concern in this study), melodrama. He went to a particular kind of melodrama, formalized in the series of films Douglas Sirk made for Universal Pictures in the fifties. These films—particularly *Written on the Wind* (which not only had its influence on Fassbinder, but is the progenitor of the American television series *Dallas*), *All That Heaven Allows, Magnificent Obsession,* and *Imitation of Life*—are the *summa* of American film melodrama. Not merely because they play so richly with family intrigues, despondent women and idealistic men, the sexually hyperactive and the passively homey; not only because they give us the expected situations of thwarted loves and crumbling business empires, conniving and denying, emotions too large and too demanding ever to exist in the plain air of experience; but because on an unobtrusive level they are aware of exactly what they are doing. Sirk was an intelligent European filmmaker in an unintelligent American business, contracted to make unintelligent films. He survived his obligations by crafting spectacular soap operas, in which he emphasized the grand operatic gestures of the genre and exaggerated the glowing pastel colors of fifties Technicolor (his cinematographer was Russell Metty, adept at sweeping crane shots and a rich, expressive lighting style; he photographed *Touch of Evil* for Orson Welles).

Sirk was in no position to make Brechtian cinema or indicate in any obtrusive way that he was aware of the absurdities of his material. But he was able to extend these absurdities just to the point of stylization—that is, almost to the point where, as in Chabrol's films, they reveal themselves as being absurd. The crazed, masturbatory dance that the nymphomaniac Dorothy Malone character performs in her room while her father has a heart attack downstairs, his cries drowned out by her music, does not quite leap out of its context in *Written on the Wind.* We expect that in melodrama a bad girl will carry on while her father dies. Sirk fulfills our expectations (that is the greatest obligation of the melodramatist), but gives us slightly more; he exaggerates the already exaggerated, but then holds back. He will not deny us our feelings, but try on some level to enhance our understanding of them. The Malone character is an overstated figure of the explosion of destructive sexuality, of passion breaking through the corporate propriety of a male-dominated society. The more she uses her sexuality as a weapon, the more she is seen as the victim of repression, of the distortion of sexuality by power—as, finally, she stands under a portrait of her father, fondling a very phallic model of an oil well.[73] Sirk makes the lack of subtlety a virtue. For with it he shows us what melodrama is about, if we care to look: the various forms of repression. The deer that appears at the window at the end of *All That Heaven Allows* is not merely a sappy image in a film drenched with our tears, but a necessary punctuation, a symbol (with all its connotations of gentleness and innocence) of two passive and quiet people who are the objects of abuse and forced to deny their desire by the proper townsfolk and family who see their union as unseemly. One may groan as the deer sadly looks in the house where Jane Wyman sits at the bedside of her young lover, Rock Hudson. Groan or not, its appearance is *necessary*. Sirk cultivates all the groaning silliness of melodrama, recognizes its silliness, but stops just short of showing it up. Instead by overdecorating it, embellishing it with color and movement and reflections in mirrors, he attempts to redeem the form.

But he cannot. Melodrama cannot be redeemed from the inside, primarily because it is so absorptive. It can suck any subject and almost any attitude into its center and adapt it, a fact demonstrated by the way American film has, with only a few recent exceptions, used melodrama to encompass all of its non-comedic statements. Almost all of the filmmakers I have been discussing have tried to confront and examine this phenomenon, but only Fassbinder confronted it head-on by, in effect, yielding to it. He enters the melodramatic structures of Sirk's films and reemerges able to make them comment upon and reveal themselves. It would be misleading to imply that his attraction to Sirk was based only upon an unsullied intellectual understanding of their expressive possibilities; he was also attracted to the garishness, the pastel tackiness of the Sirkean *mise-en-scène*. But he could make use of that garishness, along with the exaggerations and posturings of the fifties faces and bodies that populate Sirk's films, to manifest psychological states and social situations relevant to contemporary Germany. There is an undeniable campiness in Fassbinder's work and with that a homosexual subtext that some believe runs through all of his films (Fassbinder was an outspoken gay). Richard Dyer has tried to analyze the double perspective that arises from this attraction to the gaudiness and posturings of fifties American cinema and the functional, analytical use Fassbinder turned it to:

> On the one hand camp is relentlessly trivializing, but on the other its constant play with the vocabulary of straight society (in particular, the excesses of male and female role-playing) sends

> up that society in a needlingly undermining way. . . . One . . . has to recognize that it is Fassbinder's camp that has allowed him to develop the kind of foregrounding techniques which critics have usually preferred to ascribe purely to Brechtianism.[74]

Camp, when it functions beyond nostalgia or the glorification of the trivial (as it does not in the works of Andy Warhol, to whom Fassbinder is often and incorrectly compared), is a method of "making strange." Fassbinder's melodrama sometimes reaches outrageous proportions and refuses to resolve into the conventional repose melodrama always offers (the deer looking through the window as Jane Wyman comforts Rock Hudson). By exaggerating the characters and their situations through parodying fifties melodramatic techniques, Fassbinder is able to analyze the personal and social relationships between his characters and between his characters and ourselves. The stereotypes created by non-reflexive melodrama—even the melodrama of Sirk, which exaggerates and plays itself up rather than reflecting upon itself—when placed in a different context, a different country, a different time, become something other than stereotypes.*

Unlike Dyer, I would not substitute the model of camp for the model of Brecht. Fassbinder's "campiness" is rather a part of the greater Brechtian strategy he uses throughout the Sirk-influenced films (which include most of his output from *Merchant of the Four Seasons,* 1971, through *The Desire of Veronika Voss,* 1982). The primary result of bringing melodramatic posturing to the fore, making the viewer observe it as if for the first time, is to create an estrangement from it. Suddenly we must examine what was taken for granted. The desire to draw our attention to the way we look at the image and its contents is something Fassbinder shares with all the filmmakers ex-

* Not always. There are films in which Fassbinder's outrageousness does not yield insight. In *Satan's Brew* and *Chinese Roulette* (1976), in *The Third Generation* (1979) and, after a point, in *Despair* (1977), the bizarre turns to the silly and Fassbinder loses himself in the very lunacy of the events he creates. Curiously, three of these films, very different from one another, try to deal somewhat directly with fascism, and one, *The Third Generation,* with modern terrorism. The seriousness of the subjects either evades his grasp or is too complex for him to confront head on.

amined here, but none of the others, not even Chabrol or Russell, is willing to come so dangerously close to the foam rubber and satin soul of fifties melodrama as is Fassbinder in his attempt to transmogrify it. Nor is anyone quite so willing to play with his audience, to allow them to think they are coming to an emotional understanding of a situation, only to break that closeness by having the characters freeze into a tableau or by composing them within the frame of a doorway so that the viewer must observe them through the screen frame and then through a frame within that frame—often while those characters stand motionless and stare as we sit motionless and stare at them.

Fassbinder works many variations upon his basic model. At one extreme, he pays direct homage to Godard. *Effi Briest* (1974), based on a story by Theodor Fontane, is about a woman (played by Hanna Schygulla) destroyed by nineteenth-century cultural and sexual restrictions. Fassbinder films it in cold black-and-white episodes, rigorously composed and static, in the style of *My Life to Live,* a film that influenced him tremendously.[75] Here the melodrama is squelched before it has a chance to emerge, and we are forced to observe block after block of imagery that bespeaks the character's willingness to be passively abused by a closed social order. On the other end, he makes an almost straightforward commercial narrative. In *The Marriage of Maria Braun,* the melodrama of a woman who refuses to be passive, who makes her career by any means, is played against another, hidden melodrama, the German "economic miracle." In both the overt melodrama of the rise to power of a lower-middle-class survivor of the war, and the hidden one of the rise to power of a lower-middle-class country that survived the war, Fassbinder examines the prostitution of good faith and the manipulation of everyone by everyone else that are necessary for continued survival in a capitalist milieu. Maria Braun's universe is created by explosion, as the old Germany is blown up at war's end. She and her new husband lie on their bellies in the rubble, signing their marriage contract. The film concludes with an explosion when her husband, Hermann, returns after serving a long prison term and a self-imposed exile, having taken the blame for killing Maria's postwar lover, a black American soldier. Maria did the killing to prove her attachment to her husband; but Hermann, long-suffering soul of the nation, took the punishment. As he suffers in prison, Maria works and whores her way to corporate preeminence. In their strained reunion, in an enormous house in which Maria lives alone, while the radio blares the commentary of a soccer match (it is 1954 and the match is the first world cup Germany ever won), Maria absent-mindedly leaves a gas burner on.[76] When she goes to light her cigarette on it, she blows up the house and herself.

The Marriage of Maria Braun, more than any other Fassbinder film, depends on plot, on the interaction and continuity of events, to inform its structure, rather than on the way those events are cinematically observed (this may help account for its great popularity with American audiences). But even in this tumbling accretion of events and the double, almost allegorical text that Fassbinder asks us to read, he forces a necessary distance. By refusing to make a pure allegory in which each step in Maria's career can be used as a key to understanding postwar Germany, but hinting enough so that we may not fall in with the outrageous episodes of Maria's career without considering their political significance, we are kept jostled and removed enough to perceive the ambiguities of an individual and a country on the make, as well as of the garnering of power and all the destruction inherent in that process.

While *The Marriage of Maria Braun* is not filmed in the zero-degree style of the conventional Hollywood film, neither does it give a complete example of Fassbinder's stylistic and ideological methodology. If we go back to some earlier films, to *The Bitter Tears of Petra von Kant* (1972) and *Fear Eats the Soul* (1973), we can see more clearly the structuring principles he employs. *Petra* is another film deeply influenced by Godard. Its subject is a dress designer who lives with her mute, black-dressed, red-lipsticked secretary and slave, Marlene (played by Irm Hermann, whose mean, pinched face causes the spectator discomfort in many of Fassbinder's films). Petra (Margit Carstensen) has an affair with Karin, a young working-class model (played by Hanna Schygulla), that involves a back-and-forth shift of

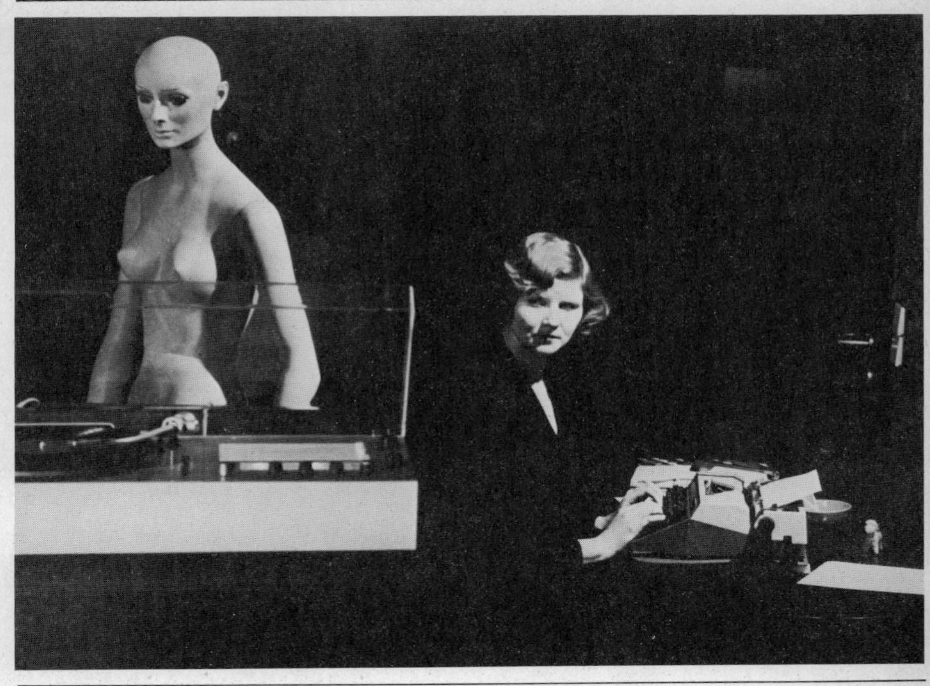

Marlene, who looks (Irm Hermann). *The Bitter Tears of Petra von Kant* (New Yorker Films).

power and humiliation, ownership and abuse in which Fassbinder uses the lesbian situation to indicate how insidious the patriarchal codes of domination and subservience are no matter which gender adopts them. The hurtful struggles for control are shaped by means of a carefully designed shooting style and a *mise-en-scène* that defines the characters at every instant. The action takes place in one room; the shots are long and precise; the characters speak slowly and deliberately. A mural of a Baroque painting covers one wall. In it, a number of reclining nudes are dominated by a central male figure, and the characters in the film are placed beneath this figure at various points in their rise and fall. Three white mannequins stand about the room, composed as the bleached, lifeless surrogates of the principal

Petra, Karin, and the mural (Margit Carstensen, Hanna Schygulla). *The Bitter Tears of Petra von Kant* (New Yorker Films).

characters. At one point, after Karin has left and a hysterical Petra is surrounded by her daughter, her mother, and her cousin, two of the dummies are seen lying on top of each other, while the third looks on. They function as the dumb reminders of the power-hungry affair between Petra and Karin and of Marlene's mute witness to it all. With the mural and the dummies, Fassbinder is able to create a modified expressionism. Along with carefully made compositions that stress the emotional locations of the characters at any given moment, they allow him to extend the limited physical space and indicate the psychological struggles going on.

"Indicate" is the operative word. The strained, sometimes hysterical confrontations of the characters are transposed to their gestures and reflected in the design and objects of the room. We watch the reflections of their psychological state rather than the states themselves. "Melodramatic films are correct films," Fassbinder once said. "The American method of making them, however, left the audience with emotions and nothing else. I want to give the spectator the emotions along with the possibility of reflecting on and analyzing what he is feeling."[77] Petra suffers to an extraordinary degree, but our emotional access to her suffering is blocked by the static, almost incantatory style of the acting; by Fassbinder's refusal to show us everything we want to see; or by his covering what we want with a distraction—the sound of Marlene's typing, for example, which accompanies the sequence of Petra and Karin's first meeting. A point is reached where the suffering is suffering *about* suffering, a sign of the thing itself. And we finally are not allowed to experience a resolution, even when the character seems to resolve her own problems. Three distinct climaxes are created in the film, each one skewing us away from a satisfying closure, forcing us into a position of confrontation with our own perceptions. When Karin leaves her, Petra has a nervous breakdown. But it is for us no intimate and horrifying expression of loss and despair. Instead, Fassbinder manufactures the elements of every such breakdown suffered by a woman in an American film of the forties or fifties. Petra is sprawled on the rug of the room, which is now emptied of all furniture. The mural, however, still dominates. She lies with a whiskey bottle, a doll that looks like Karin, and a telephone. She writhes and yells. Every time the phone rings she leaps for it, expecting to hear Karin's voice, slamming it down when it proves not to be her. Through it all, the camera stays at her level, distorting the space, emphasizing her abysmal situation. Her mother, daughter, and cousin visit her; the spectral Marlene watches over everything. Through it all, Petra rants and insults. She hurls her whiskey bottle at the mural. She appalls her mother by telling her of her lesbian affair, and finally tries to throw them out, threatening suicide.

At which point Fassbinder literally puts a stop to the proceedings. With the camera at floor level, looking at Petra on the rug with her phone and her doll, her mother's legs in the right foreground, her cousin and daughter back by the mural (whose dominant male figure centers the composition), Marlene in the rear at the left looking on, the characters freeze into a tableau. On the sound track, a male voice sings an aria from Verdi. The shot holds for some seventy seconds as the complex situation of the frozen characters, the aria, and our gaze slowly pulls us away and rearranges our perspective. The grand opera of Petra's passions is now seen to be just that: a prolonged aria about emotion, but not emotion itself. We have been made spectators to it (as we always are) but are now permitted to comprehend not the emotions, but the *playing* of emotions. Fassbinder is saying a great deal about sexual politics in this film; he is saying even more about the politics of spectatorship, about how the viewer is controlled by melodramatic form, and how he or she can be given back that control and allowed to judge the propriety of image and event. It is one of the fine distancing moments in contemporary cinema.

The tableau finally fades to black. We have been given distance and an opportunity to resolve the problems of the film and its characters. Now Fassbinder gives the characters an opportunity to resolve their problems. When the image fades back in to Petra, she has achieved a new calm. She lies in bed and talks to her mother (Marlene stares from the doorway). For the first time since the beginning of the film she is without wig and makeup. She now realizes that her attraction to Karin was not love at all, but the desire for possession. Karin calls, but Petra, once hysterical, is now restrained and refuses to see her. She says she is at peace and Mama leaves. In the finest tradition of Joan Crawford, our heroine has discovered an inner strength. The only thing left for her is to make amends to her slave, Marlene. As she approaches her, Fassbinder composes Petra in a shot that indicates that her new-found understanding may not be very thorough. She is seen (as often throughout the film) through a set of wooden shelves that frame her face. Opposite her face is a doll. The peace and kindness she claims to have discovered are challenged by the blocked, restricting frame, the toy doll, the objects that cause us to pull away from a direct observation of the character. Petra is still removed, from herself and from us. We may not sympathize with her new calm and understanding any more than we could with her old hysteria. Marlene, the dumb chorus to all the proceedings, has a dim comprehension of the treachery of feelings and reacts accordingly. Petra offers her freedom and joy, promising that they will work together. Marlene smiles and, still the slave, kisses Petra's hand. But her mistress refuses the gesture and instead, as she has earlier done with Karin, urges Marlene to tell her about herself.

Marlene looks at Petra and immediately walks off. Petra puts on a record, the Platters singing "The Great Pretender" (fifties rock becomes an interesting analogue to the nineteenth-century operatic aria). In a far shot of the room, darkened, with Petra lying in bed, Marlene returns with a suitcase. She moves back and forth, packing her things, which include a gun that she casually drops in. She takes her case and the doll that looks like Karin, and leaves. Petra turns off the light and goes to sleep, and the film ends. The only certainty is that Marlene has come to some understanding of the tyranny of feelings and of the danger of proprietorship inherent in the words "Tell me about yourself," while we have learned about the possibilities of overcoming the proprietary assumptions of films that manipulate our emotions.

In *The Bitter Tears of Petra von Kant* Fassbinder created the kind of enclosed, hothouse confessional that Ingmar Bergman is so attracted to (he recognized the connection, and in one shot, when Karin tells Petra the amazing story of how her father killed her mother and himself, he frames the two in imitation of the famous two-shot of Alma and Elizabeth in *Persona,* one character facing front, the other turned slightly). But the hothouse quality is continually punctured by the absurdity of the characters' gestures, their overreactions, the very clothes they wear, which are parodies of high-fashion chic. In short, Fassbinder reveals the absurdities of excess that lie just below the surface of Bergman's melodramas and exposes them baldly for the conventions they are. The exaggerations and the highly stylized cinematic treatment of them constitute not reality, but one of many possible ways of observing it.

Petra is a formal exercise, one approach to the complexities of

sexual relationships. It provides an alternative to the abstractions of *Effi Briest,* where the action is stopped at regular intervals, formed into discrete episodes of faltering and blocked passion. *Petra* employs exaggeration and indirection to point up the dangers of emotions overindulged and manipulated. What it does not do (apart from persistently reminding us of the patriarchal order) is demonstrate Fassbinder's skill in dealing with socially determined relationships, particularly those of working people, a class he has been more successful in treating than any filmmaker since the neo-realists. In 1974 he in effect remade *Petra* from the perspective of male homosexuality. The film, called *Fox and His Friends* in English–though its original

The famous Bergman two-shot from *Persona* (*opposite;* Bibi Andersson, Liv Ullmann), and (*above*) one by Fassbinder from *The Bitter Tears of Petra von Kant* (both Museum of Modern Art Film Stills Archive).

title, *Faustrecht der Freiheit,* which roughly means "Might makes right," is more precise–concerns a working-class gay, played by Fassbinder, who is taken up by a group of bourgeois men who proceed to exploit and humiliate him. Like *Petra,* the film is less concerned with homosexuality–something taken for granted by both works–than with manipulations for power that, in the case of *Fox,* depend on class structure more than on sexual proclivity. In both films homosexuality is a primary distancing device. We are presented with what is for many of us an alien world. The milieu is then used by Fassbinder to get at other important problems. *Fox* does not close itself off from the world, as does *Petra,* and its narrative parallels the standard

Hollywood melodrama of the woman who falls in love with a man out of her class and suffers for it, until snobbery and bigotry are swept away by the force of love. The difference here is that it is a man falling in love with another man, and rather than class bigotry, Fassbinder concentrates on the exploitation of one class by another. Love does not conquer, and poor Fox dies on a subway platform from an overdose of Valium. His body is ignored by his friends and rolled by two young boys.

Fox is a direct and straightforward film. The analysis of class structure it performs is simple and moving and proves that emotions can be valid expressions of conflict if the psychological and social realities of the conflict can be perceived beneath the conventions. Less straightforward, though more moving and acute in its analysis of social structures, is *Fear Eats the Soul* (*Ali*). Like *Fox, Ali* is closer to the conventions of cinematic realism than is *Petra.* That is, it does not attempt an abstract contemplation of its form, but instead envelops that contemplation within a traditionally "well-made story"—well made, that is, except for Fassbinder's insistent breaking of the action by tableaux, by the hard and exaggerated stares of the people who observe the main characters, and by the rigorous and distancing double framing of those characters within doorways, arches, and open spaces. The content of the story also creates a built-in alienation effect. *Ali* is based on Sirk's film *All That Heaven Allows,* in which well-to-do widow Jane Wyman falls in love with young nurseryman Rock Hudson and receives the scorn and derision of her children and friends. Love conquers (albeit with some difficulty) at the end. *Ali* is about a young immigrant Moroccan worker who falls in love with an old German widow and marries her to the scorn and derision of her children and neighbors, who finally come around when they discover that Ali and Emmi can be of use to them. Here Emmi begins showing Ali off and he leaves her for a whore. They have a reconciliation in the Arab bar where they first met, during which Ali collapses from an ulcer, which, we are told by a doctor, is a common ailment of migrant workers in Germany. Like *All That Heaven Allows, Ali* ends with Emmi sitting at Ali's bedside. There is, however, no deer

A touching joke: love between Emmi and Ali (Brigitte Mira, El Hedi Ben Salem). *Fear Eats the Soul* (New Yorker Films).

at the window; only the doctor looking over them, who has assured Emmi that Ali's ulcer will simply keep recurring until it kills him. The doctor in Sirk's film assures Jane Wyman that love and care will help the injured Rock Hudson.

The pleasure of *Ali* is gained from the subtle layering that Fassbinder achieves, first by presenting us with a touching joke—the perfectly nonsensical notion that an old German woman, a former Nazi Party member, would marry a foreigner, and not merely a foreigner, but a young black man—and then using the joke to express some very warm emotions, eliciting pity and compassion for the couple, and finally discovering in their plight some complex social and political problems. *Ali* is concerned with the isolation of foreign workers and native old people from the society in which they live, and the further isolation of one foreign worker and one old person from those who immediately surround them, an isolation caused by their attempt to overcome their loneliness by being together. It is the perfect melodramatic situation: one or two people (it cannot be more, for melodrama depends upon individual struggle) attempt to find happiness and are made more unhappy because others will not let them be. "Happiness is not always fun," is Fassbinder's epigraph for the film. Emmi and Ali are oppressed on every level, by the society at large, by their neighbors, Emmi by her family (in a fit of exquisite outrage over her marriage, a son kicks in Emmi's television), and finally by each other.

When neighbors and family begin to accept them, because Ali is strong and can help the neighbors move things, because the family needs Emmi to babysit, because the local racist grocer needs their trade, Emmi and Ali begin to oppress each other. She shows off his muscles to the neighbors. She refuses to make him couscous. He leaves her and seeks solace with a whore. He and his workmates laugh at her when she comes to take him home. The mutuality and generality of meanness redoubles, extends. Ali stares at himself in a mirror and repeatedly slaps his own face; Emmi and her now friendly co-workers sit on the steps in the building they clean and ostracize another worker, a woman from Yugoslavia—another immigrant, isolated the way Emmi and Ali were a short time ago. The worker is observed, sitting alone on the steps, in exactly the same shot that isolated Emmi earlier. Oppression and cruelty return like a rhyme.

Fassbinder refuses to allow his characters to learn anything. There is no liberal sentimentality in his work and absolutely no hope that everything will be all right in the end. He reveals the material facts of exploitation on all levels and counterpoints them with the false emotional security offered us by melodrama, the security that comes from believing that repression and emotional suffering will be repaid by a higher and more lasting peace. Fassbinder knows that peace on any level is impossible in a culture divided by class and overdetermined by an ideology of competition that depends upon the exploitation of one individual or group by another. The only hope he can offer is the ability to make us see this. And the only way he can make us see is to cut into the pathos at every possible point, give us the emotions we feel are our due and at the same time reorient our gaze so that we may analyze why we are feeling them and what is going on in the narrative to make us feel them. At one point Ali and Emmi sit in an empty outdoor cafe. Emmi weeps copiously and convincingly over the treatment that she and her husband have been getting. It is a high point of pathos in the film, the focus of our identification with these two apparently innocent sufferers. Two things shatter this identification. Through it all, the owners and waiters of the cafe stand in the background like statues, staring at the couple. When Emmi reaches the height of her passion, weeping, clutching Ali's hands, the actors both suddenly stop acting, freeze, the camera pulling back, past the tables and chairs, isolating the figures in tableau. We are once again forced to leave the fiction and judge the cause of and reaction to emotions.

Fassbinder died in 1982. In his work he took over from Godard the role of interrogator of everyday life and the cinematic images that attempt to explain it. A new cycle may be starting. In *Sauve qui peut* (*La Vie*), Godard reentered the world of everyday struggle, sexual gamesmanship and the oppressiveness of social roles. As the New Wave films influenced a new generation of filmmakers, so those filmmakers are now having their effect on their teachers. The communal web that marked the vitality of sixties cinema may be reasserting itself, and the creative and commercial success of the Germans may have helped to call Godard out of his isolation.

The communal web is not all-inclusive. One major figure of the German renaissance, Werner Herzog, attempts to create for himself the romantic image of the lone artist, whose work is born out of individual struggle and deals with human mysteries in a landscape of awesome natural forms. Herzog is an extraordinary self-promoter, eager to do or to fabricate great personal deeds (walking 300 miles to visit the film critic Lotte Eisner on her sickbed; threatening a cantankerous actor, Klaus Kinski, with a gun on the banks of the Amazon; traveling with a film crew to a Caribbean island threatened with volcanic annihilation). And his films are dedicated to an evocation of the mysterious, the ineffable, a world apparently outside the immediate materialist concerns of Fassbinder or Wenders, Alexander Kluge or Volker Schlöndorff.

Herzog is so dedicated to an almost metaphysical contemplation of the spirit that from film to film he runs the risk of being condemned as a mystic—or worse, a mystifier—a filmmaker with few ideas, but a distinct talent for creating a *mise-en-scène* evocative of the unknown and unknowable. Yet clearly Herzog does not completely ignore the realities of the world. He is capable of creating films like *Aguirre: The Wrath of God* (1972) or *Heart of Glass* (1976) or *Woyzeck* (1978), in which the taste for mysteries is put at the service of an investigation of the madness of power (and the powers of madness), the distortions and turmoils of early capitalism, the infinite abuses heaped upon the lowly and the powerless.

Perhaps Herzog is the only contemporary filmmaker who can reach for metaphysics while still infusing his meditations with a recognition of history and human activity within it. If so it is as much a result of the way he builds his films as it is of the subjects encompassed and created by them. Had *Aguirre* been made by a conventional filmmaker, it would have turned out to be an exotic costume picture about man versus nature in the tropical jungle. Herzog does this, but also manages to create out of the confrontation a reverie on the unspeakable attractions of fascism. This is accomplished in part by the particular way he observes his characters in their environment: a distant, seemingly uninvolved gaze that refuses to explore or to explain, and that accepts equally everything that is put in the frame. This method sets out a range of relationships and perspectives. Aguirre is a lunatic, a maniacal, physically distorted individual crazed by the belief that he can discover El Dorado. He and the conquistadors he forces to accompany him travel up the Amazon, defying its terrors and blind to the impossibility of their quest. Only we, as secure onlookers, discern their smallness and Aguirre's insanity. The images of destruction, the decimation of the men by Aguirre's wrath, disease, starvation, arrows shot from shore by unseen natives; images of nature's presence and indifference to the madness of the intruder—such as the monkeys that take over the raft and are adopted by Aguirre as his new followers—are viewed with a matter-of-factness that becomes hallucinatory. There is no sense of climax, no consciousness on the part of Aguirre or his men of their self-destruction (and certainly no consciousness of the destruction they and their fellows visit upon the country), only a persistence that is admirable and appalling, a monomania as impossible and unyielding as the jungle through which they move.*

Herzog has a most curious relationship to the neo-realist tradition, that part of it at least that calls for objective observation of figures and landscape. Like the neo-realists, he very carefully manipulates what he wishes the camera to see; but he is more willing than the neo-realists to absent himself from the act of observation, or, more accurately, create an illusion of an omniscient eye, looking but not judging. In 1970 he released a narrative feature called *Even Dwarfs Started Small,* an odd, Buñuelian allegory with an all-midget cast, involving revolt and cruelty and a notion that the small are as terrible as the large, the oppressed as vicious as the oppressors. *Dwarfs* manages most successfully to demonstrate Herzog's ability to treat the bizarre as if it were normal without removing or diminishing any of the bizarre characteristics of his subjects. It also contains the anomalous images that are essential to Herzog's *mise-en-scène,* images that have no immediate connection to the narrative, but by entering it fill it with an enigmatic, even awesome quality: a crucified monkey; a kneeling camel; an old truck that goes endlessly around in circles. What is incomplete in this film is the landscape—physical and, through metaphorical transformation, psychological—that extends the narrative, adding connotation, attenuating rational analysis. *Dwarfs* is a claustrophobic work. Herzog still must find the way to observe a fully articulated world to complement the characters—or swallow them up.

The way is found in *Fata Morgana* (also released in 1970), a "doc-

* This may sound familiar. Coppola based *Apocalypse Now* very closely on the structure of *Aguirre: The Wrath of God* and even borrowed many of its images.[78]

Even Dwarfs Started Small (New Line Cinema Corporation).

umentary" of the North African desert (Herzog continually alternates his narrative film production with documentaries, and the methods used in both are similar and feed into one another), though in fact more a dadaist expression of the region than a record.[79] In this film, narrative is kept separate from the images. An idea of narrative structure is laid over the images by means of a voice-over commentary reading a South American Indian creation myth. The film itself is divided into three parts: "Creation," "Paradise," and "The Golden Age," but the relationship of the images to the commentary and the headings is ironic at best, in general non-existent. After an introductory series of shots that shows, eight times in succession, a jet plane landing, the first section of the film proceeds, made up largely of left and right tracking shots of a desert landscape. As the "creation" narration continues, remnants of human habitation are seen: oil refineries with burning smokestacks, a wrecked airplane, junkyards. When human figures appear here and in the later sections, they are connected to the landscape only by their poverty and isolation—more accurately, by the poverty and isolation Herzog creates for them in his refusal to make any links between the figures and where and how they live. He is perfectly content to photograph a native of the region in full figure, staring at the camera, his features distorted by a wide-angle lens. The figure becomes one object among the others, contemplated and unexplained. When he photographs the Europeans who live in the region, the sense of disconnection is even more startling. A German holds up a lizard and gives a lecture on the desert heat; another dives for tortoises in a pool. At the beginning of the "Golden Age" section the camera stares at a man and woman sitting at a piano and drums, singing terrible Spanish pop songs, on what appears to be the stage of some wretched ballroom. (The man wears a pair of goggles similar to those worn by some of the dwarfs in *Even Dwarfs Started Small.*) Meanwhile the commentary has broken down into perfect dada nonsense: "In the Golden Age man and wife live in harmony. Now, for example, they appear before the lens of the camera. Death in their eyes. A smile on their faces [the couple we see are not smiling]. A finger in the pie. . . ."

The film keeps moving from the strange to the silly and back again. At its strongest Herzog merely lets his camera move by the derelict structures of Western building companies, with a Leonard Cohen song on the sound track, or stare impassively at the dried-out animal carcasses that stain the ground. *Fata Morgana* is about impassive observation and refusal: the camera's refusal to become involved in, or even inquisitive about, what it sees. "There is landscape even without deeper meaning," says the commentary at one point, and it is a statement without much irony. The images Herzog makes from this landscape have no past and no future. Even though many of them contain the remnants of a colonial past, the distance Herzog keeps from them (there is a preponderance of telephoto shots in the film) disassociates us from any historical analysis. One need only refer to Jean-

The surreal landscape. Herzog's *Fata Morgana* (New Line Cinema Corporation).

Louis Bertucelli's film *Ramparts of Clay,* released in the same year as *Fata Morgana,* to see how the same landscape can be entered not as a place of mystery, a surreal world to be gazed at from a distance, but as the habitation of people struggling to live, coming to consciousness of their economic and social circumstances. Bertucelli's North African desert has deeper meaning, and while he does not entirely ignore its otherness–like Herzog he tracks persistently, here around the walls of the desert village–his tracking shots also embrace the landscape, attempt to comprehend it, as opposed to Herzog's telephoto, lateral tracks that only emphasize its strangeness. Bertucelli does not yield to its mysteries, but rather wishes to understand them.

The political landscape. Bertucelli's *Ramparts of Clay* (Cinema 5).

The people he observes are not aliens; they attempt to survive the landscape, not become one of its objects.

This comparison reemphasizes the dilemma of dealing with Herzog. Whenever a sense of otherness can be asserted, he will assert it. Whenever possible, he will attempt the impossible and merge a neo-realist observation of people in a landscape with an expressionist's desire to make that landscape a state of mind; if he can, he will turn people themselves into a state of mind. Like most of the filmmakers discussed here, Herzog is less interested in the individual psychology of his characters and the motivations for their situations and actions than he is in the way those situations and actions can be observed. More than the others, he refuses most analysis and chooses instead to make his characters enigmatic, self-contained objects, passive suf-

The Herzogian landscape. *Every Man for Himself and God Against All* (Museum of Modern Art Film Stills Archive).

ferers of the world's stupidity, sometimes defying the world by withdrawal into a kind of heroic innocence, in any case falling in defeat with their grace intact. Whether a proto-fascist like Aguirre, an *idiot savant* like Kaspar Hauser (in *Every Man for Himself and God Against All*), or a mythic figure like Nosferatu, the Herzog character moves through a landscape that (in the films following *Fata Morgana*) is a German romantic's dream of nature—oblivious to it while we are hypnotized by it—and finally disappears.[80] "My characters have no shadows . . . ," Herzog says. "They are characters without a past, or whose past does not matter. They come out of the darkness and people who come out of the darkness cast no shadow. The light is something that always hurts them, so the character is there, at the moment, and then is gone to his obscurity. Their actions are somehow oblivious, it seems, to themselves."[81]

Though not to us. We attempt to understand, though blocked at every instant by the landscape and by the characters (whose strangeness on screen is often compounded by their extra-narrative existence—Bruno S., who plays Kaspar Hauser, is a part-time schizophrenic "in real life"; Klaus Kinski is a bizarre personality both in and outside the films; the actors in *Heart of Glass* are hypnotized throughout). Blockage, awe, dis-ease—these reactions link Herzog's work to the expressionist tradition. He is able to turn a landscape or a figure into an expression of oddity, separation; his gaze isolates and makes strange, more strange in fact than that of the original expressionists. They separated their work from the natural world and painted the world they wanted inside the studio, creating an extreme chiaroscuro that helped provoke a perceptual anxiety (an effect Herzog achieves in *Heart of Glass,* the film that closely approaches the visual and acting styles of the expressionists). Herzog achieves somewhat similar results by the prolonged gaze upon distant, natural landscapes, shots held so long that the natural becomes artificial and troubling. It is a technique that he in fact learned from one of the last of the expressionists, F. W. Murnau. In Murnau's *Nosferatu* the artificial settings are punctuated by shots of actual landscapes, and while these are never held as long as Herzog holds his shots, they showed him a way of delivering up the natural world so that it is perceived as obdurate, unpliable, unknowable. Perhaps Herzog's remaking of *Nosferatu* is somewhat less interesting than we would expect it to be because he demonstrated what he had learned from Murnau's film before remaking it. His *Nosferatu* is a direct homage to a kind of filmmaking he had already been practicing and, with the exception of Klaus Kinski's reading of the central role—his melancholy rat's face giving the vampire a despair missing in Murnau and all other film versions of the Dracula myth—he does not add to or deepen the myth to any great extent. The film does not completely evoke the original nor find its own style, suffering from too conscious an attempt to pay homage rather than intelligently extend an influence.

Perhaps the problem with Herzog is that he seems to insist on denying his own intelligence by adopting the guise of the romantic, attacking rationalism, evading analysis, dealing with history and psychology almost exclusively in the forms of allegory, and most concerned with anomalous states of mind and perception. His subject is always the outsider, the individual or group alien to the rationally constructed bourgeois world, whose strangeness makes the world strange by his or their presence. Even in *Stroszek* (1977), his one fiction film that does deal with the modern world, Herzog is more interested in observing the absolute alienation of his three unlikely German immigrants (one simpleton–Bruno S. again–one little old man who studies animal magnetism, and one prostitute) from the flat American midwestern landscape and its flat inhabitants than he is in understanding it. As I have said, Herzog's eye is obsessively drawn to otherness, and his preference in observing the strange and bizarre is to let it remain inviolate and make the rest of the world other by its very presence. Nature and society remain untouched by the appearance of the shadowless other. At the end of *Aguirre,* the imprisoning camera eye swoops wide circles around the raft upon which stands the lunatic conquistador, surrounded by the dying and dead and overrun by monkeys. Despite the movement, despite the allegory of the fascist personality contained in the narrative, the final image entraps the character and the spectator's comprehension of him in stasis. History is canceled by wonder–even admiration for the heroic madman.

In *Heart of Glass,* Herzog attempts to create an allegory of the rise and fall of industry. The inhabitants of a nineteenth-century glass-making town become crazed because they have lost the secret of their manufacturing process. A seer voices apocalyptic visions of the death throes of capitalism. But just as the megalomania of *Aguirre* becomes more attractive to Herzog than the prophecy of fascism inherent in the megalomania, so the mysterious breakdown of the town in *Heart of Glass* (and the manifestation of that breakdown in the zombie-like actions of the hypnotized players) becomes more attractive than a comprehension of economics and its cultural effects. Herzog gets caught up in a fascination with obsession, with the attraction to megalomania, and he short-circuits his allegory and his prophecy.

François Truffaut in his film *The Wild Child* (1969) attempts to understand the ramifications of bringing language and reason to a child who has known neither most of his life. The film is about education and learning, the need to give up nature, and the melancholy nostalgia for the life of nature that is given up. The *mise-en-scène* echoes the rusticity of D. W. Griffith, as Truffaut parallels his character's acquisition of language with the simple visual language of early film. In *Every Man for Himself and God Against All,* whose subject is an individual who has been locked in a dungeon, perhaps since birth, Herzog attempts to assume the point of view of the half-formed man, suddenly released upon the world not knowing language or reason, and to understand what the rational world of the nineteenth century can learn from him. The answer, he finds, is nothing. Kaspar Hauser becomes an obstacle the bourgeois world must overcome, and the world for Kaspar becomes an extension of his dreams. The form of the film slides the internal and external worlds into one another, and Kaspar gets stuck in a prison house in which kindness and brutality become two poles of incomprehension. In his version of the wolf-boy myth, Truffaut has his wild child almost educated by the bourgeois world; Herzog is content that the world will never be educated by the child-like mind.

Finally, there is a certain self-satisfaction that determines Herzog's films. Beyond the discomfort, the awe, even the semi-hypnosis they tend to create through the long-held shots of sublime landscapes, they are works very content with themselves—a phenomenon that further connects them with the expressionists (and perhaps with romanticism in general), whose films never inquired about their own nature; whose images were silent about their genesis and meaning. Of all major contemporary European filmmakers, Herzog is most willing to allow his images to stand uninterrogated; to allow them, and the carefully selected music he insinuates under them, to generate amazement, promote reverie, and frustrate analysis. His films, like his characters, are without shadows, and, like the landscape of *Fata Morgana,* without deeper meaning. His images are astounding, but his discourse is attenuated. The films are more incantations than narratives.

Herzog has taken the movement from neo-realism to modernism

to a curious dead end. He de-politicizes the neo-realist image so that observation becomes its own end. His landscapes and his inward-looking characters suffer our gaze but take no cognizance of it, make no response. The modernist thrust, in either its Brechtian or its non-Brechtian mode, is to make the image accountable to our perception of it and permit a mutual interrogation to occur. Even the most simple gesture, such as the frame-by-frame slow motion that Godard uses in *Sauve qui peut* (*La Vie*), reveals a desire on the filmmaker's part to excite desire in the viewer to consider the complexities of the illusion that film is (that life is). Herzog has rerouted this desire back to an acceptance of mysteries and the mystery of film.

But, after saying all this, I must point out that Herzog does share the modernist's ability to disturb the spectator, to force him or her into dealing with some elements of the imagery, even if the result is frustration when the images do not yield to coherent analysis (as opposed, for example, to Straub and Huillet's images, which will yield after much work). Those images are so well made and seductive that it is impossible to dismiss them, no matter how banal their content proves to be. There are few filmmakers who can turn the simplest image—like the blowing wheat field that opens *Every Man for Himself and God Against All* or the shot of Bruno S. gazing at a newborn infant in *Stroszek*—into an evocation of awe and strangeness, or who can make the most complex images—like the one that ends *Aguirre* or those that close *Heart of Glass*—suggest the eternal ambiguities and contradictions of a Faustian desire. But it is precisely the embracing of such eternal ambiguities that I find troubling. Herzog's is a cinema of impasse. The provocation of ambiguity, the ironies of the yearning hero frustrated by the rational controls of the social order or the irrational controls of nature are attractive to any of us still suffering the remnants of romanticism. But these provocations and ironies and the desires of doomed heroes, when allowed to go unanalyzed, invite us to remove ourselves from a world in which ambiguities must be sorted out and understood, and in which ironies provide only temporary refuge. Amos Vogel once wrote about Herzog's films, "To reveal a metaphysical element in life or art without becoming a reactionary is one of the challenges of the day."[82] Herzog just barely meets the challenge. Neither a metaphysician nor a reactionary, he creates a romantic, allegorical universe which excites the eye and threatens to muffle the mind.

Most of the filmmakers I am discussing have tried with varying success to attack the old romanticism of form and content and to dislodge the notion that form is the glass that permits us to gaze into a world of passions and mysteries, yearnings and transcendings. Herzog is by no means attempting to re-create the old zero-degree style, but he is trying to promote cinema as something of a magic glass that can reveal the extraordinary beyond our ordinary vision. Filmmakers like Fassbinder and Godard, Chabrol and Buñuel, Antonioni, and many others we have yet to discuss, attempt to show that in the ordinary lies the possibility for cinema to reveal the complexities of reality, a reality constituted by the intersection of cinema with our own experience, each addressing the other without mystifications. From the various formal concerns of these individuals has come an understanding that film is not limited to mere description or to the simple transmitting of moral platitudes. Nor must it be dedicated to the opulence of spectacle, to entertainment by excess. Rather, film can set itself the role of examiner and revealer of things hidden. Not mysterious things, though perhaps those things that societies and their politics have a stake in making mysterious. As filmmakers have begun to reveal that theirs is a work of artifice, of making images, they have also been able to reveal what makes up images—both those of film and those of our day-to-day lives. In the process of interrogation film has reflected back to us the questions that it had—until the mid-forties—largely ignored. In revealing the methods of its looking it is able to reveal things not looked at before by film. This work of demystification has helped us regain control over what we see, and see where we can exercise some control.

CHAPTER THREE

POLITICS, PSYCHOLOGY, AND MEMORY

In my time streets led to the quicksand.
Speech betrayed me to the slaughterer.
There was little I could do. But without me
The rulers would have been more secure.
This was my hope.

Bertolt Brecht[1]

FEW THINGS make an American film critic more uncomfortable than a movie with an overt political discourse. The critical commonplace is that "politics" somehow diminishes a work, narrows it, turns it into "propaganda." "Propaganda" is limiting; it denies richness and ambiguity because it propounds (propagates) a narrow, predetermined point of view. To be "realistic" a film must be open to the fullness of experience, with characters roundly developed, given a past and a future, their behavior clearly motivated, living in a world that seems to be based on the world as we know it from everyday experience: continuous, spontaneous in presenting events, and unencumbered by a defined political point of view. A filmmaker must not have "an axe to grind." Tacit permission is sometimes granted to include a political or social "theme" in an American film. Statements against bigotry, against corporate tyranny, more recently statements about a woman's right to determine the direction of her life, may be woven into a film's pattern. Usually, however, these statements take the form of inoffensive populist arguments—if we all worked together we would achieve an equitable solution to our problems—or, conversely (and particularly since the early seventies), the notion that exposing the problems also exposes our inability to do anything about them. We have, if anything, only our individual strengths to fall back on. The work of exposure is usually placed in the frame of a chase thriller: will Robert Redford and Dustin Hoffman reveal corruption in time to alert the country? Will Jane Fonda and Michael Douglas reveal the perfidy of the nuclear power company before it silences them? The race against time and evil pursuers constitutes a genre into which any subject can be molded. Even European filmmakers are not immune to it. In *Z* (1968), Costa-Gavras made a powerful political thriller about murder and repression in Greece in which, as in so many recent American films, a reporter runs down the dismal facts.[2]

The fear of determined political analysis, of raising a clear and unencumbered political voice in commercial American film, is part of a greater political phenomenon. In the United States "politics" usually connotes the machinations of vote-getting rather than the realities of the structures of power. When politics in this more general sense is theorized about, or discussed in a fictional narrative, any deviation from the conventional ideologies of individualism, free enterprise, and equal opportunity for all members of the society to better themselves is considered not so much subversive as unseemly and the expression of an alternative, analytical political discourse is therefore made very difficult. In current commercial cinema (in America, and to a growing extent in Europe and elsewhere) a simple economic censorship operates to keep dissenting voices unheard. Financing is difficult to find for political works, indeed for any work which in form or content deviates from the standard comedic or melodramatic conventions of realism. Just as the larger, conventional ideology that encompasses it presents itself as the only viable ideology (even when it does not represent the real situation of most individuals), so conventional realism presents itself as the only way experience is to be understood cinematically. Radical variations in form and content are condemned as being "unrealistic," and worse, not entertaining–the final form of censorship awaiting a film that does manage to go beyond the conventions. Film is only entertainment; if it defies that boundary it has denied its function.

There are differences in the ideologies of European and some developing countries that make this censorship less rigorous, that enable (or enabled) the cinema of these countries occasionally to give voice to an alternative discourse or assume a political perspective different from the one that dominates the culture. Many European countries are socialist, and since it is the socialist–the leftist or Marxist–perspective that insists cinema (and imaginative expression in general) deal with people in social and political contexts, the ideological repression, on that level, is less severe there. But other difficulties emerge. Some socialist ideology denies the appropriateness of dealing with subjective, psychological problems in film as vigorously as capitalist ideology denies the appropriateness of dealing with social and political problems. There is also the burdensome history of socialist realism—the refusal to permit experiment, the promotion of formal simplicity and easily grasped conventions that restricts inquiry as much as any other unquestioned form of "realism" does. Fortunately the strictures of socialist realism have loosened considerably in Eastern Europe (even somewhat in the USSR, as can be witnessed in films such as Andrei Tarkovsky's *Solaris,* 1972). In social democratic Europe, there is not the paranoia and arrogant dismissal of leftist ideology to the degree that exists in the United States. There is (or at least was) less difficulty in creating and finding an audience for films that inquire about social and political realities and that offer leftist alternatives to them.

Considerably less inquiry of this kind is going on in the 1980s, and some filmmakers, like Godard, Bertolucci, and Costa-Gavras, are retreating to less inquisitive modes of filmmaking or to downright, unquestioning melodrama.* Much of this retreat may have to do with a desire simply to get their work funded and distributed, a problem less oppressive in the sixties and seventies than it is now.

In a sense I have been discussing political film throughout this book. An essential component of the neo-realist endeavor was its concern, really for the first time in film, to deal objectively with the working class. That it could not avoid sentimentalizing its subject is ultimately unimportant. The fact is that by consciously choosing to concentrate upon a socially and economically defined entity, the neo-realists politicized their images and narratives. They replaced psychological inquiry with depictions of external struggle with the so-

* Signs of change? After a romantic film, *Clair de femme* (1979), Costa-Gavras has made a political thriller for Universal Pictures with Jack Lemmon and Sissy Spacek called *Missing* (1982), about an American whose son was killed in the Chilean military coup of 1973.

cial environment, the government, the economic and political state of postwar Italy. As neo-realism became the founding movement for contemporary cinema, its political initiative was never lost, although the focus moved from the working to the middle class, if only because European filmmakers were and are middle-class intellectuals, more comfortable dealing with their own class (a fact which does not obviate the troubling question of how the working class will get films made by it and about it). Of course the process of politicizing the image was not universal; some major, popular filmmakers, like Bergman, Fellini, and Truffaut, avoided overt political concerns. And in many instances (Godard's is the classic example) the politicizing of content followed the experimentation with form—an experimentation, I must reiterate, that was itself a political act.

When in the early part of the century the surrealists and dadaists set out to disturb the refined conventions of the fine arts, they were addressing a limited audience and playing upon the value of shock and surprise. When Antonioni, Resnais, and Godard set out to redefine the conventions of narrative cinema in the early sixties they were subverting a form known to millions of people who had found it comfortable and undemanding. These filmmakers began implying that happiness is not always fun, that the pleasures of narrative had to be sought out and worked for, and that this work would be liberating. It was precisely the comfort and security of the old, closed forms of filmic storytelling that allowed film to be the repository for conventional wisdom, melodramatic morality, dollar-book Freud, and the subliminal whisperings of the dominant ideology. Modernist and Brechtian cinema attempted to remove the security and dislodge old conventions and viewer attitudes. This was a political process in the sense that it broke the authoritarian grasp of the old, closed forms and gave the viewer freedom to think and feel, to draw conclusions rather than only accept them. It was a psychological process as well, preventing the viewer from identifying with the events on the screen, instead inviting the viewer to judge their value and use.

The films of Godard are an index to these processes. In his early generic experiments and tryings-out of the Brechtian model, he probed not only the relationship of image to viewer, but the nature of images themselves. He discovered that the image had become a fetish, a projection of desire that acted as a substitute for the reality of things and people. In *Les Carabiniers,* the brave and stupid soldiers bring home the spoils of war, a trunk filled with picture postcards that they divide, catalogue, and covet. The Parthenon (which they do not like because it is damaged); the leaning tower of Pisa (which they have to bend over sideways to see); photos of trains and boats and foreign countries; the Technicolor factory in Hollywood; Cleopatra (a photo of Elizabeth Taylor); dozens of pictures of things which are to them as real as—more real than—the things themselves, which they have never seen. The sign replaces what it signifies and the owners fetishize the image, the way the audience fetishizes the images on the page or the screen, embracing them as a reality. In *A Married Woman* (1964), Charlotte, a woman torn by the demands of sexuality as advertised in fashion magazines and the uncertainties of the sexuality she herself feels, all but disappears into the lingerie ads she obsessively reads. Godard creates a montage of lingerie layouts that Charlotte looks at in a magazine. On the sound track is a pop song, "Sad movies always make me cry." As the montage proceeds, Charlotte appears suddenly in front of a brassiere ad, and not until the camera moves do we realize that it is an enormous wall poster that she is walking in front of. Our first reaction to the image is that somehow she has literally entered her fashion magazine and become part of it. The image absorbs life, and Godard sees culture disappearing into the signs once created to explain it.

"The signs take root and pile up with no foundation in the axis of appearances," he says in *Le Gai Savoir* (1968). And in his later films he attempted to query those signs and the way they have deformed us intellectually, sexually, politically. He piled them up himself, cataloguing them roughly, until finally he discovered the possibility of explaining them by means of a Marxist model. He began to work out for himself the Marxist ground of Brecht, developing explanations of why and how we are forced to allow ourselves to surrender to images. But for Godard an explanation always resulted in more questions. He saw clearly that images have an oppressive function, and that this oppression is the result of our yielding to the unexamined assumptions of work, ownership, play, love, sexuality that our culture tells us are correct (in *Le Gai Savoir* there is a set of graphics with the words "Henceforth we refuse to accept any self-evident truths," ending with a drawing of a television set with the words "self-evident truths" on the screen, guarded on each side by a storm trooper). Godard understood the tyranny of images and the way that individual needs and desires—personal, social, and economic—are shunted aside by the pictures of false security and stability presented by advertisements and the romantic delusions of film and television fiction. But how to reorder the ideological sign system, realign it with the realities of everyday life, was still a problem. Even the assumption of the Marxist perspective did not allow him to shake off self-doubt and a certain romantic pleasure in his own uneasiness, most clearly expressed in *Two or Three Things I Know about Her* (1966). Here a narrative whose subjects are urban renewal in Paris, the Vietnam war and its effect on the consciousness of the West, and the obscenities of a consumerism that threatens to turn people themselves into objects (the central character takes up prostitution to supplement her husband's income) is overlaid by Godard's own voice questioning the appropriateness of his images and his ability to combine his subjectivity with objective analysis. In the films of the Dziga Vertov period (1969–71, made in collaboration with Jean-Pierre Gorin), he attempted to undermine this romanticism by ridding himself of fictional narrative completely and bringing to the foreground the essayistic quality that was always part of his work. Films like *Wind from the East, British Sounds,* and *Vladimir and Rosa* go beyond the process of Brechtian alienation by denying themselves and the audience any possibility of emotional rapprochement. They are teaching tools, demonstrations of Marxist models for the appropriate use of images and sound; demands for understanding these images and sounds in the context of class and class struggle. The taxonomy of images that goes on in these cinetracts, the explanations of how images fool us into believing they are real, are clear and indisputable. But the arrogance and coldness with which the explanations are sometimes made do more than make us distant, agitated, and inquisitive; they make the explanations difficult to deal with.

These films go beyond those of Straub and Huillet in the distance they create and the unyielding manner in which they state their analyses, and they tend to negate the dialectical method inherent in the Brechtian approach. In *History Lessons* (1972), based upon Brecht's fragment *The Affairs of Mr. Julius Caesar,* Straub and Huillet present the spectator with extended interviews in which actors in togas expound upon the economic history of ancient Rome and the growth of the merchant class, interviews which are intercut with even longer shots from within a car traveling through the markets, slums, and poor and middle-class neighborhoods of modern Rome. In the association of these images with the actors' speeches lies the history lesson: the attitudes voiced by the actors speaking for the ancients result in the urban structures of the present, and these in turn reflect the past. The arrogance and exclusivity of proprietary economics is made clear in words and in the concrete images of a class-structured urban society. Godard's Dziga Vertov films refuse the delicacy of this kind of dialectic and tend to hector the audience. Made in the spirit of the events of May 1968, they are full of revolutionary certainty and clarity. But, perhaps like those events themselves, they had nowhere to go. The student and worker uprisings in France were an outpouring of emotion and ideas, but stopped short of convincing the bourgeoisie of their power and hope. After the government called upon the electorate to reaffirm its power, the movement died out rapidly. Godard's films of the period are also an outpouring of emotions and ideas, but they are detached and raw, too cold and abstract to effect a change in attitude or understanding. To the audience that most needs to be convinced, the films are dismissible as "rhetoric" (the term used by the dominant ideology to negate the language of Marxism). With some heroic endeavor, Godard turned away from the narrative skill and visual fluency he had developed over a decade to experiment with direct agit-prop, full of questions and analyses of images and sounds and their political forms.[3] But he forgot briefly that stories are the best way film has to communicate ideas, and that the ancient Horatian dictum that art must teach *and* delight still holds true. Brecht never forgot it. Neither did the filmmakers of Latin America—distant students of Godard and the New Wave, of Pasolini, of the neo-realists—who learned their filmmaking lessons under the oppression of military dictatorships or in the excitement of a post-revolutionary society.

In *Wind from the East* there is a sequence in which the late Brazilian filmmaker Glauber Rocha is seen standing, arms outstretched, at a crossroads. A pregnant woman with a movie camera slung over her shoulder comes to him and says: "I beg your pardon for disturbing you in your class struggle. [Contrary to majority opinion, Godard had not lost his sense of irony in these films.] I know it is very important. But which is the way to the political film?" The woman kicks a red ball as Rocha points in one direction and says: "That way is the unknown cinema, the cinema of adventure." He points in the other direction and says: "That way the Third World cinema, a dangerous cinema—divine, marvellous. . . . A cinema of the oppression of imperialist consumption is a dangerous, divine, marvellous cinema, a cinema out to repress the fascist oppression of terrorism. . . . It is a cinema that will build everything—technique, projection rooms, distribution, technicians, 300 movie makers to make 600 films a year for the entire Third World. It's the cinema of technology, it's for the people, to spell it out to the masses of the Third World. It is cinema."[4]

A cinema that will repress oppression: the dialectic moves back and forth. Latin American cinema, perhaps more than any other, is dominated by American distribution, American product, American attitudes. The rise of national cinemas in South America has been sporadic, often repressed, but occasionally—as in the Brazilian Cinema Novo movement of the sixties, of which Rocha was a major member and whose purpose was very much defined in the statement quoted above, bursting with imagination and political vitality. In Cuba, where revolution succeeded, Rocha's dream of an independent cinema, with its own apparatus and distribution, was realized. The Cubans dedicated their cinema to ideology, an ideology that would clarify history, correct the misrepresentations of American film, and propagate socialism. They have experimented in many forms—documentary, fiction, fictional documentary and documentary fiction. Like the French New Wave, Cuban filmmakers practiced with various genres, posed questions about history; about the representation of history in film; they inquired about the relationships, public and private, between individuals; and about how those relationships are understood in the light of history. In short, theirs is a Marxist cinema that at every instant accepts the validity of Marx's central position: "It is not the consciousness of men that determines their being, but, on the contrary, their social being that determines their consciousness."[5] Like many of the major filmmakers we have examined, the Cubans turned away from the cinema of psychological realism to the cinema of psychological and social materialism, where subjectivity and individual experience are examined in the context of a culture and its history, of human beings in relation to each other and to their world. Their inquiries, however, are always in a revolutionary context.

Within their revolutionary Marxist framework, these films maintain a complexity of statement, an inquisitive and multi-leveled narrative structure that prevent them from being dismissed as simple "propaganda." The films of the Cubans and the political cinema of other Latin American countries are neither hortatory nor reliant on unexamined rhetorical structures separated from cultural analysis and emotional response. On the contrary, the filmmakers understand that Brecht's reevaluation of drama did not deny spectacle, performance, pleasure. Quite the contrary, he demanded them. But he demanded as well that the work and the viewer be placed in the mutually enlightening perspective of history.

> We need a type of theatre [read "cinema"] which not only releases the feelings, insights and impulses possible within the particular historical field of human relations in which the action takes place, but employs and encourages those thoughts and feelings which help transform the field itself.[6]

The most successful of the Latin American filmmakers are able to combine emotion, insight, and calls for change within narratives that are engaging at all of these levels, that are didactic and moving simultaneously.

In the Cuban cinema, the didacticism sometimes occurs in counterpoint to the narrative. A film will guide the audience through a proper reading of it, commenting on the images and the narrative, deconstructing them in order that the audience may better understand them. Sergio Giral's *The Other Francisco* (1975) begins in a mode of high melodrama. We see a black slave in the woods meeting his lover. As a romantic score swells on the sound track, they exchange longing glances; the camera swoops down as they embrace and Dorothea tells Francisco that they cannot be married, their master and mistress have forbidden it. As a final blow, she tells him that she has slept with her master. She leaves Francisco distraught; he runs through the woods, throws himself on the ground, and in the next shot he is found hanged from a tree, as a voice-over narrator tells of his grief and suicide.

There is something wrong with this. While the gestures of the characters, the movements of the camera and the music are overdone, they remain just to one side of parody. The action is only slightly more ripe than the romantic hysteria we are accustomed to in film (and that is something of a staple in "non-political" Latin American film). Our uncertainty is continued into the next sequence. From the hanged Francisco, the scene changes to a nineteenth-century Cuban literary salon. A man is reading aloud a story that follows the events we have just seen. We learn that after Francisco's suicide, Dorothea wasted away and died. The reader is applauded by the fancily dressed guests. At this point another voice-over narrator is heard. He locates us in time and place, telling us that the reader is one Anselmo Suárez y Romero and the work he is reading is his own, Cuba's first anti-slavery novel. We see the salon's host and are told he is a prominent reformist and bourgeois intellectual. There is also a British diplomat, who is in Cuba to study breaches in the anti-slavery pact. The historical moment is defined, and our place in the fiction is questioned. We learn that we are viewing a reconstruction of the time when slavery had just ended in Cuba and the liberal businessmen who brought it to an end are celebrating by congratulating themselves and enjoying romanticizing the past. The voice-over narrator questions whether the novel being read is in fact an adequate description of slavery in Cuba or merely serves the interests of people like those gathered in the salon. Can we find, he asks, another Francisco than that character invented by Suárez y Romero?

The rest of the film provides answers to the questions, or, more accurately, continues a process of question and response, a dialectic of liberal attitudes toward the passive sufferings of the slaves and another, radical reading of history that sees the slaves as actively rebellious. This reading interprets the freeing of the slaves not as a liberal, humanitarian gesture, but an act of economic self-interest (it is better to pay cheap wages and let the workers fend for themselves than to keep and support them) and of conflicting fears (there have been successful slave uprisings in the Caribbean, a fact that makes the slave owners want to tighten their grip but also points to the futility of their situation). The film narrative is continuously stopped, interrupted by the narrator asking questions, by turning to discussions of economics by the owners, on the plantation, or to the salon, where the motives of the author of the original novel and his once slave-owning audience are investigated, by alternative readings of the events on the plantation where the main action of the film takes place. At one point the opening sequence of the film is replayed, and the narrator asks if it is likely that a slave would hang himself because of a romantic triangle. The contrast between the activities of Francisco and Dorothea and the larger brutalities committed against them and the other slaves has made it clear that romantic involvements were not of paramount importance in their lives. The film continually works against the romanticizing of individuals and toward the observation of large-scale actions by slaves as a group, a class, who can achieve their freedom only by acting together. In the film they do and revolt against their masters. The film becomes a history lesson and a reading lesson. It clarifies the economic causes of past events and teaches an audience how to probe the "realistic" face of narrative fiction in order to understand what it says and does not say.

The interrupted narrative, in the style of Godard, is one method

Cuban cinema employs to break the spell of conventional film stories. Also, like Godard, the filmmakers layer the discourse of their films so that many voices and perspectives grow out of or cluster around a central subject. *One Way or Another* (directed by Sara Gómez, written by Tomás Gutiérrez Alea and Julio García Espinosa, 1977) uses a central metaphor of slum clearance to develop a complex discussion of other "clearances," social and cultural changes made in a new society. Using fiction and non-fiction devices, professional and non-professional players, the film weaves problems of machismo and misogyny, relationships between workers, anxieties over informing on malingerers, factual reports on the modern holdovers of old, male-centered tribal rituals, and the new care offered to recalcitrant slum children in and out of a love story with the repeated image of a wrecker's ball linking them all. The film is a multivalent discussion of societal alteration and integration, with various concrete problems presented as questions and possibilities, as needed areas for study. But again "study" and "didacticism" are not the same as "lecture." The film intercuts its stories and documentaries to achieve a sense of connection and vital interrelationship. Unlike traditional narrative cinema, it includes rather than excludes, indicating that problems between individuals are reflections of problems shared in the community at large. It refuses to isolate its form from its content, its fiction-making from its fact-reporting, and allows the interrelationship of modes to become a metaphor for the interrelationship of social attitudes that is its subject. Narrative and reality reflect each other instead of presuming to take the place of one another.

This work of narrative deconstruction is only one kind of cinema made in Cuba. As in the other socialist countries, there is a variety of approaches, though the ideological scrutiny given the subjects remains strong and prominent no matter what the narrative form. Tomás Gutiérrez Alea, for example, is more comfortable with less experimental forms. His *Memories of Underdevelopment* (1968), the Cuban film best known in the United States, is a rather gentle study of a Cuban bourgeois unable to embrace the revolution, suffering from ennui, discomforted by the new society, yet unwilling to leave it. Alea breaks up the subjectivity of the narrative by inserting reminders of the political realities of the country, the military threats against it, the social reorientation it is going through, the people who move actively around the central character. But the continuity of its story is basically unimpeded.

In 1977, Gutiérrez Alea made *The Last Supper,* which, like *The Other Francisco,* deals with slavery, this time in late-eighteenth-century Cuba. Although this film is somewhat closer to the conventional modes of story-telling than is Giral's film, its straightforward construction also reveals a revolutionary direction. Its arguments develop from the confrontations of the characters in a traditional fashion. However, these confrontations are so carefully clarified, the positions of the characters so clearly contrasted, that the viewer is offered a persistent exposure of oppression.

The film traces the development of a slave rebellion during Easter week, using the theological structure to break down the Christian underpinnings of slave ownership. A devout sugar mill owner wishes to teach his slaves humility by setting a Christian example. He ministers to them, washes their feet, and invites a select group into his home. In the long set piece of the film, a supper given by the owner for his slaves on Maundy Thursday, a shifting of power takes place. The entire sequence is played out against a dark background, with the camera picking out the dramatic shifts and reactions around the table as the religious apology for oppression is revealed and elucidated for the mystification it is. As everyone, master and slaves, sinks into drunkenness, the owner reveals the innate racism that makes slavery possible. As if discovering new truths, he voices the old clichés: blacks are created to work and suffer; they are resistant to pain; they are the living manifestation of the Christian imperative to learn humility and forbearance in the face of the unhappiness of the world. In a gesture to demonstrate his own humility, he gives one old slave his freedom. The blacks, for their part, react with amusement to the owner's homilies; one, whose ear was cut off as punishment for an attempted escape, expresses his disgust and defiance. They dance and mock the owner. The revelations become

Master and slave. *The Last Supper* (Unifilm).

clearer on the following day when the owner's profession of humility is contradicted by the plantation overseer, who demands that the slaves work, even though it is Good Friday. They revolt, killing the overseer and his wife and burning the mill. The owner has the rebels hunted down, and on Easter Sunday places crosses on a hill to mark the death of his overseer. The heads of the rebel blacks are put on stakes.

Alea plays with the contradictions of Christianity without subtlety, revealing it as an ideology that excuses cruelty and murder by raising them to the level of the spiritual in which the owners can hide. Humility and piety become self-satisfying gestures for the whites and weapons they can use against their slaves. The slaves, free of that ideology, aware of how it hurts them, are able to take action against their condition. Most of the rebels are captured and killed, but the one who had attempted to escape before gets away, and the film ends with his running through the hills to freedom. The closing montage, in which his escape is intercut with images of wild horses, birds, water, and falling rocks, reaches for a simplicity of statement that might make an audience used to ambiguity and indirection uncomfortable, and it slightly skews the direction of the film. Associating the escaped slave with the forces of nature seems to ignore the fact that his action is based on human necessity and is not a natural force. By suggesting that the escaped slave is in touch with more primitive forces than the whites, Gutiérrez Alea creates a somewhat irrelevant romanticism and perhaps too easy a way out. *The Last Supper* is an example of difficulties that may arise when radical subject matter is presented in more or less conventional form. Since form, in the last instance, determines content, the clear and direct confrontations presented in the film yield clear and direct conclusions, which are important in unraveling the mystifications of Christian ideology. But this clarity is somewhat lessened by the simplicity of the final montage. *The Other Francisco,* which also ends with a slave rebellion, takes more risks in the questioning of its formal presentation and in the way it recalls and delineates history. Although it too ends with the promise of freedom and revolution (Cuban cinema is always concerned with the success of the revolution and each film must present an analysis of history that validates that success—just as all non-revolutionary cinema must validate the ideology of uncertainty and isolation or the limited and passive success of a couple in love), the promise is based on rational understanding rather than on the romantic coupling of images of escape with images of unfettered nature.

This is not to say that *The Last Supper* is a failure, certainly not in its aim of exposing religious hypocrisies. The fact that it uses more conventional narrative forms than some other Cuban films points to the range of experimentation in Cuban cinema and to the possibilities inherent in the tensions between form and content. For although form does determine content, this does not mean the two may not struggle against each other, that conventional form may not carry subversive content—and vice versa.[7] Once more the issue is the shifting definitions of realism. *The Other Francisco* attempts to arrest some of those shifts and determine whose reality is being presented and what determines the understanding of a particular reality at a particular time. *The Last Supper* attempts a "realistic" re-creation of a period *in* which, rather than *about* which, questions can be raised. Its realism is somewhat stymied by the fanciful montage that ends it, raising the film to the level of revolutionary romanticism; yet despite that problem it is effective as a radical reading of history.

Outside Cuba, we can see yet another approach to the same subject and formal problem in an Italian film, Gillo Pontecorvo's *Burn!* (*Queimada!*, 1968). The work deals with a somewhat more complex political argument. In the loosely framed, obliquely cut, hand-held style so prominent in the late sixties, this film focuses on the machinations of an English adventurer (played by Marlon Brando, emerging from his sixties obscurity) in the Caribbean who first foments and then squelches revolutionary activity and is killed for his pains. *Burn!* is so apparently harmless a film that, in the late seventies, and with relatively few alterations, it was shown on American network television on a Saturday evening. But it deals with the same revolutionary material as does *The Other Francisco:* the economic cynicism of nineteenth-century imperialism that allowed slavery to come to an end not because slavery was abhorrent but because it was no longer economically feasible. Pontecorvo is able to sidestep the inherent romanticism of *The Last Supper* by indicating that the growth of revolutionary activity among the slaves was a direct result of white provocation—not merely oppression, but an active teaching of revolution (in this instance by Brando's Sir William Walker, who uses the blacks to overthrow Portuguese rule of an island so that it will be free for corporate domination) which then gets "out of hand." Walker returns, years later, as the officer of a sugar company, betrays the black leader he befriended and set up, destroys the rebel movement, and makes the island safe for exploitation. At the very end, boarding ship to return to England, Sir William is greeted by a black porter, similar in appearance, attitude, and social position to the man he had originally made rebel leader and then had executed. As he turns to greet this figure, the man stabs him to death. Pontecorvo thus indicates that the revolutionary spirit, once created, outstrips individuals and becomes

Sir William Walker (Marlon Brando) leads on a rope the insurgent he once supported. *Burn!* (United Artists).

not part of nature, but of the culture. The man who first formed and then betrayed it is destroyed by one of its representatives, who comes to stand for this man's own bad conscience and the country's revenge.

In the guise of an adventure story, *Burn!* is a radical analysis of history, contemporary as well as past. The narrative of foreign agents provocateurs, the images of the land burned by colonial armies to flush out the rebels, the sequences of a divided population, blacks fighting blacks, turn the film into an allegory of the French and then the American presence in Vietnam, and the corporate war that, at the time *Burn!* was made, was being waged against the revolutionaries of that country. Within its straightforward storytelling, it manages to be allegory and prophecy, connecting levels of historical and emotional realities, enlightening past and present. *Burn!* is not as extraordinary in form as Pontecorvo's *The Battle of Algiers* (1965), in which the struggles for Algerian independence are re-created in the conventions of *cinéma vérité,* but it indicates possibilities of presenting political analysis in a form that points to its content more than it does to itself, demonstrating that a more or less "conventional" cinema may be as subversive as modernist.

Thereby another dialectic has been formed. The movement from neo-realism to modernism and the use of Brechtian forms permitted cinema to examine and respond to its own conventions. Once these were understood and an audience could be shown what constituted the process of cinematic creation, perception, and comprehension, and once this process could be made to embrace social and political as well as personal and romantic experience, it became possible to call back more traditional forms to communicate less than traditional content. In other words, once the illusions of cinema are revealed as such, the forms of illusion-making can be used for purposes other than fostering more illusions. This may be an optimistic, even idealistic observation. It presumes that enough people will choose to be exposed to the new forms of cinema (or, in the case of Cuba, to be exposed to a wide range of formal experimentation) and learn from them, so they can then read the older forms with a greater comprehension of how they work. Then filmmakers can put the old forms to new use. What is so interesting about Latin American cinema, and Cuban cinema in particular, is the concerted effort made by filmmakers to accelerate this process, to teach the audience how to understand what they are watching so that all forms of cinematic communication will be demystified and thereby rendered usable again. Alfredo Guevara, founder of the Cuban Institute of Cinematographic Art and Industry, stated that their work was ". . . to demystify cinema for the entire population; to work, in a way, against our own power; to reveal all the tricks, all the resources of language; to dismantle all the mechanisms of cinematic hypnosis. . . ."[8]

One Cuban film, Humberto Solás's *Lucía* (1969), so encapsulates the process that it stands as something of an encyclopedia of progres-

The three Lucías: *opposite page: above,* 1895, *below,* 1932; (*this page,* at center, with Tomás) the 1960s (Raquel Revuelta, Eslinda Nuñez, Adela Legra). *Lucía* (Unifilm).

sive film in the sixties, and as such deserves some special attention. A long film, in three parts, it covers three major moments in the island's revolutionary history: the struggles against Spanish rule in the 1890s; the uprising against the dictator Machado in 1932 (an uprising that ultimately failed and led to the installation of Batista); and the post-revolutionary society of the sixties when the country was battling, among other things, its ingrained machismo. Each section of the film concerns a different class: the first, colonial aristocracy; the second, the middle class; and the last, the peasantry. Each section is created in a different style, a pattern of formal development that most accurately and concisely renders the history and class with which it is concerned. The central figure of each episode is a woman, Lucía, whose romantic involvement is determined by the historical events surrounding her, which are themselves determined by a particular way of observing them cinematically—a method which, as much as the events themselves, expresses the complex of social, political, and personal relationships the film is about.

The middle episode is the most cinematically conventional of the three. Because it concerns the dead center of the country's political struggle, when one dictator was replaced by another, and because it centers on an attractive couple who, while desiring a conventional romantic relationship, feel compelled to take part in a rebellion which takes the man's life, this episode indulges in a sad, contemplative attitude. It is told in flashback, through the memories of Lucía, now working in a tobacco factory, who recalls her romance with Aldo, the demonstrations they took part in, his raids on the police, their brief happiness at the overthrow of Machado, and the resumption of violent political activity that led to Aldo's death. This is a story about loss and gain, most particularly the loss of romantic love (at least of the kind portrayed in movies) which conventionally should be exclusive and isolated, but cannot be when political events intervene. The Lucía of this section wants the romance that movies have convinced us is our due, but because she and her lover are politically active that convention is not allowed to run its course. Here it is not another woman (or man) that interrupts the couple's happiness, but events they choose not to ignore. They are not forced out of romantic solitude; they decide not to indulge in it. The tensions inherent in their choice are clearly presented. After the overthrow of Machado, Aldo and Lucía attempt to settle down. She is pregnant. But Aldo is disturbed by the fact that the government remains oppressive, that his friend and co-revolutionary Antonio falls in with the decadent carryings-on of a thirties salon (in an orgiastic sequence similar in style to the work of Ken Russell).* The tensions are worked out when Aldo, Lucía, Antonio, and his wife sit in a deserted restaurant. Drunk and despondent, Antonio and his wife attempt to convince themselves that they can now devote themselves to each other and be a proper family. Aldo and Lucía cannot accept a quietism that goes against what they need to fight for. The sequence borders on hysteria, as Flora, Antonio's wife, gets sick over the anxieties resulting from the conflict between what she wants to do and what needs to be done, and as it slides close to melodrama–at least to overwrought emotionalism–it manages to portray, from within the logic of the characters' personalities and their situation, tensions unlikely to be developed in more familiar cinema. It is unusual to observe film characters struggling with personal and political feelings, desiring to integrate domesticity with the need to work for something else, agonizing over the consequences of sacrificing romance for a public cause. In the tradition of melodrama, the sacrifice is extreme. Aldo is eventually killed, and Lucía must identify his body in a morgue. She wanders the streets, is observed in a long shot under a bridge and then in closeup, staring at the camera. The long closeup allows full expression of our emotions and sympathies, and the section ends in the manner we are used to in Western cinema, with the central figure alone but determined as well as pregnant (a conventional sign of female strength and solitude in the face of heavy odds), and with the connotation that her life and Aldo's will be continued in the next generation. The section leaves us with ambiguous feelings of sadness and hope, and with the individual prominent.

* The similarity is probably coincidence, unless Solás had seen Russell's television films.

But this is not the end of the film. Obviously a Cuban audience, and any other aware of recent history, knows that this Lucía's loss and the country's political defeat were not an end, but a middle stage. Solás can allow us to luxuriate in the sadness and loneliness of the final images of this section, knowing full well (as we do not know in other films) that they are not the end of a historical process. The third section of the film takes for granted that certain battles are now won. The revolution has occurred and was successful. There is not loneliness but community. The subjects are not politically struggling bourgeoisie, but people in the countryside struggling with new revolutionary policy and old oppressive tendencies. The formal construction is the loosest of the three sections. The gray tones of the middle part are replaced by a clear, hard-edged black-and-white cinematography, hand held and loosely framed in an imitation *cinéma vérité* fashion. In fact, Solás is here documenting one aspect of Cuban revolutionary struggle, and the loose documentary form creates a proper sense of movement, vitality, and instability.

The opening shots of fields and workers seem to the Western viewer made wary by her or his own ideology to threaten a socialist realist piece about happy peasants working the land, a celebration of mindless labor. It is a celebration, but not mindless, nor is it socialist realism in the clichéd sense; it is rather a comedy of struggle, a condemnation of sexism, and a satire of revolutionary machismo set among rural workers. Lucía, a mulatto peasant worker (the mixture and integration of races is taken for granted), has married Tomás, a strutting, cigar-smoking buffoon who claims that he and not his wife is the revolution. He refuses to let her work and in a fit of jealous rage nails shut the door and windows of their hut. When a schoolteacher from Havana comes to teach Lucía to read and write as part of the literacy program, Tomás hovers over them and gets into fights. When Lucía does learn to write, her first words are "I'm leaving. I'm not a slave." Language makes her free and she leaves her husband. Tomás chases her while the other women chase after him and hold him back. The final images are among the most moving in contemporary political film. Tomás and Lucía confront each other on the beach, talking out their fears and desires, Lucía demanding that she must be allowed both to work and to love him, that she cannot do only one or the other. The struggle becomes quite literal, as the two run and wrestle by the sea. All the while, a young girl in a white shawl watches them. Her face is intercut with the battling couple, making her a silent, bemused observer, who, as the fighting continues, laughs and runs off to a crescendo of music (a politicized, feminist version of "Guantanamera" has acted as commentary to all the action; this and Leo Brouwer's score throughout the film help develop our response to the images), and the screen fades to white.

At the end of Fellini's *La Dolce Vita* there is also a young girl by the sea who looks at the hero and then at the camera. The difference in signification of these similar figures is an index to the difference of intent of the filmmakers. *La Dolce Vita* is about decadence, about the falling into despair and hopeless pleasure-seeking of a journalist who finds no satisfaction or reason in his life or work. The young girl on the beach is a conventional symbol of innocence, the freshness and delight the hero has lost, the offering of freedom and new beginnings to which he is now deaf and blind. The young girl at the end of *Lucía* is a figure of continuity. Her presence does not signify the hopelessness and despair of the central characters, but the promise of their and her own ongoing battles for equality. She is the next Lucía for whom the present Lucía and Tomás prepare the way. The film ends with images that speak to the possibility of social and personal progress, an optimism that may be beyond the reach of the culture to realize immediately; but it is a statement of hope and good feeling missing from most contemporary cinema.

In comparison to the romantic melancholy of the second part and the vitality and optimism of the last, the first part is a complex, explosive mixture of styles and attitudes, an attempt to link historical and dramatic form with psychological aberration and to relate the destructive nature of colonialism to the destructive nature of melodramatic love. Solás works an analogy: as a powerful country takes over and destroys the nature of one less powerful and more docile, so male domination, and the acceptance of that domination by a docile woman who believes in masculine strength and feminine weakness, destroys her nature. The only curative that may reverse the process is, on one hand, a revolution of the colonized country against the colonizers and, on the other, a desperate revelation on the part of the woman that will enable her to destroy the oppressive charade of melodramatic gestures. The story line is simple. In the late nineteenth century a peasant uprising is taking place in Cuba against the Spanish. Lucía is the daughter of an aristocratic Havana family and her brother is fighting on the side of the rebels. She falls in love with Rafael, who poses as an apolitical Spanish businessman. He seduces her; she reveals the location of the plantation where the rebels are hiding. He launches an attack in which her brother is killed, and in maddened revenge she stabs him to death.

This is, in outline, a melodramatic plot with a political subtext, in some ways similar to Visconti's film *Senso,* in which an Italian noblewoman falls in love with a soldier of the Austrian occupation. He betrays her romantically and politically, and she in turn betrays him. But where Visconti cultivates the (soap-) operatic posturings of his characters and uses political intrigue as the underpinning of their sufferings, Solás gives the posturings themselves political significance and subverts the conventions of psychological realism, showing them to be a kind of language system of self-abasement, delusion, and the suppression of liberating action.

The episode is structured in, literally, a black-and-white frenzy. Most of it is shot on high-contrast stock, washing out the gray tones, making the images harsh and obtrusive. Action is cut to action without continuity. Lucía and her friends gossiping, fanning, flitting about a Victorian drawing room are intercut with bizarre battlefield scenes. The women see out the window (or see as if out the window, for the spatial juxtapositions are deliberately confused) a madwoman wandering the streets, among carts filled with war dead, exhorting Cuba to awaken from its colonized slumber. One of Lucía's friends tells the story of this madwoman (and we "see" the story, intercut with the friend's telling of it). Fernandina was a nun who blessed the dead on the battlefield. She and her colleagues were attacked and raped by

The nuns on the battlefield. *Lucía* (Unifilm).

Spanish soldiers presumed dead. This nightmare vision is filmed silently, with non-synchronized sounds of screams and sighs, the shots rushing and fragmented. Like the orgy sequence in the second episode, it bears similarities to Ken Russell's work, particularly in *The Devils.*

The mad Fernandina emerges as a major figure in the episode, as chorus to the action and as Lucía's "other." The juxtaposition of proper aristocrat and maddened harridan allows a comparison and an allegorical coupling. Fernandina is the "response" to Lucía's upper-class madness; she is the maddened spirit of the people, raped by their oppressors, wandering the streets, attempting to give them a voice. Lucía is herself figuratively raped by the Spanish, but the violence of that act is displaced and deflected in the gestures of conventional romantic passion, of the woman suffering for love. The climax of this destructive passion occurs in the sequence in which Lucía and Rafael seduce one another. At once hilarious and terrifying, it is a parody of movie passion, full of rolling eyes and heaving breasts in the best tradition of D. W. Griffith—pointedly so, for the episode reflects the period whose acting style Griffith imitated, and the ways lovers express themselves in film have changed little since Griffith. Though moderated somewhat, they are qualitatively the same.

The seduction takes place in a ruined building in the country. The participants pursue each other, grabbing, pulling, kissing, weeping in exaggerated closeups and two-shots. Rafael leans against a wall, in sensual dishevelment, breathing heavily; in the background, Lucía looks distraught and runs her fingers through her hair. She yields and comes to him, pulls open his shirt to a crash of music and kisses his chest. Her passionate yielding is punctuated by the next shot, a high tower rising out of a forest with the couple seen very small in the foreground. The sign for intercourse in older films is a discreet cutaway to water or rain, perhaps a storm. Here the phallic image predominates unashamedly, but not uncritically. The game has been Rafael's and for a while will continue to be. Love's melodrama was created by men and Lucía abides by its rules. She plays the foolish virgin and pays a price for allowing the phallus to control her, a control emphasized by the shot of the tower.[9]

She has allowed not only her body but her spirit to be seduced, and even a direct warning from Fernandina to keep away from Rafael does not make her understand—cannot, for she only acts out the repressions and delusions of her class. After the seduction Rafael says he wants to be alone with her, to take her away from the turmoils of the world, and convinces her to take him to the plantation. On the way, the troops he leads (for the man who claimed to be without politics is in fact a leader of the Spanish colonial army) overtake them; she is unceremoniously dropped from Rafael's horse and abandoned as he leads the attack.

Parody is not the same as lampoon, but on first viewing it is not exactly clear what all of this exaggerated passion and abandonment is leading up to (although we are certain, from Rafael's first proclamation of political neutrality and his questions about Lucía's brother, that the result will not be happy). When the betrayal occurs, the events preceding it are rendered lucid, not comic. The exaggeration of gesture is understood in a double perspective. The posturings and proclamations of love are part of the baggage of Lucía's class. More accurately, they are part of the fictional representations of that class. Lucía behaves like the heroine of Victorian melodrama (or the modern popular romance novel), the cinematic version of which goes back to Griffith. At the same time Solás makes the viewer aware of the fictional nature of Lucía's behavior and turns it all into an ideological analysis; the exaggerations and phallocentric compositions enable the viewer to understand the nature of her illusions and the results of accepting the stereotypes of the compliant woman. Solás's viewers are far removed from nineteenth-century aristocracy and Griffith melodrama, but they still bear the burdens of male-dominated images of romantic love and passive surrender. By classifying these images through exaggeration, Solás turns them into instructional tools.

In the film, passivity ends with Lucía's betrayal. The battle that follows between the peasants and Spanish troops is one of the most dynamically filmed of its kind, and while it has some antecedents in John Ford's cavalry-and-Indian pursuits, its main inspiration is the battle in Orson Welles's *Chimes at Midnight* (*Falstaff,* 1966). Like Welles, Solás cuts sweeping movements of charging soldiers with small fights in the mud–gruelling, filthy beatings and skewerings. In the wide shots, the ride of the black, naked peasants, waving machetes and whooping like Indians, is an exciting image of unfettered energy (and based on historical fact).[10] In the closer shots, the action is seen only as vicious slaughterings. However, there is no liberal statement here about war being hell. The black troops and their battle are the focus of admiration (reversing Ford, the black "Indians" are the heroes of this battle, not the Spanish cavalry). The fight is necessary *and* awful; it is part of the battle for the country's political liberation and for an ideological liberation as well. Lucía wanders crazed through the battlefield and discovers her brother's body. Her hysteria grows and carries over to her return home, where, seeing Rafael in the square, in white Spanish uniform, she stabs him repeatedly. A religious procession surrounds the action. Again, Solás's frenzied style communicates the hysteria and through it the break Lucía makes with her past. The killing of Rafael might be just another melodramatic gesture of a scorned and betrayed woman. But the presence of Fernandina changes and deepens it. As Lucía is dragged from Rafael's body, Fernandina touches her, caresses her face, and calms her. It is a meeting of two classes, both betrayed and driven to madness, now making contact. The aristocracy to which the first Lucía belongs will ultimately disappear, rendered irrelevant by history. Fernandina's class will ascend. The contact of the two in the fiction indicates the linkage and points ahead to the changes in class structure that the rest of the film will elaborate.

As a whole *Lucía* is a work of optimism and confidence. Its complexity is the sign of a culture aware of questions that remain unanswered and problems that stay unsolved. The fact that the film does not despair, even when its tone is melancholy, is also a sign that there is purposive movement. Other political films from Latin America, from countries also still struggling with older ideologies but which have not had a revolution, are less confident in outlook, though no less so in execution. There are fewer of them, for they are, obviously, not supported by their governments, and they tend to appear in cycles as the governments go through periods of greater or lesser repression of the left. Outside Cuba, Brazil has been the center of Latin American filmmaking activity. It was the origin of the Cinema Novo movement that spread briefly in the sixties to Argentina, where Fernando E. Solanas's and Octavio Getino's *The Hour of the Furnaces* became a major example of agit-prop filmmaking–a work in this case fashioned to be shown to small groups with pauses for questions and discussion–and to Peru, Bolivia, and, in its brief moment of democracy, Chile. Many of these works, like *Hour of the Furnaces,* are documentary in nature, though with specific left-wing social and political perspectives. Some, like Jorge Sanjinés's Bolivian film *Blood of the Condor* (1969), document a terrifying oppression in the form of narrative fiction–a form, in this case, close to neo-realism.

The Bolivian Indians. *Blood of the Condor* (Unifilm).

The subject of the film is the forced sterilization program carried out by the government with the aid of the American Peace Corps (here called the "Progress Corps"), which many on the left considered an attempt to annihilate the Indian population. Around this event Sanjinés clusters a number of terrors facing these people, who are abused in their mountain home and in the city and have little to fall back on but their native rituals. The film does not have the sophistication of the Cuban and Brazilian cinema, although it too avoids straightforward exposition by intercutting past and present events, building its indictments through a series of oppressions, humiliations, and brutalities committed by the government upon the Indians. Unlike neo-realist film it does not observe the people and events from a sentimentally engaged distance. Rather it pursues the events coldly, with anger and with despair. An Indian, Ignacio, is wounded by soldiers and taken by his wife to the city for treatment. At the hospital, his brother is informed that, if he cannot find a blood donor, he will have to buy the blood Ignacio needs to survive. The body of the film is the brother's humiliating and futile search for blood paralleled with flashbacks that explain the shooting. The Indians discover that the American "clinic" set up in the jungle is a sterilization center, a place for controlled genocide; they surround and capture the Americans who run it. "You're killing life in our women's wombs," Ignacio tells them; "we'll do the same to you." "We only sterilize women who have too many children," says one of the American women. "You can't do this, I'm a scientist," she insists. "My embassy won't allow it." Violence is the only response the Indians have to the violence committed upon them, and they castrate and kill the Americans. Ignacio is shot by the police for his part in the action. His brother is finally unable to find blood for him, even though he breaks into a meeting of American doctors in an attempt to procure it, and Ignacio dies in the hospital.

For an American or European audience, the film acts as a grim lesson, a demonstration of ways of life and death rarely thought about or discussed. Its simplicity, crudeness even, does not permit it to escape into easily assimilable conventions as does, say, Costa-Gavras's *State of Siege* (1973). That film, a European's attempt to expose United States power in Latin America by analyzing how it teaches methods of police surveillance and techniques for the capture and torture of leftists, loses its analysis in a well-made thriller format. Costa-Gavras's American agent (based on a historical figure) is played by Yves Montand, a figure too sympathetic to reveal even the banality of evil. Finally, the careful structuring of suspense and expectation and the concentration on the methods of the guerrillas in capturing the American and those of the police in pursuing the guerrillas diffuse attention, subordinating the politics of repression to the special interest of engaging the audience. *State of Siege* is an exciting film and manages to teach the innocent viewer about reprehensible behavior, but unlike the structure of *Burn!*, form overtakes its content and understanding gives way to suspense engendered by the chase. *Blood of the Condor* concedes little to excitement or expectation, requesting our interest with its desire to reveal unhappy realities, offering hope only through the hint of possible rebellion against brutality (in the last shot rifles are raised defiantly). It is narrow in its focus; unpolished in its execution; enormous in its implications.

Blood of the Condor examines the Indian population of Bolivia in almost documentary fashion, making them the subjects of its investigation. In an alternative approach, the filmmaker may subject his or her imagination and that of the audience to the indigenous population, entering its mythologies and from them constructing a narrative out of which the social and political patterns of the culture emerge. This is a peculiar kind of imaginative endeavor, for the filmmaker has to submerge him or herself in legend, explain it, mold it into coherency, and yield a point of view. The film that results must trace a path between obfuscation (a deliberate refusal to explain its events) and a sort of liberal universalism ("We are all the same the world over"). This approach, which was attempted by the Senegalese director Ousmane Sembène, has been most successfully realized by a major filmmaker of the Cinema Novo movement, Glauber Rocha. Rocha's films of the sixties, including *Barravento, Black God, White Devil, Terra em Transe,* all search out ways of dealing with a coming to political consciousness of an oppressed people. In *Antonio Das Mortes* (1969) the elements dealt with in the earlier films are patterned into a complex mixture of folk opera, musical comedy, western, and a Latin American–African version of the myth of Saint George and the dragon. The result is an enormous spectacle of the birth of revolutionary consciousness.

The film is set in the *sertão,* the barren northeast section of Brazil which, along with the slums of the cities, has epitomized for most of the Cinema Novo the poverty of the country. Within this area Rocha places a number of figures created out of the legends and the social experience of the people who live there. Some are allegorical: the Colonel, Horácio, a blind landowner; Laura, his mistress, draped in purple; Matos, his sheriff, a representative of the middle class, desirous of foreign investment in the country, a keeper of law and order. He is in love with Laura (they sing a musical comedy duet as he showers her with jewels; they plot Horácio's death on a balcony bordered with withered plants growing out of pots made from American oil cans). There is a Priest who moves indecisively until he learns militancy, and a Professor, a schoolteacher and intellectual, who suffers from despair until he finds a political purpose. Other characters come directly from religious mythology: the black man, Antão, associated with Africa and its myths, passive and fearful among the people until he emerges as Saint George and spears the dragon, Horácio; the Santa, a holy woman, who is the silent center of the activity. Finally there are figures from folk legend: the title character, Antonio, the hired killer in cape and hat, who in the past slew Lampião, the leader of the *cangaceiros* (bandits who fought for the poor), and is called upon by Horácio to kill Lampião's current incarnation, Coirana. Finally there are the *jaguncos,* the band of hired killers (Antonio started as a *jagunco*) Horácio brings in at the last moment when Antonio begins to move away from the side of the oppressor.[11]

In form and structure, the film builds from a Godardian base. Rocha photographs individuals or groups at a ninety-degree angle against a bright-colored building or room. Space is flattened; the shots are complex and long in duration. Cutting is done against temporal continuity, so that the time of even a single sequence is fractured and shuffled. But where Godard makes the conflicting forms, voices, and signs of contemporary realities clash with one another, Rocha mixes levels of reality, enwraps the present within the past and the past within the present, creating a fictional world at the confluence of various cultures and their myths, always focusing on the simple polarity of the rich who own the land and the poor who must learn the means to get it back. In a montage worthy of Eisenstein we see Horácio railing against his people and their demands, vowing no one will take his land from him, rejecting agrarian reform, and blaming the unrest on the atomic bomb—*"a bomba atômica."* On these words, Rocha cuts from this blind, foolish old man to a rocky gorge in which the people are dancing and singing. He zooms back from them slowly, allowing full recognition that the "bomb" the Colonel fears is quite human and, in these circumstances, more powerful than any technological weapon.

But this power held by the people has to be analyzed with care. There is no revolution imminent in Brazil, and the forces of reaction are powerful; so Rocha must examine the fears and passivity of the people that need to be overcome before an active rebellion is possible. His method in *Antonio* is to identify and integrate the disparate mythological, religious, and legendary figures and stories of the culture. When proper linkages and identifications are made and the history of the people's myths can be linked to their present lives, a force for change may be created. First, however, history must be rehearsed and repeated. The Colonel calls Antonio to the *sertão* to destroy Coirana, as before he has destroyed Lampião. Antonio and Coirana are each other's double, one fighting on behalf of the peasantry, the other against it. All that is needed to put Antonio on the right side is a shift in consciousness. Their connection is visualized in the fight between them. In front of the people who dance and sing about the confrontation, "the duel between the dragon of evil and the warrior saint," Antonio and Coirana take machete and sword to each other while holding either end of a red sash in their teeth. Antonio slashes Coirana, and the latter's slow, operatic death throughout the rest of the film provides a ground for the shifting positions of the other characters and the slow revelations they undergo.

Antonio comes to recognize his evil and his isolation. The Professor comes to an awareness of the role of the intellectual, caught between the people who employ him and those for whose welfare he needs to work. His indecisions and paralysis parallel Antonio's, for both have been caught under the landowner's rule and both become aware of its destructiveness. Laura, unsuccessful in convincing Matos to kill Horácio, herself kills Matos, stabbing him viciously after they have been discovered and humiliated by their blind master. In a bizarre sequence, she and the Professor, chased by the Priest, drag Matos's body through the desert, wrestling over it, clawing at one another. The Priest dances madly around them, begging the Professor to attend to the living rather than the dead; the Professor beats him, and atonal, electronic music accompanies this lunatic ballet of misdirected passion and romantic necrophilia. While the Professor in-

The fight between Antonio and Coirana. *Antonio Das Mortes* (Museum of Modern Art Film Stills Archive).

sulates himself within these passionate agonies, Antonio carries Coirana's body onto the plains and the Colonel's hired guns shoot down the peasants.

Rocha continuously shifts the events he portrays among various levels of representation in order to fashion his dialectics of religion and politics, of social, mythic, and psychological realities. Through the interplay of general and particular, abstract and concrete, past and present, he avoids an anthropological study of a particular people (the perspective of *Blood of the Condor*), a neo-realist lament for the still, sad state of humanity, and the confusions that arise when conventional cinematic forms siphon off attention from the political matter being dealt with. The structure of his film continually challenges the viewer to go through precisely the kind of integrations his characters face, to place the fragments of expression in an order that leads to understanding.

The peasants are slaughtered; the Professor returns from his orgy with the sheriff and Laura, the dead and dying middle class. The mythic and holy representatives of the people, Antão and the Santa, are first tied back to back amid the dead peasants and then freed. Antonio recalls the Santa's proclamation of an everlasting holy war. But everything waits in suspension until the Professor and Antonio discover their loyalties and their function. At this point Rocha briefly pulls both of these characters out of the fictive place. They leave the village on the *sertão* and enter a world more recognizably "real," a place of trucks and highways, movement and commerce, the world of industrial economy. Their wanderings among the trucks are intercut with shots of the Santa in a montage that counterpoints the people of the *sertão* and the capitalism that is their economic ruin. The religious peasants (the *beatas*) are cut off from this world by the oppressive landowner, by an economy that bypasses them, by a spirituality that is out of place in the grime of the highway. The visual contrast points up the social-economic distance that exists between them, a distance that Antonio, continuing his movement from hired killer to protector of the people, must cover. Moved by the Santa and the people's suffering, he continues his progress as a holy warrior. He begins to pull the Professor out of his intellectual and emotional paralysis and drags him back to the *sertão* to the music of a pop tune playing on the sound track: "Get up, shake off the dust. Start climbing up the path. . . . A strong man doesn't stay down. He doesn't need a woman to give him a hand. . . ." Like Godard, Rocha finds that all levels of discourse, from the profound to the banal, can serve to define the complexity of his film's argument. The silly words and music of a pop song become as relevant to the images of Antonio's attempt to lead the confused Professor away from his attraction to Laura and his depression amid the trucks as the folk and religious chants were to the images of the fight between Antonio and Coirana, surrounded as it was by the aura of myth and legend. A culture moves and expresses itself through varied modes of expression, any one of which reveals something about it; and even more is revealed when seemingly anomalous modes are played off each other.*

As Rocha continues mixing these modes, one moment of understanding, change, and action follows another. Antonio takes the Professor to view the body of Coirana, in a sequence which is edited to create a revelatory climax. The gunfighter and the intellectual, composed together in the frame, look out of it in wonder and a cut is made to the object of their gaze: Coirana draped in a barren tree, a primitive tableau of crucifixion. As the camera dollies in on the strange, colorfully dressed figure in the tree, another song begins on the sound track, a comic folk ballad about the legendary Lampião who harrows hell and releases the blacks held prisoner there. The long narrative of this song weaves in and out of the rest of the film. The Professor takes Coirana's sword and pistol; the Santa hands Antonio his hat and rifle. The Priest is armed. Horácio, Laura, and the *jaguncos* meet them for a final confrontation. There is a long

* The sexist content of the pop song, as well as Rocha's treatment of Laura—who is associated with the Great Whore of Babylon—may not be defensible, but does need to be seen in context. Unlike his Cuban contemporaries, he was unable to come to terms with the machismo of his culture or see it as part of the great complex of oppression.

tracking shot in which Horácio and Laura are carried across the desert by the hired assassins, as the song about Lampião continues. They all meet at a church, for it is here that all the forces of Brazilian society converge, and here that the film's second climax occurs. In a low shot of this white building with blue shutters, the Professor emerges wearing the dead hero's sword. He announces the moment of revolution as if it were the apocalypse:

> Colonel! . . . the time is come! The eyes of this town will be opened. . . . I have never shed one person's blood. But I am prepared to shed my own to avenge the oppressed and humiliated *sertão*. And I borrow the words of the Bible to say: "An eye for an eye. A tooth for a tooth!"

After this grand call for action Antonio and the Professor divide their duties, solving the old problem of theory versus practice, idea versus action. "You'll fight with your courage, and I'll fight in your shadow," says the Professor. "No," responds Antonio. "Fight with your ideas. They're worth more than I am." And they proceed to do battle with the hired killers, in a sequence most surprising of all in this film of surprises. The shoot-out is done in the style of a Sergio Leone western, full of exaggerated gestures, leaping, falling, screaming, and blood. It is the western turned into revolutionary grand opera. The American genre so admired outside America is given a function and a purpose: to reveal the essential artifice of its gestures and at the same time show how these artifices can themselves express a powerful and useful fantasy of action and victory over evil. The sequence reveals as well the essentially speculative nature of the film. Rocha cannot predict with certainty that any revolutionary activity will occur in Brazil, nor can he predict how that activity will manifest itself if and when it does occur. What he is certain of is the necessity for the culture to draw fully upon all its resources and integrate those that are foreign to it. Exclusion is counter to political and social understanding. Exclusion is what created the oppression of the people that *Antonio Das Mortes* addresses. Therefore, if the popular form of the western shoot-out can be made to signify revolutionary

St. George slays the dragon. *Antonio Das Mortes* (Museum of Modern Art Film Stills Archive).

activity, to function as an image of social change, it has as much place as any of the other apparent anomalies in the film.

The process of integration continues in the third climactic event. As the shoot-out reaches a frenzy, Antão, with the Santa behind him, rides up the hill to confront the Colonel. The black warrior has now become Saint George and, in a series of temporally overlapping shots that imitate Eisenstein's technique of repeating a single action from several temporal perspectives, he spears the Colonel to the ground. The dragon is slain. Myth and history reach a junction and a revolutionary moment is realized *in the film*. Possibilities for action outside it are left to the spectator. The films ends with a number of atemporal tableaux of the main figures–the Professor, Antão, the Santa, and the armed Priest, who guards the people's guardians. The ballad of Lampião concludes by telling us that the hero burned Satan's rule-book and broke his clock. Antonio returns to the "real" world, and the final shots of the film show him walking down a highway in his cape and broad hat, a Shell Oil sign prominent, cars roaring by, and birds circling. On the sound track, a song about the wandering killer of *cangaceiros* accompanies him. Because there is no revolution in Brazil, Rocha must end the film with the notion of quest, of continuance. The figure of Antonio, killer of the people turned killer for the people, remains ambiguous and alone, skulking down the highway with its signs of American ownership, looking for a place to rest, his role still incomplete and uncertain, as was Rocha's own role as a revolutionary filmmaker.

Shortly after making *Antonio Das Mortes,* he left Brazil, quite probably as a result of government censorship, and went to the Congo, where he directed a less complex work on colonialism called *Der Leone Have Sept Cabezas* (*The Lion Has Seven Heads,* 1970). He traveled about Europe, filming where he could, and returned to Brazil in 1976, where he made *The Age of Earth* (1980). This is an enormous, not quite fully formed allegory of contemporary Brazil, which draws somewhat on the methods of Godard's Dziga Vertov films, though it is less politically radical and, because of the political circumstances in Brazil, less overtly revolutionary than *Antonio Das Mortes. The Age of Earth* mixes styles, is abstract, meandering, and repetitive, yet fully as passionate as Rocha's other work and firmly committed to the physical, cultural, and political context of his country. He died in 1981, and his death marked the end of the Cinema Novo movement which had barely survived repressive governments and various aesthetic shifts during the sixties and seventies. Some political film continued to be made in Brazil during the seventies (such as Nelson Pereira dos Santos's *Tent of Miracles,* 1977), but by and large the political impetus has dried up or gone underground. The major distributor of films in Brazil is now state owned and censorship is extreme.* If a Brazilian film is now seen in America or

* Robert Stam reports that the Brazilian government has a booklet of censorship guidelines. It refers to the " 'subversive techniques' of Jean-Luc Godard and other leaders of 'international leftist cinema' "; Joseph Losey is called the

Europe, it is likely to be something like *Dona Flor and Her Two Husbands,* a repugnant sexist comedy whose argument is that a woman will accept all manner of ill treatment as long as her husband is good in bed—a film some distance from the political passion of Cinema Novo.

Political cinema has come a long way from its roots in Eisenstein and his colleagues and the work of the neo-realists. Like neo-realist cinema, some political film of the sixties and early seventies is concerned with the poor and exploited, subjects usually ignored by mass entertainment cinema. But unlike the neo-realists, most of the makers of these films are not concerned with creating an illusion of a disinterested gaze at ongoing phenomena, but with manipulating the phenomena and the audience into a position of understanding and participation, so that the film work and the work of the audience are mutually engaged. These films make no pretense at being value free; that is one of the many illusions they avoid. They are unashamedly Marxist in orientation and they explore their subjects through that perspective, for it offers an analysis of class difference and of economic and social struggle. But it is important to repeat that the Brechtian-Godardian model which most of these films follow presents ideology indirectly. While they are not obscure or ambiguous in the tradition of non-political modernist art, they are always rich in the complex details of their cultures and in the analysis of relationships among traditions. They are rich also in the possibilities offered the viewer to understand and make sense of those relationships—as rich as ordinary cinema is poor. Conventional "non-political" film insists

---

" 'world leftist leader' of North American cinema, Sidney Pollack is an 'intransigent anti-American,' Robert Altman sees North American society as a circus . . . , John G. Avildsen (who directed *Rocky*) is an enemy of North American authorities who actively attacks democracy, and Arthur Penn is an imitator and follower of Godard who satirizes and attempts to destroy religious faith—as well as the more thoroughly subversive filmmakers targeted in the booklet like Bertolucci, Chabrol, Resnais, Bellocchio, Antonioni and Ken Russell. In Brazil, Glauber Rocha and Ruy Guerra are singled out as being particularly dangerous."[12]

that social, personal, and political experience remain separate and discrete. Political film insists they are connected and co-determine each other.

Filmmaking in the socialist countries of Europe offers further insights into this relation-making process. Polish and Hungarian cinema offer a variety of approaches and methodologies, among the most exciting of which are the films of the Hungarian Miklós Jancsó. Jancsó is an example (if one is still needed) of the fact that socialist realism—the demand for an easily assimilable plot and hero-centered celebration of working-class life—is no longer the only aesthetic model for Marxist art. His films are rarely centered on individuals, but rather on the activities and movements of large groups, out of which individuals emerge and into which they are absorbed. Movement itself is the focus of Jancsó's attention. There is rarely a moment of stasis; the camera and its subjects—whether they be opposing armies in *The Red and the White* (1967), prison guards and captives in *The Roundup* (1965), students in *The Confrontation* (1968), or peasants in *Red Psalm* (1971)—move constantly, vertiginously. Groups shift sides and allegiances, change roles of domination and repression. The movement of history itself is abstracted and concentrated within the limits of the screen.

These films work through a number of the formal and contextual concerns we have been examining. Jancsó is a committed revolutionary filmmaker, and most of his work deals with particular historical periods in Hungary in which pre- or post-revolutionary events occur. He expresses these events dialectically, indicating the intricacy of relationships between opposing sides; the shifts, changes in balance, movements, and negations of ideological attitudes; and generating of ideas and events out of their opposite. When Eisenstein confronted the problem of creating dialectical structures in cinematic terms, he solved it through montage, the conflict of shot against shot, so that the elements within one shot contribute to the other, creating a perception that is greater than the conflicting parts. Jancsó works in the opposite manner. He avoids montage, cutting only when it is necessary to change an angle, move to a different area, or replace the reel of film in the camera. For him, the dialectical process is fluid and continuous and must be perceived as such. Rather than presenting it as the collision of discrete entities (shots), he develops it as the movement of forces, manifested within shots in the activities of his characters.

This political aesthetic would seem to align Jancsó with André Bazin, perhaps even the neo-realists. In fact, Jancsó's practice makes clear some of the contradictions inherent in Bazin's theory. According to Bazin, the long and complex shots Jancsó uses should create a temporal and spatial wholeness that is faithful to "reality." But there is in fact no reality of the conventional cinematic (or even everyday perceptual) variety in his films; there is rather the reality of a particular perception of history: not history as fact, but history as progress, as a series and simultaneity of social and socializing events determined by a revolutionary perspective. The world created in his long takes exists on a rolling, featureless landscape, peopled with groups in constant motion, changing sides in a seemingly endless choreography of despair and brutality, victory and celebration. The events and the landscape are often ambiguous, though not with the kind of ambiguity that Bazin wanted revealed in his integral, open realism. Jancsó is clear as to the way he wants history read, even though he makes that reading multi-layered and emphasizes history's complex movement. Like the Latin American filmmakers, Jancsó begins with the reality of oppression and the necessity of change, a reality that disallows the withdrawal of the observer that is a structuring principle of the neo-realists and the basis of Bazin's aesthetic. The construction of Jancsó's films takes change as the reality of history, change that is never direct or immediate, clear or quite fulfilled, yet always moving toward fulfillment, rejecting continuity and wholeness as they are perceived in everyday reality or the reality constructed by conventional cinema. Like Eisenstein, Jancsó would create out of his images something that is greater than the images themselves—thought perhaps, even history itself.

A fine example of his method can be seen in *Red Psalm,* a film somewhat close in its general approach to *Antonio Das Mortes.* Like Rocha's film, Jancsó's is about the failures and successes of peasant revolt; like *Antonio* it takes place on a wide, barren plain. But the plain of action for *Red Psalm,* with its gentle undulations, is not the same as the brutal *sertão,* and unlike the *sertão* it is not a "real" geographical location. It is instead a locus, a stage upon which this and most of Jancsó's films take place, the field where the history of Hungary is played, danced, and sung. For like *Antonio,* this film intermixes a variety of kinds of performance that grow out of folk legend and myth, and like *Antonio* examines the archetypes of death and resurrection.

The film's subject is peasant rebellion against landowners and the military who protect them in late-nineteenth-century Hungary. But as always in Jancsó's work, the subject provides only a rough score with which he elaborates his dance of history. Here the choreography involves, on one side, young peasant revolutionaries and older, more traditional men and women, still bound to religion, unsure of a new order; and, on the other, the landowners and their representatives, the bailiffs, priests, and soldiers (these last two closely related—at one point a priest appears in a soldier's cap). The groups engage in a series of confrontations in a film that lasts eighty-eight minutes and is divided into twenty-seven shots (the average American film contains in the neighborhood of six hundred shots), each shot presenting one element in the shifting of power and domination between the groups.

Early in the film there is a typical Jancsó gesture. The peasants move among the soldiers, singing, the women forming a separate group. One woman proclaims, "With too many masters, there is no freedom. . . . With too many rich there are even more poor. . . ." As she moves on, another woman opens her blouse. Two more women do the same and the group walks off into the distance, three women with their blouses open, flanked by two female guardians. The woman in the middle turns toward the camera, then turns her back again as she and her two comrades remove all of their clothing and link arms in a circle. The omnipresent soldiers yell and run to them, forming a circle, then breaking it and running past them. The female guardians await on either side as the other peasants come up, link arms, and circle the entire group of women.

The continual encirclements constitute a Jancsó signature: threatening when done by soldiers (as later in the film they circle the entire peasant group and shoot them down) and protective when the peasant men and women link arms. The women disrobing is another act repeated in almost every film. Sometimes it is a mark of humiliation, as in *The Roundup,* where the women are reduced and diminished by their captors, unclothed and unprotected. Here it is a sign of defiance and liberation. Karen Jaehne writes,

> . . . Jancsó uses nudity as a celebration of humanism, providing his actors with the grace and anonymity of classical statuary. The human form as the measure of all things offers a cinematic barometer for the uses and abuses of power. It evokes an eroticism in whose presence we too feel naked, vulnerable, and therefore afraid. No matter how beautifully or peaceably juxtaposed, the contoured forms of the human body together with the meticulous uniforms of figures representing authority present such incompatible violence.[13]

The "humanism" in this instance has a deeper and more specific significance than the centrality of the human figure, though that too is present. The three nudes become, for a moment, a precise and classical icon; they are the three Graces, figures painted often in the Renaissance as an image of spring and rebirth (as in Botticelli's *Primavera*). In this instance, Jancsó focuses on the human body not only as a vulnerable and heroic form, but as an ancient figure of renewal, an idea central to the film and referred to frequently in other figures and events. In a later shot, soldiers pass a revolver from one to the other. One shoots it, wounding a peasant woman (one of the three Graces) in the hand. A soldier who originally held the revolver but refused to shoot, joining instead in the peasant's dance, is himself shot. He falls, is kissed by a peasant woman, and rises. In the following shot, the wounded woman appears with her hand raised; on her palm instead of a wound is a red ribbon, a sign of revolution that will reappear, worn finally by all the peasants.

These magical risings from death constitute a celebration of the peasantry, their power and persistence—a power that Jancsó also celebrates by its opposite, a magical death. A man in a leather jacket

The Three Graces on the Hungarian plain. *Red Psalm* (Museum of Modern Art Film Stills Archive).

comes to talk to the peasants. He crouches by a tree and delivers a standard free-enterprise speech: "Supply and demand is a fundamental principle of economics. . . ." He calls for thrift and a withdrawal from political activity. "Thus will Hungarian farm workers acquire moral capital and, ultimately, land." In response, an old peasant reads a proclamation to him: "The leaders of the present social system will never voluntarily improve the conditions of the workers. . . ." The man in the leather jacket says to the old man, "I don't wish to offend you, but you can't even read." The old man has obviously been reading! Something odd begins to happen: the man in the leather jacket attempts to continue, but begins rolling over on his side. "Shouldn't people be educated and rights given later . . . ?" he asks, halting, rolling over completely, and finally dying. This may be the first time in film that a character dies from the internal violence of his own oppressive ideas. If the clichés of capitalism are deadening and destructive, there is no imaginative reason why their destructiveness cannot affect one who generates them. In a film that depends on presenting an abstract concentration of history in which events are foreshortened and there is a desire to draw socialist ideas out of the myths of the peasantry and their closeness to the cycles of nature, the events of the film may take on mythic, even magic proportions themselves.

Not all of the destructive acts in the film are as non-violent as the death of the man in the leather jacket. At one point an old peasant, unable to comprehend fully or accept the new ideas of socialism, cuts his wrist with a meat cleaver. But his death shows a way toward a reconciliation of the people's old religion with the new politics. From the death comes a celebration; the peasants combine mourning, feasting, and religious sacrament into a revolutionary act, a movement of solidarity and defiance against the owners and the military. By the old man's body is a crucifix wrapped in a red ribbon. One of the peasant leaders reads a socialist version of the Lord's Prayer (". . . People, deliver yourselves from the universal suppressors of human rights. But do not forgive the tyrants their debts. . . .").[14] There is more celebration and dance—and the soldiers, as always, are in the background. More violence ensues: the peasants are shot down by the troops while celebrating around a maypole (itself an ancient symbol of rebirth). A stream runs red with their blood. The young soldier who was earlier killed and revived kneels in it, baptizing himself. A confusion of shooting, assassinations, and betrayals follows, until the very last shot. This begins with a closeup of a rifle being loaded. The camera pans down bayonet and barrel to other bayonets held at the ready by the soldiers. We see one of the remaining peasant leaders join his surviving, or perhaps resurrected, comrades in a circle, itself encircled by soldiers. The soldiers' commander and a fancily dressed lady cross the field. The peasant women, one naked, join each other on the field as the camera observes various symbolic objects and figures: a dead musician lying naked with a dead dove by his fiddle; bloodied white dresses lying pierced by swords on the ground. The white gloved hand of the commander raises a drink as a woman in a red dress wanders amidst the soldiers. A military band plays. Suddenly and quietly she pulls a soldier off his horse, takes his gun, and fires; she kills a soldier, she shoots the lady; one by one she kills all of them. She turns to the camera and sings one of the main songs of the film: "We are workers. We have no freedom. Whatever happens, we're the losers. Long live the workers' society." She holds up her pistol, wrapped in a red ribbon.

There is an enormous problem of reductiveness in describing the action of such a film. Jancsó's revolutionary optimism—at least in *Red Psalm*—runs the risk of being condemned as romantic no less than *The Last Supper*—even though its level of abstraction is more consistent. Anti-leftists may dismiss the film as glorifying revolutionary violence without questioning the outcome of such violence. Jancsó's optimism might be questioned in light of the difficulties East European countries have in maintaining their revolutionary fervor and autonomy (though Hungary has been relatively successful in maintaining this autonomy during recent years). Yet if we can bracket out the difficulties and disappointments of practical politics, we can see in the film's rhythms, the purposive choreography, the fantastic, mythic movements, and the refusal to bring its argument down at any point to individual and subjective psychology (figures do emerge; spokesmen for the peasants move throughout the film, arguing, acting, but always reintegrating themselves into the whole) the force of imaginative necessity, a powerful call to liberating action. It may not convince any viewer not already sympathetic to its ideology. No film will do that. What it can do is instruct the receptive viewer in Marxist perceptions of history and the ways such perceptions can be aesthetically realized. What is more, *Red Psalm* demonstrates a strong sense of artistic continuity. In the Renaissance, the humanists integrated pagan mythology into Christian theology. *Red Psalm* is anxious to integrate pagan mythology and Christian theology into socialism and to show that revolution, rather than being a break with the past, is a radical reabsorption of the past, one that is alert to contradictions, to struggle, and to the need to deny the past at the very moment of attempting to absorb it. Jancsó is as alert to the violence of this denial and absorption as he is to the harmony attainable by recalling tradition and using it for the sake of liberation rather than repression.

Because he takes such a speculative and abstract view, Jancsó is able to avoid the predicament that Bertolucci gets into in *1900.* Bertolucci individualizes his peasants and owners, placing them in a context that mixes conventional realism with epic abstraction, and he therefore loses his perspective and is forced into a conclusion in which nothing is concluded. Peasant and *padrone* remain in constant, even eternal battle. *Red Psalm* maintains its speculative point of view throughout and its narrative retains a high degree of historical abstraction. The victory it celebrates at the end is somewhat fanciful, yet it proceeds from a revolutionary conviction inherent in the form and content of the entire film. Such certainty may be utopian (I must emphasize that it is rare even for Jancsó to announce such positive victory); but so was the poet William Blake, and *Red Psalm,* with *Antonio Das Mortes,* shares with Blake a vision of struggle leading to an apocalyptic victory, a great burst of imaginative revolutionary activity that succeeds in creating the vision of a new order. Films such as *Red Psalm* and *Antonio Das Mortes* reveal a continuity of revolutionary art from seventeenth-century literature through the drama of Brecht and into the filmmaking of the sixties and seventies. This is a major tradition, though one not often recognized in conventional critical history, and a response to the literature and cinema of despair that predominates in Western culture.

Jancsó's approach to filmmaking is unique, perhaps as unique in terms of political content as Bergman is in terms of psychological content. No other Eastern (or Western) European director indulges in the long take, the complex choreography of movement, or the abstracting and compressing of history to the extent he does.* Other

* Jancsó is another major figure to suffer in the U.S. from lack of commercial viability and therefore lack of distribution. Few of his films since the early seventies are available or have even been seen outside film festivals. It is re-

recent filmmakers in Hungary, for example, stay within the bounds of a more conventional expository style and are content to deal with small subjects and individual studies, somewhat in the tradition of the Czech filmmakers of the mid-sixties. Unlike the Czechs, however, they are not sentimental and tend not to play upon audience sympathies quite as much. There is also a persistent recognition of political realities and problems which the Czechs avoided (or had to avoid), either by setting their films in the past (Jan Kadár's *The Shop on Main Street* or Jiří Menzel's *Closely Watched Trains*), or through the creation of elaborate allegories (Jan Schmidt's *The End of August at the Hotel Ozone* or Jan Němec's *Report on the Party and the Guests*). In their relatively short period of creative filmmaking, the Czechs indulged in a good deal of experimentation, adapting many techniques from the French New Wave, early Godard and Truffaut in particular. They were most successful when dealing with the ordinary and everyday, as in Ivan Passer's film *Intimate Lighting* (1965).

This is a quiet, almost recessive study of a family in a rural town. The father is a musician; he, his wife, children, and grandparents entertain a friend who comes with his lover to play cello in the local orchestra. The film presents scenes of family life, small joys and frustrations, the containments and pleasures of living outside the city and is distinguished by its attempt not to expand or comment upon its observations of unprepossessing middle-class life, to add no intrigue, suspense, or mystery. And no politics: it could take place in any small European town. The Hungarian András Ferenc's *Rain and Shine* (1977) uses a similar gambit. Again a small town and large family are observed, in this instance on the occasion of a national holiday and a visit from the mother's sister and her boss, a dull and complaining functionary from Budapest. Like Passer, Ferenc is interested in small gestures and family portraits, the rituals of meals, faces

---

ported that his version of a Sophocles play, *Elektreia,* has only twelve shots. It is also reported that a more recent film, *Allegro Barbaro,* while containing only twenty-two cuts, uses some of these to make comments through the juxtaposition of shots rather than merely linking one shot to another. This may indicate some interesting changes in his style.[15]

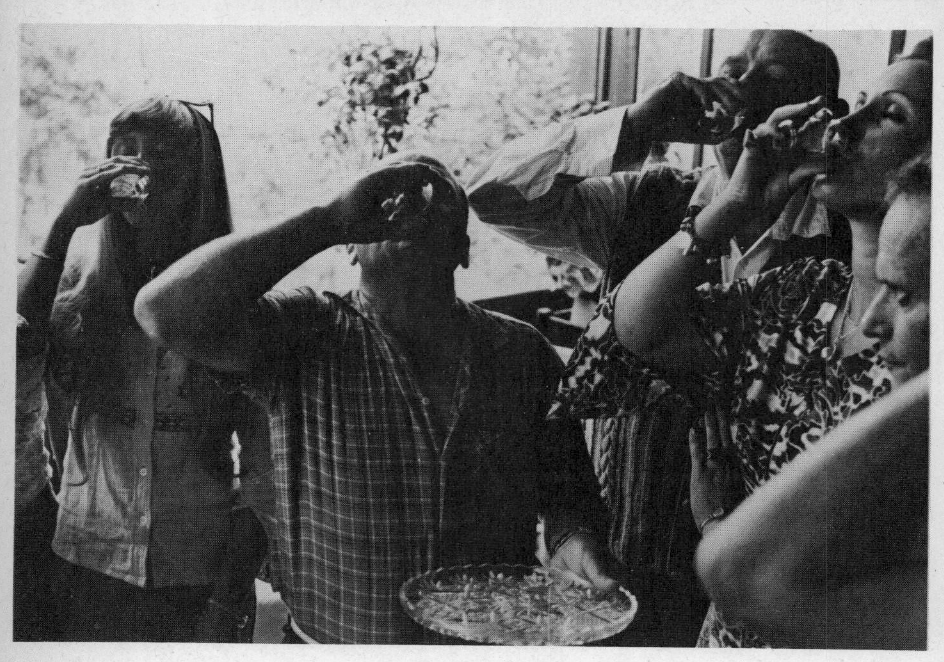

Family life. *Rain and Shine* (New Yorker Films).

reacting to each other. But he manages as well some small reflections on social and political tensions. The city bureaucrat has not the least interest in the country family, their past or present, and is totally uncomfortable with them. The family are separated from him by their vitality and warmth, and of all things, by money (they are successful wine growers), enough to build a new home for themselves. *Rain and Shine* becomes a film about differences in occupations and interests, the dullness of government representatives, and a culture splitting its rural and urban traditions while attempting to cover the split with television. The bureaucrat leaves to attend a public event, which is seen later on the family's television set. He cuts a ribbon, the TV commentator discusses the latest five-year plan. But the television plays to an empty room: the family is in the garden drinking.

Hungarian cinema in the late seventies seemed intent on probing the country's political discomforts—both quietly, as in Ferenc's film or the work of Márta Mészáros (in such films as *Women,* 1977, and *Just Like Home,* 1978), and with some degree of pain and sadness, as in those films which examine the transitional period to socialism in the late forties and early fifties, when suspicion and betrayal threatened to undo the political reorientation taking place after World War II. These films (two of which have been seen in the United States, András Kovács' *The Stud Farm,* 1978, and Pál Gábor's *Angi Vera,* 1979) present an interesting contrast to Jancsó's films of revolution, both in form and content. They have none of the celebratory and ceremonial qualities of Jancsó's work, and are rather straightforward in narrative development and visual style. Both—indeed all of the recent Hungarian films I have seen—pay careful attention to their image-making, using color as a quiet and expressive function of the *mise-en-scène.* But these films do not use their *mise-en-scène,* as Jancsó does, to subordinate the conventional details of narrative development to the formal movements of figures and ideas. Rather they develop, in the traditional sense, a "story," though like Jancsó, a story that comes out of political history and reflects its agonies.

Angi Vera concerns a young woman who is chosen by the Communist Party in 1948 to be trained for official government work. She is chosen because, in her position as a nurse, she spoke out against the bad conditions in her hospital and the special treatment given to patients with money. As a reward she is offered the protection and care of the party and receives a period of study that brings about a reduction of her spirit. At the training center she and her comrades are diminished physically by the gray damp winter and by the party officials who sit at tables before them; they are emotionally and intellectually shrunk by the constant pressure to re-form their thought and remain alert to an ill-defined and shifting notion of proper ideological behavior. The film is careful to avoid a suggestion of direct force. None of the workers who attend the training session are "brainwashed" or threatened into conformity. But the long self-criticism sequence, in which a glib and self-satisfied party representative humiliates and cajoles the members of the group into a perception of their ideological errors, demonstrates a good measure of emotional brutality. The film points out forcefully the way Stalinist authoritarianism forced its subjects into ideological rigor mortis, but it does not condemn the socialist cause—a discrimination difficult for Western audiences to understand.

In the West we tend to look at any manifestation of overt political indoctrination, particularly when combined with personal attack, with horror. Gábor re-creates the horror of that time but also attempts to comprehend the situation, to indicate the cruelty that emerges from a desire to change an old political order swiftly and without question, a desire that led to the threats, suspicions, and destruction that marked the Stalinist period. He is concerned with what the party did to the individuals who accepted its tenets without question and with a zeal that left them in turn marked and deformed. Vera emerges as a figure eager to pursue an ideological purity that she can use as a way to justify her personality more than her politics. She becomes so easily made over into an ideological model that she appalls the very ideologues who molded her. The extent of her ferocity is measured against four other figures. Traján is a woman hardened by her fight in the Resistance and an unhappy love affair with her married teacher, who was captured and killed by the Germans during the war. She first shows Vera the ease of informing when she has her get the name of an old man who offered them hospitality but is in trouble with the party (which ignores his legitimate grievances). Maria is a younger woman, as dedicated to her own sensuality as she is to the party. She acts as normative figure, a good party worker who is also concerned with her own and her comrades' emotional well being. There are two men. One is a miner, bumbling along as best he can with political theory that is foreign to him and methods he barely comprehends. Vera is first noticed at the training school when she offers to tutor this man. The other, István, is one of the course leaders, a young intellectual, both gentle and dedicated, who is eventually ruined by Vera's misdirected enthusiasm.

She falls in love with him (he is married), sleeps with him, be-

Angi Vera and her mentor, Traján (Veronika Papp, Erzsi Pásztor). *Angi Vera* (New Yorker Films).

comes fearful when she thinks Traján has seen her go to his room and confused when Maria stops her from going there, and finally confesses the affair in front of the self-criticism meeting. The moment is so shocking and stupid that Traján publicly condemns Vera and attempts to excuse her in front of the committee as a hysteric. István understands the damage done to his personal life and his political career by Vera's confession. At the meeting he insists that he loves her and denounces the whole apparatus of self-criticism as inhuman and productive only of liars and masochists. He is not seen again. While Vera shows some sadness over the event, it is Maria who shows the emotion that Vera should be suffering. She beats Vera and weeps bitterly over her emotional death—a death rewarded by the party, which praises Vera for perseverance and her ability to overcome transitory emotions. She is given a job as a journalist. At the film's end Vera and Traján ride together in a chauffeured car. Vera is following in the older woman's footsteps, but she is already colder and more unyielding. Their car passes Maria, doggedly riding her bike, still a good party worker but cut off from the privilege Vera has earned with her coldness. Vera calls to her, but Maria does not hear.

Angi Vera is a difficult film for a cold war audience to deal with, precisely because it appears to be a cold war film. In other words, its ideology is altered by the ideology that perceives it. For a Western audience it confirms all the horrors we have been taught are the natural products of communism. For a Hungarian audience (I would imagine) it is part of the de-Stalinization process, an attempt to understand the near past and correct its errors, and perhaps an attempt to criticize the present in a relatively safe way, by filtering the criticism through the past. At the same time, Gábor seeks to affirm—by criticizing its negative side—the humanity that should be the basis of socialism (an idea that István expresses in his defense in the film). That Hungarian filmmakers can express these problems in well-made films that get distributed abroad is a sign of a certain freedom of expression in their own country and their talent in integrating political analysis with more conventional modes of cinematic drama, "bourgeois" concerns of love and emotional involvement, self-questioning and doubt.* Their films provide one way of examining the possible conjoining of areas of experience—the subjective and the political—that in Western film are usually kept distinct.

* A postwar film from Eastern Europe, Andrzei Wajda's *Ashes and Diamonds* (1958), concentrated on these very concerns in its examination of a young man hired to assassinate a communist leader. A more recent film by Wajda, *Man of Marble* (1977), attempts an inquiry into Poland's Stalinist past by tracing the career of a young worker who was made a hero in the fifties, disgraced, and then left to oblivion. But Wajda attempts to bring history into the present. The documentary filmmaker who is searching for the worker discovers that he was killed in the uprising of 1970. The Polish government forbade Wajda to retain the sequence of that discovery in his film. During the brief liberalizing of the government in the early eighties, Wajda reclaimed the sequence for his 1981 sequel to the film, *Man of Iron,* which attempts to communicate, though not really explain, the events of the Solidarity movement.

In some cases, the attempt to mix them might just indicate the advisability of keeping them apart. In the early seventies, the Yugoslav filmmaker Dusan Makavejev received some recognition for his lunatic investigations of sexuality and politics in films that mixed documentary and fiction, acted sequences and archival footage in a formal collage that brought some of Godard's techniques to a curious dead end. Godard's complex inter-layering of political, social, commercial, and psychological discourses, his allusions to painting, poetry, advertising, cinema, comic books, Marx, Freud, Laurel and Hardy, Rimbaud, Che, and whoever else may fit even tangentially into his encyclopedia of culture, allow him to make a film an ordered focus of disorder that directs us how to find our way through the oppression of cultural signs. Makavejev's disorder is both greater and narrower. He attempts to deal with the fracturing and repression of sexuality in contemporary society and to examine that fracturing as a political phenomenon. His theme is that political and sexual liberation must go together. In his best-known film, *W.R.: Mysteries of the Organism* (1971), he creates a kind of flip-card effect in which a variety of images—some making up a documentary on the life and work of Wilhelm Reich, others documenting early-seventies sexual-encounter therapies (much of the film was made in America), still others creating a narrative fiction of a sexually active Yugoslav who attempts to liberate a Russian ice-skating champion and gets her head cut off for her pains—knock against each other in an ultimately futile attempt to figure patterns of sexual life that are therapeutic rather than destructive. Makavejev cannot find the pattern, and his film keeps slipping away from points of discovery to areas of confusion. It is pro-socialist, anti-communist, celebrating sexuality with an adolescent's fervor, advocating sexual anarchism while laughing at it, and finally, perhaps even inevitably, equating sexuality with brutality. The repressed Russian responds to the Yugoslav woman's offer of sexual freedom by decapitating her. But her head lives! And at the end it smiles and speaks: "Cosmic rays streamed through our bodies. We pulsated to the vibrations of the universe. But he couldn't bear it. He had to go one step further. Vladimir is a man of noble impetuousness. A man of high ambitions, of immense energy. Romantic. Ascetic. A genuine Red fascist! Comrades, even now I'm not ashamed of my Communist past!"

Irony mixes with childishness, Reichian jargon with political confusion, and in the end little is revealed.[16] Makavejev is at his best when he indulges his technical facility at manipulating footage from various sources. At one point he cuts from a shot of Milena (the liberated Yugoslav) looking up at Vladimir (who has knocked her to the ground) to a shot of Stalin—that is, an actor playing Stalin in a late forties Soviet hagiographic film—looking down at her. The idea is interesting and the effect successful; based on the theories of the Russion filmmaker Lev Kuleshov, who pointed out that editing could erase any spatial barrier, it quickly establishes Makavejev's point about the sexual repressiveness inherent in conservative communism.

More importantly, this effect exemplifies the playfulness that is Makavejev's major talent and is revealed to better effect in an earlier film, *Innocence Unprotected* (1968). Here footage from the first Serbian talking picture (made in 1942)—a standard romantic melodrama—is intercut with newsreel footage of the Nazi occupation of Yugoslavia and a documentary on the surviving makers of the original film. Makavejev has a figure in the 1942 film look out a window and "see" the occupied city; the rape of a character is intercut with shots of Nazis. He connects melodrama with fascism and allows history to reveal itself as a combination of fictionalized reality and the reality of fiction—a dialectic common to many cinema modernists. But when that playfulness is applied to the complexities of sexual politics Makavejev gets confused and turns silly; in retrospect, *W.R.* appears not so much the revolutionary film it was thought to be, but a prophecy of the inward-turning, "self-realization" fetishism that diverted political activity—in America, at least—during the seventies.*

Sexuality is the most difficult subject for any artist to deal with, perhaps most difficult for a filmmaker, who must work either with or

* I have not seen *Sweet Movie,* which Makavejev made after *W.R.* By all accounts it continues his inquiry into sexual liberation more graphically, moving further toward pornography, as does his more recent *Montenegro.*

against the prevailing conventions of romantic love and decide where the boundaries of pornography lie; how to show—whether to show—the actual contact of bodies. But these are the least of the problems. The filmmaker who attempts to make some untraditional commentary on the subject, desires perhaps to extend the sexual into a wider context, has to fight a number of other conventions and contradictions. There is a prevailing belief that sexuality is a human activity separate and cut off from a political and social context. Sexuality is seen as withdrawal, a removal of two people's presence from the social realm that involves an unassaultable claim to privacy and involvement only with one another. But at the same time, "too much" sexuality, or sexuality not legalized by marriage or homosexually oriented, challenges societal norms and is looked upon as dangerous precisely because the withdrawal it threatens is too great. Homosexuality represents not only an unknown experience to a majority of people, but a threat of anarchy, a denial of procreation and of the ordered, accountable process of pairing which is a major event upon which societies base their continuity. Feminism as well threatens the orderly perpetuation of hierarchies in a culture, not to mention the romantic myths of dominance and passivity that have made possible both the melodramatic dreams of societies and their oppressive realities.[17] That sexuality and the social order are intimately connected, the ideology of power reflected from one to the other, is clear to any rational analysis. Yet the conventions that keep them separate are powerful.

Thus a double prohibition faces a filmmaker who attempts to examine sexuality as part of the social order. Not only is art supposed to be separate from politics; sexuality is too. Intertwining the sexual, psychological, and political into an imaginative form, insisting they are inseparable, runs high risks of condemnation and confusion, high enough so that few filmmakers will take on the task. Ingmar Bergman's work is obsessed with the psychology of sexuality, but refuses to look at it beyond the couple or the individual. His studies in emotional agony and the pains of relationships are made in a vacuum. His characters live on the periphery of the world—on an island, if possible—working out their sufferings among themselves, tearing at one another, confessing, accusing, hurting, being hurt. They continually seek a universal and never-defined love without the benefit of understanding how "love" operates outside the confines of the Bergman two-shot. The background—the world—stays in soft focus. Even when he chooses a subject that forces him to confront history, as he does in *The Serpent's Egg* (1977), set in Berlin in 1923, world events become a foil against which his characters can be tested and destroyed. For Bergman, if history exists at all, it is a paranoid force that crushes rather than explains. As I noted earlier, his work is the contemporary consummation of melodrama, and makes clear the difficulties that need to be overcome by a filmmaker who would examine sexuality and its attendant psychology in other than a closed, melodramatic context.

We have already seen some attempts at probing and questioning the limits and delimitations of sexuality, love, and the psychology of relationships. Solás's film *Lucía* and Fassbinder's work in general explore the way melodrama has deformed sexuality and how that form can be reworked so that both it and its content contribute to an understanding of how we are affected by it. The extraordinary thing about a film like Fassbinder's *Fox and His Friends* (*Faustrecht der Freiheit*) is the way it takes the sexual orientation of its characters for granted and thereby removes much of the threat this might otherwise have. By placing its homosexual characters within the conventional melodramatic context of a poor workingman falling in love out of his class and suffering for it, Fassbinder makes form and content clash. His emphasis on the economic opportunism and class snobbery practiced by Fox's middle-class lover, and the lover's friends and family (including an obligatory dinner scene in which Fox appalls the company by the way he eats), places sexuality in a social perspective, demonstrating that emotional suffering is as much a product of class and social attitudes as it is of psycho-sexual attitudes and that oppression occurs on many levels simultaneously. A homosexual is oppressed by the culture as a whole because of his sexual choice and within the subculture he chooses is oppressed further by hierarchies and betrayals that duplicate the attitudes of the larger culture.

Fox approaches the problem of linking subjectivity, sexuality, and the behavior of the society at large through a parody of melodramatic modes. Three other very different works offer alternate approaches. Godard's *Masculin-féminin* (1966) explores various points of contact between the personal and the social worlds. Fassbinder's *In a Year of Thirteen Moons* (1978) goes far beyond *Fox* in its examination of sexual oppression, developing a critique of the fascism of everyday life. Bertolucci's *Last Tango in Paris* has become the reference point for the treatment of sexuality in contemporary cinema.

From *Breathless* through *Sauve qui peut* (*La Vie*), Godard has tried to figure out how a man and a woman could exist together. The ideal for his couples was always *tendresse,* a notion of mutual care and understanding often thwarted by the demands their own individuality made upon them and the demands upon that individuality made by others. The Godardian male was either too sensitive or too insensitive, the woman too independent or confused. By the time he reached *Pierrot le fou* (1965) he had run down most of the possibilities contemporary middle-class culture had to offer, and many of the formal possibilities his cinema had to offer in investigating the problem. He had invented new ways to confront it, forced the audience into a stance of objective contemplation, overlapped the concerns of the various couples he examined with impositions from the culture at large, counterpointed their lives with the intolerable directives on how to live those lives that came from the various commercial apparatuses of the culture (pimps in *My Life to Live,* advertising in *A Married Woman,* computerized control in *Alphaville*). In *Pierrot* the external directives are finally overwhelming. The inability of the Godardian male to deal with the intractability of an independent woman and discover an alternative to the romantic conflict of dominant and passive roles becomes destructive. Marianne, his gun-running girlfriend, betrays the film's would-be hero, Ferdinand. He shoots her, paints his face blue, wraps his head in dynamite, admits his lunacy, proclaims "a glorious death for a little man," and before he can finish the words blows himself up. With the explosion, Godard may have hoped to wipe out the romantic longings of hapless men that had plagued his thinking and remain so much a part of the romantic tradition. His success was only partial. For one thing, in the film the characters' spirits survive their destruction. In a final burst of romanticism, they meet in an apotheosis: the camera drifts skyward from the exploded Ferdinand and we hear his voice and Marianne's as if they have met in heaven.

This is a delightful learned allusion; the heavenly voices refer to events in a film by the Japanese director Kenji Mizoguchi. But they are also an indication of how difficult it was for Godard to throw off his romanticism. Despite his sensitivity he could not, and still cannot, deal with a situation in which his men and women struggle equally together. Only the Jane Fonda character in *Tout va bien*—the film in which Godard most successfully examined the way sexual roles are determined by social hierarchies—comes close to being a fully formed and eloquent individual who does not destroy her male partner. Otherwise, even in the most radical films of the late sixties and early seventies, where he adopted a feminist critique, there was still the sense that he was forcing himself into a rational stance on this particular issue—a stance so forced that he could easily slip out of it. *Sauve qui peut* returns to the perspective of *Pierrot le fou.* The film begins with an image of the sky, the camera panning left, back down to earth, returning to the realm of *Pierrot* and the same despairing examination of heterosexual relationships.

This is not to say that Godard was completely at the mercy of romantic conventions. He always questioned them, examined them for their ironies and lies, and after *Pierrot* always attempted to see them as part of larger events within the culture. In *Pierrot* something important happens: allusions to the Vietnamese war make their appearance; and the ramifications of that war nag at Godard's conscience and his characters' in every film he makes from then to the mid-seventies, another obstacle to the withdrawal of a couple into themselves. In *Masculin-féminin,* the film that followed *Pierrot,* the war, the conflicts created by an awareness of a troubled culture and a violent society, provide a context for a more objective study of the romantic couple. Here Godard reverted to the small black-and-white

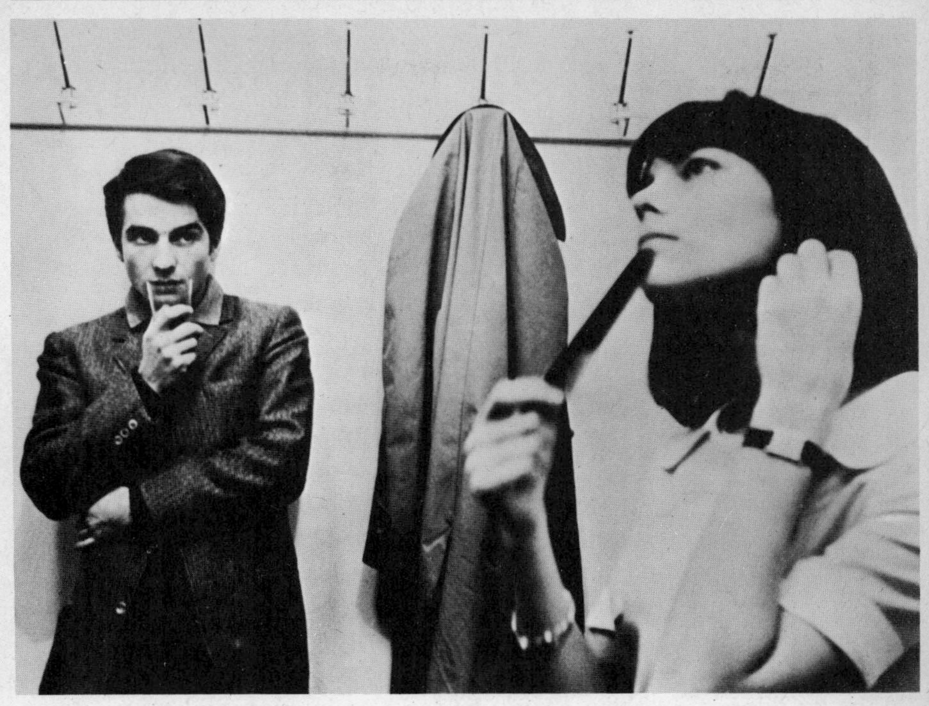

Paul and Madeleine (Jean-Pierre Léaud, Chantal Goya). *Masculin-féminin* (Museum of Modern Art Film Stills Archive).

image (*Pierrot* was in wide-screen color). The film is set in Paris (*Pierrot*—Godard's *North by Northwest*—follows its couple through the country to the Mediterranean); its subjects are late adolescents, who are observed coolly, from a distance, in long gray shots, their dialogue struggling against the noises of cafés and traffic, their attempts at understanding themselves interrupted by people killing each other on the subways, knifing themselves on the streets, immolating themselves in protest against the war. Sections of the film are introduced with titles that destroy continuity and with the sounds of gunshots. There is an almost neo-realist observation of individuals and their social environment; but unlike the neo-realists, Godard does not see them integrally; each section introduces new distractions and strains on the main characters and their relationships. The focal figure is Paul (Jean-Pierre Léaud), a young man who works as a public opinion survey taker and who attempts to love Madeleine, a budding pop singer. Their love is continually imposed upon by violence, by the commercial world Madeleine inhabits, by the world of consumers imposed upon Paul in his work. In one sequence he interviews a celebrity, "Mademoiselle 19 ans," a vacuous young lady with vacuous responses, a woman rubbed clean of any personality and insight. Godard titles the sequence "Dialogue with a Consumer Product," and ends it with the sound of a ringing cash register.

Masculin-féminin is a statement about intrusion, about the inability of couples to disengage themselves from the world and enter exclusive relationships. The random violence of that world, and even the gentle words of Paul's revolutionary friend Robert, disallow comfort, demand attention. And in the end, Madeleine finds it impossible to give herself over to romance, while Paul discovers that his work confounds and confuses individuality, distorts his own ideas and those of the people he interviews. She is caught up in the pop world (and may also be involved in a lesbian affair); he seeks an interior wholeness: "A philosopher is a man who pits his conscience against opinion: To have a conscience is to be open to the world. To be faithful is to act as if time did not exist. Wisdom would be if one could see life, really see, that would be wisdom."[18] But this is a dream of a past humanism that is no longer possible, for Paul or for Godard, because "life" is not whole and open to a clear perception; time *does* exist and history demands attention to all its unresolvable fragments. To be open to the world is to receive the shocks of its random violence. The major act of perception would be to understand that this violence is in fact not random, but an expression of an economic and political system that does violence to its members in a variety of ways, from war to turning people into things whose major function is to consume. That we begin to consume each other is less of a mystery when we are allowed to see how small consumptions grow and become overwhelming. Paul is himself overwhelmed. He dies at the end of the film, though we don't see it, only hear the reports given to the police by Madeleine and her friend. The death may have been suicide, or an accident. Paul wanted to take a photo of their new apartment; he stepped back to get a good composition and fell out the window. He died, that is, attempting to compose a view. For the "children of Marx and Coca-Cola" an attempt to see the world in all its parts is dangerous, even destructive. The filmmaker can just barely keep one step ahead of the characters and their sufferings and attempt to see the jagged parts of their lives that they cannot fit together. The characters themselves are subjected to those parts and hurt by them. The last words of Madeleine, the last words in the film, are "I don't know . . . I'm not sure."[19]

Masculin-féminin is a cold and funny film. The emotional and physical atrocities committed around the main characters are terrible only in their resonances, not their presentation. The dialogues of Paul, Robert, Madeleine, and Catherine are cool and detached, and the more intriguing for that. Godard (as always) allows us to listen and observe without directing our feelings. Though the film has been called grim and despairing, these are emotions that would have to be slipped into it by the viewer.[20] As a reverie about potentials for despair, it does not look upon the potentials despairingly. Rather it sees them as material upon which to build perceptions of how individuals operate among themselves and others. Paul's persistence is full of energy and delight, and his failure not tragic because its context is so clearly delineated. His failure in fact becomes our success and Godard's. The film permits us to integrate those elements that act to disintegrate the characters. In *Masculin-féminin* Godard observes disintegration lovingly. He still has tenderness for his characters and hope for what his audience may learn from them. The tenderness vanishes in *Weekend* (1967), where the voraciousness of the consumer extends to cannibalism, and the human form, as well as human relationships, is picked clean of any imaginable gentleness.

The cannibal metaphor, the devouring of the soul, was taken up years later by Fassbinder. *In a Year of Thirteen Moons* is a film of such despair that only Fassbinder's determination to regard his subject distantly, persistently, and with grim humor, to diminish emotional intensity by denying spectator identification with the characters, makes it bearable. More subjective than anything Godard has done, it was made as a response to a dreadful event in Fassbinder's own life—the suicide of his lover—and it was made almost singlehandedly, written, photographed, and edited by the director. Perhaps it is a mark of Fassbinder's talent that, given the personal nature of its origin and creation, the finished work does not stand as a subjective lament, nor does it indulge in the hermetic or obscurantist façade that is sometimes associated with "subjective cinema." Fassbinder was as antiromantic a filmmaker as any working today (matched only by Buñuel). Therefore, the pain suffered by the filmmaker and expressed in the film is situated objectively, and although the film studies the breakdown and death of an individual, that process occurs in a way that parallels a larger breakdown in social relations. Like all of Fassbinder's films, it becomes an analysis of capitalism and the distortion of relationships created by that economic system on every level.

The film is about mutilation and self-destruction. Its central character is a transsexual named Elvira (*née* Erwin, played by Volker Spengler, a frequent actor in Fassbinder's films whose chameleonlike talent makes him hardly recognizable from one film to the next), a figure of such innocence that her/his grotesqueness emerges not from what she has allowed to be done to his body but from the matter-of-factness with which she accepts it and allows it to destroy her. Elvira's past is pieced together throughout the film in the various narrative episodes that roughly knit it together. As Erwin, she was married and had a child. Erwin went to work for, and fell in love with, a certain Anton Saitz, a man who was in a concentration camp during the war, wanted to go to America when he was released, and got as far as Frankfurt, where he became a small-time racketeer in the meatpacking business and ran a whorehouse along totalitarian lines. He is now an enormously powerful landlord, a ruler and a destroyer. He has become a fascist, an embodiment of that which once imprisoned him, and the password that gains one entrance to his presence is "Bergen-Belsen." "Foreclosing is the big field with a real future,"

Elvira is told by Anton's guard when she goes to visit him in his skyscraper office after a long separation. Anton, who forecloses on his tenants, foreclosed on Elvira, took advantage of weakness and put her out of her body. When Erwin expressed his love, Anton told him it was too bad he was not a woman. So Erwin went off to Casablanca and returned as Elvira.

If the relationship between Saitz and Elvira parallels that of master and slave, on another level it parallels that of Dean Martin and Jerry Lewis: a relationship of fraudulent sophisticate and childlike fool, user and abused. The association is made quite literal. In one of the most lunatic sequences in the film, when Elvira comes to confront Saitz, she discovers him and his lieutenants watching a videotape of a routine from a Martin and Lewis movie. The men prance about, mimicking the movements on the TV screen, and Elvira joins them. The sequence confirms Elvira's status as passive follower and willing victim;[21] it continues the bizarre, almost dreamlike aura that surrounds every episode in the film; and it climaxes a phenomenon of contemporary European cinema: the almost perverse love of Jerry Lewis by many a major *cinéaste* since the late fifties. Godard has stated that he admires Lewis as an *auteur* and as a composer of comic sequences, but it is in Fassbinder's film that the darker side of the admiration appears. European intellectuals admire Lewis (more accurately, the Lewis persona) because he is such a perfect fool, with no sophistication, no self-awareness, no leavening to his simplemindedness other than an equally simpleminded sentimentality and childlike morality. No such characters exist in contemporary European film, nor in European literary history, where the character of the fool is almost always craftily insightful and wise. The admiration for Lewis is therefore made up of amazement and condescension, which in Fassbinder's film is turned into pity and sadness. Although Saitz mimics Lewis's antics, it is ultimately Elvira who is mocked as the Lewis surrogate and continually humiliated; while lacking Lewis's protective silliness and innocence, she has a sentimentality that helps destroy her.

In *Masculin-féminin,* the acts of destruction that surround the characters and finally involve them are, from the spectator's point of view, dialectically constructive. That is, the filmmaker positions the spectator so that relationships can be made by understanding the *un*making of relationships that occur within the film. We are not permitted such a privileged positioning in *Thirteen Moons*. Fassbinder does not allow us into the fiction or let us lose sight of any of its elements; but neither does he allow us a place of intellectual and emotional security from which to judge it. To some extent this is due to the expressionist nature of the film, for here Fassbinder yields to that major tradition of his country's cinema and subdues the usually rigorous Brechtian structure of his work. Every space that Elvira inhabits, every sequence of the film, echo the mutilation and disintegration of her self. The *mise-en-scène* is dark; each shot seems to have been made in available light with little enhancement. The viewer must often seek out the image, discern it, locate it, and then deal with the emotional terrors it contains, which reflect those of Elvira's psyche. Early in the film, after being thrown out by a lover, knocked down by a car, and looked after by Zora, a whore who literally picks her up from the gutter, she visits the slaughterhouse in which she once worked and where she first knew Saitz. "Blood and death give an animal's life meaning," she says in a kind of fascistic reflection that indicates the state of her confusion and damage.

During the slaughterhouse sequence, Fassbinder intercuts shots of Elvira and Zora with shots of the killing and dismemberment of the cattle, while on the sound track Elvira comments on her past and recites hysterically the lines she used to read with her lover (who was an actor). The sequence spins off a number of allusions. Primarily it reflects, in a hideously comic manner, Elvira's own butchered state, what she permitted to have done to her body; the way she allowed her personality to be devoured. The butchers in the abattoir cut the cattle into smaller and smaller bits as Elvira's disembodied voice speaks of the transformation of her former lover from a would-be actor to "the kind of man they tell us we're supposed to be: active, willing to make decisions, independent," while all the time he lived off her. By the time she recounts how he used to ask about the size of the penises of the men she slept with to support them, Fassbinder is cutting to the small remains of the cattle lying about the floor. Emotional and physical degradation are linked, and the obsession with physicality is given a brutal literalness.

The sequence calls to mind Georges Franju's short film *Le Sang des bêtes,* a documentary of slaughterhouses which begins with an ironic image of two lovers kissing in a pastoral setting. Even more it evokes the slaughterhouse montage in Eisenstein's *Strike.* That sequence is purely political in nature: the killing of cattle is intercut with the killing of strikers by soldiers, and its political point is made by the brutality of both sets of images, the indication that workers are considered to be no better than cattle. The sequence in *Thirteen Moons* is not a montage in the Eisensteinian sense. All the action is set in one place and the actual montage is of image and spoken word. (This is a kind of montage that Eisenstein, in fact, encouraged for sound film.)[22] If such a hybrid term can hold meaning, it might be called an expressionist montage. The state of Elvira's body and mind is made present–perhaps suggested into presence–by the images of the slaughterhouse and her accompanying commentary. Instead of discrete images conflicting with each other, the slaughterhouse reflects Elvira's subjective state, giving distressing meaning to her words.

She has been and is being dismembered and consumed by the intolerable demands of sexual role-playing. Fassbinder and Spengler so construct her character that she becomes a screen on which are projected almost all the conflicting patterns of sexual and emotional manipulations that can be acted out by one person upon another. Erwin/Elvira has played most of them: man, woman, husband, father, worker, provider, passive lover, abused lover, chattel, willing surrenderer of identity, of sexuality, of personality. The slaughterhouse becomes a manifest image of the brutalities latent in the roles, a metaphor for the fascism of the spirit. Other versions of spiritual murder and dismemberment follow. Elvira seeks out Saitz and finds, across the street from his office building, a man who stares. He worked for Saitz until he got cancer of the kidney, and since Saitz cannot stand having sick people around, he was fired. For seventeen months he has stared at Saitz's office every day from ten until six. In a long take, broken only by a shot of Saitz's building, we see this man stand and stare and deliver himself of a monologue in which we learn of Saitz's past and this man's present as a starer, one more defiled individual whose impotence is manifested in his obsessive need to keep the cause of his defilement perpetually in sight, fetishizing the building of his former boss (who, as a landlord, is duly represented by a building), compounding his own status as an object.

Later, when Elvira finally enters Saitz's building, she meets a black man in a lobby preparing to hang himself. The space is shadowy and cavernous, with a red light flashing on and off, creating the most dreamlike sequence in the film and, despite what happens in it, the most detached and contemplative. Because the setting is so dark and the events so strange, a distancing effect occurs, and because the two participants are so matter of fact the whole sequence takes on aspects of bizarre comedy, something in the manner of Samuel Beckett. The man goes about the business of setting up his noose; Elvira, in a black dress and veil, sits in a corner, eating bread and cheese, chatting with the suicide (commenting upon how campy it is to eat bread and cheese, recalling that Anton, the former meat packer, hated meat, and deciding that life would be very sad without a little nostalgia). Their discussion reveals further the self-loathing Elvira feels as well as the ease with which she accepts the words of others. The suicide delivers a ridiculous speech about life and death, a nihilist's call (though based roughly on Schopenhauer) to end misery in the most direct way possible. "By the way," he says, "it is wrong to see the negation of the will to live in terms of suicide as a negative act. On the contrary, negating the will to live is in itself an acceptance of the will, since negation means renouncing not life's suffering but its joys. The suicide accepts life, rejects only the conditions under which it has been offered to him. . . ." Elvira can only respond by saying, "I think you better do it now." He invites her to watch and carries out his task, swinging in the blinking red light.[23]

I imagine that, for someone who has not seen this film, this description may confirm a suspicion that it, and perhaps all of the new Ger-

Reflections of despair: Elvira (Volker Spengler). *In a Year of Thirteen Moons* (New Yorker Films).

man cinema, is unbearably grim. But even in this most despairing of films, Fassbinder, like his colleagues, like all of the filmmakers discussed here, refuses to subject his audience to unearned and unnecessary emotional stress or to a state of emotional complicity. The despair the film deals with is observed through expressionist blocks of grotesque exaggeration and ironic comment. Even at its most conventionally melodramatic, the film prevents any forcing of emotions that would allow us to evade confrontation with its images. The images instead negotiate these emotions with us, offering us not the emotions themselves but ways of comprehending them. At one point we learn about Elvira's childhood, a bit of exposition that, in a conventional film, would make us secure by offering the "motivation" for the current state of the hero. His father was in a concentration camp when

Erwin was born, and his mother had the child brought up by nuns. A couple fell in love with Erwin and wanted to adopt him. That was impossible because he was a legitimate child and his father—who apparently never learned of the child's existence—could not give his consent. The resulting tension turned Erwin from a cunningly affectionate child to a withdrawn little thief whom the nuns feared and hated. This atrociously touching and unhappy story is undercut by the telling. The information is provided by one of the nuns (played by Lilo Pempeit, Fassbinder's mother), who brought Erwin up and who tells the tale as the camera follows her pacing around the cloister, a copy of Schopenhauer under her arm. Zora, who has come with Elvira to learn about the past, is dressed in her prostitute outfit; Elvira is in a white hat and polka-dot dress. They make an unholy trio, with a fourth party present, figured in Saitz's building, which looms over them.

The sequence ends, appropriately enough, with Elvira swooning at the retelling of her past. We, however, learn very little but that she was unloved. In the telling, however, more elements of perversity are added to the narrative, more marks of Elvira's disbarment from human community, and more reminders to the spectator of his or her own disbarment from a direct understanding of this character and the world she inhabits. The elements of the sequence refuse to yield rational and coherent information; the sentimental content of the nun's tale is contradicted by the form in which it is told and we get, finally, no satisfying explanation of why Elvira has become what she is. Nothing here or in any of the film's sequences offers comfort or affirmation of love, friendship, support, security, or even emotional continuity other than a basic and insistent sadness.

When at one point in the film Fassbinder does introduce a familiar, domestic scene, he disrupts it by indicating how out of place it is. Elvira visits her wife and daughter, who are having a meal in a lovely, sunlit garden. It is one of the brightest sequences in the film, filled with domestic chatter. The mother wants Elvira to tell her daughter to eat more; they discuss what the daughter will do with her life. Elvira tells them her despair and asks if she can come back to them.

But once again, a number of elements make this sequence both terribly sad and terribly ridiculous. Just prior to it, Elvira has brought Zora and Saitz back to her apartment. Immediately, the prostitute friend and the destroyer-landlord begin making love as Elvira watches: further humiliation that leads to further mutilation. Elvira attempts to deny her present state, cuts her hair off, dresses in men's clothing, and goes off to her family. In that sunlit, domestic place, their first reaction upon seeing the reincarnated husband and father is laughter. The entire situation is skewed; the woman-father cannot find a center, a place of emotional safety, and this lack is echoed in the composition of the scene: when the daughter regains her composure and embraces her father the camera pans away from them slightly, unbalancing the frame. The sequence is as dark as every other event in which Elvira takes part, and no less expressionistic than the others, despite its sunniness. The domestic unit is as unreceptive to Elvira as any other, for her initial act of mutilation has cut off all chances for integration.

But this does not imply that Fassbinder made a cautionary, moral-ridden film: if you have yourself castrated you deny nature and will live a life of such misery that it will only result in the ultimate castration, the removal of your life itself. Elvira is passive and pitiable, but she becomes part of a trauma greater than her own, a trauma at once psychological and political. She is the victim of fascism past and present, and all the characters of the film carry the spirit of Bergen-Belsen with them. (A glimpse of Chilean dictator Augusto Pinochet on a television set confirms the extended metaphor.) It is no fanciful joke that this is Anton Saitz's password, for the former concentration camp inmate and present Kapo of free enterprise manifests the camp's spirit, and Elvira, like Saitz himself, remains its victim. But again a warning against reducing the film's meaning is necessary, for it is not an allegory offering a simple proposition that we are all victims of fascism, suffering together in the great concentration camp of life. On some level Fassbinder wanted us to understand this, but he was not a maker of universal statements. He was rather the maker of large indiscretions, of unseemly and tasteless acts committed by one character against another or the self, acts that simply repeat the brutalities that are part of history and therefore part of the present. The ease with which these brutalities are submerged within the familiar patterns of melodrama makes it necessary for him and for us to wrench them out, reposition them so that they can be seen more discretely—or more indiscretely. They are not permitted to remain on the personal level of aberrant acts committed by perverse individuals. Fassbinder forces them into the context of their culture, and this makes them more disturbing than they would be if left as individual aberrations.

During the last sequences of the film, as Elvira's acquaintances come to her apartment and discover her body on the bedroom floor (she has committed suicide, though we do not see the act), with Zora and Saitz making love in the bed next to it, we hear her voice on the sound track delivering a long confessional. In it Fassbinder permits the expression of sentiments we are used to hearing in film. Elvira says her need for love is like a scream. She weeps and talks of her suffering: "Love is . . . or was . . . hope, some kind of hope, I guess. I mean things like tenderness or maybe need . . . or desire. Maybe I wanted to find out what those words really mean. . . ." What those words really mean for her are castration and death. "As long as movies are sad, life remains fun," says a character in *The Third Generation*. And Fassbinder must have his fun, or the pathos would overwhelm him and us. As Elvira's voice incants her misery, the acquaintances gather, passing inspection by Saitz's black guard who stands at the door. The nun who earlier told the sad tale of Elvira's childhood comes up the stairs to the apartment. The guard frisks her.

The fear of being overwhelmed is not the only thing that forced Fassbinder simultaneously to embrace melodrama and to push it away. He also needed to find out what there is in melodrama that still speaks to us about suffering without inviting us to share it (which obviates our understanding it) or directing us how and when to feel. *In a Year of Thirteen Moons,* like most of Fassbinder's work, is disruptive in the extreme, much more than Godard's. In this disruptiveness lies the desire that he shared with Godard to give the emotional life a context and provide a way of seeing connections. Anton Saitz—former concentration camp victim, whoremonger, butcher, landlord—is not just a convenient villain, any more than Elvira, who changed her sex on a whimsical suggestion, is a simple victim. The roles shift about easily in a society that provides justification and encouragement for the perpetuation of villainy and victimization. Psychology and sociology merge. Saitz victimizes as many people as possible in his role of grand landlord—"foreclosing is the big field, with a real future." Elvira victimizes herself, mutilating her body and spirit, letting herself be devoured until there is nothing left but death. But her self-mutilation and her suicide are the only irreversible acts in the film; everything else can be changed.

Fassbinder's "left-wing melancholy" (a phrase borrowed from Walter Benjamin by Richard Dyer)[24] shows itself in his reveries upon oppression and the self-defeat that occurs when that oppression is internalized by the individual and thereby perpetuated so that it acts as a destructive force on all levels. His characters are not "alienated" from society but are rather too much a part of it (and Fassbinder makes sure we see the connections), too ready and willing to play its hurtful games. In the cruelties visited upon them and that they visit upon each other are the clues as to how those cruelties might be avoided.

Bernardo Bertolucci's perspective is similar; his methods of inquiry utterly different. Neither melancholy nor perverse, he is more interested in broad gestures and intense confrontations than in distancing the spectator. He luxuriates in his *mise-en-scène,* opening the screen space to political or psychological investigations in which history and the individual struggle, with the individual usually losing. Time is often a central subject in Bertolucci's work. Like Alain Resnais, whose characters are determined by the obsessive presence of time and memory, Bertolucci subjects his characters to structures of the past that help to define, if not explain, their actions and entrap them in their own past or that of others. This gambit is developed in *The Spider's Stratagem* (1970), a film Bertolucci made for Italian television, and the one in which his lush and active camera style is first manifested. Based upon a Jorge Luis Borges piece, "Theme of the Hero and Traitor," it probes the Borgesian principle of imaginative slippage, the movements, sometimes barely perceptible, between various layers of the realities created by fiction and the perfectly undependable temporal relationships within those creations. Working in film, and influenced by his native neo-realism, Bertolucci articulates these slippages in carefully defined images which create at once a strong physical presence and an uncertain temporal space.

In the film, a young man, Athos Magnani, Jr., returns to his home town of Tara (the never-never land of *Gone with the Wind*) to seek information about his father, a great anti-fascist hero and martyr during the reign of Mussolini. He discovers that, far from being a hero, his father in fact betrayed the town, was probably a fascist spy, and when discovered as such by his friends, planned an elaborate theatrical death for himself, "a legendary death of a hero. . . . All Tara will become a great theater." He arranged for his friends to assassinate him during a performance of *Rigoletto* (as with Visconti, a major influence, the opera metaphor reigns over Bertolucci's work), an assassination replete with literary devices, warnings, and prophecies. The plan seems to have worked, and too well, for Tara became locked into the moment of Magnani senior's death, slipping out of history, confusing the man with the image he created for himself, existing in the eternal delusion of its fascist past. The delusionary and hallucinatory state of this existence outside time is expressed in a number of ways. First, the movement of the camera as it follows Magnani junior's quest for the past is insistent and ominous—advancing before him as he walks through the town, enclosed by its buildings on either side; tracking with him along walls; and entrapping him even when it is held steady, as in an extraordinary set of shots in which we see two men talking to each other in closeup, while behind them in the night Athos approaches from the distance with his bicycle. When he gets up to them, Bertolucci cuts to a complete 180-degree reverse shot of the two old men, still talking face to face, though their faces are now on opposite sides, as Athos retreats in the distance.

(The so-called 180-degree rule constitutes a fundamental stricture in American filmmaking. A cut must never be made 180 degrees across the compositional plane to the "other side" of the image, for this would be inexplicable to the audience. Bertolucci, along with many another European filmmaker, relishes the opportunity to "break" this rule and thereby break the illusory spatial continuity of the American style.)

Within the foreboding and seductive visual design of the film, Bertolucci does other things to impress upon us the town's drop from time. In the flashbacks with which Magnani junior pieces the puzzle together, the characters do not change in age, and the actor who plays Magnani junior plays the father as well. "Present" and "past" will occur within the space of the same shot, or collide in a montage. This is not merely technical gimmickry; in fact Bertolucci transcends his considerable technical facility to create something like a dream vision—a dream based not in the subjectivity of a single individual, but in the shared aberration of a group who impose their dream on an intruder. Young Athos cannot escape his father or the paralyzing myth his father created. At the end of the film, Athos junior waits for the train that will take him from Tara. The loudspeaker announces its increasing delay, and the camera tracks along the tracks, which become increasingly overgrown with weeds. Athos does not leave. He may not even have arrived, perhaps has existed there continually, entangled with his father in the same web.

In Godard's *A Married Woman,* someone recounts a story told him by a Monsieur Rossellini, about a parade along the Champs-Elysées of former concentration camp victims, dressed up in their old striped prison uniforms. "Ten years after. Well, naturally, they weren't still as thin as skeletons like when they came out of Dachau, or Mauthausen. They had eaten, they'd earned money since then . . . Of course, they were living normally, they'd got fat . . . It just didn't look right on them. Memory had got it all wrong, because they just didn't remember that they had changed. . . ."[25] The fallacy of historical memory intrigues both Fassbinder and Bertolucci, though in very different ways. One success of fascism is its ability to make people forget about it; its brutality is so enormous that it is difficult to believe when it occurs and readily forgotten when past.[26] Many European filmmakers attempt to refresh the memory, correct the fallacies, and remind us of the reality of its presence then and now. Fassbinder demonstrates in film after film the fascism of everyday life. In *The Spider's Stratagem,* Bertolucci alludes to fascism as a web of betrayal, theatrical gesture, and lies that entraps everyone permanently. In the films that followed—*The Conformist* and *Last Tango in Paris*—Bertolucci deals in different ways with the realities and memories of fascism: in a re-creation of history in the first film; displaced and confused in the contemporary world in the second. In each this subject is filtered and reflected through sexuality.

The Conformist is one of a group of films, beginning with *Rome, Open City* and of which Visconti's *The Damned* is a major example, that attempt to discuss fascism as a manifestation of perverted or misaligned sexuality. One source for this is perhaps Wilhelm Reich's *The Mass Psychology of Fascism* as well as the historical realities of Nazi experimentations, eugenics, and fascism's obsessively male-centered ideology. Fascism is an ideology of denial and destruction, the romance of sacrifice and conquest brought to a climax in the abjuring of any human quality but the ability to kill and die. In truth it does not emerge from aberrant sexuality nor lead to it. Aberration occurs in its turning sexuality, as it turns any other human activity, into a thing to be used in a destructive way. Fascists are not degenerates (that is too easy an excuse) but the cause of degeneration; yet sexual perversity remains a favored means of explaining fascism or demonstrating its effects.

Rossellini does not make much of the matter in *Rome, Open City,* beyond allowing his Nazi commandant to be fey. Visconti in *The Damned,* however, attempts to define Nazism as an incremental series of sexual perversions. Bertolucci is more subtle. His conformist is an ordinary Italian fascist who, fearing he is outside the bourgeois norm of sexual behavior, decides that the best way to prove his normalcy is to work for the party. Marcello Clerici (Jean-Louis Trintignant) is a little man who recalls a homosexual incident as a child during which, as he remembers, he shot the man who attempted to seduce him. His adult response to this event is a lunge toward respectability, away from his drug addict mother and his father in a lunatic asylum (he was maddened by his own early contact with the fascists—he once met Hitler) and into the arms of a dull middle-class woman and the party, which gives him a job as petty spy, finger-man, and assassin.

The narrative content of the film has the proper components of political melodrama: an anguished protagonist with a disturbing past; an assignment to kill a Resistance worker living in Paris who was his professor in college; two sexual interests, his own wife and the professor's, who offers herself both to Clerici and to his wife in order to save her husband. Rather than squelch the melodrama, Bertolucci instead internalizes it, makes it part of the perceptual pattern of the central figure, creating a complex first-person point of view. First-person narrative in film is not the same as in literature; we do not see "through" Clerici's eyes but rather are permitted to inhabit his world with his sensibilities, perceive it in a manner that is analogous to his own state of mind. And since that mind is caught in a shadowy world of repressed desire and misdirected energies, all of its activities colored by an uncertain perception of the past, the narrative develops by means of perceptual dislocation, contemplating an individual who sees things only partially and misunderstands the little he sees.

Bertolucci constructs a complex time scheme for his character, beginning his narrative in the midst of things, in a *film noir* hotel room in Paris complete with blinking neon sign outside where Clerici awaits final directions for the political drama he hopes to enact. The drive to the place where the assassination will occur, a purposive movement through a wintry landscape during which Clerici and Manganiello, the agent assigned by the party to watch over him, discuss their job, provides a frame into which are inserted flashbacks—in achronological order—that gather together the incidents leading to this moment. The incidents themselves are disruptive and disrupted, visually disorienting, some of them bordering on the surreal. Bertolucci adapts three seemingly unadaptable styles and mixes them within his own *mise-en-scène:* the temporal montages of Resnais, the expressive architecture of Antonioni, and the vertiginous movements and engulfing spaces of Welles—particularly the Welles of *The Trial* (made in 1962, attacked by critics, unknown by audiences, but an influence on directors such as Godard, Herzog, Fassbinder, and Bertolucci).* Out of the mix, Bertolucci develops images of confusion and blindness and fragments of memories in reflections and half-light. Clerici is introduced to a party official in a radio studio where three women imitate the Andrews sisters and the reflection of a blind man (Clerici's friend and political guide) broadcasting Fascist Party propaganda that he reads with his fingertips can be seen on the studio glass. The images obscure figures and disorient the viewer; together with the narrative they reflect Clerici's disoriented state of mind. He goes to confession, where he recalls the childhood seduction by a chauffeur (Pierre Clementi) with flowing hair in images of long corridors and empty rooms, of sexual arousal and the shooting of his seducer. The priest takes enormous interest in the crime. Clerici assures the priest he wants now to atone, to build "a normal life" with a middle-class girl. "I'm confessing today for the sin I will commit tomorrow. Blood washes away blood. Whatever price society demands from me I will pay." The priest asks him if he belongs to a secret organization or a subversive group. "No, no. I'm a member of the organization which hunts down subversives." "Then you are absolved of all your sins."

It is the illogic of this kind of interchange that informs the film, an illogic that is chosen *as* logic by the fascist mind, with the result that it blanks out a clear understanding and coherent reading of experience. Bertolucci finds a controlling metaphor for Clerici's confused perceptions in Plato, in the great myth of the cave from *The Republic,* the story of chained prisoners facing a wall on which are projected

* While influenced by Welles, *The Conformist,* and to lesser extent *Last Tango,* have themselves had a great effect on two Italian-American directors, Francis Ford Coppola and Martin Scorsese. The visual and narrative style of Scorsese's *Taxi Driver* owes much to *The Conformist,* as does the lighting style of the two *Godfather* films. In *Godfather II,* Gastone Moschin, who plays Manganiello in *The Conformist,* acts the role of Fanucci, the Black Hander. For *Apocalypse Now* and *One from the Heart* Coppola used Bertolucci's regular cinematographer, Vittorio Storaro.

the shadows of real objects carried behind the backs of the prisoners by their captors. Clerici wrote his thesis on the subject and its explication forms the central set piece of the film, where Clerici and his former professor confront each other in a room and discuss the myth of the cave as their movements and the camera's in and out of shadow and light echo the words of the myth. It is a bravura passage in which the filmmaker calls attention to his own clarity of vision at the expense of the characters and by so doing focuses attention on the formal execution of the film, its thematic content, and the illusory quality of Clerici's life. He is one of Plato's prisoners, accepting as real his own shadowy memories, assuming the chains of an ideology built on falsehoods.

In his self-imposed blindness, Clerici sees things both he and we cannot be sure we are seeing. The shifting patterns of light and shadow in the sequence in which he and his professor discuss Plato, the movement of the characters in and out of silhouette, express the shifts in Clerici's own perceptions, shifts and confusions which Bertolucci occasionally allows us to share. For example, Anna (Dominique Sanda) turns up in the narrative twice before her main appearance as the professor's wife. At one time Clerici sees her lying across the desk of a fascist official in an enormous hallway that dwarfs the figures. On his way to Paris, when he stops to get further information about his assignment, he sees her again, this time as a prostitute in a strange museum-cum-brothel, where they embrace as she pronounces herself mad. There is no explanation given for her appearance in these two places, nor even any narrative assurance that it is supposed to be the same woman (though it is clearly the same actress, and Clerici tells Anna he met a woman who looked like her). As a visual enigma it is another echo of Clerici's emotional dislocation, the way in which he looks at all women as whores, and the way Anna presents herself as a whore in her attempts to prevent Clerici from murdering her husband.

She needn't have tried, for Clerici proves finally to be a simple coward, incapable of assassinating anyone or anything but his own conscience and memory. Manganiello, the good soldier, is left to carry out the task. "For my money, cowards, pederasts, Jews are all the same," he tells Clerici in disgust. "If it was up to me I'd line them all against the wall. Better, kill them at birth." Bertolucci is attracted to this bizarre murderer, this unthinking executor of orders, no doubt because there is no perversity to his actions, no apparent or hidden motives as with Clerici. He is not mysterious or devious and therefore perfectly understandable for what he is, a fascist killer. But the two make a fine pair. In fact, there are two fine pairs; Manganiello and Clerici, Clerici and the professor. Clerici is caught in the middle, right and left surround him; he is finally incapable of attaching himself to either; and like many a centrist gets destroyed by the movement around him. At a dance to which Clerici and the professor go with their wives (a sequence introduced by the camera's observing them next to a picture of Laurel and Hardy as if to emphasize Clerici's bumbling relationship to his former mentor as well as Manganiello, who watches them), he gets caught up in a swirl of bodies, drowning in the middle of activity, swept along in movement he wants no part of. That he seems to want to be part of the fascist movement and abjures the professor's Resistance work (Bertolucci himself does not seem to approve of the way the professor works, for he is depicted as weak, living in some luxury in Paris while his colleagues are imprisoned in Italy) only further indicates his passivity. Too frightened to act against the majority, he yields to it, though is still unable to act and in the end appears neither enigmatic nor confused, but merely despicable.

The assassination takes place in the snow. The professor and his wife are trapped by Manganiello on the road. Clerici sits paralyzed in his car as Manganiello's men stab the professor (in a sequence that, despite its setting, recalls the stabbing of Caesar in the Forum), then run down and shoot his wife, who is unable to get Clerici out of his car to aid her. This is the point to which the film's various time sequences lead, the point where all of Clerici's confusions and self-delusions are manifested in further self-delusion, confusion, and murder. ("Murder and melancholy," intones Clerici's father in the lunatic asylum, yielding up his arms to a straightjacket.) It is a sequence

Clerici (Jean-Louis Trintignant) at the dance: repressed, isolated. *The Conformist* (Museum of Modern Art Film Stills Archive).

that simultaneously clarifies and further disturbs our perception. The time leaps forward some years to the fall of Mussolini. We see Clerici, his wife, and a little daughter in a poor flat. The sequence is an imitation, a kindly parody even, of neo-realism and its squalid apartments and poor tenants. The flat is dark; there is a crucifix on the wall. An old man sits in the corner cradling a chicken on his lap. Clerici, older and plumper, puts his daughter to bed in a room with clouds painted on the walls. The radio announces Mussolini's downfall. The lights go out. Clerici goes out to the streets, "to see a dictatorship fall" and to meet his old friend, the blind propagandist, Italo. Once outside, the hallucinatory style that marks so much of the film returns. Lights flicker and swoop around the dark streets. Crowds flow by; a stone head of Mussolini is dragged through the streets.

As Clerici talks to Italo, telling him to remove his Fascist Party badge ("something has stuck to you"), he passes a familiar figure sitting in a wrecked courtyard with another man. It is Lino, the chauffeur, the man Clerici believes attempted to seduce him as a child and whom he thought he had killed. As Clerici confronts him, the camera tracks nervously around them in the dark by the fire the two gay men have lit for warmth. Clerici becomes hysterical and shouts at Lino that *he* is an assassin, that *he* killed the professor. Clerici's past–the "motivation" for his life–has come back and is now given the blame for his own bad conscience. His hysteria mounts and he denounces Italo as well. Lino flees. A crowd marches through and, like the dancers earlier, surrounds Clerici, sweeping Italo away and leaving Clerici alone with the other gay man in the dark. The camera, from the other side of an iron fence, tracks slowly to Clerici, who sits by a fire, his back to us. In the last shot of the film, Clerici turns toward the bars of the gate that separates him from our own gaze and looks, his face lit by the firelight.

These final images suggest again the myth of the cave, and Clerici is left imprisoned by shadows and his own bad memory. The images offer an easy reading and a simple explanation: a repressed homosexual has sublimated his insecurities into vicious political activity. But this is not enough. Certainly men have killed out of the anxieties of their own homophobia, but Bertolucci is not interested in presenting the case history of someone pathologically ill. He uses Clerici's sexual terrors as a place from which to begin an analysis rather than as the end of it, as a site of confusion that initiates a series of willful misinterpretations, wrong choices, and a desire for passive absorption into the ideological mainstream. One of the paradoxes of fascism is that it requires enormous cultural passivity for its brutalities to exist. Individuals must yield unquestioningly and agree that wrong choices are correct ones, that force and fear will gain for them what their own active engagement in political life will not. Shadows on the wall are accepted as real events and chains are mistaken for freedom.

Clerici is indeed like one of Plato's prisoners, living in a perceptual half-light, willing to accept the darkness and confuse cowardice and murder with a normal life.

Paul (Marlon Brando) in *Last Tango in Paris* is Clerici's precise opposite. He actively pursues not an entrance into, but an escape from, bourgeois life. In the pursuit he makes enormous errors, the creator of the film makes enormous errors, and this study of withdrawal into sexual anarchy becomes a male fantasy of a lunge for power and a desperate loss. But the mistakes of the film are only apparent as tracings beneath a powerful surface of rich images that attempt to articulate a web of despair. As in so many of the films we have been discussing, Bertolucci begins with the assumption that the contemporary world is, to a person of any sensitivity, a place of sadness and isolation, intractable to the spirit, resistant to intellect and emotions. The very first image of *Last Tango* (after the credits, behind which are portraits by Francis Bacon of distorted and anguished male and female figures) is a violent booming of the camera to Paul, who stands under the roar of the Paris Métro, hands over his ears, shouting, "Fucking God!" A middle-aged American in Paris whose wife has just violently killed herself, he is a figure of desolation, a heterosexual version of Fassbinder's Elvira, emotionally mutilated, his coherency destroyed.

But unlike Elvira and, more important, unlike Clerici, Paul does not seek a fruitless conciliation with the destroying world. Instead he attempts to withdraw completely into anonymous, solipsistic sexuality, to live in defiance of societal order and ritual, the nicety of "relationships" and the conventions of romance. His partner is Jeanne (Maria Schneider), a young girl and erstwhile free spirit, willing at first to engage with a stranger; more ambivalent and confused as they go on. Both attempt to find a solace from the unconscionable demands of a bourgeois life. Paul was a wanderer in the world until he married Rosa, who owned a poor Parisian hotel that was little better than a whorehouse. He was her helper in proprietorship; he shared her with another man; he was, it is implied, sexually at her mercy; and his final humiliation was her suicide. Jeanne is the

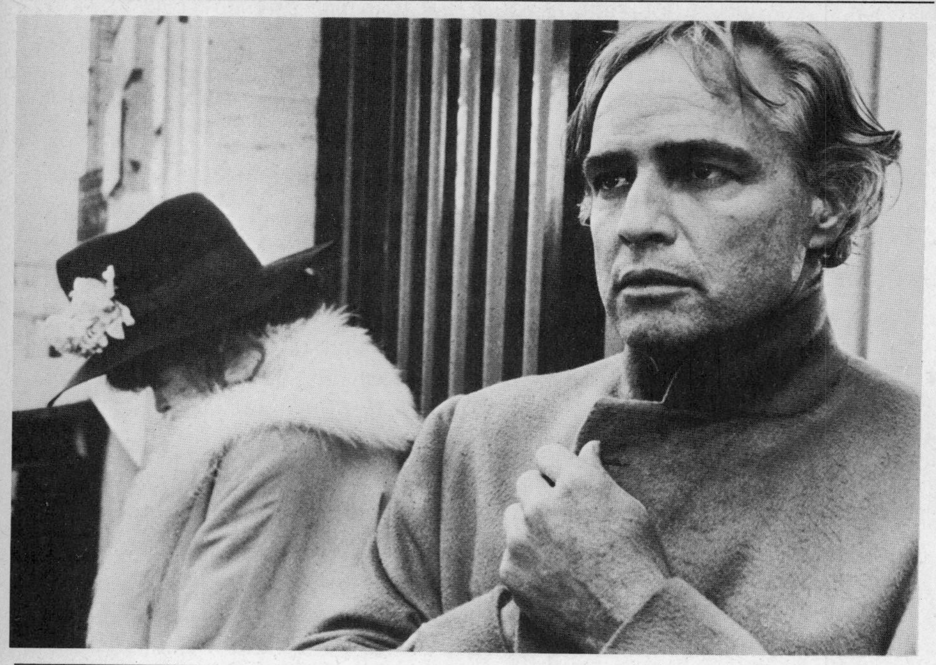

A figure of desolation. Paul (Marlon Brando) in *Last Tango in Paris* (Museum of Modern Art Film Stills Archive).

daughter of the French military middle class; her father fought against the Algerians in their war for independence. At the moment of her meeting Paul she is attempting to settle her own life by marrying Tom, a filmmaker, a hilarious parody of a New Wave film fanatic played by Jean-Pierre Léaud, who parodies the persona he himself created in many a Truffaut and Godard film.

The narrative of *Last Tango* is built from a series of confrontations and humiliations as Paul and Jeanne use each other to escape from a past and present made inescapable and inevitable by these very attempts to escape them. Paul tries to construct a sexual sanctuary for himself and Jeanne in an enormous flat in the Rue Jules Verne, a fantasy world bathed in shadow and golden light, where the only responsibilities will be to the penis and vagina. It will be a world of games and confessional and surrender of the self. Like any fantasy world, it does not hold up to the demands of reality, and whenever they leave their room, both become reabsorbed in the very demands they attempted to avoid. Jeanne's fiancé makes her into an object for his camera, turning their life into *cinéma vérité.* His superficiality is a direct (and perhaps too obvious) contrast to Paul's intensity and desire to deny any external impediments to what he regards as unsullied feeling and expression. For his part, whenever he leaves the room Paul is confronted by his immediate past and its refusal to yield to his comprehension. He has painful meetings with his mother-in-law and his wife's lover, Marcel,* who wears a robe identical to one that Rosa gave Paul. Marcel inhabits a small room, clipping newspaper items, chinning to keep himself fit. He shows Paul where Rosa clawed the wallpaper with her fingers in her unnamed and never-explained despair. "I wonder what she ever saw in you?" Paul asks him, misdirecting his inquiry. He does not understand that Marcel, isolated and withdrawn, chinning instead of fornicating, is his own mirror image. Later, confronting his wife's corpse decked out in hideous makeup in a room full of flowers, he is once again confronting himself, in a further attempt to understand his own subjectivity. "Who the hell were you?" he asks her. He says that during their life together he felt like one of her hotel guests. He curses her and asks her forgiveness, crying: "I'm sorry. I don't know why you did it. I'd do it too if I knew how. . . ." And he is called away by another of the hotel's "guests," a whore whose client he scares away, runs after, and beats up, as if he were attempting to relive or settle his past and deal violently with its sexual torments.

Although Paul attempts to eradicate the violent enigmas of his wife and his past while in the room with Jeanne, all he can do is relive them, acting out his anger and self-hatred with her. Their sexuality is briefly joyous, and then cruel. Paul attempts to be a destroyer of bourgeois ideology, to grind into detritus the demands of propriety

* Both played by old neo-realist actors: Marcel by Massimo Girotti, who played the lover in *Ossessione;* the mother-in-law by Maria Michi, who acted in *Rome, Open City* and *Paisan.*

and manners, of self-importance, of sanctified relationships and the forced stability of families. He would like to see himself in fact as an atom smasher of the nuclear family, breaking its repressiveness and sanctified hypocrisy. He sodomizes Jeanne and forces her to repeat as he reaches climax: "holy family . . . church of good citizens . . . the children are tortured until they tell their first lie . . . where the will is broken with repression . . . where freedom is assassinated by egotism . . . the family . . . you fucking family. . . ." But his invective is contradicted by its physical form. Paul assaults the repressiveness of the family by assaulting another person; he attacks repression by being repressive himself. His anarchic violence against societal order is misdirected and finally as hurtful as that order itself. In his withdrawal, in his attempt to make Jeanne into an object of scorn and an echo of his own self-loathing, he allows his emotional turmoil to turn into the very thing he wishes to destroy. The bourgeois love he professes to despise will soon become the love he wishes once more to experience.

In neglecting to deal with Jeanne as a discrete individual, he neglects the consequences of her personality reasserting itself. In the sequences that follow Paul's attack on Jeanne's body and the body of the family, a number of significant events occur. We see Jeanne and Tom acting for Tom's cameras in a boat. He tells her he will marry her and places about her neck a life preserver with the name "L'Atalante" printed on it. She immediately throws it overboard and it sinks like a shot. *L'Atalante* is the name of Jean Vigo's 1934 film of strained lyrical romanticism, which carries with it an aura, a legend perhaps, of fragile beauty by a fragile artist who died before it was even released. The work carries as well some of the seeds of *Last Tango* itself in its exploration of the romantic couple, the education of a young girl by an old man, its melodrama of love lost and rediscovered. Jeanne's act of throwing overboard the life preserver with its sacred name proclaims the death of romantic fantasy. Paul attempts to destroy and then revive conventional romance, without success; Jeanne consummates its end by destroying Paul and embracing the security offered by Tom. Bertolucci cuts from the sinking life preserver to Jeanne's mother beating the dust from her late husband's military jacket on the balcony where Jeanne will eventually shoot Paul. Jeanne puts on the father's uniform, looking every bit like a depraved Shirley Temple. The very family Paul attempted to curse out of existence is reincarnated before our eyes as daughter and father merge before the mother, herself startled by the transformation.

When Jeanne returns to Paul he practices his last bit of humiliation and self-abasement. He torments her with a dead rat on their bed. She tells him she is in love with someone, and Paul accuses her of seeking an impossible security. He has her thrust her fingers up his rectum as he curses her and reviles himself, demanding she confront death to free herself of loneliness. This act precedes the sequence in which Paul visits the corpse of his wife, and the structure of events forms a narrative pattern of Paul's fall and Jeanne's ascent. When Paul is gone she is momentarily distraught and lonely, and invites Tom to see the apartment that has, until now, been inviolate. Inside they talk of marriage and children (she will name a boy Fidel, he will name a daughter Rosa–after Rosa Luxemburg, though, ironically, Rosa was the name of Paul's wife). Bertolucci treats the invasion of the sanctuary from a distance. The apartment seems huge and cold. Jeanne and Tom's discussion of becoming adult and acting serious sounds ridiculous within that space where Paul attempted to recover from the wounds of adulthood. They decide the apartment is not for them.

The apartment is for no one. It was all along an imaginary space, with golden light and strange, draped objects, guarded over by a concierge who laughed maniacally. It was an expression of Paul's fantasy and purgation. Once entered by someone else, it is just a huge ugly place. And once Paul encounters Jeanne outside it, the privilege it offered him, the sanctuary from polite middle-class manners and discourse, vanishes. Back in the world with Jeanne, Paul becomes reinfected by the romantic disease he attempted to cure in the quarantine the apartment offered. The dance hall they visit in the film's penultimate sequence offers images of paralyzed, polite sexual ritual, sterile, decorous, and bizarre. It is too much for Paul, who bares his backside to the offended judges of the last tango. But it is more than his ass that he bares; he makes the mistake we least expect from him, and bares his soul to Jeanne. He announces his love and asks to live with her. "In your flophouse?" she asks. "What the hell difference does it make if I have a flophouse or hotel or a castle? I love you. What the fuck difference does it make?" It is a question that echoes back through every romantic melodrama ever filmed, the lover's statement that should (and in those films usually does) transcend every reality: "I love you. What difference does anything else make?" Of all the moral frauds committed by the movies, this stands among the greatest. That Paul falls for it only emphasizes the difficulty of overcoming its seductiveness and indicates how much emotional need falls into pre-established patterns. The absurdity of his statement is emphasized by the response of the outraged judges of the dance contest to his excuse for his indecorous behavior. "It's love," he tells them. "But it's a contest," a judge responds. "Where does love fit in? Go to the movies to see love."

Fassbinder once wrote, ". . . I am more convinced than ever that love is the best, most insidious, most effective instrument of social repression."[27] The romantic love ritualized and stereotyped by film demands a hierarchical order. One member of the couple, most often the male, takes control, the other a relatively passive role. The stereotype demands as well that certain culturally prearranged moves occur. Love leads to marriage, which leads to the construction of a family, which removes itself from wider contact with the society. The exclusivity of the couple and the demands upon it to raise children, to work, to consume, recapitulate and further the order of society. Individuals are removed from concern for the operation of society and locked into a concern for the operation of the family. Within the family, the larger repressive modes of the culture are mirrored, and hierarchies, rules, restrictions are taught, practiced, perpetuated. The love that Paul and Jeanne first attempt to practice seems to deny this process. Though a withdrawal, it is an anarchic one, seeking to reject the recapitulative roles society demands. When Paul decides to break this pattern and impose the established one,

Jeanne refuses. She has decided already to give herself over to those demands with Tom, for whom she is an object to be filmed.

Tom is as domineering, in his own way, as Paul; but it is a safer domination. The humiliations he inflicts on Jeanne are of a lesser order and not as physically or emotionally threatening. Jeanne's reactions to Paul's proclamations of love are panic and violent refusal. While she entertains his aggressive introspections in the anonymity of their apartment as a kind of adventure, once that aggressiveness is put at the service of a public proclamation of "normal" love, it is Jeanne's turn to withdraw. She indulges in her own final, anarchic, "anti-social" gesture and masturbates Paul while they sit at a table in the dance hall, an act of rejection and farewell, which Bertolucci emphasizes by having his camera arc around them and pull away, leaving them surrounded by empty tables.[28] Jeanne leaves and Paul pursues her to her mother's apartment. His new-found romantic litany continues: "I ran through Africa and Asia and Indonesia and now I found you. And I love you." He asks her name for the first time (anonymity was one of the games they played in the apartment) and as she tells him she shoots him with her father's gun. Paul staggers out on the balcony, calls out, "Our children . . . our children," places his chewing gum under the balcony railing, and dies in a fetal position.*

During the final confrontation, Paul has put on Jeanne's father's military cap, assuming, momentarily, the guise of the kind of figure most repugnant to him. The gesture calls forth a Freudian reading—and beyond that a mythic one—suggesting that Paul assumes, despite himself, the role of father, the dominating, destructive male ruler. Jeanne's killing him could therefore be interpreted as transcending the local narrative to become a kind of ritual destruction of the Fisher King. Francis Ford Coppola attempts to re-create just such an arche-

* The placing of the gum is one of those fine Brando gestures, the kind that details a character and inflects a sequence; it is so outstanding that Bertolucci remembered it, and in *Luna* had a character "find" the wad of gum under a balcony railing, commenting, "Jesus Christ, he leaves his gum all over the place."

type in *Apocalypse Now* when he has Willard cut down Kurtz (Marlon Brando again) and recycle the pattern of rule. But such a reading overgeneralizes *Last Tango*. It is clear that Paul does expand from the lost, desolate, diminished figure he is at the beginning of the film to a man confident enough to want to re-establish the pattern of domesticity that almost destroyed him in the first place. That his reassertion of dominance scares Jeanne is clear; she kills Paul because he is too overpowering, the way her father was; the way fathers are. But Paul also kills himself. The rush of melodrama that carries his renewed romantic emotions sweeps away the memory of what his past romantic emotions did to him. That he begins talking like the eternal film lover—"I ran through Africa and Asia and Indonesia and now I found you. And I love you"—is too much for Jeanne, the film, or the viewer to bear. The reestablishment of romantic discourse is the most comforting thing in the film, but it breaks into a context that has been contradicting that discourse and parodying it. The sudden appearance of that discourse demands a violent reaction. It is not too far fetched to say that it is the *film* that kills Paul, eliminates him for making the mistakes it has been trying to expose.

This reading has attempted to save the film, and perhaps makes it more insightful than it really is. Godard removes his Paul from *Masculin-féminin* quietly, as an absence. We do not see his death. His absence, like his presence, is a complex of personal and social confusions, a sign of his inability to find a model through which to perceive his world and avoid succumbing to it. Bertolucci's Paul does discover a model—romantic passion—and it undoes him with a violence that assures a passionate response from the spectator and runs the risk of deflecting us from the larger concerns of the film. *Last Tango* is a conflicted work; looked at with some dispassion, we find that it never does depart very far from the romantic model that Paul so fully embraces at the end. Formally, Bertolucci creates a design of such sumptuous movement and grace (as opposed to the cool and distant observation in *Masculin-féminin*) that our perceptions are directed into the soul of Paul even more than they are into the tortured hearts of many other sufferers in film fiction. In a word, we are asked to *identify* with Paul to the exclusion of everyone else in the film, Jeanne most particularly. *Last Tango* is, simply put, a sexist film, in which the emotionally tortured man is allowed to be the focus of our sympathies, and the woman given the role of object through which he can work out his sorrow and destroyer when his sorrow turns to affection for the object. There is no question that *Last Tango* is a political film that examines sexuality and domesticity as part of the order of culture, seeing them as reflecting the repression and brutality of that order. There is a great question, however, as to whether Bertolucci has great success in clarifying the connections, in seeing exactly how intimate relations mirror larger struggles for power and domination in the manner of Godard or Fassbinder.

There is no real indication that he is aware that, even in their withdrawal from the world, Paul and Jeanne are mirroring the same dominant/passive roles of the world at large. Put another way, Bertolucci and Brando (who is very much responsible for the character, which was originally meant to be played by Jean-Louis Trintignant) are deeply concerned with the wounding and eventual destruction of the male by the vagaries of female emotions. The abuse given to the character of Jeanne can be seen as a way of taking revenge for the damage allegedly caused by those emotions. Jeanne is most closely associated with the destructive order. Riot police are on the streets when we first see her, and her donning of her father's uniform completes the association that is climaxed when she kills Paul with her father's gun. There is only a glimmer of an awareness of the male responsibility in the destructive process (aside from the generalized and ghostly figure of the father). In one sequence, Jeanne, nude, goes through the pockets of Paul's clothes and pulls out a razor. It is a moment when the audience is tantalized in a Hitchcockian manner. We know that Rosa killed herself in a violent and bloody way; we have seen the bloody bathroom. It is not clear whether the razor is the suicide weapon, but Jeanne's finding it in Paul's pocket makes it clearly threatening, particularly because she is naked (the image of a naked woman and a razor or knife is a central film icon of misogyny). This sequence of discovery is built up in such a way as to suggest that Paul is a physical danger to Jeanne, a suggestion that is carried through later in the sequence when we see Paul stropping the razor so that he can shave with it, while in the foreground of the shot, we see Jeanne's nude torso. Nothing further happens, as far as the razor is concerned (although Jeanne does ask, half in jest, whether he is going to cut her up). But in this same sequence Jeanne says that Paul hates women. His response immediately diverts this crucial insight and puts us back on his side: "Well, either they always pretend to know who I am, or they pretend that I don't know who they are. And that's very boring."

Whenever possible, responsibility is removed from Paul, and this allows unacknowledged tensions to develop in the film's crucial arguments. Bertolucci understands that the agonies of romantic love are reflections of the patriarchal order, but he has difficulty creating a female character who might provide a response to that order. Jeanne accepts it as a given; Paul suffers from its burden but cannot shake it off. The difficulties Bertolucci has in clarifying this social-sexual-political complex diminish the film, which is a pity, for *Last Tango* deals with the intensities and complexities of heterosexuality with less exploitation and more passionate analysis than almost any other film. That the analysis falters on Bertolucci's inability to structure a female response to sexuality and the emotions that surround it that is equivalent to the response of his male character should not come as any surprise. No male filmmakers are able to do this. Bertolucci sees the oppressive structure of the culture at large and the destructive powers of the romantic myth; but he cannot quite link them, and no matter how clearly he sees the threat of male domination, he seems unable to rid himself of the old notion that woman is the ultimate destroyer. Neither can he rid himself of a certain melodramatic intensity. *Last Tango* sheds most of the modernist accoutrements that allow *Spider's Stratagem* and *The Conformist* to negotiate with the audience an understanding of the intricate relationships of consciousness and history. Both of those films dealt with fascism as a counterpoint between historical circumstances and individual perceptions of and reactions to those circumstances. The fascism dealt with in *Last*

Tango is muted and removed, present only in the ghost of the father and the idea of societal repression that looms over Paul's withdrawal from the world and his reentry into it as a reborn, and therefore doomed, romantic.

Bertolucci, like Visconti before him, finally gave over to the melodrama of violent emotion, rather than confronting those emotions and investigating them. We have seen that one reason for the failure of *1900* was a loss of perspective; in a film about history, individual conflicts were allowed to eclipse the history they should have embodied. *Luna* (1979) fails because the filmmaker lost all perspective on the individuals he created, foundered in their emotions, presuming that what he found interesting in an opera singer with an incestuous desire for her drug-addicted son would also interest an audience. The resulting film moves wildly between sensationalism, hysteria, and contemplation, unable to determine a consistent structure for observing its characters, only occasionally managing to capture an appropriate detail of gesture or create a disorienting movement or cut. There are moments of insight and visual acuity, but Bertolucci cannot move *Luna* beyond its sensational subject matter, and its lack of distance and analysis is typical of much commercial European cinema in the late seventies and early eighties.*

With the first stage of the modernist/Brechtian movement over, and (except for the Germans) with commercial European filmmakers returning to relatively safe structures and themes, serious cinema began to regress. The passion for cinema to scrutinize the world and clarify the relationship of people to it and to each other peaked in the years right after the May events of 1968, when that passion spilled, for a moment at least, into the world itself. When the student and worker uprisings led nowhere, however, there was a slow but steady movement back to introspection, in cinema and about cinema. While the introspection *about* film created new theoretical models

* Bertolucci's latest film as of this writing, *Tragedy of A Ridiculous Man* (1981), is a cool and distanced political work and indicates a reassertion of control and direction.

and important insights into the connections between film, spectator, and ideology, filmmakers themselves began to regress to conventional modes. Distributors grew wary of experiment, filmmakers grew weary of probing or inquiring into the ways of their art.

One curious film from France manifested this decline, simultaneously reflecting and commenting upon it, and announced, in 1973, the end of political film the way *Weekend* announced the end of conventional narrative cinema in 1967. Jean Eustache's *The Mother and the Whore* is hardly conventional, at least not in length. At 215 minutes, it competes with the films of Rivette for the patience of its audience. This great length is filled with talk, offering a superficial analogy with the films of Rohmer. Most of the talk and some of the action concern sex and sexuality, offering an analogy with *Last Tango.*[29] But neither of these analogies holds on close examination, and *The Mother and the Whore* reveals itself finally as a film that goes against the work of Rohmer and Bertolucci (at least their work up to that time), closes the door on the multi-layered inquiries of Godard, and in short states that the New Wave is over. The film moves away from openness and toward introspection, from an interaction of characters with their environment and culture to an introverted concern with a limited set of personal feelings and reactions. One of the women in the film, the "mother," who lives with the central male character, Alexandre, despite his love affairs and his maltreatment of her, tells him of some graffiti she has read in a café toilet: "My passion opens out on death like a window on a courtyard." To which, she says, someone has added, "Jump, Narcissus!"

Narcissus in this case is Alexandre, played by Jean-Pierre Léaud, whose very presence in the film hooks it into some thirteen years of influential French cinema. The Léaud persona grew up in the films of François Truffaut, from a shy, inquisitive child in *The 400 Blows* to the inquisitive *naïf* in *Stolen Kisses* and *Domicile conjugal.* His self-effacing earnestness and ironic self-consciousness also made him an excellent character for Godard—as the would-be lover impinged upon by the world's chaos in *Masculin-féminin,* as Saint Juste preaching revolution and a young man singing love songs in a phone booth in *Weekend,* as one of the leaders of the Maoist cell in *La Chinoise,* and as the earnest inquisitor of cultural images in *Le Gai Savoir.* In *The Mother and the Whore* the self-effacement and irony are gone. The self-consciousness remains, but the earnestness has turned to obsessiveness. Alexandre is a parody of the mythological French bohemian, the passionate observer of the world from a seat in an outdoor café, in flowing scarf and dark glasses, with no job and many acquaintances, a number of lovers, and a greater number of opinions. But the parody is a dark one. This bohemian observes not the world but himself; though witty, he is without humor; though full of passion (at least verbal passion), devoid of compassion. He is brutal–he tells a new lover of how he beat up an old one, a story which, even if untrue, makes evident his hatred of women–and he uses his lovers essentially as mirrors in which to observe himself.

The two women who most concern Alexandre are Marie, the "mother," who houses and cares for him, and Veronika, the "whore," a promiscuous nurse who both glories in and loathes her sexuality. She becomes Alexandre's lover and engages in a masochistic *ménage à trois.* The film observes the three of them in nondescript black-and-white tonalities, using a compositional and cutting style that interferes as little as possible with the monologues and dialogues the three carry on, stubbornly refusing to comment upon them. Eustache seems to reach toward a psychological neo-realism, notably devoid of melodramatic effects and insistent in maintaining its illusion of casual observation. But it can only reveal emptiness, an emotional and intellectual vacuum. There is no revelation of spiritual torment as in Bergman, no longing for discovery or contentment with searching as in the films of Wim Wenders, and certainly not the emotional engagement of Truffaut or the intellectual rigor of Godard. And unlike Rohmer's characters, Eustache's merely talk; their words enlighten neither them nor us, there is no sense of the delights of conversation or the ways language proves or disproves the moral structures individuals create for themselves. Unlike that of *Last Tango,* the sexuality does not become a metaphor for social and political relationships. Even the way the inhabitants of the film use it to manipulate one another reveals nothing. The characters are so lacking in self-respect, and the filmmaker so lacks an attitude toward them, that their mutual abuse merely collapses in upon them.

Perhaps it is breaking a butterfly on a wheel to go after this film with such vehemence, but I do so because it so clearly marks a change in the direction of European narrative film. Beneath the façade of its non-bourgeois characters, beneath the challenge of its length and its casual structure, it reveals a very safe and somewhat reactionary perspective: the old perspective of conventional cinema, inward upon characters concerned only with themselves. Eustache's trio sit, drink Scotch, listen to records, fornicate or talk about fornication, recall 1968 as a bad dream, and ruminate obsessively on their emotional state. In 1973, James Monaco wrote that *The Mother and the Whore* "is one of the first films to display the sensibilities of the seventies."[30] And he was as prophetic as the film. Eustache's characters close themselves in, forget the world, and look to the self as refuge, promoting its importance, forgetting that as important as it is, it can only be understood in relationship to the complexities of external political events that manipulate individuals, perhaps allowing some to exist in a carefree state of introspection while others are not permitted this leisure.

In 1969, Jean-Pierre Léaud had appeared in Pasolini's remarkable film *Pigsty* (*Il Porcile*) as the catatonic, pig-loving son of an old Nazi, who looks like Hitler and cheerfully admits to being a caricature born of Brecht and George Grosz. Pasolini juxtaposes this neo-fascist industrialist and his friends with a strange cannibal figure (Pierre Clementi), who forms a tribe and wanders the volcanic hills of some medieval world until caught and murdered by "civilized" people. But Pasolini is not making a simple analogy in which fascists equal cannibals. Rather the son and the cannibals form a shifting perspective through which the father and his activities may be seen. The son is the repressed and emotionally ruined offspring of this family of political pigs. He seeks refuge with actual pigs who–like his family, but more literally–devour him. The cannibals are savage like the family, but in a state of nature; violent, but not yet repressed as the son is. They are primal man, and when captured, their chief can only repeat, "I killed my father; I ate human flesh; I trembled with joy." The son is already and perpetually captured and devitalized, victimized, and, like the cannibals, destroyed. His father and his father's cohorts talk delightedly about their past, their slaughter of the "Jewish-Bolshevik-Commissars," and about a future from which humanism and conscience will be expunged. As the cannibals roam the barren hills and are caught the son slips into and out of catatonia, unable to rebel, unable to find alternatives in subjectivity, finally eaten by the pigs he loved. At the end of *The Mother and the Whore,* after an evening of drunken confession and self-abasement by the three characters, Alexandre takes his lover home to her miserable nurse's quarters while Marie stays in their flat listening in silence to an Edith Piaf record. Alexandre, in the face of Veronika's hysteria and her fears of being pregnant with his child, screams his love and asks to marry her. She says yes and throws up. The last shot of the film shows us Alexandre sitting on the floor of Veronika's room, tapping his fingers, grimacing, and finally looking just blank. Where the Léaud character in Pasolini's film is destroyed by the conflicts of history and personality, in Eustache's film he is unrooted and without direction, trapped by the vagaries of subjectivity, a careless regard for himself and others, without reason for his condition beyond an almost terminal self-absorption.

The two films are obvious opposites: Pasolini's a Brechtian fantasy of psycho-political destruction; Eustache's a "realistic" observation of contemporary Parisian bohemians. In the opposition of their subjects and approaches we find a summary of the elements and problems inherent in both forms. We expect the realist mode to allow the characters to play out their personalities, perhaps defined by their setting, class situation, and emotional makeup. We expect the Brechtian mode to remove us from direct contact with personality and instead create political tableaux in which temperaments and ideologies are played out through characters whose conflicts are determined by and whose emotions are filtered through the filmmaker's analysis of the subject. Eustache chooses, within his realist approach, to create characters who have forgotten they exist in the world and have chosen to retreat into their sexual insecurities. He avoids melodrama, ordininarily associated with the realist mode, and at the same time narrows the range of his inquiry. Like the New Wave filmmakers, he focuses loosely on a specific set of characters and experience and allows a prolonged and open observation of them; but he does not try to reveal a social and economic environment. He rather seals his characters into a hermetic world in which they talk their lives out without achieving a coherent discourse. Pasolini achieves coherence by, paradoxically, seeming to avoid it. The relationship of the modern political caricatures and the ancient cannibals is only suggested by the intercutting of the images (at one point the cannibal looks up and there is a cut on his gaze to the home of the fascist industrialist, as if the man in the past were seeing the present; a minor character appears in both past and present narratives). As part of the Brechtian process, the spectator must draw the links, help the film construct its historical analysis and create narrative sense. In *The Mother and the Whore,* the images process themselves. Their chronology is secure, their spatial coordinates familiar, and the characters speak their feelings. Eustache does not probe those feelings or seek motivation for them, but also does not seek a context for them. We are given no material to work with beyond the characters' words and faces, no ideas beyond those stated by them.

Between the extremes of a realism in which we are asked to believe we are watching the bared souls of ciphers and a formalism in which we are forced to knit a continuity of meaning out of images adamant in giving us pleasure only through labor lies a range of cinematic expression. There are films which combine an analysis of history, politics, and class with characters created in rich detail, inhabiting a world that is both recognizable and significantly structured to reveal and comment upon aspects of contemporary life. Alain Tanner's *Jonah Who Will be 25 in the Year 2000* (1976—co-written by John Berger and co-produced by Swiss television) demonstrates a particular response to Eustache's political amnesia. He examines the lives of various characters who preserve an intellectual strength and a knowledge of themselves and the changes in Europe since May '68, who seek survival without sealing themselves off from the world and keep asking questions. With a sensibility as warm as Jean Renoir's, Tanner embraces a number of characters–laborer, teacher, farmer, immigrant worker, banker, journalist, old resistance fighter, transcendental meditator–and gently, persistently shows that political conscience is not dead and that the ability of film to speak to an audience about ideas held with passion did not die when Godard turned away from narrative in the early seventies. *Jonah* has few Brechtian elements and is not as spare or schematic in its examination of the post-'68 consciousness as Godard and Gorin's *Tout va bien.* Unlike that film it is not concerned with how narratives of love and work are made, though it shares with it a love of narrative-making, of storytelling, and even more a love of observing people attempting to find their way in ideas and emotions.

The new German cinema has indicated the range of formal and contextual approaches possible without giving up responsibility. Volker Schlöndorff works comfortably in a conventional realist mode, yet manages to keep his fictions in touch with history and politics. Wim Wenders develops subjective analyses of the consciousness of his characters, yet at all times attempts to detail, if not explain, how that consciousness is touched by the larger culture, formed and deformed by the material world that surrounds it. Werner Herzog turns the material world into a dreamscape through which half-crazed characters wander in narratives that subjugate time and history to the interior spaces of irrational longings and barely defined battles between desire and reason. But even though subjugated, time and history do exist. R. W. Fassbinder, after Godard the major heir of Brecht, fractures desire and diminishes the subject by placing him or her in a landscape of oppression. He calculates his images and narrative structure so that the viewer, kept alert to information about the subject and sensitive rather than only reactive to the emotions experienced by the subject, is forced continually to question the subject's actions, decisions, and motives. In no instance do these filmmakers take anything for granted–not the forms they use, the characters they create, or the response they expect from the spectator. They will mix melodrama with distancing devices; continuity with leaps in internal and external space and time; a realistic *mise-en-scène* with expressionist interiors and landscapes.

The political economy of German filmmaking has so far permitted them to search out a variety of methods and subjects that, in the seventies, were largely abandoned by the filmmakers of other Western European countries for lack of financing and because the pressure to inquire was lost. The abandonment should be temporary only, for serious cinema, like the novel, has never stayed long in a creative slump. American film may be a lost cause for the present; some Latin American cinema may remain suppressed until the brutality of military regimes is ended. But the continual intellectual ferment of Europe and the desire and ability of governments to provide money so that ferment can be realized in images bode well. The struggles and successes of East European cinema; the independent filmmaking in England–rarely seen in America, but still in existence despite being ignored; state television's support of Italian filmmakers; and the phenomenon of German film in the late seventies are all optimistic signs.

Although serious European film is getting more and more difficult to see in America, some films are getting made. And because this is a celebration rather than an elegy, I want to end by discussing two figures who have endured many cycles of creative, economic, and political changes in the course of their careers and have managed to keep on making films that get distributed and seen, and that sum up many of the problems we have looked at in course of this study. I have already talked of Luis Buñuel; the other filmmaker, Joseph Losey, has managed to evade discussion, perhaps because a career that began in Hollywood, moved to England, and spanned forms as diverse as science fiction and the cinematic rendering of Mozart opera defies the categories criticism needs to give its subjects order.

Joseph Losey is an American, and therefore really does not belong in this study at all. However, he left the United States in the early fifties because of the blacklist and became so thoroughly involved in

European production and attuned to European sensibility, so at ease at filmmaking in England and France, that he is a European director for all intents and purposes. Losey is also a Brechtian, perhaps the most traditional Brechtian of all contemporary filmmakers. He knew Brecht and directed the first English-language stage performance of *Galileo* with Charles Laughton (although when he finally filmed it in 1974, for the American Film Theater enterprise, he could not transcend its theatrical limits). He does not engage in the radical distancing devices and the foregrounding of ideological analysis found in the work of Godard, Straub, Pasolini, or Fassbinder. Instead, in his most successful work, he achieves an analytical distance in a different way. He absorbs character into class (giving the representatives of a class very specific character) and makes his narrative function within carefully defined spatial coordinates. The way he deals with space, the way he makes architecture function as a defining structure, detailing the interior of a house with as great care as the characters who inhabit it, places him in the tradition of Bresson and Antonioni in the West, and also of Yasujiro Ozu. Ozu makes his habitations comfortable; they secure his characters. The rooms of Bresson are an expression of his characters' desolation, sparely furnished for the most part, often mean and constricting. Antonioni turns rooms, buildings, and landscapes into oppressive forms that defy human habitation and deny human comfort.

Losey uses a different strategy; he makes a house and its rooms a place in which to build a point of view that determines the situation of a particular character and the way that character is to be interpreted. In those films written by Harold Pinter—*The Servant* (1963), *Accident* (1967), *The Go-Between* (1971)—the treatment of interiors is made a visual equivalent of Pinter's language. The observation of place provides pauses in the action, sometimes indicating threat, often cutting off one character from another, always providing commentary and perspective. *The Servant,* for example, is on one level an abstract allegory of class hatred and revenge, in which the master, Tony (James Fox), and servant, Barratt (Dirk Bogarde), play increasingly vicious games of role alternation to the mutual destruction of their personalities. The inquiry into the fragility of character, the fragility of any structure that depends upon dominance and submission, is rendered concrete by enclosing it within Tony's house. Not only does the house become the center of most of the action, but the changes it undergoes and the places within it from which these changes are seen provide our own visual field in which to judge what is happening, rendering it more concrete than do the events themselves. There are specific places of importance: the ground floor dining room and lounge are where, at the beginning, Tony and Barratt act out the conventional roles of servant and master. The upstairs rooms are at first discreetly separated into the master's bathroom and bedroom and the servant's quarters; as they are taken over by Barratt and his lover, Vera, these spaces become threatening, palpable expressions of the vulnerability of power and privilege. The downstairs kitchen, the conventional place for the servants, becomes an ominous area with a loudly dripping faucet: the place where Vera seduces Tony. The stairs that connect the levels become the major point of transition and the place of the film's climax, marking ominously the transitions of the narrative. Tony and Barratt's role reversal is played out on the staircase; they play ball with each other, shifting personalities, altering their psychological makeup as we watch.

The exchange of personalities is a favorite literary and cinematic gambit. In Bergman's *Persona,* the struggle between Elisabeth Vogler, the actress who decides to cease speaking, and Alma, her nurse, confidante, double, and victim, occurs in a barely defined landscape—a hospital room, a house on the beach, the surface of the film itself, to which Bergman calls attention in order to remind us how easily images are manipulated and the surfaces of personality shifted. In Bergman's treatment, the causes of the encroachment of one persona upon another arise from some dark recesses of the psyche and from the metaphysical pressures of the need for communication. His characters seek assurance that they are emotionally alive in a deadening world, a need so powerful that it results in one character attempting to suck another dry. But whereas Bergman dislocates both us and his characters, Losey attempts to locate both in a more defined context. By making the house the locus of activity, by giving it a presence and allowing it to fashion our perspective on the fragile psychological imbalances that ownership (in all its manifestations) creates, Losey roots his analysis in the material world.

This allows him great flexibility. *The Servant* is both a critique of the British class system and an investigation of sexual manipulation and psychological cruelty that could exist independently of that system but are defined and clarified by it. The two couples, Tony, his lover Susan, Barratt, and Vera, stalk each other, reflect and deflect each other (quite literally, as a distorting mirror in the foyer of the house reflects their features), and use each other emotionally and physically. The degradation they cause is determined by their social attitudes, but is played out through the weakness of each, the readiness of each to use and be used, and the absolute ripeness for degeneration that Losey and Pinter observe in all of them, as well as in those who surround them. In a restaurant sequence a number of individuals appear, peripheral to the main narrative, but each playing out a role of domination or submission that echoes the events and attitudes occurring in the house. The result is a concurrence of microcosm and macrocosm—the house, the restaurant, the world—in which class and psychological cruelty demean and destroy individuals.

The Go-Between takes a similar view, though here the social-psychological dialectic occurs not only within a house and its environs but in the environs of memory as well. In the early part of the century, Leo, a lower-middle-class child, is taken in for the summer by an aristocratic Norfolk family. One member of that family, Marian (Julie Christie), uses him as a message-bearer to her lover, a tenant farmer, Ted Burgess (Alan Bates). The activity brings ruin to both men: Burgess commits suicide after he is discovered in bed with Marian by her mother; Leo is emotionally ruined by seeing their sexual activity. This plot appears thoroughly melodramatic, full of potential for emotional excess, sexual exploitation, and moralizations about the abuse of children. Instead, Losey creates out of Pinter's script (itself based on L. P. Hartley's novel) a study in temporal

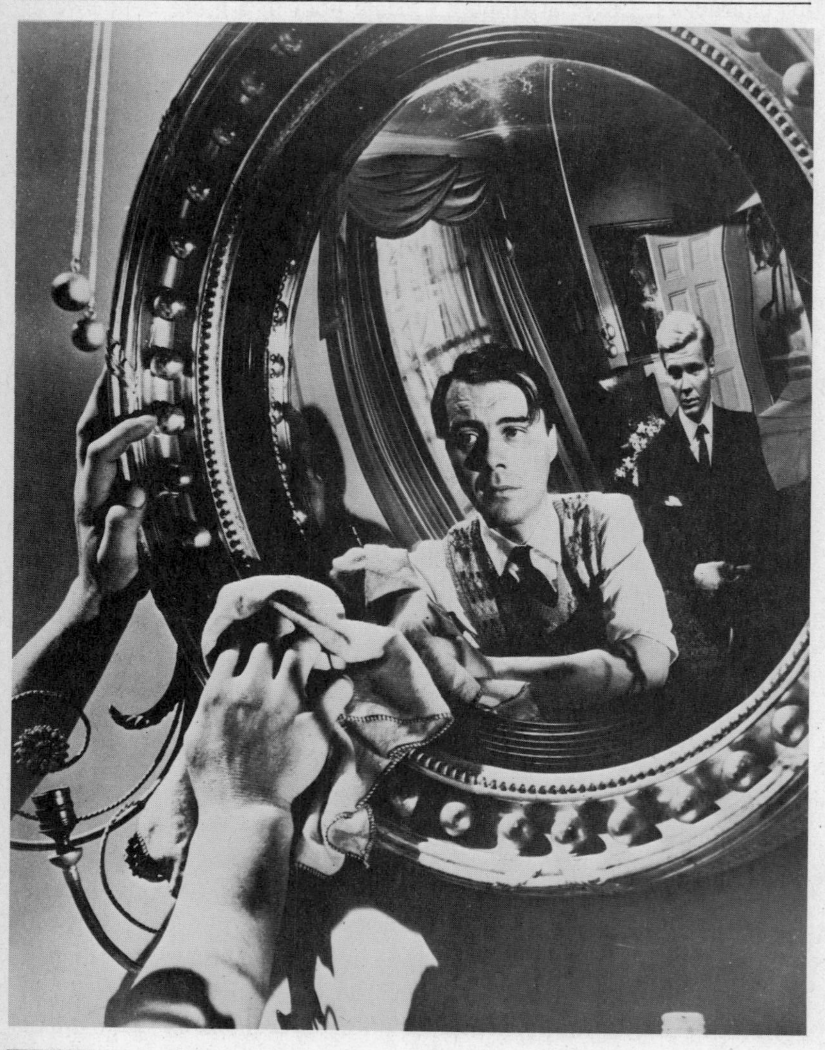

Servant and master (Dirk Bogarde, James Fox). *The Servant* (Museum of Modern Art Film Stills Archive).

point of view, an almost Proustian structure in which not only various times, but perceptions of those various times, cross.* "The past is a foreign country. They do things differently there" are the first words we hear in the film, spoken by Michael Redgrave, who plays Leo as an old man, whose perceptions partially determine the narrative structure. Though only partly. The film is not "told" in flashback; if anything, it is told in flash-forward. The body of the film takes place in the warm summer of young Leo's ruin, when he is admitted into the ritual-ridden world of the aristocracy and falls in love with Marian and Burgess (whose vitality is continually contrasted with the paralysis of the rich family). Used by both, he is finally damaged by the exploitation, rendered an emotionless, loveless man. At strategic intervals within this narrative there are shots—of varying duration and out of chonological order—of another time and place: a gray and rainy time as compared to the sunny green of the main narrative. The shots gradually reveal themselves, through objects such as a car and a television set, to be of the "present."

The quotation marks are important. The time scheme of *The Go-Between* is not as complex as that of a Resnais film—*La Guerre est finie,* for example, which is interrupted by flash-forwards to possible events in the central character's life, or *Je t'aime, je t'aime,* which is like a mirror of the past shattered into hundreds of bits, each shiver reflecting a small fragment of the central character's memory. Rather than juggle the cinematic conventions of time past, present, and future, Losey creates a convergence of times and a point of view caught in that convergence. Again buildings serve as a focus for that point of view. Shots are composed and edited within the aristocrats' house so as to create an effect of seeing things twice: we see things out a window just after or just before Leo actually looks at them, as if someone else were recalling events slightly out of sync. Young Leo visits the cathedral in Norwich. Inside there is a sudden and unexplained leap to an extreme high angle of him from the ceiling.

* Not coincidentally, Pinter has written a screenplay based on Proust that Losey would like to direct. Given the taste of most producers at the moment, such a project is not imminent.

Throughout the film there are distant shots of deer on the lawn of the estate that act as punctuation marks, suspending the action, reminding us that a particular act of observation is occurring, that there is a consciousness separated from the individuals in the immediate drama before us, which may be recalling or reflecting upon events and memories. The events in the film are seen from our point of view, from the perspective of an omniscient author, and from the consciousness of Leo as a child and Leo as an old man.

The result of this confluence is an effect of time suspended and an unlocalized reverie of regret, longing, and fear as the various temporal planes are played out one against the other, culminating in a shock when time present takes over and the old Leo, puffy and emotionally deadened, is approached by an old Marian and asked once more to be a go-between—this time between herself and her grandson. As in *The Servant,* class and power are used as a weapon, and everyone's emotional well-being is damaged by it. By indicating the temporal spread of the damage, its movement across time, Losey is able to deepen the notion of its virulence. But at the same time, *The Go-Between* hides its social perspectives. Less abstract than *The Servant,* even with its careful and complex temporal pattern; visually more engaging, more "pretty" in a conventional photographic sense; and using well-known stars and a sexually oriented story, it was a commercially viable film and a measure of Losey's ability to weave perception of history and class into an attractive narrative form and substance not threatening to an audience, but not obsequious to it either. He can deal with the emotional entanglements we expect from movies and at the same time construct a point of view that permits the spectator to take an analytic stance, if he or she is willing.

Losey has struck a careful, even enviable, balance between the modernist/Brechtian urge for a politically engaged cinema that disrupts the ordinary pattern of spectator involvement and the "commercially viable product" that offers a sexy story and recognizable faces. He is engaging and subtle, deeply aware of the relationship between emotional, sexual, and social experience, suspicious of class motives and satisfactions but willing to entertain them while investigating them. "The bourgeois life has its compensations, doesn't it?" asks Michael Caine's well-to-do novelist in *The Romantic Englishwoman* (1975). "What would it be without them?" responds the German drug runner–cum-poet who is about to steal the author's wife. *The Romantic Englishwoman* is a kind of ironic elegy for the middle class, a mid-seventies summation of the pressures of domesticity, the growing discomfort of women in their hitherto predetermined roles of mother and supporter, the insecurity of men in response to that discomfort, and the general fantasizing of an adventurous life that might transcend discomfort, insecurity, boredom, and fear. It is an elegant film that at the same time parodies elegance and the elegant fantasies of bourgeois film. Elizabeth (Glenda Jackson), the novelist's wife, runs off with the German adventurer, attempts to live out a fantasy of escape, danger, and romance, and inadvertently lives out her husband's fantasy "plot" for his own cuckolding. But if the film parodies, it also reassures; husband and wife reestablish their domestic unit. The novelist interferes in the "plot," runs after his wife, puts himself in danger with the drug runners, and brings her home with the most gentle of words: "I don't want you to come to harm."

What would bourgeois life be without its compensations? Losey and his screenwriters, Tom Stoppard and Thomas Wiseman, confront a question basic to all middle-class, left-wing intellectuals, that of finding alternatives to the life they themselves lead and at the same time find abhorrent, particularly when placed in a wider cultural-political context. The elements of middle-class life—order, security, predictability; the freedom, within defined limits, to act and think independently; the cultivation of individuality; "honesty, scrupulousness, discrimination, protectiveness, tenderness, aversion to violence and the conscious practice of terror" (qualities catalogued by a character in Resnais's *Providence*)—are so deeply inscribed as to be almost impossible to erase. They may be mocked and excoriated, they may be examined in a global context and seen to be limited and even dangerous when forced upon societies that have other needs and values. But when examined at home, within the domestic unit, they are almost impossible to reject—on moral if not political grounds. Sometimes they can only be examined by being stripped away, exposing a vulnerability of feelings and a desperate need for the security that bourgeois values were created to protect. *The Romantic Englishwoman* deals with the need for assurance, safety, and continuity in a somewhat frivolous way. Losey treats it more profoundly in *Mr. Klein,* a film made in France in 1976, written by Franco Solinas (one of the major political screenwriters of Europe).

Mr. Klein is another entry in what might be considered a genre of European film: the inquiry into the fascist period of the thirties and early forties, an almost obsessive probing into a period which is historically close, yet so appallingly distant from what we imagine our political behavior should be that it must be examined over and over. Images of fascism are created and re-created in an attempt to understand and expunge them, but only rarely—as in some of Fassbinder's films, Resnais's 1955 documentary *Night and Fog,* and Marcel Ophuls's *The Sorrow and the Pity* (1971)—are they seen as historically continuous, still with us in disguised form. In *Mr. Klein,* Losey and Solinas choose a small facet of the phenomenon and elaborate from it a psychological fantasy. The moment is Paris during the Nazi occupation, and the subject is the problem of complicity, the way all people, but most especially those who imagined they were outside political events, were deeply involved in the round-up and massacre of the Jews. The narrative structure of *Mr. Klein* develops the idea of the *doppelgänger*—the other self. Robert Klein (Alain Delon) is a wealthy art dealer in 1942. The Paris police are rounding up Jews. Klein's discovery of a Jewish newspaper left at his door, addressed to him, leads him to discover the existence of a Jew with his name whom he feels compelled to find, partly to clear himself of a dangerous association and partly—increasingly, as the film progresses—to discover what it means to exist as a person in danger. The body of the film follows Klein as he follows various clues, visiting people who know the "other" Klein, examining the wretched flat where the other Klein lived, chasing after rich acquaintances and poor ones in a diminishing circle that leads, finally, to his own deportation.

Losey and Solinas use the theme of the double as a device upon which to build a larger structure of inquiry. Mr. Klein is a figure who has every reason to believe that he can remove himself from the realities and demands of history. A rich bourgeois, encased in the elegance of a respected trade, he considers himself something of a disinterested helper of the persecuted. The first time we see him, he is buying the art works of a Jew who needs money. He does it coldly and with arrogance, describing the painting in the impersonal tones of the doctor who, in the very first sequence of the film, is seen examining and cataloguing the traits of a woman for the state's records of racial origins. The woman, who is naked, is treated like a thing to be dealt with, classified, and sent away. The cut from the doctor's office to Klein's rich and secure surroundings, with pictures of human figures on the wall and his mistress lounging in bed, immediately indicates a connection between Klein's private world and the horrors that are occurring outside it. He too turns the human body into an object, something to be observed and used. And once again the house becomes a primary sign for Losey, an objective indication of Klein's tenuous security which breaks down as he becomes more obsessed with discovery. For much of the film its elegance stands as a separation from and contrast to the streets where police activity quickens, where barriers and detention centers are set up. But when the police begin to accept Klein *as* his double, refusing to see a separation, they invade the house and strip it. The other Klein invades it too, by means of his dog, which appears and is adopted by Mr. Klein. When the police search the house, a friend of Mr. Klein's discovers a piece of music on his piano which Klein says was written by his double. He tells the friend to play it. It is the "Internationale."

Invaded both by the police and by his double (who, it becomes more and more apparent, is a left-wing member of the Resistance), Klein is forced into history—partly by default and by accident, partly by his own active participation in seeking out the mysterious other Mr. Klein. But here we are not dealing with a psychological convention of confused identities; this is not the microcosm of *The Servant,* nor the displacement of self that occurs in Fassbinder's *Despair* (1977). (That film, set in Germany in the thirties, involves an intricate perceptual dislocation in which an individual adopts and kills a double who looks nothing like him as part of a psychotic escape from a psychotic society).[31] Rather, Losey is depicting a kind of forced march into the world, led by an unseen figure who becomes more of a conscience than a character. The "other" Mr. Klein is that other which is and is not the self (significantly, on a number of occasions when Mr. Klein hears about his double, his first reaction is to glance at himself in a mirror), and which the self must attempt to appropriate.[32] Klein becomes hunter and hunted, his elegance and security finally peeled away until he unconsciously chooses to be the other. That ghostly figure no longer has a separate identity. As the police sweep the city, rounding up its Jewish population (including the "other," who is turned in by Mr. Klein's friend), Mr. Klein is loaded into a bus with the other deportees. At the stadium where the Jews are being collected, Klein's name is called out. A faceless figure in the crowd raises his hand, and we assume that here we may actually see the elusive other Klein. But Mr. Klein, despite the fact that a friend has arrived with a clearance for him, runs after his fugitive self, whose face is never revealed, and is swept up by the crowd and placed in a cattle car. Behind him is the Jew from whom, at the beginning of the film, he purchased a painting.

Klein does not merely "become" his other; he becomes part of the enormous group collectively turned by the Nazis into a cultural "other," a group determined by the facist ideology to be its enemy and threat, its dark side that must be destroyed. The irony is that fascism is itself the dark side of bourgeois complacency and self-centeredness. The "Jewish Question" was the Nazis' invention of a dialectic where there was none, and an attempt to erase their own relationship to a history they pretended to control. The paranoid view of history, which is a major component of fascism, demands the creation of enemies, the turning of people into things. This is, of course, what Mr. Klein has done, to a lesser extent, in his private life. Now that he is forced to confront history, to see and be his other self, his ability "to be objective" is gone. The world's terrors become his own, seen by Losey in extraordinary images of commonplace violence.

In the film's final sequences, Losey observes with a removed horror the city in which the Jews are rounded up, noting in the faces of those caught and awaiting deportation a combination of hysteria and stillness, a frantic action and a dumbfounded passivity, an expression of disbelief so thorough as to be paralyzing. The most active figure in this grouping is Mr. Klein, who embraces his destruction with the anticipation of someone making a discovery he cannot resist.

The movement to irresistible discovery is a major quality of Losey's films. He does not care for epiphanies, for sudden revelations, but for steady processes of understanding and seeing through; he places characters in environments in which they either lose or discover something, often both simultaneously—Mr. Klein loses his life when he discovers that he is, like everyone else, a part of history. Losey allows us as spectators safely to observe the effects of class barriers or political amnesia and perceive what occurs when the safety they offer is removed. That is what all of his best films are concerned with. When he came to film Mozart's *Don Giovanni* (1979), he interpreted it as a legend that can only exist in a culture where economic privilege permits one individual leisure and power to abuse others. He opens the film with an epigraph taken from the writings of Antonio Gramsci, the Italian communist theoretician: ". . . The old is dying and the new cannot be born; in this interregnum, a great variety of morbid symptoms appears." His fluid, architectural version of the opera becomes, under the aegis of this quotation, a prelude to revolution, a notation in legend of the morbid obsessions of dying classes.

The quotation could well be the epigraph for the whole canon of contemporary Western European political cinema. Unable or unwilling to see the new born, horrified and delighted at the dying of the old, some filmmakers fight history or explain it, some succumb to it, many try to show we are not impotent in the world. Others simply observe its morbid symptoms. No filmmaker does this with greater joy than Luis Buñuel. I have already examined two phases of Buñuel's work: his mid-career adoption of neo-realism—certainly one of the more bizarre relationships in the history of cinema—and his later rejuvenation by the New Wave, certainly one of the more heart-warming examples of an old master learning from the young who, in their turn, had learned much from him (although the term "heart-warming" would ordinarily be one of the last to come to mind in considering Buñuel).

I want to look at his work yet again as a point of summary and examine what happens when an anarchic-surrealist-socialist-misanthrope active since the late twenties moves into the late seventies and attempts to deal with its problems. Buñuel's voice, in his early and middle films, is that of an angry and bemused, more than slightly perverse fantasist who despises bourgeois arrogance and self-centeredness with such a passion that he would like to take the entire class by its collective neck, wring it until its eyes split, and make it see its own oppressive absurdities and presumptions. In the seventies bemusement seems to win out over anger, and in *The Discreet Charm of the Bourgeoisie* and *The Phantom of Liberty* he seems more content to laugh than to rail. He looks at the upper middle class as performers on a stage, dreaming one another's acts and acting each other's dreams. *The Discreet Charm* is a dream film with no levels of reality except for the reality of its own perceptions of the class it excoriates. A group of people attempt to have a dinner party, keep attempting to have it for the length of the film, but are unable ever to eat because all their dreams of love and terrorism, of military maneuvers, of a bishop who shoots a dying old man who has murdered his parents, and a South American diplomat who deals in drugs, keep interfering. At one point in their long march to nowhere, the group comes to the home of an army colonel for dinner. Their host is not present, but servants bring them two rubber chickens to eat, which are dropped and tossed around. Suddenly loud tapping noises are heard. Lights go on. The red curtains on the dining room wall part and a theater audience is revealed looking at the guests. They attempt to leave, but a prompter stops them and attempts to direct them into a performance of (perhaps) *Don Giovanni*: "To prove your courage, you invited the Commander's ghost to dinner. . . ." This does not work; general chaos ensues; the audience grows restive; one of the guests admits he does not know the text he is meant to play—then wakes up and goes to the Colonel's dinner, only to become an actor in someone else's dream.

The film is a wonderful parody of the Hollywood convention of resolving difficult situations by revealing them to be only dreams. But Buñuel goes many steps further. All of the actions in the film are dreams and dreams of dreams. Buñuel used to employ dream images to express, at crucial parts in a narrative, an explosion of the unconscious, the outward manifestation of his characters' fears and repressions. They were not always presented as dreams. Buñuel's images, indeed entire films, are eruptions of repressed material pouring out of the seams of cultural rituals. For example, the nun's progress from virgin to poker player, with an interlude of a beggar's banquet that takes the form of the Last Supper, makes *Viridiana* (1961) not so much an attack upon Catholicism as Catholicism's confession of its own nightmares of defeat. Buñuel found in religion a structure of repression so obvious that he merely had to invert a few of its terms to reveal piety as self-hatred, sacrifice as masochism, self rightousness as a terrifying vulnerability. The good priest in *Nazarin* (1958) travels about in poverty to improve the lot of the world and leaves chaos and death in his wake. Finally led off to prison, he stops by a fruit stall where a woman wants to make him an offering. He is dumbfounded at this expression of kindness, the first he has received in some time. The viewer is confounded at the offering made and accepted—a pineapple, hard and sharp, a symbolic crown of thorns for this would-be Christ marching across country to prison.

Buñuel's film-dreams perpetually surprise, offend, confound, and outrage. They invert the codes that govern waking life in order to reveal some deeply implanted desires for revenge and destruction and dismantle the hypocritical gestures that are themselves destructive. No one comes off unhurt. Priests and nuns, saints, dwarves, blind men, legless cripples, insects, dogs, chickens, people in gowns or top hats, workers, soldiers, orchestra leaders, diplomats, terrorists become victims of their liberated repressions. The only figures that come out less damaged than others are old lechers. Although Viridiana's uncle (who makes her dress in his late wife's wedding gown) hangs himself, and although Tristana hastens the death of her ward and seducer, Don Lope, these old foot fetishists and destroyers of virginity—invariably played by Fernando Rey—are the only characters Buñuel permits to keep even a modicum of self-respect and dignity. They act upon instinct without first filtering their acts through layers of hopeless fears and restraints. The sexism here is rampant, though slightly offset by the fact that everyone in Buñuel's realm is inhibited and hurt by inhibitions, men as well as women. His women, however, can be seen to suffer doubly: from the social and religious structures that oppress both sexes and from the men who are the administrators of the oppressive structures.

The heroine of *Tristana* (1970; one of Buñuel's most "realistic" narratives, only slightly dependent on the intrusion of the fantastic) achieves a rare victory over her seducer. She kills him. But the cause of her revenge is the complete repression of desire, so great that it is manifested as a kind of castration. Tristana has a diseased leg which must be amputated. The inability to deal with desire becomes self-destructive. As Joan Mellen indicates, she becomes a kind of figure for Spain itself—the country of Buñuel's birth, with which he has had a hateful relationship all his life and in most of his films—a land impassioned and imprisoned, so fearful of expression that its history is pockmarked by religious and political repressions barely distinguishable from each other.[33] The film is set in the early thirties, a period of political upheaval. Tristana (Catherine Deneuve) is an orphan, given over to her old guardian Don Lope (Fernando Rey), who, without much resistance on her part, seduces her. Their relationship is confused and repressive. "If you want an honest woman," Don Lope says (with some prophetic irony), "break her leg and keep her at home." He tells her "I am your father and your husband, and I can be one or the other as and when it suits me."[34] Tristana takes a lover, an artist, who knocks old Don Lope down and takes Tristana away, only to bring her back when she refuses marriage and gets sick. Her own leg amputated, she sits at the piano with her prosthetic leg lying on the bed (images that climax the foot fetishism that works its way into all of Buñuel's films) and plans her vengeance on passion in general. Her vision of Don Lope is a dream of his head as the clapper in an enormous bell, and what remains of her sexuality is expressed by her exposing herself to a young mute worker, who flees into the woods to masturbate, a sequence followed by a cut to a church, where Tristana and Don Lope are married.

It is a marriage made for further revenge. Tristana will not sleep with her husband and ends by refusing to call a doctor as he lies dying. The destructive woman (that most ancient of film figures) is here given a context for her evil, and an explanation. The repression of emotion, like the repression of class conflict (here, as so often in Buñuel's work, the rumblings of revolution intrude upon the characters and act as foil to their perversities), leads to eruptions: the unrest of the denied classes; the perverse expression of denied desires in the ruling classes. The woman in Buñuel's work is both social and sexual victim; she internalizes her victimization and then externalizes it by victimizing the poor old Buñuelian man—who, in the old Latin tradition, wants very little more than to get laid. The result of the inhibitions, victimizations, desires, and their collapse is a perversity of event, a dreamlike discontinuity in what are conventionally considered as logical and humane activities (desire, love), and a transformation of the screen into a space of fantasy, debilitation, and absurdity, with a point of view—always tightly controlled by Buñuel—of humorous disengagement and downright joy at the earned misery and meanness of the characters he creates.

In *That Obscure Object of Desire* (1977), his most recent film (and, given his age, quite likely his last), Buñuel attempted a summation of his attitudes in what is, for him, something approaching an understanding of the woman's situation. Like *Tristana, That Obscure Object* is constructed in a fairly conventional way. Although the body of the narrative is in flashback—as Mathieu (Fernando Rey, again) tells his traveling companions on a train from Seville to Paris about his unhappy love for Conchita—the events told move (with one major exception) with an almost old-fashioned continuity. The fantastic eruptions of the unconscious that we are used to in Buñuel's work appear offhandedly, almost unobtrusively. There are some familiar

Buñuelian characters, such as a dwarf, in this instance a psychiatrist, who is one of the people on the train. When the little man first enters the compartment, a little girl unhesitatingly attempts to lift him onto the seat. Some Buñuelian mysteries occur. A group of old women meet Mathieu on the street, finger his palm, and show off a pig wrapped in a blanket. There is an old man who wanders after Mathieu carrying a brown sack (carried occasionally by Mathieu himself) whose contents are not revealed until the very end. Offhanded jokes and absurdities abound. All the people in the train compartment turn out to know one another or each other's relatives. Scattered throughout the film are references to the catching of flies and mice. In a restaurant where Mathieu bemoans his difficulties with Conchita, he discovers a dead fly in his drink. The waiter tells him he's been chasing that one for days. "One fly less," remarks Mathieu. And when Conchita's mother asks him if he plans to marry her daughter, a mousetrap is sprung.

In the Buñuelian world flies and mice are caught as man and woman are caught in each other's traps. Entrapment is Buñuel's theme, whether it is Viridiana, the priest Nazarin, or the would-be saint of *Simon of the Desert* entrapped in the illusions of religion, the dinner guests of *The Exterminating Angel* so trapped in bourgeois rituals they cannot escape the dinner party they attend, or the corrupt hypocrites of *The Discreet Charm of the Bourgeoisie* who are trapped into trying to have a dinner party they can never bring off. The traps in *That Obscure Object* are the usual ones: sex and politics. Mathieu, like all of the characters Fernando Rey plays for Buñuel, is looking for a mistress. Around him, political factions are looking for a way to deal with the European bourgeoisie. The manifestation of both quests is terrorism.

European filmmakers have had no more success than any one else in dealing with the concept and reality of terrorism. The fear and anger it arouses, combined with the all but inexpressible understanding that some terrorist acts originate from deeply felt frustration and need for change in rigid political structures, works to prevent rational comprehension and either a passioned or dispassioned analysis of it.

When terrorism is confronted in film it is usually shown as the work either of misguided and uncohesive groups, as in Chabrol's *Nada* (1974), or of middle-class fools, as in Fassbinder's *The Third Generation*. (Chabrol, however, depicts the organization of the state against the terrorists as more brutal and foolish than anything the terrorists themselves can manage; while Fassbinder sees terrorism as an unwitting aid to repression by the state.) Costa-Gavras's *State of Siege* and Pontecorvo's *Battle of Algiers* have made engaged attempts at analyzing the politics of left-wing terrorism, and Manuel Guttiérrez Aragon, one of the filmmakers working to revive a Spanish national cinema, has attempted to examine neo-fascist terrorism in *Black Brood* (1977). In Buñuel's case political analysis is, as always, joined to, even submerged in, psycho-sexual analysis. The terrorist activity that occurs in *That Obscure Object,* under the leadership of a group that only Buñuel's perverse intelligence could have invented–the Revolutionary Army of the Infant Jesus–is reflected into and out of the terrorism committed upon one another by Mathieu and his Conchita, or rather Conchitas. Despite the apparent "realistic" continuity and the straightforward narration of events, something occurs in this film that denies every bit of reality, as well as the security of our point of view, our location in the narrative organization as spectators. Conchita is played by two different actresses. One, Carole Bouquet, is slim and adolescent. The other, Angela Molina, has a more conventionally sensual "Latin" appearance. The maddening aspect of this is that, like all the other surprises in the film, it is done with no attention called to the fact. They may appear in the same sequence, one coming into a room the other has just left; they speak with the same voice; their actions and attitudes do not change very much from one actress to the other; and Mathieu takes absolutely no note of their different appearances. They are the same person for him, with two different physical manifestations for us.

The immediate result is a subdued act of terrorism committed upon the viewer, a disruption in the way we are used to looking at characters on the screen, particularly women who are presented as objects of desire. The disruption in this instance goes beyond mere confusion

Mathieu (Fernando Rey) and one incarnation of his Conchita (Carole Bouquet). *That Obscure Object of Desire* (Films Incorporated).

over seeing two people acting one role; it attacks our expectations about the erotic object on the screen. In a seminal study of the phenomenon, Laura Mulvey writes:

> In a world ordered by sexual imbalance, pleasure in looking has been split between active/male and passive/female. The determining male gaze projects its phantasy on to the female figure which is styled accordingly. In their traditional exhibitionist role women are simultaneously looked at and displayed, with their appearance coded for strong visual and erotic impact so they can be said to connote *to-be-looked-at-ness*. . . . Traditionally the woman displayed has functioned on two levels: as erotic object for the characters within the screen story, and as erotic object for the spectator within the auditorium, with a shifting tension between the looks on either side of the screen.[35]

There is no question that Conchita serves as the erotic object—the obscure object of desire—for Mathieu. But what about the spectator? Why are only we able to discern a difference? All women are the same to Mathieu; they are all merely objects of desire. Conchita knows this, for her purpose throughout the film is to tease, to promise him her sexuality and then deny it, proclaim her independence, demand that love and fornication are not the same thing, offer and withhold continually. She does to him precisely what his own misogyny demands. But as the object of viewer desire the two Conchitas frustrate and confuse the male gaze. If Mathieu is blind to women as individuals, the spectator may not be; if the male gaze has been perpetually satisfied by the screen's image of the sexually desirable woman, it will be no longer. The object of desire in film was always unattainable, merely the reductive image of woman as thing. Now it is both unattainable and incomprehensible. In an older film version of the 1898 novel by Pierre Louÿs, *The Woman and the Puppet,* which is Buñuel's source, Josef von Sternberg's *The Devil is a Woman* (1935), Marlene Dietrich is the conventional erotic object for both male viewer and male participants in the fiction. She is the center of all gazes, the glittering focus of desire. Buñuel fractures the security and the object of the gaze; he makes the spectator look twice at the same character and twice at Mathieu who looks and sees no difference. The effect of distancing he achieves is not as extreme as in a Godard or Fassbinder film, but perhaps more subtle and therefore more subversive. We are made uncomfortable by a difference that goes unacknowledged in the film and forced to view the proceedings as something other than one more tale of a man pursuing a reluctant and calculating woman. We are forced to pursue the ramifications of our own looking.

For her part, Conchita is very much aware of the function of woman as the object of the look. As part of her design to undo Mathieu, who bought her from her mother (though too much should not be made of this, for Buñuel's characters rarely act out of simple melodramatic motivations like revenge), Conchita makes Mathieu the spectator of her erotic performances. She wears an elaborate and nasty chastity belt to amaze and infuriate him. She sees to it that he watches her dance nude for tourists in a nightclub. She locks him out of the house he buys for her and makes him watch her make love with her guitar-playing boyfriend in the courtyard. After each performance, she denies his perception of her activities, insists that she is not owned by him, and is, anyway, still a virgin, an argument that always renews his interest. The point of view is shifted back and forth between Mathieu and Conchita. Her teasing is unconscionable, hilarious, deserved. When, out of his frustration and damaged machismo, he beats her, Buñuel runs the risk of creating a conventional response in which the woman is confirmed as worthy of masculine hatred and brutality. The bitch-goddess is an ancient figure of misogyny, created to reflect men's fears and hatred of a woman who will not be a passive object, and the history of film is filled with her presence. Such a figure is (within the logic of misogyny) worthy of the wronged man's revenge and may be physically hurt for the emotional hurt she causes. In this film, it is, happily, not so simple. Throughout their story, Mathieu and his Conchita(s) play their roles of lecherous old man and reluctant virgin knowingly, willingly, and with some delight (it is with great delight that Mathieu tells his story to his traveling companions, who listen eagerly). The sexual terrorism they enact upon each other is not as vicious as that committed by Elvira upon herself in *In a Year of Thirteen Moons* or by Paul and Jeanne upon each other in *Last Tango in Paris*. Mathieu and Conchita keep seeking each other out, chasing each other away, returning, meeting by accident and by design (accident and design are often interchangeable in Buñuel's work). Around them their games are echoed by acts of the political terrorists, who create a general havoc paralleling the individual havoc created by the two (three) would-be/reluctant lovers.

The despair of sexuality, so evident in the work Fassbinder, Bertolucci, and Godard, is replaced here by its absurdity. That people should engage in objectifying desire, buying and selling love, playing out spectacles of pursuit and conquest and denial and revenge seems worthy only of derision. Barter and exchange present serious enough problems in the economic world. When the emotional environment mimics middle-class notions of proprietorship and involves the exchange of favors and the turning of humans into objects, the resulting terrors can eventually only destroy.[36] Which is precisely what happens to Buñuel's two (three) terrorists of sexuality. When Mathieu finishes his story (his bourgeois traveling companions–judge, dwarf psychiatrist, proper lady–all agree that Conchita got the beating she deserved),[37] she reappears in the compartment and repays him by dumping a pail of water on his head, as he did to her when the film began. They leave the train together, passing in the station the workman with the mysterious brown sack who has constantly been following Mathieu (earlier in the film someone has referred to women as "sacks of excrement," and we begin to associate this figure and his burden with this woman-hating remark).

They proceed to a shopping arcade, where the sack appears in a store window. Mathieu and Conchita walk by, arguing, pausing to look in the window where they see a lady pull not excrement, but various bloodied linens and laces out of the sack and mend them. Buñuel the old surrealist endures; Mathieu's dirty linen is literally aired in public. As the lovers look and walk on a radio report is broadcast from a loudspeaker, one of the funniest pieces of news ever created:

> Police report the formation of a strange alliance. Several extreme left groups, known to the public as the P.O.P., the P.R.I.Q.U.E., the G.R.I.F., and the R.U.T., have suddenly joined in a campaign of violence under the direction of the R.A.I.J., the Revolutionary Army of the Infant Jesus. These attacks, launched at random, are aimed at throwing our society into total confusion. Extreme right-wing terrorist groups, in particular the P.A.F. and the S.T.I.C., say they'll meet the left's challenge and are going into action, too, collaborating in this devastating act of subversion. . . . Msgr. Fiessole, Archbishop of Sienna, remains in a coma. One bullet that hit him in last week's attack struck the carotid artery. His state is critical. His breathing is normal, thanks to medical science, but his brain is practically dead. Msgr. Fiessole's living death could continue for months. The

> Roman Curia has protested the attack. The Communist Party itself has issued a vigorous denunciation of this odious act. . . . And now, to change the mood a little, here is some music.

Strains of Richard Wagner are heard. Mathieu and Conchita walk away, arguing still. In a sudden blast of flame and smoke, they are blown up.

The final act of terrorism is Buñuel's. Of all the filmmakers who have offered responses and alternatives to the melodramas of sexuality and love's difficulties, who have tried to help themselves and their audience to an understanding of the tyrannies of the romantic myth, only Buñuel, the old anarchist, has decided there is one thing to be done: blow it up.

Perhaps of all the filmmakers discussed in this book Buñuel is old enough and has the authority to indulge in such a simple, direct, even apocalyptic conclusion. "The screen's white eyelid would only need to be able to reflect the light that is its own, and it would blow up the universe," he once said.[38] And from the eyeball split open at the beginning of *Un Chien andalou* to the exploding of the ridiculous lovers at the end of *That Obscure Object of Desire* he has tried to cleanse our perceptions and explode the repressive stupidities of convention and ritual. The other filmmakers, by comparison, work in more restrained ways; yet most have tried to discover through the cinema eye ways of clarifying history and relationships of people to history and to each other, to analyze and clear away obscurity and those parts of tradition that blind. Their success is measured in the ways they have made film reflect an inquiring and informed intelligence and a passion for seeking images that explain, and, perhaps, show a way to change.

NOTES

1. THE VALIDITY OF THE IMAGE

1. Quoted in David Overbey, "The Other Bertolucci," *Sight and Sound* 48 (Autumn, 1979), 240.
2. David Overbey, ed. and trans., *Springtime in Italy: A Reader on Neo-Realism* (Hamden, Conn.: Archon Books, 1978), p. 32n. See also Pierre Leprohon, *The Italian Cinema,* trans. Roger Greaves and Oliver Stallybrass (New York and Washington, D.C.: Praeger Publishers, 1972), p. 86. Leprohon's discussion of the movement is influential on my own.
3. The notion of neo-realism as genre was developed in discussion with Stephen Prince.
4. Louis Althusser, *For Marx,* trans. Ben Brewster (New York: Vintage Books, 1970), pp. 32–34. Althusser takes the concept of the "break" from Gaston Bachelard.
5. A convenient summary of recent theories in cinema historiography can be found in the essays contained in Blaine Allan, Valentin Almendarez, and William Lafferty, eds., *Film Reader 4* (Evanston, Ill.: Northwestern University Film Division, 1979).
6. "A Thesis on Neo-Realism," in Overbey, *Springtime,* p. 69.
7. See, for example, Robert Sklar, *Movie-Made America* (New York: Vintage Books, 1975).
8. Noël Burch has done the important preliminary studies in the "zero-degree" style. See his *Theory of Film Practice,* trans. Helen R. Lane (New York and Washington, D.C.: Praeger Publishers, 1973). The original concept (applied to literature) is Roland Barthes's. "Form

. . . becomes more than ever an autonomous object, meant to signify a property which is collective and protected, and this object is a trouble-saving device: it functions as an economy signal whereby the scriptor constantly imposes his conversion without ever revealing how it came about." *Writing Degree Zero,* trans. Annette Lavers and Colin Smith (Boston: Beacon Press, 1967), p. 27.

9. In *Film Form,* trans. Jay Leyda (New York: Harcourt Brace Jovanovich, 1949), pp. 238–39. The italics are Eisenstein's.
10. Ibid., pp. 233–34.
11. Ibid., p. 35.
12. *The Haunted Screen* (Berkeley and Los Angeles: University of California Press, 1973), p. 151. For the production history of *Caligari* see Siegfried Kracauer, *From Caligari to Hitler* (Princeton: Princeton University Press, 1971), pp. 61–71.
13. A fact recognized by Roland Barthes in "The Third Meaning: Research Notes on Some Eisenstein Stills," in *Image, Music, Text,* trans. Stephen Heath (New York: Hill & Wang, 1977), pp. 52–68. It is a phenomenon of the perception of fiction in general: "In the direct experience of a new work of fiction we have a sense of its unity which we derive from its persuasive continuity. As the work becomes more familiar, this sense of continuity fades out, and we tend to think of it as a discontinuous series of episodes, held together by something which eludes critical analysis. . . . Hence we need a supplementary form of criticism which can examine the total design of fiction as something which is neither mechanical nor of secondary importance." Northrop Frye, *Fables of Identity* (New York: Harcourt, Brace & World, 1963), p. 30.
14. In *The Haunted Screen,* Lotte Eisner briefly points to some relationships between late Weimar film and neo-realism; see pp. 330–35. Franco Venturini discusses the influence of *Kammerspiel* in "Origins of Neo-Realism," Overbey, *Springtime,* pp. 169–97. For *Die Neue Sachlichkeit* see John Willett, *Art and Politics in the Weimar Period: The New Sobriety, 1917–1933* (New York: Pantheon Books, 1978), pp. 111–49, et passim.
15. André Bazin, *What Is Cinema?,* trans. Hugh Gray, 2 vols. (Berkeley and Los Angeles: University of California Press, 1968, 1971), I: 27. For a response to Bazin's reading of Von Stroheim, see Charles Wolfe, "'Resurrecting *Greed,*" *Sight and Sound* 44 (Summer, 1975), 170–74.
16. See Herman G. Weinberg, *The Complete "Greed"* (New York: E. P. Dutton, 1973), Foreword.
17. *Jean Renoir,* trans. W. W. Halsey II and William H. Simon (New

York: Simon & Schuster, 1973), p. 87. Bazin discusses Von Stroheim's influence on Renoir, pp. 15–17, 19, 80–81, 152.

18. Raymond Durgnat, *Jean Renoir* (Berkeley and Los Angeles: University of California Press, 1974), p. 99.
19. George Sadoul, *Dictionary of Films,* trans. and ed. Peter Morris (Berkeley and Los Angeles: University of California Press, 1972), p. 380.
20. Quoted in ibid., pp. 379–80.
21. "A Few Words about Neo-Realism," in Overbey, *Springtime,* p. 90.
22. "A Thesis on Neo-Realism," p. 72. For a discussion of the political atmosphere in Italy at the end of the war, see Guiseppe Ferrara, "Neo-Realism: Yesterday," in Overbey, *Springtime,* pp. 199–205, and Overbey's introduction, pp. 10–11.
23. "The Philosophical Basis of Neo-Realism," in Overbey, *Springtime,* p. 121. In his quest for stylistic simplicity Morlion is able to detect that Welles's editing is in fact complex, a fact usually forgotten in discussions of Welles's shot construction.
24. *What Is Cinema?,* II:60.
25. In Overbey, *Springtime,* p. 121.
26. *What Is Cinema?,* I:13.
27. *Ibid.,* II:37.
28. See *Film Form,* p. 37.
29. *What Is Cinema?,* II:66.
30. "A Discourse on Neo-Realism," in Overbey, *Springtime,* p. 150.
31. Ibid., p. 142.
32. *What Is Cinema?,* II:81.
33. Stefano Roncoroni, ed., *Roberto Rossellini: The War Trilogy,* trans. Judith Green (New York: Grossman Publishers, 1973), p. 217.
34. Ibid., pp. 314–16.
35. Ibid., p. 348. The English commentary in the film that is quoted here differs from the screenplay.
36. *What Is Cinema?,* II:36–37. An early attack on "psychological realism" occurs in an essay by Bazin's young follower, François Truffaut, "A Certain Tendency of the French Cinema," in *Movies and Methods,* ed. Bill Nichols (Berkeley and Los Angeles: University of California Press, 1976), pp. 224–37.
37. "A Thesis on Neo-Realism," p. 71.
38. Ibid., pp. 72, 73.
39. Ibid., pp. 71, 72, 73.
40. Cf. Eric Rhode, *A History of the Cinema from Its Origins to 1970* (New York: Hill and Wang, 1976), pp. 458–60.
41. Ibid., p. 441.

42. For the political and literary influences on the film see Geoffrey Nowell-Smith, *Visconti* (Garden City, N.Y.: Doubleday, 1968), pp. 39–44.
43. Ibid., pp. 40, 50–51.
44. Cf. ibid., p. 40.
45. Ibid., p. 42. Nowell-Smith sees this as a creative tension. I do not.
46. Rhode, *History of the Cinema,* p. 459.
47. *What Is Cinema?,* II:69.
48. Vittorio De Sica, *Miracle in Milan* (Baltimore: Penguin Books, 1969), p. 120.
49. Ibid., p. 11.
50. Quoted in Overbey, Introduction, *Springtime,* pp. 26–29.
51. ". . . A dangerous inclination to aestheticism . . . ," wrote Bazin in 1948. *What Is Cinema?,* II:45.
52. James Roy MacBean, *Film and Revolution* (Bloomington and London: Indiana University Press, 1975), p. 211.
53. MacBean offers a similar analysis of these sequences, ibid., p. 213. Geoffrey Nowell-Smith goes further and calls Rossellini a political opportunist although he also points out his aesthetic consistency. *Visconti,* p. 32.
54. *What Is Cinema?,* II:88.
55. Ibid.
56. Siegfried Kracauer, *Theory of Film: The Redemption of Physical Reality* (New York: Oxford University Press, 1965).
57. *Film Language,* trans. Michael Taylor (New York: Oxford University Press, 1974), p. 14.
58. For an overview of this period in British filmmaking see Roy Armes, *A Critical History of the British Cinema* (New York: Oxford University Press, 1978), pp. 236–79; Alexander Walker, *Hollywood, U.K.* (New York: Stein and Day, 1974).
59. See David Thomson, *A Biographical Dictionary of Film* (New York: William Morrow, 1976), p. 465.
60. Quoted by Randal Johnson, "Brazilian Cinema Today," *Film Quarterly* 31 (Summer, 1978), p. 45n.
61. Freddy Buache, *The Cinema of Luis Buñuel,* trans. Peter Graham (London and New York: Tantivy Press and A. S. Barnes, 1973), pp. 40–42. Francisco Aranda suggests Buñuel wrote some of the film. *Luis Buñuel: A Critical Biography,* trans. and ed. David Robinson (New York: Da Capo Press, 1976), p. 128. For a more complete treatment of this period, including discussion of features and documentaries in which Buñuel probably had a hand, see Aranda, pp. 100–136.

62. Buache, *Cinema of Buñuel,* p. 42.
63. Luis Buñuel, *The Exterminating Angel, Nazarin, Los Olvidados,* trans. Nicholas Fry (New York: Simon & Schuster, 1972), p. 299.
64. Ibid., p. 238n.
65. *What Is Cinema?,* II:25–26.

2. THE SUBSTANCE OF FORM

1. Bertolt Brecht, "Against Georg Lukács," trans. Stuart Hood, *New Left Review,* no. 84 (March–April, 1974), p. 51.
2. Roy Armes argues that the modernist movement in film connects directly to the sophisticated image-making of the silent era. *The Ambiguous Image* (Bloomington and London: Indiana University Press, 1976), pp. 7–8. For a slightly different view of the relationship of form and content in postwar cinema, see Dudley Andrew, *André Bazin* (New York: Oxford University Press, 1978), pp. 180–82.
3. Cf. Burch, *Theory of Film Practice,* pp. 36–37.
4. Arnold Hauser, *The Social History of Art,* trans. Stanley Godman, 4 vols. (New York: Vintage Books, n.d.), IV:244. See also Willett, *Art and Politics,* pp. 108–10.
5. Margot Kernan pointed this out to me.
6. Cf. Rhode, *A History of the Cinema,* pp. 117–55.
7. Stig Björkman, Torsten Nanns, and Jonas Sima, *Bergman on Bergman,* trans. Paul Britten Austin (New York: Simon & Schuster, 1973), p. 29.
8. *Social History of Art,* IV:250.
9. *Ambiguous Image,* p. 14.
10. See Andrew, *Bazin,* for a discussion of postwar film culture in France.
11. The most important analysis of the effects of the gaze in the shot/reaction shot style is Daniel Dayan, "The Tutor-Code of Classical Cinema," in Nichols, *Movies and Methods,* pp. 438–51. The essays on point of view in *Film Reader 4* are also helpful. See also Nick Browne, "The Spectator-in-the-Text: The Rhetoric of *Stagecoach,*" *Film Quarterly* 29 (Winter, 1975–76), 26–38. My reading of the film parallels Thomson, *Biographical Dictionary,* pp. 494–95.
12. *What Is Cinema?* II:98.
13. The notion of closed form is similar to that of Leo Braudy, *The World in a Frame* (Garden City, N.Y.: Anchor Press/Doubleday, 1976), pp. 94–103.
14. The notion of "making strange," re-situating the familiar objects of the world so that we perceive them differently, is a central concern

of Russian formalist criticism. See Fredric Jameson, *The Prison-House of Language* (Princeton: Princeton University Press, 1974), pp. 50–54.

15. *What Is Cinema?*, I:27.
16. Ibid., p. 26.
17. Ibid., p. 35.
18. Ibid., pp. 35–40.
19. Jean Narboni in Jonathan Rosenbaum, ed., *Rivette: Texts and Interviews,* trans. Amy Gateff and Tom Milne (London: British Film Institute, 1977), p. 81.
20. See Brian Henderson, *A Critique of Film Theory* (New York: E. P. Dutton, 1980), pp. 16–31.
21. Narboni in *Rivette,* p. 81.
22. The notion of the enigmatic code in a narrative, that which prods us into continuing by making us wonder what will happen, comes from Roland Barthes, *S/Z,* trans. Richard Miller (New York: Hill and Wang, 1974).
23. See Jonathan Rosenbaum, "Tati's Democracy," *Film Comment* 9 (May–June, 1973), 36–41; Lucy Fischer, "Beyond Freedom and Dignity: An Analysis of Jacques Tati's *Playtime,*" *Sight and Sound* 45 (Autumn, 1976), 234–39 (with an afterword by Rosenbaum).
24. Analogue and digital theories of language and communication are numerous and complex. One source is Umberto Eco, *A Theory of Semiotics* (Bloomington and London: Indiana University Press, 1976), pp. 189–90.
25. Alain Robbe-Grillet, *Last Year at Marienbad,* trans. Richard Howard (New York: Grove Press, 1962), p. 90. The monologue in the film itself is somewhat different.
26. For the concept of play in the film—and a reading which is generally close to this one—see Alan Thiher, *The Cinematic Muse: Critical Studies in the History of French Cinema* (Columbia and London: University of Missouri Press, 1979), pp. 166-79. Thiher also recognizes the subversive activity in modernist film.
27. Robbe-Grillet, *Marienbad,* p. 12.
28. *Alain Resnais* (New York: Oxford University Press, 1979), p. 8.
29. See Peter Wollen, *Signs and Meanings in the Cinema* (Bloomington and London: Indiana University Press, 1972), pp. 155–74; Bill Nichols, *Ideology and the Image* (Bloomington: Indiana University Press, 1981), pp. 69–103.
30. Cf. Thomson, *Biographical Dictionary,* pp. 566–67.
31. "The Cinema of Marguerite Duras: Sound and Voice in a Closed Room," *Film Quarterly* 33 (Fall, 1979), 25.

32. *Bergman on Bergman,* pp. 29, 32.
33. *Godard on Godard,* ed. Jean Narboni and Tom Milne, trans. Tom Milne (New York: Viking Press, 1972), pp. 146–47.
34. Manny Farber, *Negative Space* (New York: Praeger, 1971).
35. In 1957, Eric Rohmer and Claude Chabrol wrote a monograph on Hitchcock, one of the first large-scale studies of an American film-maker. Published in English as *Hitchcock: The First Forty Four Films,* trans. Stanley Hochman (New York: Frederick Ungar, 1979).
36. John Hess's analysis, "La Politique des Auteurs," can be found in *Jump Cut,* nos. 1 and 2 (May–June, July–August, 1974), 19–22, 20–22.
37. Truffaut, "A Certain Tendency of the French Cinema," in Nichols, *Movies and Methods,* p. 234.
38. Astruc, "The Birth of a New Avant-Garde: *La Caméra-Stylo,"* in *The New Wave,* ed. Peter Graham (Garden City, N.Y.: Doubleday, 1968), p. 22.
39. James Monaco draws interesting parallels between Astruc's notions of "writing" and those of Roland Barthes. See *The New Wave* (New York: Oxford University Press, 1976), pp. 8–9.
40. *Godard on Godard,* p. 175.
41. Ibid., p. 28. And see Monaco, *New Wave,* pp. 104–7.
42. *Godard on Godard,* p. 39.
43. Ibid., p. 40.
44. Ibid., p. 173.
45. For *Claire's Knee,* "I didn't look for locations to fit a story I had written; I found the places first and it was only afterwards that I wrote the film." Quoted by Rui Nogueira, "Eric Rohmer: Choice and Chance," *Sight and Sound* 40 (Summer, 1971), 122.
46. Joe Miller and Barbara Bowman were helpful in this discussion of *The Marquise of O.*
47. Robert Phillip Kolker, "Angle and Reality: Godard and Gorin in America," *Sight and Sound* 42 (Summer, 1973), 132. Jean-Marie Straub said that his film on the life and music of Bach, *The Chronicle of Anna Magdalena Bach,* "was his contribution to the fight of the North Vietnamese against the Americans." Quoted in Richard Roud, *Jean-Marie Straub* (New York: The Viking Press, 1972), p. 71.
48. E. H. Gombrich, *Art and Illusion: A Study of the Psychology of Pictorial Representation* (Princeton: Princeton University Press, 1969).
49. *Critical Essays,* trans. Richard Howard (Evanston: Northwestern University Press, 1972), p. 74.
50. "Against Georg Lukács," p. 50.

51. *Brecht on Theatre,* trans. John Willett (New York: Hill and Wang, 1979), p. 37.
52. "A Short Organum for the Theatre," in ibid., p. 193.
53. *Screen* 15 (Summer, 1974) contains a number of articles on *Kuhle Wampe*. For the theater of Piscator and Brecht see Willett, *Art and Politics,* pp. 149–58.
54. "Short Organum," p. 201.
55. *Film Language,* p. 100. For Godard's camera practice, cf. Burch, *Theory of Film Practice,* pp. 119–21.
56. In Jean Collet, *Jean-Luc Godard,* trans. Ciba Vaughan (New York: Crown Publishers, 1970), pp. 146–48.
57. See ibid., pp. 34–35.
58. Roud, *Straub,* p. 78.
59. See Jonathan Rosenbaum, "Interruption as Style: Buñuel's *Le Charme discret de la bourgeoisie," Sight and Sound* 42 (Winter, 1972/73), 2–4, and Armes, *Ambiguous Image,* p. 39.
60. Cf. Roud, *Straub,* pp. 19–26.
61. For a more detailed study of Bresson's recent films see Michael Dempsey, "Despair Abounding: The Recent Films of Robert Bresson," *Film Quarterly* 34 (Fall, 1980), 2–15. *The Devil Probably* (1977), Bresson's most recent film as of this writing, never got into distribution in the United States, presumably because its producers, believing there existed a large market for such a work, demanded too much money for it.
62. "Bressonisms," *Sight and Sound* 46 (Winter, 1976/77), 21. Bresson's complete text is in *Notes on Cinematography,* trans. Jonathan Griffin (New York: Urizen Books, 1977).
63. Thomas Elsaesser, "The Postwar German Cinema," in *Fassbinder,* ed. Tony Rayns (London: British Film Institute, 1980), p. 4.
64. Quoted in ibid., p. 8.
65. Much has been written on the financial arrangements that make the work of the new German filmmakers possible. See the Elsaesser article cited above; Hans-Bernhard Moeller, "New German Cinema and Its Precarious Subsidy and Finance System," *Quarterly Review of Film Studies* 5 (Spring, 1980), 157–68; Richard Collins and Vincent Porter, "West German Television," *Sight and Sound* 49 (Summer, 1980), 172–77; Jan Dawson, "A Labyrinth of Subsidies," *Sight and Sound* 50 (Winter, 1980/81), 14–20.
66. The political climate in West Germany is discussed by Jan Dawson, "The Sacred Terror: Shadows of Terrorism in the New German Cinema," *Sight and Sound* 48 (Autumn, 1979), 242–45; Jack Zipes, "The Political Dimensions of *The Lost Honor of Katharina Blum,*"

New German Critique, no. 12 (Fall, 1977), 75–84; Hans Magnus Enzensberger, "Civil Liberties and Repression in Germany Today," trans. Sophie Wilkins, *October,* no. 9 (Summer, 1979), 107–17.

67. David Wilt, "Driving the Rough Road: The Outlaw Couple in American Film, 1937–1976," (M.A. thesis, University of Maryland, 1980), analyzes the image of the road in American film.
68. *Pierrot Le Fou,* trans. Peter Whitehead (New York: Simon and Schuster, 1969), pp. 28–33. I have slightly modified the translation.
69. Mike Bygrave and Joan Goodman, "Meet Me in Las Vegas," *American Film* 7 (October, 1981), 41–42; Lynda Myles, "The Zoetrope Saga," *Sight and Sound 51* (Spring, 1982), 93.
70. "Short Organum," p. 193.
71. See Richard Dyer, "Reading Fassbinder's Sexual Politics," in Rayns, *Fassbinder,* p. 58.
72. Quoted in J. C. Franklin, "The Films of Fassbinder: Form and Formula," *Quarterly Review of Film Studies* 5 (Spring, 1980), 169.
73. See Christopher Orr, "Closure and Containment: Marylee Hadley in *Written on the Wind," Wide Angle,* vol. 4, no. 2 (1980), 29–35.
74. Dyer, "Fassbinder's Sexual Politics," pp. 62–63.
75. "That's one of the greatest films in the world." Fassbinder in an interview with John Hughes and Brooks Riley, "A New Realism," *Film Comment* 11 (November–December, 1975), 15.
76. The film is full of radio news reports, which, like the broadcast of the soccer match, provide a necessary historical background. The subtitled version does not translate them. My thanks to Peter Beicken for pointing out the significance of the soccer match.
77. Quoted by Franklin, "Films of Fassbinder," 174. See also Judith Mayne, "Fassbinder and Spectatorship," *New German Critique,* no. 12 (Fall, 1977), pp. 61–74; Paul Thomas, "Fassbinder: The Poetry of the Inarticulate," *Film Quarterly* 30 (Winter, 1976–77), 2–17.
78. Michael Dempsey, "Apocalypse Now," *Sight and Sound* 49 (Winter, 1979/80), 6.
79. See William F. Van Wert, "Hallowing the Ordinary, Embezzling the Everyday: Werner Herzog's Documentary Practice," *Quarterly Review of Film Studies* 5 (Spring, 1980), 183–92.
80. Peter Beicken pointed out the relationship of Herzog's landscapes to one German romantic painter, Caspar David Friedrich (1774–1840). The notion of a "neo-realistic expressionism" was offered by Maxmillian Schell at an early point in the New German Cinema movement. See David L. Overbey, "From Murnau to Munich: New German Cinema," *Sight and Sound* 43 (Spring, 1974), 101.

81. Quoted in Alan Greenburg, *Heart of Glass* (Munich: Skellig, 1976), p. 122.
82. "Herzog in Berlin," *Film Comment* 13 (September–October, 1977), 38.

3. POLITICS, PSYCHOLOGY, AND MEMORY

1. From "To Posterity," in Bertolt Brecht, *Selected Poems,* trans. H. R. Hays (New York: Grove Press, 1959), p. 175.
2. Cf. James Monaco, "The Costa-Gavras Syndrome," *Cineaste* 7 (1976), 18–22.
3. For a less harsh treatment of the Dziga Vertov films, see Monaco, *New Wave,* pp. 213–52. See also Sylvia Harvey, *May '68 and Film Culture* (London: The British Film Institute, 1980).
4. *Wind from the East,* in *"Weekend" and "Wind from the East,"* trans. Marianne Sinclair and Danielle Adkinson (New York: Simon and Schuster, 1972), pp. 164–65.
5. Karl Marx, "Preface to *The Critique of Political Economy,"* in *Karl Marx and Frederick Engels: Selected Works* (Moscow: Progress Publishers, 1968), p. 182.
6. "Short Organum," p. 190; see also pp. 180–83.
7. In their seminal article "Cinema/Ideology/Criticism," in Nichols, *Movies and Methods,* pp. 22–30, Jean-Luc Comolli and Jean Narboni offer a variety of interactions possible between form and content and discriminate between ideologies hidden, expressed, or criticized. See also Julianne Burton, "Revolutionary Cuban Cinema: First Part: Introduction," *Jump Cut,* no. 19 (December, 1978), 17–20.
8. Quoted in John Mraz, *"Lucia:* Visual Style and Historical Portrayal," *Jump Cut,* no. 19 (December, 1978), 21.
9. Ibid., pp. 25–27. Mraz's reading parallels mine in many instances.
10. Ibid., p. 23.
11. A breakdown of the characters is offered by Thomas M. Kavanagh, "Imperialism and Revolutionary Cinema: Glauber Rocha's *Antonio-das-Mortes," Journal of Modern Literature* 3 (April, 1973), 201–13.
12. "Censorship in Brazil," *Jump Cut,* no. 21 (November, 1979), 20. This and the following number of *Jump Cut* contain a thorough history and analysis of Brazilian cinema. See also Julianne Burton, "The Hour of the Embers: On the Current Situation of Latin American Cinema," *Film Quarterly* 30 (Fall, 1976), 33–44.
13. "Hungarian Rhapsody," *Film Quarterly* 34 (Fall, 1980), 55.
14. This prayer was current at the time of the events of the film. See

Graham Petrie, *History Must Answer to Man: The Contemporary Hungarian Cinema* (Budapest: Corvina Kiadó, 1978), p. 97.

15. William Kelly, "Allegro Barbaro," *Film Quarterly* 34 (Fall, 1980), 47–53.
16. For a similar argument, see Joan Mellen, *Women and Their Sexuality in the New Film* (New York: Horizon Press, 1973), pp. 179–90.
17. Cf. Herbert Marcuse, *Eros and Civilization* (New York: Vintage Books, 1955).
18. Godard, *Masculine Feminine,* ed. Pierre Billard and Robert Hughes (New York: Grove Press, 1969), pp. 176–77.
19. Ibid., 183–84.
20. Cf. Jim Hillier, *"Masculin-Féminin,"* in *The Films of Jean-Luc Godard,* ed. Ian Cameron (New York: Praeger, 1969), pp. 124–25.
21. Cf. Martyn Auty, "A Fassbinder Suicide," *Sight and Sound* 49 (Autumn, 1980), 266.
22. Eisenstein's essay "A Course in Treatment," in *Film Form,* pp. 84–107, outlines his ideas on the use of internal monologue. Paul Taney pointed out the association.
23. Stephen Prince directed my attention to the Schopenhauer allusion.
24. In "Fassbinder's Sexual Politics," p. 55.
25. *A Married Woman* in *Godard: Three Films,* trans. Susan Bennett (New York: Harper and Row, 1975), p. 85.
26. This, of course, is a basic insight of Hannah Arendt; cf. *The Origins of Totalitarianism* (New York: Harcourt, Brace & World, 1966), pp. 430–57.
27. Quoted by Roger Greenspun, "Phantom of Liberty: Thoughts on Fassbinder's *Fist-Right of Freedom," Film Comment* 11 (November–December, 1975), 10.
28. Cf. Mellen, *Women and Their Sexuality,* p. 144. My reading of the film is close to Mellen's.
29. James Monaco makes these analogies in "Mother's' Day Will Be a Little Late This Year," *The New York Times* (December 2, 1973), D13.
30. Ibid.
31. *Despair* (from a Nabokov novel and a screenplay by Tom Stoppard) is not one of Fassbinder's most successful films, though structurally it is among his most complex. A thorough reading of it is offered by Thomas Elsaesser, "Murder, Merger, Suicide: The Politics of *Despair,"* in Rayns, *Fassbinder,* pp. 37–53.
32. The film is related to the psychological theories of Jacques Lacan, examined in more detail by Peter Mayer, *"Mr. Klein* and the Other,"

Film Quarterly 34 (Winter, 1980–81), 35–39. Mayer's reading of the film's opening sequences are similar to mine.

33. See Mellen, *Women and Their Sexuality,* pp. 191–202.
34. *Tristana,* trans. Nicholas Fry (New York: Simon & Schuster, 1971), pp. 48, 76.
35. "Visual Pleasure and Narrative Cinema," *Screen* 16 (Autumn, 1975), 11–12.
36. Cf. David Overbey, *"Cet obscur objet du desir,"* *Sight and Sound* 47 (Winter, 1977/78), 8.
37. Ibid.
38. Quoted by Buache, *Cinema of Buñuel,* p. 7.

BIBLIOGRAPHY

Allan, Blaine, Valentin Almendarez, and William Lafferty, eds., *Film Reader 4*. Evanston, Ill.: Northwestern University Film Division, 1979. A major collection of essays on point of view and historiography that incorporate recent theoretical approaches.

Althusser, Louis. *For Marx*. Trans. Ben Brewster. New York: Vintage Books, 1970.

———. *Lenin and Philosophy and Other Essays*. Trans. Ben Brewster. New York and London: Monthly Review Press, 1971. Althusser's work forms the ground for recent ideological studies in film.

Andrew, Dudley. *André Bazin*. New York: Oxford University Press, 1978. Although not strong on Bazin's theories, Andrew's evocation of postwar French cultural life and Bazin's part in it is important.

Aranda, Francisco. *Luis Buñuel: A Critical Biography*. Trans. and ed. David Robinson. New York: Da Capo Press, 1976.

Arendt, Hannah. *The Origins of Totalitarianism*. New York: Harcourt, Brace & World, 1966.

Armes, Roy. *Patterns of Realism*. South Brunswick, N.J., and New York: A. S. Barnes, 1971. A survey of the neo-realist movement.

———. *The Ambiguous Image*. Bloomington and London: Indiana University Press, 1976. An introductory study to the modernist movement in film.

———. *A Critical History of the British Cinema*. New York: Oxford University Press, 1978. An avalanche of titles with some social-economic analysis.

Astruc, Alexandre. "The Birth of a New Avant-Garde: *La Caméra-Stylo*."

The New Wave. Ed. Peter Graham. Garden City, N.Y.: Doubleday, 1968. With Bazin, a major influence on the French filmmakers. Graham's collection, long out of print, contains many important documents of the movement.

Auty, Martyn. "A Fassbinder Suicide." *Sight and Sound* 49 (Autumn, 1980). On *In a Year of Thirteen Moons*.

Barthes, Roland. *Writing Degree Zero & Elements of Semiology*. Trans. Annette Lavers and Colin Smith. Boston: Beacon Press, 1970.

———. *Critical Essays*. Trans. Richard Howard. Evanston, Ill.: Northwestern University Press, 1972.

———. *Mythologies*. Trans. Annette Lavers. New York: Hill and Wang, 1972.

———. *S/Z*. Trans. Richard Miller. New York: Hill and Wang, 1974.

———. *Sade, Fourier, Loyola*. Trans. Richard Miller. New York: Hill and Wang, 1976.

———. *Image, Music, Text*. Trans. and ed. Stephen Heath. New York: Hill and Wang, 1977. Barthes is to literary theory what Godard is to film: he goes back to zero and rebuilds our perceptions bit by bit.

Bazin, André. *What Is Cinema?* Trans. Hugh Gray. 2 vols. Berkeley and Los Angeles: University of California Press, 1968, 1971. A selection of essays that formed the thinking of the new French filmmakers.

———. *Jean Renoir*. Ed. Francois Truffaut. Trans. W. W. Halsey II and William H. Simon. New York: Simon and Schuster, 1973.

Benjamin, Walter. "The Author as Producer." *Reflections*. Trans. Edmund Jephcott. Ed. Peter Demetz. New York and London: Harcourt Brace Jovanovich, 1978. Presented in 1934, an early appreciation of Brecht's theories.

———. "The Work of Art in the Age of Mechanical Reproduction." *Illuminations*. Trans. Harry Zohn. Ed. Hannah Arendt. New York: Harcourt Brace & World, 1968. Written in 1935, the classic essay on film as mass art, and a definition of fascist and socialist aesthetics.

Björkman, Stig, Torsten Manns, and Jonas Sima. *Bergman on Bergman*. Trans. Paul Britten Austin. New York: Simon and Schuster, 1973.

Braudy, Leo. *The World in a Frame*. Garden City, N.Y.: Anchor Press/Doubleday, 1976.

Brecht, Bertolt. "Against Georg Lukács." Trans. Stuart Hood. *New Left Review*, no. 84 (March–April, 1974). A major aesthetic-political statement in response to theories of traditional realism.

———. *Brecht on Theatre*. Trans. John Willett. New York: Hill and Wang, 1979.

———. *Selected Poems*. Trans. H. R. Hays. New York: Grove Press, 1959.

Bresson, Robert. "Bressonisms." *Sight and Sound* 46 (Winter, 1976/77).

———. *Notes on Cinematography*. Trans. Jonathan Griffin. New York: Urizen Books, 1977.

Browne, Nick. "The Spectator-in-the-Text: The Rhetoric of *Stagecoach*." *Film Quarterly* 29 (Winter, 1975–76). A major discussion of how point of view is structured in film.

Buache, Freddy. *The Cinema of Luis Buñuel*. Trans. Peter Graham. London and New York: Tantivy Press and A. S. Barnes, 1973.

Buñuel, Luis. *Tristana*. Trans. Nicholas Fry. New York: Simon & Schuster, 1971.

———. *The Exterminating Angel, Nazarin, Los Olvidados*. Trans. Nicholas Fry. New York: Simon and Schuster, 1972. Filmscript.

Burch, Noël. *Theory of Film Practice*. Trans. Helen R. Lane. New York and Washington, D.C.: Praeger Publishers, 1973.

———. *To the Distant Observer: Form and Meaning in the Japanese Cinema*. Ed. Annette Michelson. Berkeley and Los Angeles: University of California Press, 1979. A foremost theorist of modernist cinema. This book is something of a model for this study.

Burton, Julianne. "The Hour of the Embers: On the Current Situation of Latin American Cinema." *Film Quarterly* 30 (Fall, 1976).

———. "Revolutionary Cuban Cinema, First Part: Introduction." *Jump Cut*, no. 19 (December, 1978).

Bygrave, Mike, and Joan Goodman. "Meet Me in Las Vegas." *American Film* 7 (October, 1981). On Francis Ford Coppola's bungling his role as great producer-director.

Cahiers du Cinéma. "John Ford's *Young Mr. Lincoln*." *Movies and Methods*. Ed Bill Nichols. Berkeley and Los Angeles: University of California Press, 1976. Written in 1970, this collective text combines ideological, psychoanalytical, and formal analysis into what has become a model for film criticism.

Collet, Jean. *Jean-Luc Godard*. Trans. Ciba Vaughan. New York: Crown Publishers, 1970.

Collins, Richard, and Vincent Porter. "West German Television." *Sight and Sound* 49 (Summer, 1980).

Comolli, Jean-Luc, and Jean Narboni. "Cinema/Ideology/Criticism." *Movies and Methods*. Ed. Bill Nichols. Berkeley and Los Angeles: University of California Press, 1976. Originally an editorial in

Cahiers du Cinéma, 1969, this is a major statement of the direction of post–1968 French criticism.

Conrad, Randall. " 'I Am Not a Producer!'–Working with Buñuel: A Conversation with Serge Silberman." *Film Quarterly* 33 (Fall, 1979).

Covino, Michael. "Wim Wenders: A Worldwide Homesickness." *Film Quarterly* 31 (Winter, 1977–78).

Coward, Rosalind, and John Ellis. *Language and Materialism: Developments in Semiology and the Theory of the Subject.* London and Boston: Routledge and Kegan Paul, 1977. An invaluable survey of recent theory.

Dawson, Jan. "The Sacred Terror: Shadows of Terrorism in the New German Cinema." *Sight and Sound* 48 (Autumn, 1979).

———. "A Labyrinth of Subsidies." *Sight and Sound* 50 (Winter, 1980/81). On the economics of the new German film.

Dayan, Daniel. "The Tutor-Code of Classical Cinema." *Movies and Methods.* Ed. Bill Nichols. Berkeley and Los Angeles: University of California Press, 1976. Originally appearing in *Film Quarterly,* based on the theories of Lacan and others, this is a groundbreaking essay on the way the spectator is situated in the visual field.

Dempsey, Michael. "Despair Abounding: The Recent Films of Robert Bresson." *Film Quarterly* 34 (Fall, 1980).

Derrida, Jacques. *Of Grammatology.* Trans. Gayatri Chakravorty Spivak. Baltimore and London: The Johns Hopkins University Press, 1976. A major work by the theorist who helped introduce the concept of "deconstruction" into critical practice.

De Sica, Vittorio. *Miracle in Milan.* Baltimore: Penguin Books, 1969. Filmscript.

Durgnat, Raymond. *Jean Renoir.* Berkeley and Los Angeles: University of California Press, 1974.

Dyer, Richard. "Reading Fassbinder's Sexual Politics." *Fassbinder.* Ed. Tony Rayns. Rev. ed. London: The British Film Institute, 1980.

Eco, Umberto. *A Theory of Semiotics.* Bloomington and London: Indiana University Press, 1976. Important ideas about "digital" versus "analogue" perception.

Eisenstein, Sergei. *"Film Form" and "The Film Sense."* Trans. Jay Leyda. New York: Harcourt, Brace & World, 1949.

Eisner, Lotte. *The Haunted Screen.* Berkeley and Los Angeles: University of California Press, 1973. The basic work on German Expressionism and *Kammerspiel.*

Elsaesser, Thomas. "The Postwar German Cinema" and "Murder, Merger, Suicide: The Politics of *Despair*." *Fassbinder*. Ed. Tony Rayns. Rev. ed. London: The British Film Institute, 1980. The article on *Despair* is an excellent application of recent theory.

Enzensberger, Hans Magnus. "Civil Liberties and Repression in Germany Today." Trans. Sophie Wilkins. *October*, no. 9 (Summer, 1979).

Farber, Manny. *Negative Space*. New York: Praeger, 1971.

Fischer, Lucy. " 'Beyond Freedom and Dignity': An Analysis of Jacques Tati's *Playtime*." *Sight and Sound* 45 (Autumn, 1976).

———. "The Image of Woman as Image: The Optical Politics of *Dames*." *Film Quarterly* 30 (Fall, 1976). With Laura Mulvey's essay, an important examination of the way women are "seen" in film.

Franklin, J. C. "The Films of Fassbinder: Form and Formula." *Quarterly Review of Film Studies* 5 (Spring, 1980).

Frye, Northrop. *Anatomy of Criticism*. Princeton: Princeton University Press, 1957.

———. *Fables of Identity*. New York: Harcourt, Brace & World, 1963. Frye's literary theory and criticism predate and foreshadow the French structuralists.

Gay, Peter. *Weimar Culture*. New York and Evanston: Harper and Row, 1968. Somewhat sentimental but lucid account of the period that saw the birth of modernism.

Gledhill, Christine. "Recent Developments in Feminist Criticism." *Quarterly Review Of Film Studies* 3 (Fall, 1978). A summary of major critical trends, including a good account of the work of Jacques Lacan. The entire volume is devoted to aspects of feminist film criticism.

Godard, Jean-Luc. *Godard on Godard*. Ed. Jean Narboni and Tom Milne. Trans. Tom Milne. New York: The Viking Press, 1972. Critical essays and interviews by Godard, 1950–67.

———. *Masculine Feminine*. Ed. Pierre Billard and Robert Hughes. New York: Grove Press, 1969.

———. *Pierrot Le Fou*. Trans. Peter Whitehead. New York: Simon and Schuster, 1969.

———. *"Weekend" and "Wind from the East."* Trans. Marianne Sinclair and Danielle Adkinson. New York: Simon and Schuster, 1972.

———. *Three Films: A Woman Is a Woman; A Married Woman; Two or Three Things That I Know About Her*. Trans. Jan Dawson, Susan Bennett, Marianne Alexandre. New York: Harper and Row, 1975.

Gombrich, E. H. *Art and Illusion: A Study in the Psychology of Pictorial*

Representation. Princeton: Princeton University Press, 1969. Major investigation of "realism" and convention.

Greenburg, Alan. *Heart of Glass.* Munich: Skellig, 1976. A fan's notes on the production of Herzog's film, with scenario.

Greenspun, Roger. "Phantom of Liberty: Thoughts on Fassbinder's *Fist-Right of Freedom.*" *Film Comment* 11 (November–December, 1975).

Harvey, Sylvia. *May '68 and Film Culture.* London: The British Film Institute, 1980. Analysis of radical changes in film theory that resulted from a major societal upheaval.

Hauser, Arnold. *The Social History of Art.* Trans. Stanley Godman. 4 vols. New York: Vintage Books, n.d.

Henderson, Brian. "*Apocalypse Now.*" *Sight and Sound* 49 (Winter 1979/80). On Coppola's visual debt to Herzog.

———. *A Critique of Film Theory.* New York: E. P. Dutton, 1980. The essays "The Long Take" and "Toward A Non-Bourgeois Camera Style" are pivotal in contemporary cinema criticism.

Hess, John. "La Politique des Auteurs." *Jump Cut,* nos. 1 and 2 (May–June, July–August, 1974). Major analysis of the political implications of the *auteur* theory with emphasis on Truffaut.

Hillier, Jim. "*Masculin-féminin.*" *The Films of Jean-Luc Godard.* Ed. Ian Cameron. New York: Praeger, 1969.

Horton, Andrew S., and Joan Magretta, eds. *Modern European Filmmakers and the Art of Adaptation.* New York: Frederick Ungar, 1981. Some interesting essays on films and their literary sources.

Houston, Penelope. *The Contemporary Cinema.* Middlesex, Eng.: Penguin Books, 1963. One of the first books celebrating the new film.

Hughes, John, and Brooks Riley. "A New Realism." *Film Comment* 11 (November–December, 1975). One of a number of pieces on Fassbinder in this issue.

Jaehne, Karen. "*Hungarian Rhapsody.*" *Film Quarterly* 34 (Fall, 1980). Discussion of a recent film by Miklós Jancsó.

Jameson, Fredric. *Marxism and Form.* Princeton: Princeton University Press, 1971. A study of the methods of dialectical criticism.

———. *The Prison-House of Language: A Critical Account of Structuralism and Russian Formalism.* Princeton: Princeton University Press, 1972. An excellent introduction to semiotics.

Johnson, Randal. "Brazilian Cinema Today." *Film Quarterly* 31 (Summer, 1978).

Kavanagh, Thomas M. "Imperialism and the Revolutionary Cinema: Glauber Rocha's *Antonio-das-Mortes.*" *Journal of Modern Litera-*

ture 3 (April, 1973). On Rocha's use of native Brazilian mythology and history.

Kelly, William. "*Allegro Barbaro*." *Film Quarterly* 34 (Fall, 1980). Discussion of a recent film by Miklós Jancsó.

Kolker, Robert Phillip. "Ken Russell's BioPics." *Film Comment* 9 (May–June, 1973).

———. "Angle and Reality: Godard and Gorin in America." *Sight and Sound* 42 (Summer, 1973).

———. "The Open Texts of Nicolas Roeg." *Sight and Sound* 46 (Spring, 1977).

———. *A Cinema of Loneliness: Penn, Kubrick, Coppola, Scorsese, Altman*. New York: Oxford University Press, 1980.

Kracauer, Siegfried. *From Caligari to Hitler: A Psychological History of the German Film*. Princeton: Princeton University Press, 1971.

———. *Theory of Film: The Redemption of Physical Reality*. New York: Oxford University Press, 1965. On the way to being wrong, Kracauer illuminates some interesting points in the theory and history of film.

Leprohon, Pierre. *The Italian Cinema*. Trans. Roger Greaves and Oliver Stallybrass. New York and Washington, D.C.: Praeger Publishers, 1972. A thorough history.

Liehm, Antonín J. *Closely Watched Films: The Czechoslovak Experience*. White Plains, N.Y.: International Arts and Sciences Press, Inc., 1974.

Lukács, Georg. *Studies in European Realism*. New York: Grosset and Dunlap, 1964. A complex work in the socialist realist tradition, and the dialectic to the theories of Brecht.

MacBean, James Roy. *Film and Revolution*. Bloomington and London: Indiana University Press, 1975. Essays on political cinema.

MacCabe, Colin. "Realism and the Cinema: Notes on Some Brechtian Theses." *Screen* 15 (Summer, 1974). This issue of *Screen* contains many essays on Brecht and cinema.

———. *Godard: Images, Sounds, Politics*. Bloomington: University of Indiana Press, 1980. Especially important for material on Godard's work in video and for television during the seventies.

Magisos, Melanie. "*Not Reconciled:* The Destruction of Narrative Pleasure." *Wide Angle* Vol. 3, no. 4 (1980). The issue is devoted to the new German cinema.

Mayne, Judith. "Fassbinder and Spectatorship." *New German Critique*, no. 12 (Fall, 1977).

Marcuse, Herbert. *Eros and Civilization*. New York: Vintage Books,

1955. An early and influential attempt to conjoin Marx and Freud.

Mayer, Peter. "*Mr. Klein* and the Other." *Film Quarterly* 34 (Winter, 1980–81). A reading of the film from the perspective of Lacanian psychology.

Mellen, Joan. *Women and Their Sexuality in the New Film.* New York: Horizon Press, 1973. Among the best of the books of feminist criticism.

———. *The Waves at Genji's Door: Japan Through Its Cinema.* New York: Doubleday, 1976. The culture and politics of Japanese cinema.

———, ed. *The World of Luis Buñuel: Essays in Criticism.* New York: Oxford University Press, 1978. Wide-ranging collection.

Metz, Christian. *Film Language.* Trans. Michael Taylor. New York: Oxford University Press, 1974.

———. *Language and Cinema.* Trans. Donna Jean Umiker-Sebeok. The Hague: Mouton, 1974.

———. *The Imaginary Signifier.* Trans. Celia Britton, Annwyl Williams, Ben Brewster, Alfred Guzzetti. Bloomington: Indiana University Press, 1982. Metz is abstruse, sometimes almost unreadable. He is also indispensable for an understanding of contemporary film practice and criticism.

Moeller, Hans-Bernhard. "New German Cinema and Its Precarious Subsidy and Finance System." *Quarterly Review of Film Studies* 5 (Spring, 1980).

Monaco, James. "Mother's Day Will Be a Little Late This Year." *The New York Times* (Dec. 2, 1973), D 13. On *The Mother and the Whore.*

———. "The Costa-Gavras Syndrome." *Cineaste* 7 (1976).

———. *The New Wave: Truffaut, Godard, Chabrol, Rohmer, Rivette.* New York: Oxford University Press, 1976. Perhaps the definitive study. My commentary on the movement depends a great deal on this book.

———. *Alain Resnais.* New York: Oxford University Press, 1979. A genial study.

Mraz, John. "*Lucia:* Visual Style and Historical Portrayal." *Jump Cut,* no. 19 (December, 1978). This and nos. 18 and 22 of *Jump Cut* contain a history and analysis of Cuban cinema.

Mulvey, Laura. "Visual Pleasure and Narrative Cinema." *Screen* 16 (Autumn, 1975). A central essay on the sexist structure of classic cinema.

Nichols, Bill. *Ideology and the Image.* Bloomington: Indiana University

Press, 1981. A major study of the ways we read the world through the image.

Nogueira, Rui. "Eric Rohmer: Choice and Chance." *Sight and Sound* 40 (Summer, 1971).

Nowell-Smith, Geoffrey. *Visconti.* Garden City, N.Y.: Doubleday and Co., 1968. A critical-structuralist study.

Ollman, Bertell. *Alienation.* 2nd ed. Cambridge: Cambridge University Press, 1977. Studies in the dialectical method.

Orr, Christopher. "Closure and Containment: Marylee Hadley in *Written on the Wind.*" *Wide Angle.* Vol. 4, no. 2 (1980). This issue contains a number of useful articles on American film melodrama.

Overbey, David. "From Murnau to Munich: New German Cinema." *Sight and Sound* 43 (Spring, 1974).

———. *"Cet Obscur objet du desir." Sight and Sound* 47 (Winter, 1977–78).

———. Ed. and trans. *Springtime in Italy: A Reader on Neo-Realism.* Hamden, Conn.: Archon Books, 1978.

———. "The Other Bertolucci." *Sight and Sound* 48 (Autumn, 1979). An interview with Bernardo's brother.

Petrie, Graham. *History Must Answer to Man: The Contemporary Hungarian Cinema.* Budapest: Corvino Kiadó, 1978.

Rhode, Eric. *A History of the Cinema from Its Origins to 1970.* New York: Hill and Wang, 1976. Rhode gives some critical perspective to historical commonplaces and sees the connections between neo-realism and the New Wave.

Robbe-Grillet, Alain. *Last Year at Marienbad.* Trans. Richard Howard. New York: Grove Press, 1962. The original shooting script.

Rosenbaum, Jonathan. "Interruption as Style: Buñuel's *Le Charme discret de la bourgeoisie.*" *Sight and Sound* 42 (Winter, 1972/73).

———. "Jacques Tati's Democracy." *Film Comment* 9 (May–June, 1973). On *Playtime.*

———. "Work and Play in the House of Fiction." *Sight and Sound* 43 (Autumn, 1974). On Rivette.

———, ed. *Rivette: Texts and Interviews.* London: The British Film Institute, 1977.

Rossellini, Roberto. *The War Trilogy: "Open City," "Paisan," "Germany, Year Zero."* Ed. Stefano Roncoroni. Trans. Judith Green. New York: Grossman Publishers, 1973. Texts of the films.

Roud, Richard. *Jean-Marie Straub.* New York: The Viking Press, 1972.

Sadoul, Georges. *Dictionary of Films.* Trans. and ed. Peter Morris. Berkeley and Los Angeles: University of California Press, 1972. A thorough reference work.

Sandford, John. *The New German Cinema.* Totowa, N.J.: Barnes and Noble Books, 1980. An excellent survey.

Screen Reader I: Cinema/Ideology/Politics. London: Society for Education in Film and Television, 1977. Collection of articles from the journal that was the main conduit of ideas from French to Anglo-American film criticism.

Simon, John. *Ingmar Bergman Directs.* New York: Harcourt Brace Jovanovich, 1972.

Sklar, Robert. *Movie-Made America.* New York: Vintage Books, 1975. An important, somewhat revisionist, history.

Stam, Robert. "Censorship in Brazil," *Jump Cut,* no. 21 (November, 1979). This and no. 22 of *Jump Cut* contain a history and analysis of Brazilian cinema.

Thiher, Alan. *The Cinematic Muse: Critical Studies in the History of French Cinema.* Columbia and London: University of Missouri Press, 1979. The movements from "realism" to post-modernism.

Thomas, Paul. "Fassbinder: The Poetry of the Inarticulate," *Film Quarterly* 30 (Winter, 1976–77).

Thomson, David. *A Biographical Dictionary of Film.* New York: William Morrow, 1976. Short, insightful essays on filmmakers and players.

Truffaut, François. "A Certain Tendency in the French Cinema." *Movies and Methods.* Ed. Bill Nichols. Berkeley and Los Angeles: University of California Press, 1976. Originally appeared in *Cahiers du Cinéma* (January, 1954); a major statement against the "Tradition of Quality" and psychological realism.

Van Wert, William F. "The Cinema of Marguerite Duras: Sound and Voice in a Closed Room," *Film Quarterly* 33 (Fall, 1979).

———. "Hallowing the Ordinary, Embezzling the Everyday: Werner Herzog's Documentary Practice." *Quarterly Review of Film Studies* 5 (Spring, 1980).

Vogel, Amos. *Film as a Subversive Art.* New York: Random House, 1974. An annotated catalogue of political cinema.

———. "Herzog in Berlin." *Film Comment* 13 (September–October, 1977).

Walker, Alexander. *Hollywood U.K.* New York: Stein and Day, 1974. The sixties revival in British film.

Walsh, Martin. *The Brechtian Aspect of Radical Cinema.* Ed. Keith M. Griffiths. London: The British Film Institute, 1981.

Weinberg, Herman G. *The Complete "Greed."* New York: E. P. Dutton, 1973. A reconstruction of Stroheim's original film.

Willett, John. *Art and Politics in the Weimar Period: The New Sobriety,*

1917–1933. New York: Pantheon Books, 1978. A rich survey of the richest cultural period in modern Europe.

Williams, Christopher, ed. *Realism and the Cinema: A Reader*. London and Henley: Routledge & Kegan Paul, 1980. Texts and commentary on the major ideas and controversies.

Wolfe, Charles. "Resurrecting *Greed*." *Sight and Sound* 44 (Summer, 1975). Pointing out the expressionist and symbolic aspects of Von Stroheim's work, Wolfe counters Bazin's realist appraisal.

Wollen, Peter. *Signs and Meaning in the Cinema*. Bloomington and London: Indiana University Press, 1972. Still the classic work on *auteur* criticism and film modernism.

Wood, Robin, "Narrative Pleasure: Two Films of Jacques Rivette," *Film Quarterly* 35 (Fall, 1981). On *L'Amour fou* and *Céline et Julie vont en bateau*.

Young, Vernon. *Cinema Borealis: Ingmar Bergman and the Swedish Ethos*. New York: David Lewis, 1971. Has the virtue of not taking its subject too seriously.

Zipes, Jack. "The Political Dimensions of *The Lost Honor of Katharina Blum*." *New German Critique*, no. 12 (Fall, 1977).

INDEX

INDEX